THE COMEDY

OF

DANTE ALIGHIERI

THE FLORENTINE

*

CANTICA III

PARADISE

⟨IL PARADISO⟩

*

TRANSLATED BY
DOROTHY L. SAYERS
AND
BARBARA REYNOLDS

PENGUIN BOOKS

PENGUIN BOOKS

Published by the Penguin Group
Penguin Books Ltd, 27 Wrights Lane, London W8 5TZ, England
Penguin Books USA Inc., 375 Hudson Street, New York, New York 10014, USA
Penguin Books Australia Ltd, Ringwood, Victoria, Australia
Penguin Books Canada Ltd, 10 Alcorn Avenue, Toronto, Ontario, Canada M4V 3B2
Penguin Books (NZ) Ltd, 182–190 Wairau Road, Auckland 10, New Zealand

Penguin Books Ltd, Registered Offices: Harmondsworth, Middlesex, England

First published 1962
21 23 25 27 29 30 28 26 24 22

Printed in England by Clays Ltd, St Ives plc
Set in Monotype Bembo

"*Ma or convien che mio seguir desista*
più dietro a sua bellezza, poetando,
come all'ultimo suo ciascuno artista."

PARADISO, XXX. 31–3

Diagrams
specially drawn for this edition by
C. W. Scott-Giles

CONTENTS

Foreword   9
Introduction   13
THE DIVINE COMEDY
    CANTICA III: PARADISE   53
Appendix:
    Note A: Astronomy in *Paradise*   350
    Note B: Pilgrim or Falcon?   352
    Note C: Animal or Silkworm?   354
Glossary of Proper Names   356
Books to Read   395

DIAGRAMS

The Three Crosses and the Four Circles   59
The Circle of Twelve Lights   142
The Two Circles of Twenty-four Lights   166
The Little Bear as a Horn   174
The Cross of Warriors   184
The Transformation of the Letter M   221–2
The Eagle's Eye   238
The Sun below the Horizon   297
The Sun and Moon on the Horizon   313
The Celestial Rose   323
The Earth's Cone of Shadow   324
The Organization of Paradise   fold-out at end
General View of Paradise   fold-out at end

GENEALOGICAL TABLES

Descent of Dante from Cacciaguida   397
Kings of France, 1223–1350   398

Contents

Kings of Aragon and Sicily, 1196–1337   399

The Della Scala Family   400

NOTE

The abbreviation *Inf.*, which occurs in the Notes and elsewhere, refers in every instance to the first volume of this translation of the *Divine Comedy: Hell*. Dante's own title for this section of his poem was *Inferno*, which by long usage tends to oust the more English rendering, *Hell*, from the mind of the reader, and seems even to have done so from the mind of the late Dorothy L. Sayers who in the second volume, *Purgatory*, refers throughout to *Inferno* or *Inf.*   B.R.

FOREWORD

WHEN Dorothy L. Sayers died on 17 December 1957, she had completed the first twenty cantos, almost two thirds, of her translation of the *Paradiso*. Of the remaining thirteen cantos, only one long section and a few fragments were found. She had not yet begun work on the Notes and Commentaries or on the Introduction.

My interest in Dorothy Sayers's work on Dante dates back to August 1946, when I attended a lecture she gave on Canto xxvi of the *Inferno* at a Summer School of Italian held at Jesus College, Cambridge.[1] This was the first of a memorable series of lectures on the *Divine Comedy*, most of which she later collected together and published in two volumes, entitled *Introductory Papers on Dante*[2] and *Further Papers*. It was evident from the beginning that she was bringing to Dante studies in this country a new and revitalizing force, and in my foreword to her *Introductory Papers* I said that she had made possible a new relationship between Dante and the present-day reader. I still think this is true. The most valuable and original service she performed for readers of Dante was to redirect attention to the literal meaning of the *Comedy*. This she did by commenting, in a stimulating and readable manner, on the story, or poetic reality, of the work. Such an approach should not be regarded as superficial or naïvely literal-minded. It is, on the contrary, fundamental to a proper understanding of the *Comedy*. It is no compliment to Dante as an artist to disregard the superb skill with which he constructed his story, related his unique adventure, devised dialogues and situations and created characters. It is not even sound intellectually to do so, for he himself said that the allegory could not be explained until the literal sense had been understood.

In interpreting the allegory, Dorothy Sayers continually drew the reader's attention to the relevance of the *Comedy* to life. By her masterly and observant handling of both these aspects, in her lectures, in her introductions and commentaries on *Hell* and *Purgatory*, and in her translation itself, she brought Dante within the reach of thousands of readers for whom he would otherwise have remained unintelligible. It is probably true to say that between 1949 (the date of the publica-

1. The lecture, entitled "The Eighth Bolgia", has been published in *Further Papers on Dante* (Methuen, 1957, pp. 102–18).
2. Methuen, 1954.

tion of her translation of the *Inferno*) and the present day, the *Divine Comedy* has had more English-speaking readers than it has ever had over a comparable length of time in all its history. This would not have displeased Dante; as Professor E. R. Vincent has said, "he wanted as many readers as possible. . . . He could not have foreseen the invention of printing and the vast reading public of today, but he certainly appealed to the widest audience known to him. The *lettor* Dante had in mind was not a learned man, and therefore neither the *Divine Comedy* nor the *Convivio* was written in a learned language. Dante wanted readers because he had a message for all." [1]

In completing this translation of the *Paradiso*, I have done my best to continue in the style of the first twenty cantos. My hope that I may have, to some degree, succeeded rests on the fact that over a period of eleven years, and particularly during the last three years of her life, I was in contact with Dorothy Sayers with regard to her work on Dante. In conversations and in letters she discussed in detail her methods of translation, the reasons for her choice of diction, her preferences as to style and rhythm; sometimes she sent as many as ten or twelve trial renderings of a single passage, and frequently she wrote long letters almost wholly concerned with the technique of verse translation. When I learned, after her death, that she had expressed the wish that I should continue her work, I found that I had accumulated a store of information, almost of instruction, as to how to proceed.

In writing the Introduction and in the Notes and Commentaries, in order to keep to the style and pattern of the two previous volumes, I have re-read the letters I received from Dorothy Sayers about the *Paradiso*, her Dante notebooks, and one or two of her unpublished lectures. I have also recalled, as best I could, conversations we had on Dante in Cambridge and Witham and elsewhere. By these and other means, I have endeavoured to ensure as smooth a transition as possible between the first two volumes and the third. [2]

The first acknowledgement which I must make, then, is to Dorothy Sayers herself, whose enlivening and delightful companionship proved so great a help to me in the task that lay ahead. My heartfelt thanks are due also to the distinguished Dantist, Professor G. L. Bickersteth, who had been in correspondence with Dorothy Sayers for some years concerning her work on Dante and, on her death, most generously placed his great learning and experience at my disposal. To him I owe

1. *On Re-reading Dante* (Annual Italian Lecture of the British Academy, 1945, p. 2).
2. Pages 16–23 are an adaptation of material left by Dorothy Sayers.

many valuable suggestions for the improvement of the verse and for the clarification of the expression. I should also like to thank Miss Muriel St Clare Byrne, Miss Marjorie Barber, and Mr Anthony Fleming for their help and encouragement, especially during the early stages. To Dr E. V. Rieu, kindest and most understanding of editors, I owe thanks, not only for his discriminating criticism but also for his initial faith in my capacity to undertake this work. I am most grateful also to Professor Cesare Foligno for his valuable comments on the Introduction, to Mr John Press for his help and advice concerning the verse, to the Rev. John Bridger for reading and discussing several of the Commentaries, to the Rev. Dr Leon Morris for enriching the notes on Atonement doctrine in Canto vii, and for his assistance with certain of the notes to Canto xxix, to the Rev. Gordon Bridger for suggesting biblical references for the notes to Canto xxv, to Mr Alan Lloyd for help concerning Dante's references to clocks, to Professor H. R. Pitt for clarifying the problem of squaring the circle, to Dr R. A. Lyttleton for his assistance with astronomical matters, to Mr David Gardiner for illumination concerning the relevance to modern physics of the experiment with the three mirrors, and to my friend and colleague, Dr Kenelm Foster O.P., who has looked through the Introduction and Commentaries with a Thomist's vigilant eye. I should also like to thank Mr C. W. Scott-Giles for his enlightening and attractive diagrams. The transformations of the letter M, for instance (pp. 221–2), can never have been so delightfully represented.

To my husband, Professor Lewis Thorpe, I owe thanks, as ever, for his encouragement and advice. It was in his company, while on a walking tour in the Euganean hills, that I finished the first draft of the translation. To all the members of my family and my immediate circle of friends, I am grateful for the patience and understanding they have shown me during this exacting and unlooked-for task. In particular, I should like to thank Miss Edith G. Reynolds, whose skill and experience in verse translation have enabled her to be of great assistance to me.

Cambridge   **BARBARA REYNOLDS**
13 June 1960

FOREWORD TO THE SECOND EDITION

I AM grateful to the editors of the Penguin Classics for allowing me to make some alterations to the notes and also to one or two of the lines of verse of this translation of Dante's *Paradiso*. In the two years since the first edition was published a number of people, bearing witness to the close attention with which they had read the notes, wrote to point out mistakes or to suggest emendations.

In almost all cases these suggestions were accompanied by letters about Dante, many of them of great interest, to which I replied and which led to a sustained correspondence. It would be pleasant if all one's mistakes had consequences like these, but I think they must be attributed to the nature of the influence which Dante's mind and work have on his readers. Though separated from us by well over six centuries (the seventh century of his birth falls next year), he still speaks revealingly to our condition, and the discovery that he does is an excitement which we feel urged to share with our contemporaries.

I should like to take this opportunity of thanking all those who wrote to me on my completion of the great task so valiantly undertaken by the late Dorothy L. Sayers. Among those who helped me to improve several of the notes of the present edition I should like to thank particularly Father Alberic Stacpoole, O.S.B., M.C., Mr Brian McCaffery, Dr Hugh Plommer, and Dr Geoffrey Lee. My thanks are due also to the kindness with which this work was received by its many reviewers.

The University   BARBARA REYNOLDS
Nottingham
28 March 1964

INTRODUCTION

It has been said[1] that the joys of Heaven would be for most of us, in our present condition, an acquired taste. In a sense, Dante's *Paradise* is a story about the acquisition of that taste. The Dante who has been down to the uttermost depths of Hell and has climbed the Mount of Purgatory, to behold on its summit the wonder and enchantment of the Earthly Paradise, is no more prepared, after all these tremendous and unique experiences, than we should be ourselves for what he finds in Heaven. He is bewildered by his ascent from earth and totally at a loss to describe how he enters the Moon; when souls first approach him, he mistakes them for reflections of people behind him; when Piccarda speaks to him of the hierarchy of bliss, he shows, by the question he asks, how much he has to learn about the nature of heavenly life; when the contemplatives in the Heaven of Saturn utter their cry of execration at the degeneracy of monastic life, he momentarily loses his wits and has to turn to Beatrice for reassurance, as a child runs to its mother; problems of grace and predestination trouble him, the very purpose of his whole experience eludes him; wonder, fear, amazement, and, at one point, even reprehensible curiosity characterize his state of mind. There is only one phase of his journey during which he may be said to feel reasonably certain of himself and that is when he undergoes the examination in faith, hope, and love, conducted, respectively, by St Peter, St James, and St John; though even then he commits the blunder of peering too inquisitively into the radiant deeps of the light of St John, hoping to glimpse the body in which, it was rumoured, the saint had been taken up into Heaven. Yet, as he mounts ever higher through the circling spheres and beyond them to the still centre of infinity which is the abode of God, his vision strengthens and he grows in understanding and love until, at last, in the unveiled presence of the Deity, his will and desire are integrated with the divine love. Although we may feel we are strangers in Heaven, Dante at least is known to us; he is our very selves.

He is, at the same time, most personally and intimately himself. Much has been written of an illuminating and edifying nature regarding the relevance of the *Divine Comedy* to life as lived by mankind in general, but the really tantalizing problem which the *Paradiso* presents is the extent to which it symbolizes Dante's own intellectual and

1. by C. S. Lewis.

13

spiritual development. Does the Beatific Vision in the last Canto represent a mystical experience which Dante himself underwent, or is it only a symbol, intellectually arrived at, of the relationship between man's understanding and divine revelation? What are we to make of the silences, the omissions, the confessions of inadequacy or downright inability to describe what he saw? Are these merely technical devices for suggesting the inexpressible, or do they represent some incommunicable phase of Dante's own intuition of the ineffable? How far, in other words, is the *Paradiso* a record of personal experience as well as a communication, in imagined form, of personal convictions?

Such questions as these, and many others akin to them, can never, perhaps, be answered, but they constitute a perennial challenge to readers of every generation and make the story of Dante's progress through Heaven one of the most fascinating and enigmatic autobiographies ever written. Yet the *Paradiso* has probably lost more readers than it has held. Many, taking Dante's warning to heart, must have turned back to "seek the safety of the shore." [1] These words by an early-nineteenth-century scholar and critic [2] have still some truth today: "Few, even among the warmest admirers of Dante, have had the enthusiasm to follow him, step by step, through the last division of his stupendous edifice." Macaulay, an ardent enthusiast for the narrative power of the poem as a whole, [3] considered the *Paradiso* by no means equal to the two preceding parts, except in regard to its style. His reasons for considering it "far inferior to the Hell or the Purgatory" stem from a misunderstanding of the very quality in Dante which he so much admired, namely, his narrative skill. "Among the beatified he appears," says Macaulay, "as one who has nothing in common with them – as one who is incapable of comprehending, not only the degree, but the nature of their enjoyment." This is a striking instance of the mistake which readers have often made of confounding the *character* Dante (who in the story is bewildered when he first ascends to Heaven and, throughout his progress, in need of enlighten-

1. Canto ii. 4.   2. Robert Bland, 1779–1825.
3. He called it "the finest narrative poem of modern times" and said: "The great source, as it appears to me, of the power of the *Divine Comedy* is the strong belief with which the story seems to be told. In this respect, the only books which approach to its excellence are *Gulliver's Travels* and *Robinson Crusoe*." (Miscellaneous Writings, ed. 1875, pp. 21–32.) It is interesting to compare with this the emphasis laid by Dorothy L. Sayers on the compelling power of the *Divine Comedy* as a narrative, an aspect of the work which has tended since the time of Macaulay to become overlaid by allegorical interpretations. (See her article ". . . And Telling You a Story" in *Further Papers on Dante*, Methuen, 1957.)

ment and guidance) with the *poet* or *creator* Dante, whose mind and soul have comprehended the nature of heavenly joy as conveyed in the dialogues and descriptions devised for our understanding. For a still more surprising reason, Schiller thought the *Paradiso* boring – because it was all praise and no blame.[1] He must have turned back early in the voyage – if he set out at all. Shelley, on the other hand, was profoundly and sensitively appreciative of the *Paradiso*, which he preferred to *Inferno* and *Purgatorio*, calling it "a perpetual hymn of everlasting love" and "the most glorious imagination of modern poetry." Mr T. S. Eliot, for whom the *Paradiso* is "never dry", but "either incomprehensible or intensely exciting" has lucidly perceived and indicated the relationship of the third cantica to the *Commedia* as a whole, and anyone wishing to be rightly orientated in this respect would do well to read his essay entitled "A Reading on the *Purgatorio* and *Paradiso*", if he has not already done so.[2]

It has long been considered impossible for any commentator to enlist the general reader's interest in this third and last section of the *Commedia* and retain it to the end. On the whole, recent studies on the *Paradiso* have shown little sign of recanting this opinion, in that they are almost exclusively intended for specialists.[3] It is often urged by scholars that the only way of understanding Dante is to put aside all knowledge and prejudice derived from the wisdom of a later age and to try to grasp the principles of his thought in the spirit of the fourteenth century, interpreting his mind in its totality by reference to the general intellectual and spiritual outlook of his time. There is much wisdom in such advice, although it is a counsel of perfection. Even so, to stop there is to remain in the realm of the relative and historical. It is perhaps the business of the commentator and critic to point to resemblances, as well as to differences, between the form of thought of a poet of the past, and our own, for it seems that unless this is done, and done repeatedly from generation to generation, works of the past cease to have significance for the ordinary reader, which is tantamount to saying that they cease to live.

Heaven has, of course, always been inconceivable, "passing man's understanding". Of the few poets or prophets who have undertaken to describe it, even fewer have dared to keep us there for long. The angel comes, the river is passed and all the trumpets sound on the

1. Goethe–Schiller Correspondence, letter to Goethe, 27 August 1799.
2. *Dante*, Faber and Faber, 1929.
3. An exception to this is the article by Dorothy L. Sayers, originally given as an expository lecture to a non-specialized audience, entitled "The Meaning of Heaven and Hell" (*Introductory Papers on Dante*, Methuen, 1954, pp. 44–72).

other side, but we do not enter the City. Milton's heaven is so distracted with wars and tumults that, except in a few isolated and magnificent lines, he is never really called upon to present us with the picture of changeless and inexhaustible bliss, and the same may perhaps be not unfairly said of the author of the Apocalypse. Of all the poets of fulfilment, Dante alone has had the astonishing courage to take us into Heaven and keep us there for thirty-three long cantos, building it to his ecstatic climax without introducing any grandiose events, any scenery, or any incantatory dreaminess which suspends disbelief by lulling the wits to sleep. His Heaven is at first sight almost disconcertingly lucid; it is only as it piles up, line upon line, dogma upon dogma, sphere upon sphere to the exquisite and mathematical exactitude of the final vision, that we realise how much of its power to convince lies precisely in its lucidity. Of the light of Heaven he says:

> *"Pure intellectual light, fulfilled with love,*
> *Love of the true Good, filled with all delight,*
> *Transcending sweet delight, all sweets above."* [1]

The word "intellectual" is significant; the light is that of reality.

It is in the *Paradiso* that we find affirmed with the utmost clarity and consistency the fundamental Christian proposition that the journey to God is the journey into reality. To know all things in God is to know them as they really are, for God is the only absolute and unconditioned Reality, of whose being all contingent realities are at best the types and mirrors, at worst the shadows and distortions – at best, the created universe, at worst the deliberately willed delusion which we call Hell.

When Dante and his poem venture, as best they may, into the world of Reality, his guide is Beatrice, who represents his own personal experience of the immanence of the Creator in the creature.[2] In her he had seen, in those moments of revelation which he describes in the *Vita Nuova*, the eternal Beauty shining through the created beauty, the reality of Beatrice as God knew her. Apart from this personal image, Dante has restricted himself to only a very few simple and traditional symbols. For the physical structure of his ascent, he has taken the accepted system of the Ptolemaic heavens and has peopled them with souls representing the stages of spiritual attainment both in the active and contemplative life. But he is careful to insist that all these spirits really inhabit only one Heaven, which is God's presence,

1. Canto xxx. 40–42.
2. For a discussion of the significance of Beatrice in *Paradise*, see below, pp. 49–51.

and is not in time or space at all, but contains within itself "every where and every when". [1] Except for Dante and Beatrice themselves, no human *form* appears between the second Heaven and the tenth. The dwellers in the Moon appear faint as reflections in clear water; those in Mercury only gleam out for a moment from the light of joy which partly shrouds them and in which all the dwellers in the heavens above them are wholly hidden. All the variety is provided by the changing colour and intensity of the lights and by the abstract patterns which they trace against a background, itself of pure light. From heaven to heaven Dante is conducted, beholding in each the reality of what each soul was in the earthly counterpart of the Heavenly City. In Venus he enters the Heaven of the Lovers, in Mars the Heaven of the Warriors who figure with Christ in a cross formed of two bands of white light constellated with radiances like rubies. He enters the intellectual Heaven of the Sun, where the great doctors of the Church, some of whom had disagreed upon earth, find all their partial truths reconciled in the One Truth and lead their shining and joyous dance in an ecstasy of mutual courtesy. In the Heaven of Jupiter, he beholds the form of the perfect Empire. There the souls gather in the shape of an Eagle and when the Eagle speaks, Dante says:

> *What I must now relate was ne'er with ink*
> *Written, nor told in speech, nor by the powers*
> *Of mind e'er grasped, to imagine it or think;*
>
> *For I beheld and heard the beak discourse,*
> *And utter with its voice both* Mine *and* Me,
> *When in conception still 'twas* Us *and* Ours.[2]

The spirits are one with another in love and will, and when that is so, then there is perfect Empire and perfect Justice. Above that is the Heaven of the Contemplatives, and above that, the Heaven of the Friends of Christ, where Dante sees Adam and the Apostles and the Virgin Mary. Above that, beyond the visible spheres, is the Primum Mobile or the Heaven of the Angels. At last Dante is taken to bathe his eyes in the River of Light, which is also the River of Time, and the flowing of time is turned into the circle of Eternity, the mystic Rose. He sees the ranks of the Blessed, rising up about him, tier upon tier, into the light of God; from the Heaven of Venus until now, he has seen them only as bright radiances, but now they are shown to him in their true shapes, wearing the body of glory which they will put on at the Resurrection.

1. Canto xxix. 12.   2. Canto xix. 7–12.

Here Beatrice leaves him, her mission fulfilled. And now, at the prayer of Beatrice herself, of St Bernard the Great Contemplative, of the Virgin and of all the Saints, his eyes are opened to the ultimate realities. At first, he sees the universe, as God sees it. The entire created universe and everything in it: its substance (that is, the true being of the thing as it is in itself), its accidents (that is, its qualities, whatever they may be) and the mode or relationship which connects one thing with another, are seen as co-inhering in one simultaneous whole, so that what to us is an immeasurable and unimaginable succession of multiple events is revealed to him as a single and perfectly lucid unity. This, says Dante, is what he saw, and knows he saw, though the vision was gone in a flash and he cannot now recapture it. The "five-and-twenty centuries" which have passed since Jason's quest of the Golden Fleece could not bury it in deeper oblivion, yet he knows he saw it, for the joy and rapture of the vision are still realities to him.

Then, as he gazes into the light, it becomes the vision of God Himself in His Tri-Unity, the Father, and the Son eternally begotten of Him, and the Holy Ghost proceeding from Father and Son, wholly distinct in Person and wholly indivisible in Substance (that is, in essential being). This, of course, the poem can only convey by an image; and it is characteristic of Dante that he chooses an image of pure geometrical form, the famous image of the three distinct spheres occupying a single multidimensional space.

But there is one thing still to come. All his life he had known that the key to reality was somehow connected with that God-bearing image which was Beatrice, and yet not she, but which shone through and made her, as the vision of God shines through and makes the vision of the universe. So now he searches the Godhead for sight of the Master-Image, the Reality of which Beatrice was the figure, the union of Creator and created in the person of Christ. He sees it, but cannot understand it, and then in a flash it comes to him, beyond all understanding and yet known. In that supreme moment, "high fantasy" reaches its limit and leaves him, but in that moment he feels his whole being re-orientated and turning upon God as its true centre, as the heavens turn upon their poles.

*

As this visual music proceeds through its shimmering variations upon the theme of light, to resolve itself finally into one great harmony of recovered form,[1] we begin to see the outline of a single over-riding

1. i.e. the Blessed in bodily form in the Celestial Rose.

pattern impressed on the whole poem, which is the pattern of salva-
tion. In Dante's personal revelation, it stretches from the first image
of the earthly Beatrice, through the loss of that image, to the recovery
of the image in the heavenly Beatrice. In the ascent to contemplation,
which is the *Paradiso*, it stretches from the faint lunar images of the
first Heaven, through the overwhelming of the images, to the return
of the images in the Celestial Rose, clear and distinct in the light with-
out addition or substraction by distance. In the life of man, it stretches
from the birth of the flesh, through the death of the flesh and the
luminous persistence of the substantial form, to the triumphant resur-
rection of the flesh. The pattern is defined by Solomon in Canto xiv:

> *"Long as shall last the feast of Paradise,*
> *Even so long," it said, "our love shall lace*
> *This radiance round us for our festal guise.*
>
> *Its brightness with our fervour shall keep pace,*
> *Fervour with sight, sight so enlarge the mesh*
> *Of its own worth as it hath more of grace;*
>
> *And when we put completeness on afresh,*
> *All the more gracious shall our person be,*
> *Reclothèd in the holy and glorious flesh; . . .*
>
> *But, as the living coal which shoots forth fire*
> *Outgoes it in candescence, and is found*
> *Whole at the heart of it with shape entire,*
>
> *The lustre which already swathes us round*
> *Shall be outlustred by the flesh, which long*
> *Day after day now moulders underground;*
>
> *Nor shall that light have power to do us wrong,*
> *Since for all joys that shall delight us then*
> *The body's organs will be rendered strong."* [1]

It would be difficult to assert more emphatically that fundamental
earthiness and particularity, that sanctity of the individual creature and
of the "holy and glorious flesh", which marks Christianity off so
sharply from the Gnostic heresies. The body, by its very nature, im-
plies difference – the Many over against the One. The heavenly life is
not absorption into, but union with, the Absolute, for the creation of
the Many is a deliberate divine act.

An act, moreover, of pure love, for the sake of the creature, giving

1. Canto xiv. 37–45, 52–60.

to every created thing the joy of existing, of being, so far as it may,
aware of its existence, and of responding to its Creator, after its own
manner, by mirroring back to Him the glory of being which it
derives from Him:

> "*Not to increase His good, which cannot be,*
> *But that His splendour, shining back, might say:*
> Behold I am, *in His eternity,*
>
> *Beyond the measurement of night and day,*
> *Beyond all boundary, as He did please,*
> *New loves Eternal Love shed from His ray.*" [1]

It is sometimes supposed that Dante and his contemporaries, living
in an earth-centred cosmos so much smaller than that to which modern
science has introduced us, had an over-weening sense of man's impor-
tance in the scheme of things. The truth is quite the contrary. For
Dante, the earth was indeed at the centre of the universe, but the
centre was the lowest and meanest point in the scale of creation. The
cosmos as he conceived it was physically smaller than ours, but its
range was greater, for it included vast orders of beings of which our
statistical frame of reference can take no note. As mediaeval man
stood upon the surface of his central earth, and gazed beyond it to-
wards that august infinitude by Whom and in Whom and for Whom
all things exist, his spiritual eye beheld, imaged by the concentric
circlings of the heavenly spheres, the ninefold order, rank above rank,
of the celestial Intelligences, his absolute superiors. Pure love, pure
mind, pure will, pure spirit, these are the Angels, the "primal
creatures", the "first effects of God". Living in perpetual contempla-
tion of the final Reality, their wills perfectly conjoined to His, they,
by His delegated authority, move and order the whole visible uni-
verse in obedience to eternal law. They and their operations include
everything that we understand by the forces and operations of Nature.
They are the Movers, controlling not only the motions of the spheres
but all natural change throughout the universe – change being, for
the mediaeval Aristotelian, simply a particular kind of motion. It is
the Intelligences who (in Dante's metaphor) imprint upon the wax
of matter the seal of form. Although they are the instruments of
change, they are themselves by nature changeless, living in the mode
of instantaneousness or (which is the same thing) of eternity. They
know what they know, not by a process of learning, but by direct
intuition as they contemplate the divine fountain of light and wisdom.

1. Canto xxix. 13-18.

Their only "proper motion", so to call it, is the perpetual motion of love by which they circle about God, the Prime Mover, whom Dante sees as the point from which the heavens and all nature hang.[1] By love, each order is attracted to the orders above and attracts the orders below it, so that "all are drawn to God and to Him draw". And in its circling, each order sweeps its own celestial sphere along with it, so that the motions of the heavens are a reflection, an analogy, an allegory, of the loves of the angels. "Love", said Dante, "moves the sun and the other stars." "They are moved", said Kepler, "by mutual attraction." "The stars", said Hegel, "are not pulled this way and that by mechanical forces; theirs is a free motion. They go their way, as the ancients said, like the blessed gods." According to Dante, they move indeed "by attraction", but theirs is also a "free motion", for their movers *are* "the blessed gods", who of their own free will perpetually move to the love that draws them.

Turning his eyes from the great celestial wheels, and looking downward at the earth, mediaeval man was aware of another section of the ladder of being, which dropped away below his feet. Immediately beneath him were the brutes, creatures endowed with an animal-sensitive soul, in addition to life and form and matter. Below them was the vegetable kingdom, whose matter had only life and form. Below this again was inorganic matter, having form only without life. And, underlying the whole, was the prime matter itself, mere being without form and as such unintelligible, scarcely being at all, but only the potentiality of being.[2] Lower than this one could not go, except to the "dreadful centre" of Hell, which was the privation of being and the contradiction of reality, a number, as it were, on the minus side of the graph and possessing only that spurious and derived shadow of real being which minus numbers have.

Between these two hierarchies, and linking them, stood man himself, like the angels an eternal spirit, and like the brutes a compound of informed matter with a vegetative and an animal soul. His unique characteristic was the possession of a *rational* soul. He was not, like the Angels, wholly intuitive, nor, like the brutes, wholly instinctive; he could reason and learn. And like the angels he had a will that was

1. Canto xxviii. 42.
2. Compare with this conception the following passage from J. B. S. Haldane's *The Inequality of Man* (Chatto, 1932), p. 113: "We do not find obvious evidence of life or mind in so-called inert matter, and we naturally study them most easily where they are most completely manifested; but if the scientific point of view is correct, we shall ultimately find them, at least in rudimentary forms, all through the universe."

by nature free in both the Augustinian senses: he had a minor liberty of being able to choose between means to an end (whether between good and evil, or between two goods which are alternative means to a good end); this was the *liberum arbitrium*; he had also a major liberty which consists in a total love-conformity of the will to God.

This was man's glory, as it was his shame, for he was the broken rung in the ladder of created being. He alone, rejecting the manner of knowledge appropriate to his place in the hierarchy, had desired to know "as God", or at least, "as the gods", disregarding the warning that no material being could know in that way without grievous damage to himself and his operations. This rebellion of the human will, of which the consequences are handed down subconsciously from generation to generation in the very act of generation, meant that man could not fulfil his functions spontaneously like the Intelligences and the lower creation. His work had to be redeemed by being incorporated into the Humanity of the Incarnate Godhead. The Incarnation is a new glory given to mankind; but that glory belongs to the act of God and not to the nature of man. The proper function of man, whether in his original or in his redeemed perfection, was, like that of the Intelligences, to draw up by love all the grades of the hierarchy below him, so that the whole material universe – organic and inorganic – might, in the Resurrection of the Body, be restored and transformed into the new heaven and new earth.

Modern science has not superseded mediaeval thought about the nature of creation, but only the physical picture which accompanied and illustrated it. In Dante's *Divine Comedy*, the form of the literal story is, of course, as much dictated by contemporary science as is that of any story of planetary adventure by Jules Verne, H. G. Wells, or C. S. Lewis. The pit of Hell, running down to the "great fundament of the universe, on which all weights downweigh"; the southern hemisphere, uninhabited and completely covered with water, in which Dante's fantasy has situated the island and the mountain of Purgatory; the nine concentric celestial spheres with their motions – all these things belonged to the accepted current cosmology; and Dante, like all writers on similar subjects, embellishes his tale with a multitude of astronomical and geographical details, so as to lend an air of conviction to his narrative. But this conventional picture is in no way necessary to his thought, or to the significance of his allegory. He could, for instance, have managed very well with a Copernican universe centred about the sun; in some ways it would have accommodated itself better to his ideas than the earth-centred universe he knew. For he has a picture of the angelic hierarchy circling about God as their centre – the nearest the swiftest, as Kepler's law demands; and Beatrice has to furnish quite an elaborate explanation of why this arrangement differs from that of the spheres themselves, of which (since they are regarded as wheeling daily about the earth) the farthest from the centre must obviously be accorded the highest velocity.[1] The sun is frequently used as a type of God; consequently a universe revolving about a central sun would have offered great convenience to poetry. An Einsteinian ten-dimensional universe[2] with no recognized centre might be supposed less appropriate for allegory, but if Dante had now to re-write his poem in conformity with twentieth-century physics he would probably seize on the interesting numerical correspondence between the ten heavens of *his* cosmology and the ten dimensions of ours, and find little difficulty in adapting his picture accordingly. Nor would a centreless universe disconcert him; it would fit in conveniently enough with the famous dictum of the Schoolmen that "God is a circle whose centre is everywhere and its circumference nowhere."

Dante's thought, then, while closely associated with the cosmology of his period, was in no way dependent on it. Philosophy in his day was the dominant branch of learning and what we now call science tended to conform its findings to the requirements of philosophy. This had long been the case. Aristarchus in the third century before Christ had suggested that the earth might revolve round the sun, but this theory was rejected on philosophic grounds. Or again, the movements of heavenly bodies were held to be circular because the circle was philosophically the perfect figure; it was not until Kepler's time that observation, fortified by improved instruments, was able to free itself from the constraints of an idealist philosophy of mathematics. But as experimental science gradually obtained the upper hand and became in its turn dominant, the ability to interpret poetic allegory and to distinguish the figure from the thing figured was lost. The poetic statements of the Bible, for instance, were mistaken for the factual statements which they were never intended to be; and it came

1. See Canto xxviii.
2. According to Einstein's law of gravitation, there are ten principal measures or coefficients of curvature of the world. "Space-time is a four-dimensional manifold embedded in . . . as many dimensions as it can find new ways to twist about in; . . . its invention is not exhausted until it has been provided with six extra dimensions, making ten dimensions in all." (See A. S. Eddington, *The Nature of the Physical World*, Cambridge University Press, 1928, p. 120.)

to be felt that if the cosmic picture which they conveyed were false to fact, then the thought behind that picture must be false too. It does not follow that because Dante's schematic arrangement of circling spheres is an inexact picture of the physical heavens, and the southern hemisphere, on being explored, is found to contain no Mountain of Purgatory, that the religious and moral ideas which his cosmos allegorizes must, logically, be discarded. It would be as though a horticulturist reading:

> *There is a garden in her face*
> *Where roses and white lilies blow*

and proving by careful experiment that flower-gardens cannot be cultivated upon the human countenance, were to conclude that Thomas Campion's lady never existed, nor his love for her either. Similarly, when Darwin's theory of evolution was made known, honest-minded Christians saw themselves faced with a choice between intellectual integrity and religious belief. Darwinism would scarcely have worried Dante, whose system of delegated creation was flexible enough to allow considerable variation in the functioning of secondary causes.

Two other obstacles, more formidable by far than an outdated cosmology, stand in the way of the modern reader's enjoyment of *Paradiso*. One is the timelessness of Heaven;[1] the other is the variation in the degrees of celestial bliss. The two are interdependent as concepts and both may be expressed in terms of a third, namely the absence of progress. This, to the twentieth-century mind, is perhaps the most disconcerting aspect of all, for one of the results of having substituted a philosophy of becoming for a philosophy of being is that the very notion of an achieved happiness has become not merely inconceivable but actually repugnant to us. Timelessness, or eternity, like Heaven itself, passes man's understanding. Like the concept of infinity, of which it is an aspect, it can only be suggested to man's intelligence by means of mathematical symbols or poetic imagery.

> *I saw Eternity the other night,*
> *Like a great Ring of pure and endless light,*
>   *All calm, as it was bright;*
> *And round beneath it, Time, in hours, days, years,*
>   *Driv'n by the spheres,*
> *Like a vast shadow mov'd; in which the world*
>   *And all her train were hurl'd.*[2]

1. The concept of timelessness, or eternity, is of course inherent in Christianity and not particular to the concepts of *Paradiso*.
2. Henry Vaughan, *The World*.

24

These lines by a seventeenth-century poet express, by means of an image very similar to Dante's, the relationship of eternity to time. It is only as a negation of, or as something beyond or outside, time and space that we can apprehend eternity at all. "Beyond the measurement of night and day, beyond all boundary", Dante says,[1] God created the universe and, with it, time. But however we express it, the experience of timelessness eludes most of us. Indeed, if and when we grasp it, we experience beatitude. That is what happens to Dante during the vision in the last Canto of *Paradiso*. "Eternity", said Boethius, "is the perfect and simultaneous possession of unending life" – unending, not in the sense of endless prolonging, but in the sense that a sphere in three-dimensional space has neither end nor beginning – and the entering into this eternity is beatitude.[2]

If Heaven is unconfined by time and space, it follows that all the Blessed are as they are, and can be no other, for eternity. Yet each spirit is content to be its true self, which now it knows, for what God wills, they also will, and His will is their peace.[3] The knowledge that other souls exceed them in beatitude in no way diminishes their own meed of joy, and the very blemishes or imperfections of character which led them in their earthly life to merit lowlier celestial grace than others are now a matter for rejoicing. Thus the notorious Cunizza, speaking to Dante in the Heaven of Venus, gaily forgives herself the influence which love had over her life, since it is now her joy to will what God wills for her:

> "... I was by name
> *Cunizza; and I glitter here because*
> *I was o'ermastered by this planet's flame;*
>
> *Yet gaily I forgive myself the cause*
> *Of this my lot, for here (though minds of clay*
> *May think this strange) 'tis gain to me, not loss."* [4]

Against the timeless, changeless beatitude of the Blessed, which, like eternity, we can conceive of intellectually but cannot experience, Dante has set the progression of his story, which moves in time and space like the hands of a clock across the motionless dial. Within the

---

1. Canto xxix. 16–17.   2. *Consolatio Philosophiae*, V, vi, and ii.
3. Canto iii, 85. From the last Canto, xxxiii, 109–14, we learn that, for Dante, the perfected life, which is the eternal vision of God, does not mean that further progress is impossible; on the contrary, eternal life means an endlessly deepening vision of the inexhaustible.
4. Canto ix. 32–6.

space-time continuum of the *story*, the souls appear to Dante in the various spheres as he ascends, though in the timeless and unchanging fulfilment of their bliss they never leave the Empyrean. Because Dante is still in the first life, impeded by the limitations of mortality, he cannot see things in their essence, as the Blessed do, but only in their sequence, which is how he is shown them; and though, in the final vision, he does for an instant glimpse the whole of life, by love "held bound into one volume",[1] he bears in mind the limitations of his mortal readers and tells the story of his approach to that instant, page by page, from the beginning to the end.[2]

If Heaven is beyond time and change, life on earth is a progression upward or downward according to man's choice. The souls in Heaven, who see all things in God, know every choice that man will ever make, but this foreknowledge, pertaining to the instantaneousness of their beatitude, does not in the least affect the freedom of man's will. As Cacciaguida, Dante's ancestor, explains:

> "*Contingence, which doth exercise no right*
> *Beyond that frame of matter where you lie,*
> *Stands all depicted in the Eternal Sight,*
>
> *Though suffering thence no more necessity*
> *Than doth the vessel down the river gliding*
> *From its reflection in the watcher's eye.*"[3]

Since man's will is free, it follows that the choice of good must be an occasion of rejoicing in Heaven and the choice of evil an occasion of wrath. And this we find to be the case. Against the ecstatic perfection of utter bliss experienced by the souls "beyond the frame of matter" is traced the crescendo or diminuendo of their joys in measure as they participate in the triumph or defeats of human life. It is difficult to grasp that the Blessed, remaining as they do untroubled in their ecstasy, are nevertheless closely and intimately concerned with the affairs of earth. The apparent contradiction is resolved if we regard the undiminished perfection of their beatitude, like their foreknowledge of contingence, as pertaining to the timelessness of Heaven, and the increase or clouding of their joy as a sign of their share in the

1. Canto xxxiii. 85–6.
2. Readers interested in the theological implications of the gradualness of Dante's approach to the Beatific Vision will find an illuminating treatment of the subject in the article by Kenelm Foster, "Dante's Vision of God", *Italian Studies*, 1959, pp. 21–39.
3. Canto xvii. 37–42.

experience of time which will continue until the Last Judgement. By means of the imagery of his story, Dante describes the souls as experiencing an ever-mounting ectasy of joy as he himself ascends and grows in understanding. As the souls in the Moon draw near, they exclaim in delight:

"Lo! here is one that shall *increase* our loves".[1] Foulquet of Marseilles, in his joy at beholding Dante,

> *... flashed forth in brilliance clad*
> *Like a fine ruby smitten by the sun.*[2]

Cacciaguida, in his foreknowledge of the event, has awaited his descendant with "a long sweet eagerness" and bids him speak, that the sound of his voice may "slake the sweet thirst and longing" of his love.[3]

Perhaps more striking even than the enhancement of celestial joy by human fulfilment is the wrath of Heaven at wrong-doing upon earth. In the Heaven of the Contemplatives, a loud cry of execration greets St Peter Damian's denouncement of the corruption of monastic life; when St Peter proclaims the Holy See vacant in the eyes of Christ, all Heaven is veiled in shame as though by the darkness which shrouded the earth at the Crucifixion; in the Primum Mobile itself, on the very threshold of the abode of God, Beatrice rebukes the covetousness of mankind and pours scorn upon petty-minded and unworthy preachers who misrepresent or neglect the Gospel in their sermons. Her very last words to Dante are a reproach to the Italians who will resist the Emperor and a prophecy of the damnation of Pope Clement V who will join Boniface among the Simoniacs in the Third Bolgia:

> "*Him in the Holy Office no long term*
> *Will God endure, but thrust him down below*
> *Where Simon Magus pays his score, to squirm*
>
> *Behind the Anagni man, who'll deeper go.*"[4]

The more gladsome the rejoicing and the more vehement the wrath, the more emphatic is the assertion that man's will is free, for both emotions are meaningless if we are puppets of necessity. This, no doubt, is why the questions of astral determinism and free will were discussed on the Cornice of Wrath in Purgatory,[5] and why Beatrice, whose expositions on the freedom of the will are among the great

1. Canto v. 105.   2. Canto ix. 68–9.   3. Canto xv. 49, 64.
4. Canto xxx. 145–8.   5. *Purg.* Canto xvi.

imperatives of the *Paradiso*, leaves Dante with this final image of judgement.

There is, of course, an important difference between celestial and earthly passions. In Heaven, the emotion of wrath is experienced with an utter detachment from all sense of guilt. In this the saints display an attitude that is in keeping with Catholic Christianity, which must always simultaneously affirm and deny the value and importance of the things of this world, being at once concerned with them and wholly detached from them. When loved in themselves and for the sake of the self they are, however intrinsically innocent, pomps and vanities, pitfalls and impediments, "falso piacer", the lust of the flesh and the lust of the eyes, the Siren who is the false Beatrice, the mere projection of the ego upon the surface of phenomena.[1] But when they are loved for God's sake, because He makes and loves them, they are vehicles of His glory and sacraments of Himself, the teeth by which love grips the soul, the leaves of the Gardener's garden, the beauty of Beatrice, the eyes of Mary, the Incarnate God and the inmost mystery of the Godhead. This Dante has learnt, and the stages by which he has learnt it are the story of the *Divine Comedy*. When St John questions him concerning the secondary objects of his love (being satisfied that his highest love is directed to God), Dante replies:

> . . ."*All ratchets which can severally*
> *Revolve the heart towards God co-operate*
> *And are indented with my charity:*
>
> *The being of the world and my own state,*
> *The death He died that I might live the more,*
> *The hope in which I, by faith, participate,*
>
> *The living truth which I conveyed before,*
> *Have dredged me from the sea of wrongful love,*
> *And of the right have set me on the shore.*
>
> *And through the garden of the world I rove,*
> *Enamoured of its leaves in measure solely*
> *As God the Gardener nurtures them above.*" [2]

As he concludes, the whole of Heaven fills with a song of praise, and Dante's sight, temporarily lost, is restored to him. His love, like that of the Blessed, has been set in order, so that concern for secondary

1. This is the substance of the doctrine of *Purgatory*. See especially Cantos xvii and xviii.
2. Canto xxvi. 55–66.

good cannot disturb his love for God. That is why, beside every line of the *Divine Comedy* that repudiates the world one can place another that eagerly exalts it; that is why the Blessed are as joyously interested in the living Dante as they are indignantly interested in the living Boniface, and why, at the same time, not even the knowledge that Hell co-exists with Heaven can make the least wound in their eternal and unchanging beatitude.

THE RELEVANCE OF PARADISO

The relevance of Dante's allegory of heavenly life to orthodox Christianity is not far to seek. What seems more difficult to establish is any connection between it and modern conceptions of the cosmos. Since the Renaissance and the Reformation, a rift, widening inexorably year by year, century by century, has divided the facts of religious experience from those of natural science. No comparable chasm existed in Dante's time; yet he, no less than modern man, was driven, by an intellectual and spiritual urge, to seek a synthesis between – what? Between matter and spirit, causation and free will, human justice and divine providence, merit and grace, time and eternity, earthly and heavenly life, man and God. This dual pattern still runs through all existence as it appears to man, and modern science, far from showing that a synthesis is irrelevant to our intellectual and spiritual condition, makes the need for it seem all the more urgent, while rendering it more and more difficult of achievement. How, then, can Dante's synthesis meet the requirements of modern man? The very suggestion that it could do so seems almost laughable. Those narrow circles revolving with the seven planets and the fixed stars – what a tight, suffocating little universe he imagines! What has it to do with the inconceivable dimensions of our expanding cosmos, with its receding galaxies, its primeval matter which draws ever nearer to the infinitesimal the further we pursue it along the scale of time, its immensity of space and duration which mathematics can symbolize but not measure, the inexpressible complexity and multiplicity of its evolution? How can the *Divine Comedy*, above all the third cantica, *Paradise*, lay claim to the serious attention of any but historians of literature and thought?

Anyone who undertakes to interpret Dante's *Paradise* for the general reader in the mid twentieth century must, in all honesty, ask himself these questions. He may, of course, attempt to evade them by seeking refuge in the values and criteria of poetry, but even there the same questions will eventually obtrude themselves. This is a poem about the universe; if the poet's data are no longer valid in relation to our present knowledge of the cosmos, does the work move us by its verbal beauty alone? Or has the poet's intuition seized and communicated transcendant truths to which we are now returning by another route?

It is beginning to look as though this may be the case. The synthesis achieved by Teilhard de Chardin in his remarkable work *The Phenomenon of Man*[1] would have delighted Dante, as it must indeed delight all Dantists, renewing as it does an awareness of the enduring validity of his poem. There can be little doubt that if Dante were writing the *Paradiso* today, Teilhard de Chardin would shine forth among that double circle of lights which are the souls of those who sought to reconcile the truth of man with that of God.

Like Dante, Teilhard de Chardin had a strong visual imagination. With all the means of verification which modern science commands, man is still, for Teilhard, at the stage of picture language, or allegory, at least as regards communication with his fellows. Speaking of the phases of life which ran their course before the appearance of thought on earth, he says: "I do not pretend to describe them as they really were, but rather as we must *picture* them to ourselves so that the world may be true for us *at this moment*." [2] What is remarkable is not so much that man still uses pictures to convey his thought, for metaphor is the very stuff of language, but that the same pictures keep recurring. The image of the circle is particularly persistent. This may have something to do with the roundness of the earth, the sphericity of man's environment, to which Teilhard attributes the intensification of man's psychosocial activity, and to which Sir Julian Huxley traces ultimately what he calls "the bounding structure of evolving man, marking him off from the rest of the universe and yet facilitating exchange with it." [3] Whatever the ultimate cause may be, it is remarkable that a poet and a scientist, separated by over 600 years and approaching the subject from what would seem to be totally opposed points of view, should both use the sphere as the image of the universe and the "Point Beyond" as the image of God or Omega. The All towards which the universe, in Teilhard's interpretation of phenomena, is shown to be

1. English translation by Bernard Wall and others, Collins, 1959. All quotations are from this edition.
2. *op. cit.*, p. 35; italics mine, B. R.
3. *ibid.*, Introduction, pp. 17–18.

converging, is imaged by him as a Point [1] beyond the sphere of the world, "which only exists and is finally perceptible (however immense its sphere) in the directions in which its radii meet – *even if* it were beyond space and time altogether".[2] Dante would be perfectly at home with such imagery; and the modern reader who concerns himself with these immense and challenging considerations – and, in our present-day dilemma and bewilderment, how can any of us fail to do so? – will find in Dante's Prime Mover existing in a spaceless and timeless Empyrean an image no more remote and no less relevant than the cogitations of a twentieth-century scientist.

On the relation of the Ego with the All, Teilhard, again resorting to the image of the circle, speaks of the three-fold property possessed by every consciousness:

(1) of centring everything partially on itself;

(2) of being able to centre itself upon itself constantly and increasingly;

(3) of being brought by this very super-centration into association with all the other centres surrounding it. Each consciousness exists for ever as itself, but can only be fully realized as itself by integration with the Whole; or, to express it as Sir Julian Huxley has done, "persons are individuals who transcend their merely organic individuality in conscious participation." [3] For the scientist, then, no less than for the theologian, personality exists; and, further, for the scientist, no less than for the theologian, it participates in, but cannot be absorbed by, the Absolute. "In and by means of each one of us," says Teilhard, "an absolutely original centre is established in which the universe is reflected in a unique and inimitable way." These centres are our very selves and personalities, which, he goes on to show, in terms of the reasoning which sustains his whole book, grow conscious of themselves the more fully they evolve, becoming more clearly distinct from others the closer they draw to the All or Omega.[4]

In both Dante and Teilhard the relationship of the Many to the One is perceived as the persistence of the personal consciousness (i.e. the

---

1. Strictly speaking, Teilhard places it beyond, though in line with, that ultimate Point which man's mind can conceive. "This is in deference to the theological concept of the 'supernatural' according to which the binding contact between God and the world, *hic et nunc* inchoate, attains to a super-intimacy (which is thus outside all logic) of which man can have no inkling and to which he can lay no claim by virtue of his 'nature' alone." (p. 298.)

2. p. 259. My italics, B. R.

3. *op. cit.* Introduction, p. 20.

4. For a full discussion of this, see Teilhard, *op. cit.*, pp. 261–2.

soul) and the centring of the consciousness upon the centre of all centres (i.e. God).

On the subject of love, also, the poet and the scientist are basically in perfect agreement.[1] This is not so surprising as it might seem, for both are concerned with the *dynamism* of love rather than its passive or sentimental aspect. According to Teilhard: "Love in all its subtleties is nothing more, and nothing less, than *the more or less direct trace marked on the heart of the element by the psychical convergence of the universe upon itself.*" [2] This statement, for all its modern connotations, would have been, with certain reservations, acceptable to the thirteenth-century poet, Guido Guinizelli, whose famous poem on the nature of love [3] conveys much the same conviction. It could stand, without alteration, as an explanation of Dante's vision of love at the end of the *Vita Nuova*.[4] He does not there describe that vision to us, but from the *Divine Comedy*, which is the fulfilment of the pledge he there makes, we may reconstruct something of its nature and of the route by which he came to see that the love he experienced was something he shared with all creation. "If there were no internal propensity to unite", says Teilhard, "even at a prodigiously rudimentary level – indeed in the molecule itself – it would be physically impossible for love to appear higher up, with us, in 'hominized' form. By rights, to be certain of its presence in ourselves, we should assume its presence, at least in an inchoate form, in everything that is. And in fact if we look around us at the confluent ascent of consciousness, we see it is not lacking anywhere." [5] Dante, in the *Convivio*, says very much the same, all due allowance being made for the different data which were available to him,[6] and he says it again, in a more condensed form and in a different context, through the mouth of Virgil in *Purgatory*.[7]

If consciousness persists and is truly realized only on being inte-

---

1. It is perhaps necessary to make clear that there is here no intention of indicating the "influence" of Dante on Teilhard, who makes no mention of him in *The Phenomenon of Man* and gives no indication of having read him. Some points of contact between them are traceable, ultimately, to a common Catholic heritage; but this does not account for them all.

2. p. 265. Italics are mine, B. R.

3. *"Al cor gentil ripara sempre amor".* It would have been less acceptable to Dante's friend and fellow poet, Guido Cavalcanti, whose Averrhoistic concept of love was in conflict with his soul's awareness. Dante quotes Guinizelli's poem in the *Vita Nuova* and by the conversation he holds with him in the *Purgatorio* shows how much he regarded himself as indebted to him (see *Purg.*, Canto XXVI).

4. See xliii.   5. p. 264.

6. Tractate III, Ch. ii and iii.   7. Cantos xvii–xviii.

grated with the All, it follows that "a universal love is not only psychologically possible; it is the only complete and final way in which we are able to love."[1] Here, expressed in terms of scientific reasoning, is Dante's Celestial Rose. "Universal love" may seem much vaguer than Dante's precise and symmetrical picture of the souls seated on thrones and all visible to him in human form despite the measureless dimensions of time and space; but Teilhard, though he speaks in the abstract, is no less specific and personalized than Dante on this question. "Love," he says, "dies in contact with the impersonal and anonymous. With equal infallibility it becomes impoverished with remoteness in space – and still more, much more, with difference in time. For love to be possible there must be co-existence."[2] Therefore, Omega, or, to use Teilhard's, no less than Dante's, image, the *Prime Mover ahead*, must be supremely present and the consciousness converging towards it must at the same time draw further and further away from anonymity, becoming increasingly actual and personal the nearer it approaches to the personalizing action of the centre of centres.

At every essential point, the image or allegory which Dante's intuition has constructed upon the basis of his admittedly limited knowledge of the material world touches and joins hands with this recent structure assembled from the disparate elements of modern scientific discovery and thought. Even the scholastic division of *substance* and *accident* has its counterpart in Teilhard's "without" and "within" of things; and the reconciliation of causation with the freedom inherent in consciousness is tentatively essayed when he asks:

Determinate *without* and "free" *within* – would the two aspects of things be irreducible and incommensurable? If so, what is your solution?[3]

Of unity-in-multiplicity, he shows three different views. The first, looking downwards, so to speak, scrutinizes the infinitesimal being of ultimate matter:

It is almost as if the stuff of which all stuff is made were reducible in the end to some simple and unique kind of substance.[4]

The second is an intermediate view, showing the conjunction of plurality with identity:

We do not get what we call matter as a result of the simple aggregation and juxtaposition of atoms. For that, a mysterious identity must

1. Teilhard, *op. cit.*, p. 267.   2. p. 269.   3. p. 57.
4. p. 41. Compare with this, *Paradise*, Canto ii. 112–20 and *note*.

absorb and cement them, an influence at which our mind rebels in be-wilderment at first but which in the end it must perforce accept.[1]

The "upwards" view, of the universe as a total aggregate within an immeasurable and unimaginable element or being, is expressed as follows:

The history of consciousness and its place in the world remain incompre-hensible to anyone who has not seen first of all that the cosmos in which man finds himself caught up constitutes, by reason of the unim-peachable wholeness of its whole, a *system*, a *totum* and a *quantum*: a system by its plurality, a totum by its unity, a quantum by its energy; all three within a boundless contour.[2]

If relevance to modern life and thought is conceded to such con-siderations as these, then relevance must also be conceded to Dante's *Paradise*, and relevance of the same kind. Both writers are talking about the same things, though in different ways and on different scales. In comparison with our cosmos, the universe of Dante seems a very miniature model indeed; but if Teilhard de Chardin has rightly described the phenomena of the universe as we now know it, he has shown that the same principles are valid, ultimately, for both.

THE DATE OF PARADISO

Scholarly opinion is divided as to the date by which Dante began writing the *Commedia*. The problem is closely related to the develop-ment of his political views and to the course of events in Italy and Europe. Two main hypotheses have the support of expert opinion.[3] According to one, the more traditional of the two, Dante began writ-ing the *Inferno* about the year 1306 or 1307, just after the completion of Book IV of the *Convivio*. A second view places the writing of the whole of the *Commedia* between the years 1313 and 1321, that is, after the death of the Emperor Henry VII. This second view has the advant-age of rendering unnecessary the supposition that Dante altered or rewrote parts of *Inferno* and *Purgatorio* after the deaths of Henry VII,

1. p. 42. Compare with this, *Paradise*, Canto xxix. 28–36 and *note*.
2. p. 43. Compare with this the Vision of the Universe in God, *Paradise*, Canto xxxiii.
3. For a summarized discussion of both views, see U. Cosmo, *A Handbook to Dante Studies*, Blackwell, 1950, pp. 137–45. For discussion of the second hypothesis, see A. Passerin d'Entrèves, *Dante as a Political Thinker*, Oxford, Clarendon, 1952. It may be added that Professor Paul Renucci places the beginning of *Inferno* as early as 1304 (probably May), and that Mr Colin Hardie favours the year 1311.

Pope Clement V and King Philip IV of France.[1] On the other hand, eight years seems a short time in which to write so detailed and complex a work, and arguments in support of the first view, which presupposes its more gradual development and even a change of heart and mind in Dante,[2] do not seem unreasonable. If the composition was spread over some fourteen years, from 1307 to 1321, history itself may be said to have taken a hand in the work's formation:[3] when Henry of Luxemburg crossed the Alps in 1310 he entered not only Italy but also the *Divine Comedy*.

However varied opinion may be concerning the composition of the whole *Commedia*, there is general agreement on one aspect of the dating of *Paradiso*. It was written, all of it, after the death of Henry. We also know where it was written. Dante was living in Ravenna at the time, in a house of his own, under the protection of Guido Novello of Polenta.[4] His sons, Jacopo and Pietro, and his daughter, Beatrice, were with him. It is even thought, despite the tradition to the contrary, that his wife, Gemma, may have joined him.[5] In Ravenna, then, in conditions of relative comfort and security, Dante wrote the concluding cantos of *Purgatorio*[6] and began the *Paradiso*, on which he continued working up to the last few weeks of his life.

According to the most probable chronology, the *Paradiso* was written in under four years, between some time in 1318 and the summer of 1321. He had no sooner finished it than danger threatened. Serious trouble sprang up between Venice and Ravenna. Some Venetian ships were seized by the Ravennese and Venetian sailors were killed. The Doge of Venice formed an alliance with Rimini and Forlì and prepared to make war on Ravenna.

The impact of these events upon Dante's peace of mind must have been disturbing in the extreme. His friend and patron, Guido Novello, the Lord of Ravenna, was in no position to meet the challenge and it

1. These events occurred in strikingly rapid succession: Henry died in August 1313, Clement in April 1314 and Philip in November 1314.

2. See for instance the phases distinguished by F. Ercole in *Il pensiero politico di Dante*, 1928.

3. This may be partly what Dante means when he says that "both Heaven and Earth have set their hand" to his poem (cf. Canto xxv. 1-3).

4. Polenta is a castle near Bertinoro, a few miles south of Forlì. Dante refers to the head of the family, Guido Vecchio, in *Inferno* xxvii. 40-2; he was the father of Francesca da Rimini and Guido Novello was her nephew.

5. See Michele Barbi, *Life of Dante*, translated by P. G. Ruggiers, University of California Press, 1954, p. 28.

6. It is thought that the description of the Earthly Paradise is based on the landscape of the pine-forest near Ravenna.

was imperative that war should be averted by diplomatic means. This was no moment for a calm withdrawal into the revision of his last cantos. In the preoccupation and tension which attend such emergencies, it is not surprising that he left a batch of manuscript at the house of a friend [1] and that there was no time to arrange for it to be copied and sent to Can Grande della Scala, as was his usual procedure. In August 1321, after, it may be imagined, much urgent exchanging of views between Guido and the more notable citizens of Ravenna, an embassy was sent to Venice. The fact that Dante formed part of it suggests that he had been prominent in the discussions that had gone before. The delegates were successful in obtaining peace terms and Dante returned to Ravenna by the quickest route, through the *lagune* [2] of Comacchio, across the Lamone and through the northern extremity of the Pineta. On this journey he succumbed to a malignant form of malaria and arrived home ill. He died during the early morning of the 14th of September.

It is understandable that in the pressure and anxiety of external affairs the last thirteen cantos of *Paradiso* came to be mislaid. Critical opinion is on the whole disposed to accept the substance of Boccaccio's story of their recovery, and even in the light of day-to-day experience the sequence of events can be reconstructed without undue distortion of the normal or probable. If it seems strange that the dying Dante did not tell his family where he had left the manuscript, one may reply that he perhaps thought they knew already, or that he may not have realized that he was dying, for in cases of malignant malaria the end comes quickly and suddenly.[3] It seems natural that in the shock and

1. It is not clear whether the MS. was left in Dante's own house, which the family vacated after his death, or in the house of his friend, Piero Giardino, with whom he sometimes stayed. There seems at any rate to have been a removal, for, when the MS. was found, the house was occupied by other tenants. Piero Giardino, whose family can be traced back to the beginning of the thirteenth century, was a notary in Ravenna. He is attested as still living there in 1348. When Boccaccio visited Ravenna in 1346 he learnt from Giardino the story of the lost MS. For the full account see *Hell*, Introduction, pp. 52–4.

2. Locally, these are called "valli" and are marshes, with little stretches of open water.

3. According to Boccaccio, the family were in time to summon a priest. It may be that the manuscript was left behind in a removal after the death of Dante, but the fact that the sons, after the vision they had of their father, called on Piero Giardino and went with him to the house in question rather suggests that it was in a former dwelling of Giardino's that the manuscript had been left. The window, covered with a curtain, in which Boccaccio says the papers were found, was probably one of those small recesses which one

grief of their father's death and in the melancholy and exhausting distractions of the lying-in-state, the funeral oration and the burial, the sons should have been unable to concentrate on the secretarial duties they sometimes undertook when he was alive and which were now more than ever incumbent upon them. However it may be, when they came to put their father's papers in order and to assemble the manuscript of *Paradiso*, they found that it did not proceed beyond Canto xx.

It is not difficult to imagine the dejected state of mind of Jacopo and Pietro when they found themselves faced with this calamity, or the sinking hearts and despairing resignation with which they must have yielded to persuasions to finish their father's work – or their relief and joy when they found the cantos, and "having cleaned off all the mould, and seen that the pages were numbered, and placed them in order, and found they were complete", they copied them out and added them to the other twenty.[1]

It is interesting that this story should be concerned with the last thirteen cantos, for they form, in a way, a distinct division or section of the work. In Canto xxi we prepare to move from the active to the contemplative life, a transition comparable to those in *Inferno* and *Purgatorio* and to the earlier division in *Paradiso* itself when, ascending to the Heaven of the Sun, Dante and Beatrice pass beyond the spheres which are tinged by the cone of shadow cast by the earth. The fact that Dante had not arranged for any of these cantos to be copied and sent to Can Grande perhaps indicates that he regarded them as forming a whole section or unit and that composing them proved to be a continuously sustained and related process. Actually, as regards content, the last thirteen cantos fall naturally into a group of ten plus three, the final triad constituting the crown and climax of the whole work. According to Boccaccio, it was his habit to send six or eight cantos at a time to Can Grande, and, in his eclogue to Giovanni del Virgilio, Dante appears to say (in pastoral metaphor) that he intends to send him ten cantos as a sample of his work.[2] That he departed

---

still sees in mediaeval houses and churches in Italy. There is one set into the wall in the Church at Arquà, close to the altar, in which the priest keeps sundry papers. It, too, is covered by a curtain.

1. By a strange coincidence, the present translation, at the death of Dorothy L. Sayers, had not proceeded beyond Canto xx, but there, unfortunately, the coincidence ends, except for the recovery of a few fragments, all of which have been incorporated in the present translation.

2. "*decem vascula*": the interpretation of this phrase is still debated: does it mean "ten cantos", or "ten eclogues"?

from his usual practice at the end is perhaps a sign that the mounting pressure of inspiration in the culminating stages was of such urgency that he was carried past the transition which occurs at the end of Canto xxx and deferred the process of revising and copying until the whole of the first draft was down. In the light of subsequent events it is most fortunate that he did so.

At the same time as writing the *Paradiso*, Dante, it is believed by some, gave lessons or lectures on the art of poetry. It has even been suggested that he held a lectureship in rhetoric at the University. He is thought to have visited Verona more than once during this period; certainly he is known to have been there on 20th January, 1320, when in the Church of Sant' Elena, before the clergy and other notables who had assembled to hear him, he delivered a disquisition in Latin on the question of the depth of water in relation to land, a problem he had heard discussed at Mantua.[1] His reputation as a poet was growing and rumours that he had almost completed his great work were arousing interest and expectation. Giovanni del Virgilio, a young poet and lecturer in rhetoric at the University of Bologna, who had read his *Inferno* and *Purgatorio*, invited him to Bologna to receive the laurel crown (or, as we would express it nowadays, to receive an honorary degree). Being young and, consequently, still impressed by the formalities and conventions in which he himself had been trained, Giovanni del Virgilio respectfully remonstrates with Dante for not writing in Latin and suggests a number of stirring subjects relating to recent history as worthy of Dante's talent (and possibly better calculated to win academic approval than the theme on which he was at present diffusing his energies) – the death of Henry VII, for instance, the battle of Montecatini, the victories of Can Grande, or the struggle on land and sea between King Robert of Naples and the Visconti for the possession of Genoa.

The correspondence, which Giovanni initiated, consists of four communications, two from the young scholar and two from Dante. All four are in Latin, the first being a *carmen* and the other three, eclogues. From Dante's first reply we learn that he is at work on the *Paradiso* (the date is probably the latter part of 1319) and that he hopes it may earn for him the poet's crown at Florence,[2] for there and there only is he willing to receive it. In the second, said to have been forwarded to Giovanni after Dante's death, there is reference to a certain "Poly-

---

1. *Quaestio de Aqua et Terra*, edited and translated by C. L. Shadwell, Oxford, Clarendon, 1909.
2. Compare with this the opening of Canto xxv.

phemus" whose presence in Bologna makes it impossible for him to accept Giovanni's invitation.[1]

THE EPISTLE TO CAN GRANDE

From these few indications of Dante's activities during the last years of his life, it is evident, sparse as they are, that he quite often allowed himself a change of occupation as a relief from the strain of concentrating on the *Paradiso*. There remains one minor work relating to this period which has not yet been mentioned. This is the famous *Epistle to Can Grande*.[2] At one time its authenticity was vigorously, even violently, contested,[3] but after the authoritative discussion of the subject by the great English Dantist, Edward Moore, it has long been regarded as genuine. In recent years, the question has come to life again and some leading Dantists[4] are now once again of the opinion that it is a forgery. Since it has a direct bearing on the *Paradiso*, it is necessary to examine the pros and cons of the matter and to try to reach a decision, if possible.

The Epistle, which is in Latin, is addressed to Can Grande della Scala in the following terms:

To the magnificent and most victorious Lord, the Lord Can Grande della Scala, Vicar-General of the most holy principality of Caesar in the city of Verona, and town of Vicenza, his most devoted servant Dante Alighieri, a Florentine by birth, not by disposition, prayeth long and happy life, and perpetual increase of the glory of his name.[5]

In the first section, Dante (assuming him to be the author) offers the *Paradiso* as a gift to Can Grande in return for his friendship and generosity. In the second part, he says a few words by way of introduction to the work, in the course of which he has occasion to indicate, in a famous passage, the four senses of the psalm, "When Israel went out of Egypt" and the two senses of the *Commedia*.[6] In the third and final section, he offers an exposition of the literal meaning of what

1. "Polyphemus" is probably the ferocious Fulcieri da Calboli who was podestà of Florence in 1302. He was elected Captain of the People in Bologna for the first six months of 1321 (see also *Purg.* xiv. 58–60, and *note*).
2. *The Letters of Dante*, ed. Paget Toynbee, Oxford, Clarendon, 1920, No. X, pp. 160–211.
3. Especially by Francesco D'Ovidio.
4. Notably Manfredi Porena and Bruno Nardi in Italy, Professor Paul Renucci in France, the late Friedrich Schneider in Germany, and Mr Colin Hardie in England.
5. *ed. cit.*, p. 195.   6. See below, pp. 44–9.

he calls the Prologue of *Paradiso*, namely the first thirty-six lines of the first canto. He breaks off with an expression of regret that, owing to "anxiety as to (his) domestic affairs", he is unable to proceed with the commentary, which he hopes, however, to be able to continue at some later date.

It is evident that if this Epistle is authentic it is a document of the very highest importance. Let us examine first some of the arguments which have recently been ranged against it. Chief among them is the objection that the early commentators seem to have been unaware of, or to have ignored, the Epistle and that many Dantists have hardly used the Epistle at all to interpret the *Comedy*, even when they have been convinced of its authenticity. Secondly, it is asked: would Dante have interrupted the flow of poetic inspiration to plod through a prosaic Latin commentary on his work as he went along? Thirdly, if he had intended to write a commentary, would he not have begun with the *Inferno*? Fourthly, there are serious discrepancies between the Epistle and Dante's other works, notably the first Eclogue, the *Convivio* and the *Commedia* itself. Fifthly, since Dante was in any case sending cantos of the *Paradiso* regularly to Can Grande, why should he offer it to him as a gift as though he did not possess it already? There are many other arguments and sub-divisions of arguments which have been brought to bear against the genuineness of the Epistle, but these five points have more relevance than others to the important issues.

The case for the defence can best be opened by considering the probable date at which Dante could have written the Epistle. Since he addresses Can Grande as "most victorious" ("*victoriosissimus*"), the Lord of Verona is evidently at the height of his success. The Epistle, therefore, is unlikely to have been written just after his disastrous defeat by the Paduans in August 1320. We may regard this, then, as the *terminus ad quem*. Since the Epistle contains an exposition of a part of the first canto of *Paradiso* and an outline of the contents of the whole cantica, the *terminus a quo* is likely to be about 1318, that is, after the completion of *Purgatorio* and when he had begun work on the third cantica. The question is, how far had he got with it? There is no need to conclude that he had written only the first canto, but the use of the future tense to describe the contents of the rest suggest that, though he had probably sketched out a draft of the whole work, the greater part of it was still to be written. There is no need, either, to assume that Dante interrupted a flow of poetic inspiration to write the brief commentary contained in this Epistle. If he wrote it at a fairly early stage, perhaps some time in 1318, the year in which Can Grande took Cremona and was elected Captain General of the Ghibelline League in Lombardy, the intellectual aspects of his creation would be uppermost in his mind and nothing would be more natural than to formulate them. In fact, it is probable that he had already formulated them for his own benefit and that part of what he writes is an elaboration of a rough draft or notes. The Italian Dantist, Umberto Cosmo, holds that it is in accordance with what he calls "the logic of the facts" that Dante visited Can Grande at Verona at about this period and not immediately after Henry's death in 1313, as is usually maintained.[1] That the author had recently returned from Verona when he wrote the Epistle is made plain in the opening paragraph:

The illustrious renown of your Magnificence, which wakeful fame spreads abroad as she flies, affects persons in divers ways, so that some it uplifts with the hope of good fortune, while others it casts down with the dread of destruction. The report whereof, overtopping all deeds of recent times, I erstwhile did deem extravagant, as going beyond the appearance of truth. But that continued uncertainty might not keep me longer in suspense, even as the Queen of the South sought Jerusalem, and as Pallas sought Helicon, so did I seek Verona, in order to examine with my own trusty eyes the things of which I had heard. And there was I witness of your splendour, there was I witness and partaker of your bounty.[2]

It does not seem relevant to object that if Dante had written a commentary he would have begun with the *Inferno*. The Epistle is not a commentary; it is a letter of thanks for hospitality, offering a gift, which it explains.[3] It was probably accompanied by a copy of the first canto. If, as seems likely, Can Grande graciously expressed his readiness to receive further cantos, we have the obvious and natural explanation of the tradition (accepted as fact) that Dante sent him regular instalments of the *Paradiso* as he progressed. It is unlikely that once his poetic inspiration got fully under way he would have interrupted it to continue the commentary; and, indeed, we have no evidence that he did so.

1. Handbook to Dante Studies, *ed. cit.*, p. 123. Concerning the Epistle Cosmo says: "My opinion is that if we relate the letter to the culture of the period we are bound to conclude that it is authentic. If Dante had written a commentary on the whole of the *Paradiso* he would have continued in similar vein, and would not have written anything substantially different" (p. 115).

2. *ed. cit.*, pp. 195-6.

3. It is, in fact, a very gracious mediaeval example of a "bread-and-butter" letter.

The objection that the early commentators did not refer to the Epistle has been dealt with in masterly style by Edward Moore, to whose article the reader is referred if he wishes to pursue the matter in greater detail.[1] Moore has, in fact, established that the early commentators display a mixture of knowledge and ignorance of the letter, a knowledge of the expository section, an ignorance of the more formal epistolary sections. This could be accounted for by the supposition, already mentioned above, that Dante had written more than one account of the meanings of the *Commedia*. The neglect by modern Dantists of the Epistle's formula for interpretation is an important matter and can best be discussed, together with the alleged discrepancy between the Epistle and the *Convivio*, in connection with the allegory of the *Paradiso*. But first, having reconstructed, by hypothesis, the circumstances which might feasibly have given rise to the Epistle, let us examine it for internal evidence or indications of its authenticity.

It is, of course, open to anyone to say, as has indeed been said: "The style of this letter is quite unlike Dante's and is totally unworthy of him"; yet it contains, for others, unmistakable traces of his mind and personality, minor points of style and expression, as well as something about the whole appeal and tone of the letter which the reader, with an inner thrill of conviction, recognizes as Dante's own.[2] To such subjective impressions, we may add the minute divisions and subdivisions of the contents, the elaborate distinctions and analyses, and the dissection of his poetry which, as Moore has shown, are wholly characteristic of the author of *Convivio* and the *Vita Nuova*. Professor Edmund Gardner saw in the Epistle an authentic admission by Dante that he had personally undergone some mystical experience which he is unable now to relate or even to recall in full:

For the understanding of which it must be noted that the human intellect in this life, by reason of its connaturality and affinity to the separate intellectual substance, when in exaltation, reaches such a height of exal-

1. *Studies in Dante*, Third Series, pp. 284–362.
2. This impression is corroborated on grounds of textual criticism by Dr Kenelm Foster, who has given me permission to quote from a letter he has written to me on the subject. He says: "Either Dante wrote this or someone who was not only intimately familiar with his writings and his style and his thought, but also a man of genius in his own right. It is more 'economical' to ascribe it simply to Dante – *e basta!*" Here Dr Foster supplies a list of twenty parallels and correspondences between the Epistle and other works by Dante and concludes: "Some of these parallels are not by themselves significant, but taken altogether they form, to my mind, clear evidence of Dante's authorship. They are the sign of his personality."

tation that after its return to itself memory fails, since it has transcended the range of human faculty.[1]

And how like Dante's tone and style is the passionate assertion of the truth of his vision despite his own unworthiness!

And should the cavillers not be satisfied, let them read Richard of St Victor in his book *On Contemplation*; let them read Bernard in his book *On Consideration*; let them read Augustine in his book *On the Capacity of the Soul*; and they will cease from cavilling. But if on account of the sinfulness of the speaker they should cry out against his claim to have reached such a height of exaltation [2] let them read Daniel, where they will find that even Nebuchadnezzar by divine permission beheld certain things as a warning to sinners, and straightway forgot them. For He "who maketh his sun to shine on the good and on the evil, and sendeth rain on the just and on the unjust", sometimes in compassion for their conversion, sometimes in wrath for their chastisement, in greater or lesser measure, according as He wills, manifests his glory to evil-doers, be they never so evil.[3]

There will probably never now be conclusive proof as to the authenticity or otherwise of the Epistle to Can Grande. The foregoing is an attempt to show for what reasons, in the opinion of one reader, the recent controversy does not appear to have impugned the case for its authenticity as established by Moore and confirmed by most leading Dantists. If the Epistle is rejected as spurious, we are left with a forged document of very little interest. If it is accepted as genuine, we are the richer for a revealing and intimate letter from the author of the *Paradiso* at a moment when the plan, though implicit from the very beginning of the *Inferno*, has been thought out again in detail, the whole scheme of the heavens newly visualized, and the poetry of the opening cantos only recently created. In this concluding paragraph, which in the original Latin has a luminous and solemn beauty, Dante describes the movement of the whole cantica:

With regard to the executive part of the work, which was divided after the same manner as the prologue taken as a whole, I shall say nothing either as to its divisions or its interpretation at present; save only that the process of the narrative will be by ascent from heaven to heaven, and that an account will be given of the blessed spirits who are met with in each sphere; and that their true blessedness consists in the apprehension of Him who is the beginning of truth, as appears from what John says: "This is life eternal, to know thee the true God," and from what Boe-

1. *ed. cit.*, p. 208. See E. G. Gardner, *Dante*, 1923, p. 102.
2. Compare with this *Inferno*, ii. 31–3.
3. *ed. cit.*, p. 209.

thius says in his third book *On Consolation*: "To behold thee is the end."
Hence it is that, in order to reveal the glory of the blessedness of those
spirits, many things which have great profit and delight will be asked of
them, as of those who behold the fullness of truth. And since, when the
Beginning or First, which is God, has been reached, there is nought to be
sought for beyond, inasmuch as He is Alpha and Omega, that is the
Beginning and the End, as the *Vision* of John tells us, the work ends in
God Himself, who is blessed for evermore, world without end.[1]

THE ALLEGORY OF PARADISE

As regards the discrepancies which are said to exist between the
Epistle and other works by Dante, the most important is that which
relates to his discussion of allegory. As this is a crucial matter, not only
for the genuineness or otherwise of the Epistle, but also for every
reader's understanding of the *Divine Comedy*, it must be examined at
some length. At the beginning of the first tractate of the *Convivio*,
Dante expresses his intention of explaining fourteen of his odes "by
means of allegorical interpretation after the literal narrative has been
discussed." [2] In the first chapter of the second tractate, he explains
what he means by the terms "literal" and "allegorical":

I say that, as is affirmed in the first chapter, it is meet for this exposition
to be both literal and allegorical. And to make this intelligible, it should
be known that writings can be understood and ought to be expounded
chiefly in four senses. The first is called literal [and this is that sense which
does not go beyond the strict limits of the letter; the second is called
allegorical], and this is disguised under the cloak of such stories, and is a
truth hidden under a beautiful fiction. Thus Ovid says that Orpheus
with his lyre made beasts tame, and trees and stones move towards him-
self; that is to say that the wise man by the instrument of his voice makes
cruel hearts grow mild and humble, and those who have not the life of
science and of art move to his will, while they who have no rational life
are as it were like stones. And why this disguise was invented by the wise
will be shown in the last tractate but one. Theologians indeed do not
apprehend this sense in the same fashion as poets; but, inasmuch as my
intention is to follow here the custom of poets, I will take the allegorical
sense after the manner which poets use.

The third sense is called moral; and this sense is that for which teachers
ought as they go through writings intently to watch for their own profit
and that of their hearers; as in the Gospel when Christ ascended the

1. *ed. cit.*, pp. 210–11.
2. W. W. Jackson's translation (Oxford, Clarendon, 1909), p. 34.

Mount to be transfigured, we may be watchful of His taking with Himself the three Apostles out of the twelve; whereby morally it may be understood that for the most secret affairs we ought to have few companions.

The fourth sense is called anagogic, that is, above the senses; and this occurs when a writing is spiritually expounded, which even in the literal sense by the things signified likewise gives intimation of higher matters belonging to the eternal glory; as can be seen in that song of the prophet which says that, when the people of Israel went out of Egypt, Judaea was made holy and free. And although it be plain that this is true according to the letter, that which is spiritually understood is not less true, namely, that when the soul issues forth from sin she is made holy and free as mistress of herself.[1]

It will be seen that, in this passage, Dante regards the three figurative senses as three possible interpretations of the literal, but does not say whether any one text could be susceptible of all three interpretations. The fact that he uses a different text to illustrate each of the three implies that he did not regard them as "layers" of meaning underlying a single text, nor even as alternatives, but as possible meanings which were relevant according to the nature of the literal sense.

In the *Epistle to Can Grande*, Dante discusses the four meanings as follows:

For the elucidation, therefore, of what we have to say, it must be understood that the meaning of this work [2] is not of one kind only; rather the work may be described as "polysemous", that is, having several meanings; for the first meaning is that which is conveyed by the letter, and the next is that which is conveyed by what the letter signifies; the former of which is called literal, while the latter is called allegorical or moral or anagogical.[3] And for the better illustration of this method of exposition we may apply it to the following verses: "When Israel went out of Egypt, the house of Jacob from a people of strange language; Judah was his sanctuary, and Israel his dominion." For if we consider the letter alone, the thing signified to us is the going out of the children of Israel from Egypt in the time of Moses; if the allegory, our redemption through Christ is signified; if the moral sense, the conversion of the soul from the sorrow and misery of sin to a state of grace is signified; if the anagogical, the passing of the sanctified soul from the bondage of the

1. pp. 73–4. The passage between brackets is a reconstruction (here translated from the Italian) of a lacuna in the text. "But no one who knows the general argument of the whole work will, I think, make serious objection to the way the editors of the accepted text have filled the lacuna." (C. S. Singleton, *Dante Studies I*, Harvard University Press, 1954, p. 84.)

2. i.e. the *Commedia*.

3. I follow here the accepted text of the Società Dantesca.

corruption of this world to the liberty of everlasting glory is signified. And although these mystical meanings are called by various names, they may one and all in a general sense be termed allegorical, inasmuch as they are different from the literal or historical.[1]

It will be seen that in this passage there is a two-fold generic division between the literal and the allegorical sense, and under the latter are listed three "species" of meaning, allegorical (in its second sense), moral and anagogical. The difference between the two systems can be shown in tabular form, as follows:

In the Convivio:

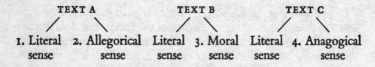

1. Literal sense   2. Allegorical sense   Literal sense   3. Moral sense   Literal sense   4. Anagogical sense

This can also be expressed as follows:

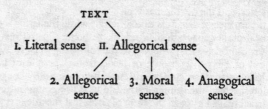

TEXT A, B, OR C

Literal sense   Allegorical, Moral or Anagogical sense.

In the Epistle:

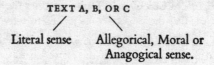

TEXT

I. Literal sense   II. Allegorical sense

2. Allegorical sense   3. Moral sense   4. Anagogical sense

In the interpretation of the psalm quoted in the Epistle, senses 1, 2, 3, and 4 are indicated. In the interpretation of the *Comedy*, also in the Epistle (see below, p. 47), senses I and II are indicated. Senses 2, 3, and 4 can be restated as sense II; sense II can be unfolded in terms of senses 2, 3, and 4.

How does this difference affect the question of the authenticity of the Epistle? According to Moore, it is an argument in support of it,

1. *ed. cit.*, p. 199.

since anyone forging the letter and hoping to pass it off as authentic would have been careful to make this passage tally exactly with the corresponding passage in the *Convivio*, the contents of which would be well known. If we consider that Dante wrote both passages, we have only to suppose that after eleven or twelve years of writing allegory (from 1307 to 1318), he had altered his view of it. The surprising thing is that he altered it so little. What he has done is to reinforce the two-fold division into literal and allegorical, a division which is in any case the one selected by him in the *Convivio* to serve as the framework for the exposition of his own odes.

The new emphasis in the Epistle on the basically two-fold pattern of meaning is of paramount importance as regards the *Commedia*.[1] In the *Convivio* Dante was concerned with distinguishing the allegorical from the literal sense of certain love poems he had written previously. At the time of writing the Epistle, he has been *constructing* an allegory for many years, and an allegory, moreover, of sublime and universal significance. One might have expected that in the process his distinctions between the possible interpretations of the literal sense would have become more numerous and complicated. On the contrary, he has reduced them from three to one:

> ... it is clear that the subject, with regard to which the alternative meanings are brought into play, must be twofold ("duplex"). And therefore the subject of this work must be considered in the first place from the point of view of the literal meaning, and next from that of the allegorical interpretation. The subject, then, of the whole work, taken in the literal sense only, is the state of the souls after death, pure and simple.[2] For on and about that the argument of the whole work turns. If, however, the work be regarded from the allegorical point of view, the subject is man, according as by his merits or demerits in the exercise of his free will he is deserving of reward or punishment by justice.[3]

Dante's *intention* is perfectly clear. If confusion arises it is because allegory, by its very nature, cannot be limited to a two-fold interpre-

1. This new emphasis has been recognized by Professor C. S. Singleton as a shift from the allegory of poets (cf. *Convivio* II, 1, 4) to the allegory of theologians. He ingeniously defines it as "not an allegory of 'this for that', but an allegory of 'this *and* that', of this sense plus that sense." For his illuminating discussion of this question, see *Dante Studies, I*, Harvard University Press, 1954, pp. 84–98.

2. The original Latin which has been translated by Toynbee as "pure and simple" is *simpliciter sumptus*. The truth, as Algernon Moncrieff said, is rarely pure and never simple. What Dante probably means is that this is the simplest and most concise way of summing up the literal meaning.

3. *ed. cit.*, pp. 199–200.

tation. A lily can signify Florence, or France, or the Ghibelline party, or the Virgin Mary, or Christ, or all these things together, in various combinations of inter-related meaning. Dante saw these possible complications, which is why he tried to clarify the matter, warning us, in the *Monarchia*, against looking for allegory "where it is not, or taking it as it ought not to be taken",[1] and firmly restricting the allegorical significance of the *Commedia* to one, and one only, in the Epistle.

This, however, is all very well. Dante chose, for the literal and the allegorical meanings of his work, a subject which by the universality of its significance and application embraces the whole of life, namely, in the literal sense, "the state of souls after death", and, in the allegorical sense, "man, according as by his merits and demerits in the exercise of his free will he is deserving of reward or punishment by justice". How are we to understand "man" ("*homo*") in this context? As mankind in history, as man in society, or as man's individual soul, or as all three? And if all three, are we to look for the meanings separately or in combination? As soon as we examine it, the very stuff of allegory divides and sub-divides before our eyes, despite Dante's determined attempt to bind it together. If we add to its inherent complexities the multiple connotations of language, and, still more, of the highly associative and emotive form of language which is poetry, we begin to understand why Dante insisted that his work was two-fold in meaning, and two-fold only. He was no doubt anxious to prevent readers (perhaps the *Inferno* and *Purgatorio* were already suffering in this way) from reducing his orderly and coherent structure to elemental chaos.

Nevertheless, as Dante himself perfectly well perceived, and as he demonstrates in the Epistle in relation to the psalm, "When Israel went out of Egypt", the two-fold *significance* (literal and allegorical) can be unfolded into a four-fold *interpretation*,[2] and commentators who avail themselves of its range are not departing from what Dante has laid down. Beyond these boundaries, however, anything can happen. The American scholar, H. Flanders Dunbar, perceived no fewer than nine levels of allegory in the *Commedia* and could no doubt have found more, for she concludes: "It is only through multiplicity of interpretation that approach to the truth is gained."[3] To this, Dante would no doubt have replied by quoting again from St

1. Book III, Ch. 4, 50.
2. Or *application*. In speaking of "two-fold" and "four-fold" meaning, the literal sense is counted as the first.
3. *Symbolism in Medieval Thought and its Consummation in the Divine Comedy*, Yale University Press, 1929.

Augustine, as he does in the *Monarchia:* [1] "It is the same mistake as is made by someone who, leaving the right path, comes by a circuitous route to the place to which the road leads ... his error should be pointed out to him for fear lest his habit of leaving the path should carry him into cross roads and wrong ones."

It is a relief to turn from the complex systems of interpretation erected by some commentators to the austere words of Umberto Cosmo: "The supremely important thing is that we should not lose sight of the poetic reality through being too meticulous in our search for the right interpretation." [2] As Dante himself said, "the literal sense ought always to come first, as being that sense in the expression of which the others are all included, and without which it would be impossible and irrational to give attention to the other meanings, and most of all to the allegorical ... I therefore will first discuss the literal meaning, and after that will speak of its allegory, that is, of the hidden truth contained in it, and sometimes I shall touch incidentally on the other meanings (i.e. the moral and the anagogical) as place and time shall permit." [3] He shows no sign of having changed his mind about this, for in the Epistle he likewise begins his commentary with an exposition of the literal meaning of the beginning of *Paradiso*.

Accordingly, in the Notes which accompany the present translation, attention has been paid first and foremost to the literal sense. The allegorical sense, in relation to the literal, is discussed chiefly in the sections entitled "Images". When the literal and the allegorical expositions have been considered, it will be found that the other meanings (the moral and anagogical) are either implied or, as Dante puts it, are touched on incidentally as place and time have permitted.

BEATRICE IN PARADISO

It is perhaps necessary to add something to what has already been said concerning Beatrice in the first volume in this series. [4] As in the *Inferno* and *Purgatorio*, so also in *Paradiso*, Beatrice in the story is what she was in real life. Like Piccarda or Cunizza or Cacciaguida, or like Dante himself, she is, first of all, a person. There can be no doubt about this, for in the Celestial Rose she returns to the place among all the other saints, all of whom are persons. For Dante, Beatrice is actively present, since like all the Blessed in Heaven, she knows clearly what happens

---

1. Book III, Ch. 4, 60.   2. *Handbook to Dante Studies*, p. 153.
3. *Convivio*, II, 1, Jackson's translation, p. 75.   4. *Hell*, pp. 67–8.

on earth. It is quite in accordance with Catholic orthodoxy for Dante
to believe that Beatrice intervened for his salvation, as it is for him to
offer thanks to her for what she has done and pray to her that she may
continue to watch over him:

> "O thou in whom my hopes securely dwell,
>   And who, to bring my soul to Paradise,
>   Didst leave the imprint of thy steps in Hell,
>
> Of all that I have looked on with these eyes
>   Thy goodness and thy power have fitted me
>   The holiness and grace to recognize.
>
> Thou hast led me, a slave, to liberty,
>   By every path, and using every means
>   Which to fulfil this task were granted thee,
>
> Keep turned towards me thy munificence
>   So that my soul which thou hast remedied
>   May please thee when it quits the bonds of sense."
>
> Such was my prayer and she, so distant fled,
>   It seemed, did smile and look on me once more,
>   Then to the eternal fountain turned her head.[1]

The last glimpse we have of her is as she folds her hands in prayer,
with all the thronging multitude of the heavenly host, that the Virgin
Mary may intercede for Dante that he may behold God.

What Dante tells us is that in real life Beatrice and his love for her
were the medium of his moral reform and of his religious salvation.
In the story, or poetic reality, he represents the influence she had on
him by, in the *Inferno*, her visit to Virgil in the Limbo, in the *Purga-
torio*, her accusation and reproaches, his confession and repentance and
the ensuing reconciliation, and, in the *Paradiso*, by the power of her
beauty to uplift him and of her knowledge and understanding to en-
lighten him.

In the allegory, Beatrice does not exclusively or specifically "stand
for" theology, the Christian revelation, heavenly beatitude, the light
of glory or any of the abstractions which, in the course of centuries,
have been put forward by critics and scholars. She is the image by
which Dante perceives such things and her function in the poem is to
bring him to that state in which he is able to perceive them directly.
To quote the great mediaevalist and Dantist, Étienne Gilson, "It is

1. Canto xxxi. 79–93.

right to mark them and associate them with the figure of Beatrice, but we cannot, without being presumptuous, infer that she actually is the Light of Glory, or Theology, or the Contemplative Life, or, broadly speaking, any of these ideas. We have not even the right to infer that she is the Christian Life regarded as a whole. The sanctity of this member of the elect does not entitle us to equate her to this any more than that of St Francis, St Dominic and St Bernard entitles us to identify them with similar abstractions." [1] The role of Beatrice in the *Comedy* is, however, more prolonged and implicated than that of any other saint and, though she is never wholly an abstraction, there are moments when the allegorical significance of her reality (or, literal sense) can be unfolded into a multiple interpretation, as, for instance, in Canto xxxi of *Purgatory*, when in the mirror of Revelation (the eyes of Beatrice) Dante sees the double Nature of the Incarnate Love – now as wholly divine, now as wholly human, or in Canto xxviii of *Paradise*, when her eyes image the theological demonstrations of the Church concerning the unity of God. The important thing is to avoid defining her too narrowly, in either her literal or her allegorical meaning. Perhaps the most comprehensive thing one might say concerning Beatrice is that she is for Dante the embodiment of his experience of love.

THE IDEAL OF JUSTICE IN PÀRADISO

For an understanding of Dante's ideal of justice, it is necessary to read his treatise on world monarchy. The issue is one on which he held the most passionate and blazing convictions and, though it is not the chief, it is a dominant theme in the *Divine Comedy*. Justice, as Dante conceived it philosophically, is an absolute standard of righteousness. In the world, in which nothing can be perfect, a maximum of justice can be found where there is a minimum of injustice. The antithesis of justice, which provokes injustice, is greed or covetousness. The sharpener and enlightener of justice is charity, which is incompatible with covetousness. The establishment, therefore, of universal love is a necessary condition of the reign of justice. How can this be brought about? Only by a universal Monarch, a single world Emperor, who alone, of all temporal rulers, would be free from covetousness and disposed, therefore, to act in accordance with the maximum justice possible on earth.

1. *Dante the Philosopher*, translated by David Moore, Sheed and Ward, 1948, p. 297.

Since these are his convictions, we can understand why Dante lashes out with such vehement invective against the enemies of justice, namely, greed and rivalry for wealth and power, particularly as manifested in the temporal ambitions of the Church and clergy, whose betrayal of their divine function he attacks with an implacable hatred.

The betrayal of his great ideal of justice Dante condemns and despises more than any other sin. Judas, the betrayer of Christ, and Cassius and Brutus, the betrayers of Caesar, are in the ultimate depths of Hell, in the very mouths of Satan. Hell itself is chiefly filled with sins of injustice in its widest sense. What he esteems and exalts above all virtues is loyalty to the ideal of justice, to the temporal powers appointed by God for its establishment on earth, to the great authorities whose origins are sacred, the Church and the Empire; for justice is rendering what is due to God as well as to man.

These are the basic conceptions underlying the cantos in *Paradise* which are an apotheosis of Roman or Imperial justice (i.e. the canto of Justinian and the cantos of the Eagle) and those in which resistance to this ideal or a falling away from it is condemned, as for instance, in Cacciaguida's denigration of contemporary Florence, or St Peter's denunciation of Pope Boniface. The whole of *Paradise* is poignant with the thought of what might have been if Henry of Luxemburg had succeeded, and exultant with the poet's faith that *one day* justice will triumph over greed:

> "*Ere January be unwintered, through*
> *The hundredth of a day which men neglect,*
> *These lofty circles shall give vent unto*
>
> *Such roaring, that the storm we long expect*
> *Shall whirl the vessels round upon their route,*
> *Setting the fleet to sail a course direct;*
>
> *And from the blossom shall come forth true fruit.*" [1]

B.R.

1. Canto xxvii. 142–8.

CANTO I

THE STORY. *Dante, who is still in the Garden of Eden, has just drunk from the river of Good Remembrance (Purg. xxxiii. 126–45). Looking at Beatrice, he sees that she has turned to gaze into the sun. He does likewise and finds he is able to endure its brilliance for a brief moment. Turning once more to look on Beatrice as she still gazes at the sun, he hears the music of the heavenly spheres and finds himself surrounded by a vast sea of light and flame. Beatrice tells him they have risen from the earth and explains the law of universal gravitation.*

> The glory of Him who moves all things soe'er
>   Impenetrates the universe, and bright
>   The splendour burns, more here and lesser there.
>
> Within that heav'n which most receives His light   4
>   Was I, and saw such things as man nor knows
>   Nor skills to tell, returning from that height;
>
> For when our intellect is drawing close   7
>   To its desire, its paths are so profound
>   That memory cannot follow where it goes.
>
> Yet now, of that blest realm whate'er is found   10
>   Here in my mind still treasured and possessed
>   Must set the strain for all my song to sound.
>
> Gracious Apollo! in this crowning test   13
>   Make me the conduit that thy power runs through!
>   Fit me to wear those bays thou lovest best!
>
> One peak of thy Parnassus hitherto   16
>   Has well sufficed me, but henceforth I strive
>   In an arena where I need the two.
>
> Breathe in me, breathe, and from my bosom drive   19
>   Music like thine, when thou didst long ago
>   The limbs of Marsyas from their scabbard rive.
>
> O power divine, grant me in song to show   22
>   The blest realm's image – shadow though it be –
>   Stamped on my brain; thus far thyself bestow,

25   And thou shalt see me to thy darling tree
          Draw near, and twine those laurels on my brow
          Which I shall merit by my theme and thee.

28   So seldom, Father, are they gathered now
          For Caesar's triumph or the poet's meed
          (Such sin, such shame our human wills allow!)

31   That the Peneian frond must surely breed
          Joy in the joyous Delphic god, whene'er
          Any aspires to make it his indeed.

34   From one small spark springs up a mighty flare;
          If I set forth, others may come behind,
          More worthy, and win Cirrha by their prayer.

37   Through divers portals rises on mankind
          The lantern of the world, but from that part
          Where the three crosses the four circles bind,

40   With happiest stars he comes conjunct, to start
          His happiest course, and seals and tempers here
          This mundane wax most after his own heart.

43   Nigh to that point he'd made the dawn appear
          Yonder, and here the dusk; all whiteness shone
          That side, and darkness veiled our hemisphere,

46   When Beatrice, intent upon the sun,
          Turned leftward, and so stood and gazed before;
          No eagle e'er so fixed his eyes thereon.

49   And, as the second ray doth evermore
          Strike from the first and dart back up again,
          Just as the peregrine will stoop and soar,

52   So through my eyes her gesture, pouring in
          On my mind's eye, shaped mine; I stared wide-eyed
          On the sun's face, beyond the wont of men.

55   There, much is granted which is here denied
          To human senses; in that gracious spot
          Made for mankind such virtue doth reside.

58   Short time I endured him, yet so short 'twas not
          But that I saw him sparkle every way
          Like iron from out the furnace drawn white-hot;

And, on a sudden, day seemed joined to day,   61
  As though the hand that hath the power had sped
  A second sun to make the skies more gay.

Beatrice stood, her eyes still riveted   64
  On the eternal wheels; and, constantly,
  Turning mine thence, I gazed on her instead;

'Twas even thus a change came over me,   67
  As Glaucus, eating of the weed, changed race
  And grew a god among the gods of sea.

Transhumanised – the fact mocks human phrase;   70
  So let the example serve, till proof requite
  Him who is called to experience this by grace.

If I was naught, O Love that rul'st the height,   73
  Save that of me which Thou didst last create,
  Thou know'st, that didst uplift me by Thy light.

The wheel Thou mak'st eternal through innate   76
  Desire of Thee, no sooner took mine ear
  With strains which Thou dost tune and modulate,

Than I saw blaze on me so vast a sphere   79
  Fired by the sun, that never rain nor streams
  Formed such a huge illimitable mere.

The unwonted sound, the bright and burning beams,   82
  Kindled my eagerness to know their cause
  Beyond the yearning of my dearest dreams;

Whence she to whom my whole self open was   85
  As to myself, to calm my troubled fit
  Stayed not my question, but without a pause

Opened her lips: "Thou dullest thine own wit   88
  With false imagination, nor perceivest
  That which thou wouldst perceive, being rid of it.

Thou art not still on earth as thou believest;   91
  Lightning from its sphere falling never matched
  The speed which thou, returning there, achievest."

But I, my first bewilderment despatched   94
  By these few smiling words, was more perplexed
  Now, by a new one which I promptly hatched.

97   I said: "I rest content, no longer vexed
         By one great doubt; but how come I to fly
         Through these light spheres? This doubt assails me next."

100   She turned on me, after a pitying sigh,
         A look such as a mother's eyes let fall
         Upon her infant, babbling feverishly.

103   Then she began: "All beings great and small
         Are linked in order; and this orderliness
         Is form, which stamps God's likeness on the All.

106   Herein the higher creatures see the trace
         Of that Prime Excellence who is the end
         For which that form was framed in the first place.

109   And being thus ordered, all these natures tend
         Unto their source, or near or farther off,
         As divers lots their divers fashions blend;

112   Wherefore to divers havens all these move
         O'er the great sea of being, all borne on
         By instinct given, to every one enough.

115   'Tis this that draws the fire up to the moon,
         The mover this, in hearts of mortal things,
         This that binds up the earth and makes it one.

118   Yea, and this bow's discharge by no means wings
         Irrational creatures only to their goal,
         But those endowed with loves and reasonings.

121   The Providence that integrates the whole
         Keeps in perpetual stillness by its light
         That heav'n wherein the swiftest heav'n doth roll;

124   Thither, as to our own appointed site,
         That mighty string impels us now, which still
         Speeds to the gold its every arrow's flight;

127   True, as the form fails sometimes to fulfil
         The art's intention, if the lumpish clay
         Prove unresponsive to the craftsman's skill,

130   Even so the creature that has power to stray
         Out of its course, though launched by that strong thrust,
         Will swerve at times, and go its wilful way,

(As lightning quits the cloud and strikes the dust),   133
  From its first impetus and upward route
  Diverted earthward by some fair false lust.

But thy ascent, if rightly I compute,   136
  Ought no more to surprise thee than to see
  A stream rush down from mountain crest to foot;

Nay, but if thou, from every hindrance free,   139
  Shouldst hug the ground, that *would* be a surprise –
  As stillness in quick flame on earth would be."

Then back again to heav'n she turned her eyes.   142

THE IMAGES. *The Sun.* In the natural universe, which Dante uses as the framework of the story, the sun is the fourth of the planets, which, together with the fixed stars and the Primum Mobile, revolve round the earth from east to west once every twenty-four hours (see Appendix, Note A). When the *story* of *Paradise* begins, it is noon on the sixth day (Wednesday) of Dante's journey. Of all the hours of the day, noon, the culminating point of the sun's light, was considered to be the noblest. The day is near the Spring equinox, considered the perfect season, for then the sun is in the same constellation as it was believed to have been at the time of the Creation. All the celestial conditions are favourable, therefore, to the beginning of the new stage of Dante's new journey. *Allegorically*, this would seem to signify that the grace of God shines with the greatest beneficence on the soul when it is most fitted to receive it.

The Ascent from Earth. In the *story*, the ascent of Dante through the nine heavens to the Eympyrean, or abode of God, constitutes the plot-mechanism of the narrative. It is what actually happens, and within the time-sequence of the ascent various meetings, conversations, and experiences occur. In the *allegory*, Dante's ascent signifies the progress of man's soul towards God.

NOTES. l. 1: *The glory of Him*: The glory of God is His light, the very being of Himself. His *splendour* (cf. l.3) is His glory reflected in His creation. *who moves all things soe'er*: God, being Himself unmoved, is the primal source of all movement in the universe. The Primum Mobile (see Glossary), moved towards God by love of Him, sets all the other spheres of heaven in motion. This conception of God as the unmoved mover is derived from Aristotle. Dante refers to God as the "prime mover" also in *Purgatory* (cf. Canto xxv. 70).

  l. 3: *more here and lesser there*: The glory of God, reflected in creation, is manifested variously according to the nature of that which receives it (see also *Para.* xxxi. 22–3).

l. 4: *that heav'n which most receives His light:* the Empyrean, the heaven which is pure light (see also *Para.* xxx. 39 and Glossary).

l. 5:*Was I:* notice the emphatic position of this statement, stressing the personal individual experience.

l. 8: *its desire:* The ultimate desire of the intellect is God, the supreme Truth.

l. 9: . . . *memory cannot follow where it goes*: As it draws near to God the intellect penetrates so deeply into the knowledge of the Supreme Good that when the experience is ended human memory is unable fully to recall it. This is an awareness common to the mystics and it is not impossible that Dante underwent a mystical experience of which *Paradise* is the reasoned, logical, humanized expression in terms of poetry.

l. 13: *Gracious Apollo!* etc.: This is the beginning of the invocation. In *Hell* Dante invoked the Muses in general and in *Purgatory* first the Muses and then, in particular, Calliope, the Muse of Epic Poetry.

l. 15: *Fit me to wear those bays thou lovest best!*: Dante hoped that his third Cantica, *Paradise*, would earn for him recall from exile and a laurel crown at his baptismal font in Florence (cf. ll. 25–7 and also *Para.* xxv. 1–12).

l. 16: *One peak of thy Parnassus* etc.: Of the two peaks of Mt Parnassus (see Glossary), Nyssa and Cyrrha, the first is thought of by Dante (following Ovid and Lucan) as the dwelling of the Muses, the second as that of Apollo, their leader. For the previous two divisions of his poem, *Hell* and *Purgatory*, Dante has deemed it sufficient to invoke the Muses; now he entreats the inspiration of the Muses and Apollo for this supreme endeavour.

l. 21: *The limbs of Marsyas* etc.: In his invocation to Calliope in Canto I of *Purgatory* (7–12) Dante has recalled her victory over the daughters of Pireus. Here he similarly recalls the victory of Apollo over Marsyas (see Glossary). As the fate of Marsyas was even more intimidating than the fate of the daughters of Pireus, so the theme of *Paradise* is even more exalted and ineffable than the theme of *Purgatory*. It may also be that Dante is here urging the god to pull his mind free from the limitations of his body. (Cf. Edgar Wind, *Pagan Mysteries in the Renaissance*, Faber and Faber, 1958, ch. xi. I am indebted to Miss Phyllis Giles for drawing my attention to this reference.)

l. 23: *The blest realm's image:* Heaven in general, all the heavenly spheres through which Dante is to journey (cf. l. 10, in which *blest realm* probably refers to the Empyrean).

l. 25: *thy darling tree:* the laurel, beloved of Apollo because it was the tree into which Daphne was transformed.

l. 31: *the Peneian frond:* the laurel. (Daphne was the daughter of Peneus, a river-god.)

l. 34: *From one small spark* etc.: The original of this line has become a proverbial saying in Italian. (Cf. *James* iii, 5.)

ll. 37–42: *Through divers portals* etc.: The "portals" are the points on the horizon at which the sun rises at different times of the year. The point where the three crosses bind the four circles is the point at which the sun rises at the Spring equinox. The four circles are the horizon, the equator, the ecliptic and the equinoctial colure. The intersection of these four circles may be thought of as forming three crosses, viz.:

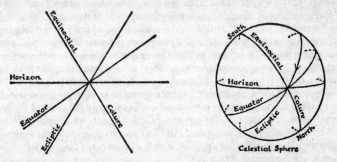

Celestial Sphere

The sun is at the point of intersection when rising at the equinox, and it was near there (*nigh to that point*, l. 43) when it rose on the first day in *Paradise*. At the time of the Spring equinox the sun is in the constellation of Aries. These are spoken of as "his happiest stars" (l. 40) because, according to tradition, the sun was in this sign at the moment of Creation (cf. *Hell* i. 37 and *note*; see also Astronomical Note to this volume). According to the early commentators, the four circles and the three crosses symbolize the four cardinal and the three theological virtues, conjoined and working together for the salvation of mankind. Thus it is that at this time of year the world ("this mundane wax") receives from the sun the most beneficent influence.

ll. 43–6: *Nigh to that point . . . when Beatrice*: Dante is here speaking of two moments, dawn and noon. At dawn, the sun had risen "nigh to" the point of the Spring equinox (not exactly at the point, since it was now several days past that date). Beatrice turned to look at the sun at noon, when the Southern hemisphere was flooded with light and our own veiled in darkness.

l. 47: *turned leftward*: Dante and Beatrice are still in the Garden of Eden. They have been facing the east, and now Beatrice, to look at the noonday sun, turns to her left, for in the Southern hemisphere the sun is seen north of the observer (cf. *Purg.* iv. 57, etc. and *note*).

l. 48: *no eagle e'er so fixed his eyes thereon*: It was believed that the mother eagle took her young up into the air in her talons so that they turned their eyes towards the sun. The eaglets that endured the sun's rays without a quiver were recognized as the true brood, but the others were allowed to drop, and perished. Dante may have read of this belief in St Augustine or in Brunetto Latini's *Trésor*. He refers again to this power of the eagle's eye in *Para.* xx. 31.

ll. 49–54: *And, as the second ray doth evermore* etc.: Beatrice is looking up at the sun. Dante, seeing her do so, does likewise. His sight of her gaze and his imitation of it are compared to a ray of light which strikes downwards (on a shining horizontal surface) and is instantly reflected upwards. This down-and-up movement of the light is compared in its turn (l. 51) to – what? That is the question. The word which Dante uses, "peregrin", or "pellegrin", is usually interpreted as meaning "pilgrim" or "traveller", and the comparison is understood to refer to the longing of the pilgrim to return home. The appropriateness of this traditional interpretation may be seen in that the simile of a pilgrim or sojourner returning home conveys the suggestion of the soul returning to its Maker, as well as of light returning to its source, which is God. In the present translation, preference has been given to an interpretation which has found favour recently with some commentators. The word "peregrin" is understood to refer not to a pilgrim but to a peregrine falcon, whose stooping and soaring is not unlike the movement of light striking down and being reflected up. (For further discussion of this controversial point, see Appendix, Note B.)

l. 56: *in that gracious spot*: i.e. the Garden of Eden. Dante's power to gaze wide-eyed on the sun, though supernaturally endowed, was natural in the first abode of mankind. Furthermore, after his purification, Dante has regained the state of Adam before the Fall and enjoys a heightening of his faculties.

l. 61: *day seemed joined to day*: Dante, without knowing it, has risen from the earth and is approaching the sphere of fire, which according to the science of his day was believed to encircle the globe at some distance between it and the moon (see chart at end of book).

l. 65: *the eternal wheels*: the heavenly spheres; Beatrice was gazing upwards.

ll. 68–72: As Glaucus (see Glossary) was changed into a sea-god, so Dante, gazing on Beatrice, who continues to gaze heavenwards, is "transhumanised", an experience so far beyond human limits that he cannot convey it in words; he can only adduce, for comparison, the experience of Glaucus.

l. 74: *that of me which Thou didst last create*: i.e. the rational human soul. In *Purgatory* Statius has explained that God breathes the soul into the body last of all (cf. *Purg.* xxv. 67–75). Dante here implies that he could not tell whether his ascent into Heaven was made in the body or by his soul alone. St Paul (*II Corinthians* xii. 2–3) expressed a similar doubt. Elsewhere in *Paradise*, however, Dante conveys that he is in Heaven in· his mortal body (cf. xxvii. 11, 61).

l. 76: *The wheel thou mak'st eternal* etc.: This is the combined rotatory movement of the heavens, of which the driving force is the desire of the Primum Mobile (see Glossary) to be conjoined with the Empyrean or abode of God. The belief that the spheres emitted music as they revolved was first taught by Pythagoras, disputed by Aristotle and revived by

Plato. In Cicero's *Somnium Scipionis* the younger Scipio, raised in his dream to the Milky Way, hears the heavenly harmony and enquires of the soul of his grandfather: "What is this great and pleasing sound that fills my ears?" The elder Scipio explains that it is a concord of tones separated by unequal, carefully proportioned intervals and caused by the motion of the spheres. The outermost sphere, the star-bearer, having the swiftest motion, gives forth the highest note, while the lunar sphere, being the nearest to the earth and the slowest in motion, gives forth the lowest tone. Macrobius, in his *Commentary* on the *Dream of Scipio*, confirms Cicero's explanation in some detail, adding that the breath constraining the spheres is stronger the nearer it is to its source. Other cosmographers, however, assigned the lowest note to the outermost sphere and the highest to the sphere of the moon. Milton evidently followed this view when he wrote of the "bass of Heaven's deep organ" in his *Hymn on the Nativity*. Dante does not reveal which view he took as to the order of the notes, contenting himself (l. 78) with referring to God as the ultimate source of all such harmony. (It is interesting to notice that Shakespeare apparently understood that the music was believed to emanate from the planets themselves rather than from the spheres in which they were thought to revolve:

> "There's not the smallest orb which thou behold'st
> But in his motion like an angel sings.
> Still quiring to the young-ey'd cherubims."
>
> *The Merchant of Venice*, v. 1)

l. 79: *so vast a sphere*: this is perhaps the light of the sun itself, or light from the moon which they are approaching, or the sphere of fire through which they had to pass (see chart at end of book).

l. 82: *The unwonted sound*: Scipio the elder had explained to his grandson: "The ears of mortals are filled with this sound, but they are unable to hear it"; and Macrobius commented, "we do not catch the sound of the music arising in the constant swirl of the spheres because it is too full to be taken into the narrow range of our ears." Dante refers to the music of the spheres a second time when he reaches the heaven of Saturn, where, for a while, he can no longer hear it (cf. Canto xxi. 58–60).

l. 92: *Lightning from its sphere falling*: the sphere of lightning is the sphere of fire (cf. Canto xxiii. 41–2).

l. 93: *returning there*: Dante is returning to *his* sphere, that is, Heaven, whence his soul came.

ll. 98–9: . . . *how come I to fly through these light spheres?* i.e. through the sphere of air and the sphere of fire. This question would seem to confirm that Dante is ascending to Heaven in the body.

l. 103: *All beings great and small* etc.: From this line until the end of the Canto, Beatrice explains to Dante how he is enabled to ascend from earth into the heavens. Her exposition may be summarized as follows: all created things are governed by order, wherein resides the likeness of the universe to God. The natural law by which fire burns upwards, heavy bodies are drawn earthwards, and brute creatures are impelled by instinct, is the same force by which creatures endowed by love and understanding (angels and men) are drawn upwards to their appointed site, the abode of God. Some, it is true, since men are endowed with free will, prove unresponsive to the upward thrust and go astray. However, since Dante has now been purged of sin and his will is rightly fixed, the fact that he is rising towards Heaven should no more surprise him than the sight of a stream rushing downhill.

On the *poetic* level, it would seem a logical continuation of the *story* that since he descended the circles of Hell and ascended the Mountain of Purgatory in his mortal state, having now experienced purification in his physical as well as his spiritual being, he should likewise ascend to Heaven in the body. On the *anagogical* (or spiritual) level, the significance of Beatrice's speech would seem to be that as God is the source of all movement, the same power which speeds all created things to their appointed ends likewise impels the soul, in whom the will is rightly directed, to ascend towards Him. Sin is the weight which keeps the soul earthbound.

l. 123 : *that heav'n wherein the swiftest heav'n doth roll*: i.e. the Empyrean, or abode of God, within which revolves the Primum Mobile, the outer-most and swiftest of the material heavens. (See also Cantos ii. 112–14, xxii, 67, xxvii. 106–20, xxx. 38–42, 52, and Glossary.)

CANTO II

THE STORY. *Beatrice gazes upwards into the heavens and Dante fixes his eyes upon her. By this means they rise beyond the sphere of fire into the First Heaven, where they enter the moon. Dante asks Beatrice for an explanation of the markings which are visible from earth on the face of the moon and which popular fancy identifies as Cain and the thornbush. Refuting Dante's own suggestion that they may be due to a variation in density of the moon's substance, Beatrice explains that they derive ultimately from varying degrees of power residing in the Angelic beings which move the nine heavens. The moon, being the furthest removed from the Empyrean, receives from it less of excellence than the other planets, with the result that the very parts of the moon so differ from one another that they receive and reflect the light of the sun unequally.*

O you that follow in light cockle-shells,
    For the song's sake, my ship that sails before,
    Carving her course and singing as she sails,

Turn back and seek the safety of the shore;   4
    Tempt not the deep, lest, losing unawares
    Me and yourselves, you come to port no more.

Oceans as yet undared my vessel dares;   7
    Apollo steers, Minerva lends the breeze,
    And the nine Muses point me to the Bears.

But you, rare souls, that have reached up to seize   10
    Betimes the bread of angels, food for men
    To live on here, whereof no surfeit is,

You may commit your bark unto the main,   13
    Hard on my keel, where ridge and furrow flee
    Ere the vext waters level out again.

The heroes that to Colchis fared might see,   16
    Amazed, great Jason at the plough-tail ply,
    But greater far shall your amazement be.

That which is born with us and cannot die,   19
    Thirst for the godlike realm, had made us skirr
    Almost as swiftly as the visible sky.

22   Beatrice gazed on heav'n and I on her;
      Then, while a quarrel might thud home, and wing,
      And from the nocking-point unloose, as 'twere,

25   I found I'd come where a most wondrous thing
      Enthralled my sight; whence she, being privy thus
      To my whole thought and secret questioning,

28   Turning to me, as blithe as beautëous:
      "Lift up to God", said she, "thy grateful sense,
      Who with the first star now uniteth us."

31   Meseemed a cloud enclosed us, lucid, dense,
      Solid, and smooth, like to the diamond stone
      Smitten upon by the sun's radiance.

34   Into itself the eternal union
      Received us both, as water doth receive
      A ray of light and still remains all one.

37   If I was body – though we can't conceive
      How two dimensions in one space can bide,
      As must be, if two bodies interweave –

40   How must our eagerness be multiplied
      To see Him in His essence, in whose being
      God's nature and our own were unified!

43   What faith holds here shall there be known by seeing;
      Not demonstrated, but self-evident
      Like those prime truths that brook no disagreeing.

46   "Lady," said I, "with most devout intent
      I give Him thanks who has advanced me so
      Out of the mortal world by this ascent.

49   But tell me now, what are the marks that show
      So dusky on this body, and suggest
      The tale of Cain to people down below?"

52   She smiled a little: "And if men have guessed
      Wrongly," said she, "where sense cannot avail
      To solve the riddle, though they try their best,

55   Thee should the shafts of wonder not assail,
      For, though sense lead the way, thou'rt now aware
      Of heights the wings of reason cannot scale.

But thou thyself, how think'st thou? Come, declare!" 58
   And I: "What shows diverse at this great height
   Derives, I think, from bodies dense and rare."

"Truly", said she, "thy thought is sunk outright 61
   In error; now, if thou wilt hear me through,
   I shall by argument refute it quite.

Full many lights the eighth sphere shows to you, 64
   And you observe how their appearances
   Differ in quality and number too.

If rare and dense alone made differences, 67
   One single virtue were in all the lot,
   Distributed all over, more or less.

But divers virtues surely are begot 70
   By divers formal principles; yet those,
   Save one, thy reasoning alloweth not.

Besides, if rarity were what bestows 73
   These stains that puzzle thee, 'twould either mean
   That of this planet parts are tenuous

All through, or else that thin leaves lie between 76
   The thick leaves of its volume – like enough
   To meat that alternates the fat and lean.

The first, if true, would offer easy proof, 79
   For when the sun's eclipsed we'd see his rays
   Shine through, as through all other tenuous stuff.

That is not so. Now put the other case, 82
   And if, belike, I quash that too, I doubt
   Thy theory's bankrupt, and can go its ways.

If this rare stuff do not extend throughout, 85
   There needs must be a point it cannot pass,
   Because its contrary doth bar it out;

This would turn back the ray that smites it, as 88
   The coloured images return reflected
   From the lead lining of a looking-glass.

But (thou wilt urge) the ray, being thus projected 91
   From farther back, is dimmer in that part
   Than in the rest: that was to be expected.

94   From this new cavil, if thou have the heart
         To try, experiment shall set thee free –
         That source whence all your science has to start.

97   Arrange three mirrors so that two shall be
         Equally distant, and the third in sight
         Between the two, but farther off from thee.

100 Face them, and have behind thy head a light
         Which, falling on them and cast back by them,
         Shows all three mirrors with its splendour bright.

103 Thou'lt see then that the farthest from the flame,
         Although in size it is inferior
         To those in front, in brightness is the same.

106 Now, as the snow that yields to the warm thaw
         Is stripped to its bare substrate, and lays by
         The coldness and the whiteness it once wore,

109 Thine intellect lies stripped; and now will I
         Inform thee with such living light as should
         Dance like a twinkling star before thine eye.

112 Within that heaven which is God's quietude
         A body spins, whose virtue doth remit
         Being unto all things which its bounds include.

115 The following heav'n, with countless beacons lit,
         Metes out this being to divers essences,
         Each one distinct from, yet contained in it.

118 The other spheres, by various differences,
         To ends and origins direct the flow
         Of those distinctive powers themselves possess.

121 The organs of the world, thou see'st, work so
         From grade to grade, as each is acted on
         By those above, and acts on those below.

124 Mark well the way I traverse, to make known
         Now to thy mind the truth which it desires,
         And learn henceforth to cross this ford alone.

127 The might and motion of the holy gyres
         Must, like the hammer in the craftsman's hand,
         So work as the blest movers' will inspires.

So too, the heaven with myriad fires made grand,   130
   In likeness of the mind that wheels it, must
   Be branded and in turn impose its brand.

And, as the soul that dwells within your dust   133
   Diffuses through the limbs, that variously
   To various powers shape themselves and adjust,

So through the stars in great diversity   136
   The Intelligence its goodness multiplies,
   Revolving still on its own unity.

With that rich body which it vivifies   139
   Virtue diverse thus makes diverse alloy,
   Blent as your life and you are blent likewise.

And as through sparkling pupils beams forth joy,   142
   Beams through the body the commingled might,
   So glad the Nature whence these powers deploy.

Hence, differences observed 'twixt light and light   145
   Derive from this, and not from rare and dense;
   This formal principle makes dim and bright,

Agreeably to its own excellence."   148

THE IMAGES. *The Moon.* In the *story*, the moon is the first stage in Dante's journey through the heavens, for in the natural universe it is the planet nearest the earth. In the *allegory*, the moon symbolizes a tendency in the soul towards inconstancy, or a will insufficiently steadfast to withstand coercion.

NOTES. ll. 1-6: Having induced in himself a humble awareness of his awesome task (*Para.* i), Dante now warns light-minded readers not to follow him into the uncharted spaces of deep Heaven lest they should lose him and destroy themselves; but those who have fed on the Bread of Angels (i.e. have attained knowledge and have studied theology and philosophy) are welcome companions. This is a disconcerting beginning, but the warning is expressed by so lovely an image that the reader who has followed so far mainly "for the song's sake" is likely (and is intended) to be led on still further by the sheer beauty of the (original) language. Cf. Note to ll. 8-9.

l. 7: *Oceans as yet undared*: The subject of Paradise had previously been treated by Giacomino da Verona in his *De Jerusalem coelesti* and by Bonvesin della Riva, in *Scrittura dorata*, but such works are slight and primitive compared with Dante's *Paradise*. (Cf. Canto xxiii. 67-9.)

l. 8–9: *Apollo steers* etc.: In this high poetic enterprise, the crown and summit of all his art, Dante submits himself to the *guidance* of the god of song, to the *inspiration* of wisdom and to the *skill* of poetic technique. The propelling force of the work is, then, divine knowledge and wisdom; poetry is the means of communicating it.

l. 16: *The heroes that to Colchis fared*: These are the Argonauts who set forth with Jason, in the first voyage ever dared, to obtain the Golden Fleece from King Aeëtes in Colchis. One of the tests which Jason had to undergo before he could gain the fleece was to plough with two wild bulls which had horns of iron and feet of bronze and which breathed fire from their nostrils. The meaning of the comparison seems to be that those who follow Dante now will be more amazed at seeing him in the role of theologian and poet of so sublime a theme than were the companions of Jason at seeing their leader turned ploughman. It is noteworthy that Dante again refers to the wonder aroused by Jason (as the first navigator) in the last canto of *Paradise* (ll. 94–6).

l. 19: *That which is born with us and cannot die*: The innate and imperishable desire in man is the insatiable longing to know God. This is the natural force by which, as Beatrice explained in *Para.* i, man divested of the weight of sin rises to Heaven. In *Purgatory* (xxi. 1) Dante has already spoken of "The natural thirst which nothing quenches" and in the *Convivio* (IV, xiii) he discourses at length on the way in which the desire for knowledge increases: "properly speaking, the enlargement of this desire is not growth but a transition from something small to something large" . . . and the final object of desire is God.

ll. 23–5: Dante and Beatrice have risen to the moon. The speed of their ascent is compared to that of a quarrel (a square-headed arrow used with the cross-bow, derived from the Latin word *quadrellus*) striking its target, winging towards it and being loosed from the bow. The order of events is reversed so as to convey an impression of a swift sequence which has taken place so rapidly that the mind is obliged to recapitulate it in reverse.

l. 30: *the first star*: i.e. the moon (see Appendix, Note A). Dante uses the words "star" and "planet" interchangeably.

l. 31: *Meseemed a cloud enclosed us, lucid, dense*: Beatrice and Dante enter the moon, which seems to enwrap them as in a dense cloud; but it is also lucid, for Dante believed that the moon not only received light from the sun but had its own luminousness, "as is evident in a lunar eclipse", he says in his treatise on world government, *Monarchia* (III, iv). The moon, however, is not a cloud; it is a smooth, solid body (l. 32). The mystery of how his own solid body interpenetrated that of the moon is discussed in the following six lines.

l. 34: *the eternal union*: the eternal pearl, i.e. the moon. The rendering of "union" for the Italian "margarita" is particularly appropriate, for "union" means, according to Pliny, an exceptionally large pearl found singly, undivided. Compare *Hamlet*, v, ii:

> "And in the cup an union shall he throw,
> Richer than that which four successive kings
> In Denmark's crown have worn."

ll. 37–42: *If I was body* etc.: Some modern commentators understand
Dante to mean here *not* "if I was in the body, and I don't know whether
I was or not", but rather "if my body interpenetrated the substance of
the moon, and still we on earth do not understand how two dimensions
can exist in the space of one, how much the more eagerly ought we to
desire to see God in His essence in Whom the human and the divine are
joined in one." (Dante, in a culminating flash of insight, does attain to
an understanding of this very mystery, but it is beyond his powers to
convey it. See Canto xxxiii. 127–41.)

l. 45: *prime truths*: these are "the prime concepts" (already referred to
by Dante in *Purgatory*, xviii. 55), the fundamental axioms, self-evident,
requiring no proof. In Heaven our knowledge and understanding of
God will be similar to our awareness of such prime truths.

l. 49: "*But tell me now . . .*: This is the beginning of the famous dis-
cussion of the reason for the markings on the moon which are visible
from earth. Although the explanation given by Beatrice is no longer
valid for the modern reader, it represented for Dante the latest thing in
scientific knowledge and an advance on his own understanding of the
question as set forth several years before in the *Convivio* (II. xiv). Though
the *information* conveyed by this passage is outdated, its *relevance* to the
reader's enjoyment and understanding of *Paradise* is as vivid and pointed
as it ever was. First, it stands as an example of the insatiable thirst for
knowledge which Dante believed was innate in us. He had good reason
to believe so, for it was insatiable in him. Secondly, the explanation
given by Beatrice is an instance of the most important aspect of Heaven
as Dante conceives and conveys it, namely its *differentiation*. The various
portions of the moon reflect variously the light of the sun for the same
reason that all creation reflects variously the unvarying power of God.
This variation is anticipated in the opening lines of *Paradise* (1. 1–3), and
will be stressed again and again throughout the work. The answer which
Beatrice here gives, therefore, to the seemingly artless question,
"What is the reason for the marks on the moon?", not only satisfies
Dante's appetite for exact information but prepares his (and the reader's)
mind for the conception of the natural order of the universe, the relations
between grace, destiny and free will, and the hierarchy of blessedness.

l. 58: "*But thou thyself, how think'st thou? Come, declare!*": Dante's
reply to this challenge is tantamount to the explanation he has already
given in *Convivio* (II. xiv) where he remarks: "For if the moon is care-
fully observed, there may be seen in it two things peculiar to it, which
are not seen in the other stars; the one is the shadow in it, which is
nothing else but rarity of its substance, upon which the rays of the sun
cannot be brought to a stand and reflected back as in the other parts; the

other is the variation in its brilliancy, which shines now on one side, now on the other according as the sun looks upon it." That is, he holds in the *Convivio* that the spots in the moon are caused by the rarity or density of its substance; and that the shadows are due to the passage of the sun's rays from behind the moon through the thicker portions of its substance. Dante was here following a suggestion put forward by Averrhoës and repeated by Albertus Magnus. It is not known how he came to alter his opinion. He may perhaps have been induced, as a result of discussion, to perform the very experiment which Beatrice recommends (ll. 97–105).

l. 64: *Full many lights the eighth sphere shows*: The eighth sphere is the heaven of the fixed stars, or starry heaven, in which are clustered the various constellations (see chart at end of book). It is situated between the Primum Mobile and the Heaven of Saturn. Beatrice here begins her refutation of Dante's theory, which she shows to be as invalid for the stars of the eighth heaven as for the moon. The intensity of light from the stars is seen to vary as from one star to another; this variation is rightly attributed not to their differing material substance but to their varying active power and influence. It it were simply a question of density or rarity, this would mean that the stars were all of an identical specific nature (ll. 67–8); but this cannot be, for the divers virtues of life on earth are due to the divers formal principles of the stars. (Beatrice is here quite properly drawing the distinction, made by the scholastic philosophers, between *material principle*, i.e. primary matter, which is the same in all bodies, and *formal principle*, i.e. the "substantial form", in the scholastic sense of the words, which constitutes the various species and the virtues, or potentialities, of bodies.)

ll. 73–105: *"Besides, if rarity . . ."*: Having shown that Dante's explanation is not tenable philosophically, since variation in the stars is not a question of quantity of primary matter but of quality of formal principle, Beatrice now proceeds to prove that it is false also according to the laws of physics. If rarity were the cause of spots on the moon, then either some parts of it must be thin right through or some strata must be dense, some rare, like the layers of fat and lean in meat (ll. 73–8). The first supposition is manifestly false, otherwise when the moon eclipsed the sun we should see the sun's light shining through the thinner parts. To disprove the second, Beatrice argues as follows: if the moon is composed of thick and thin sections, the thin, like the thick, will present a surface which will reflect light; and if Dante should object that light from the thin sections (which may be thought of as indentations or depressions on the surface) will be less bright than that reflected from the thick (because further removed) then the following experiment will disabuse his mind. Let him take three mirrors and arrange them so that two are equally distant from him, and the third, between them, set further away. (These will then represent a "thick / thin / thick" distribution of substance in the moon, the thicker portions being thought of as bulging nearer to the onlooker on earth and the thin portion as receding and presenting therefore a more distant surface from which the light is reflected.) Next, let him place a light behind him. He will then see that the more distant mirror will cast back an image which, though it is inferior in *size*, is equal in *brightness* to the images cast back by the other two. (In terms of modern physics, the conclusion drawn is correct as far as it goes. The three images of the one light will *be* equally bright and will *appear* equally bright. There will, however, be a difference in the *density* of light energy, which diminishes as the square of the distance from the source. This, it should be said, will not affect the *appearance* of brightness, for, although less light energy will come from the further mirror, it will have to illuminate a correspondingly smaller area on the retina of the eye.) (See also Canto x. Note on Albertus Magnus.)

ll. 112–20: *"Within that heaven which is God's quietude"*: Beatrice, having refuted Dante's theory, proceeds to give him the true explanation of the diversity in the moon's appearance. The "heaven which is God's quietude" is His abode, the Empyrean, the motionless heaven; within this revolves the Primum Mobile, whence is derived the existence or being of all things which it encloses within it (i.e. all creation). The heaven following the Primum Mobile, i.e. the eighth, or the starry heaven, distributes the undifferentiated virtue which it thence receives to the stars which it bears, each one of which is endowed with a distinct specific virtue and formal principle. It is in the starry heaven, then, that the universal undifferentiated "stuff" of being is first, as it were, "split up", ready for distribution by the stars. These, as they revolve, continually distribute the now differentiated and specific power to the remaining seven heavens each of which bears a planet. They in their turn direct the influences whereby the various forms of existence on earth are directed to their ends and functionings.

ll. 124–6: Beatrice intends to supply sufficient explanation for Dante to be able to perceive without further aid the answer to his question, "what is the cause of the markings on the moon?".

l. 130: *"the heaven with myriad fires made grand"*: i.e. the eighth, or starry, heaven.

ll. 136–8: *"So through the stars in great diversity"*: the virtue, power, being or "stuff" of existence, which is one and undifferentiated, becomes diverse and multiple as the eighth sphere revolves. The power causing it to revolve, here referred to as "the Intelligence", is the Angelic order of the cherubim (see also Cantos xxix and xxx).

ll. 139–41: *"With that rich body"* etc.: The "rich body" is the precious matter of each star with which the virtue or power is blended, making with each a diverse combination, just as life combined with each human individual results in a unique personality.

ll. 143–4: *"Beams through the body the commingled might"*: the power or virtue is now mingled with the star, and, as joy shines through human eyes, beams through the heavenly body.

ll. 145–8: "*Hence* ...": Beatrice leaves the last step in the reasoning to Dante (and the reader). From the varying degrees of power in the Intelligences, or Angelic beings, which move the spheres, arises the difference of light between one planet and another and between one part of the moon and another. Moreover, a lessening degree of perfection runs through all the spheres, and the heaven of the moon, being the sphere furthest removed from the Empyrean, is the one that receives the least of its excellence; even the various parts of the moon differ one from the other and receive the light of the sun in an unequal manner. It is for this reason, and not for any difference in density of substance, that some parts of the moon appear darker than others.

In her answer to Dante's question, Beatrice has extended his range to a consideration of the organization of the whole of Heaven and of existence. Everything else that Dante hears and experiences in the remaining cantos has been, ultimately, anticipated and prepared for by this discourse.

CANTO III

THE STORY. *In the pale atmosphere of the moon a group of faces appears, pearly, faint and indistinct. They are souls who were inconstant to vows made on earth. Dante speaks with Piccarda dei Donati who tells him that she and all the spirits who share her lowly estate are content in the degree of bliss which it has pleased God to assign to them, for "His will is (their) peace." Piccarda tells the story of her nunhood and enforced marriage and indicates the soul of the Empress Constance (the mother of Frederick II of Sicily) who was likewise compelled to leave her convent and enter into matrimony. Singing* Ave Maria, *Piccarda fades from sight and Dante turns once more to look on Beatrice. Her radiance, shining for an instant in its Empyrean glory, overpowers his vision and leaves him unable to frame the questions he would ask.*

The sun that warmed my bosom first with love
   Had brought the beauteous face of truth to light,
   Unveiling it by proof and counter-proof.

Corrected and convinced I must outright   4
   Confess me, and, the better to convey
   These sentiments, I raised my head upright;

But what I saw so carried me away   7
   To gaze on it, that ere I could confess,
   I had forgotten what I meant to say.

Like as from polished and transparent glass,   10
   Or as from water clear and luminous,
   Whose shallows leave the bottom shadowless,

The image of a face comes back to us   13
   So faint, a pearl on a white forehead stirs
   The seeing sense no slowlier than this does,

So I saw faces, many and diverse,   16
   Eager to speak; and straight fell in a snare –
   The pool-enamoured swain's, but in reverse;

For I, the moment I beheld them there,   19
   Taking them for reflections, turned my head
   Hastily round, to find out whose they were.

22   But I saw nothing; so I turned instead
          Straight to my dear and guiding light; she smiled,
          Her holy eyes a-flame, and then she said:

25   "What wonder if I smile, as at a child?
          Childish thy thought, which venturing not, for fear,
          Its foot on solid truth, leaves thee beguiled,

28   As is the way of it, and emptier.
          True substances are these thou dost perceive,
          Who broke their vows, and so are cloistered here.

31   Speak with them therefore, listen, and believe;
          The light of truth wherein they rest content
          Holds fast their feet, and to that truth they cleave."

34   So, to the shade that seemed most keenly bent
          On speech, I now addressed myself, although
          Over-excitement made me diffident:

37   "Soul made for bliss, enjoying in the glow
          Of life eternal those sweet mysteries
          Which, till they're tasted, pass man's wit to know,

40   If it so please thee, I should dearly prize
          Some news of you – your status, and thy name."
          And she replied at once with dancing eyes:

43   "Our love would no more turn a rightful claim
          Back from the door, than His who is indeed
          Love's self, and will have all His court the same.

46   On earth I was a nun; my present meed
          Of greater beauty should not cloud thy view;
          If thou but search thy memory with good heed

49   Surely my name will come to thee anew –
          Piccarda, that with all this blessèd host
          Joined in the slowest sphere, am blessèd too.

52   The sole good-pleasure of the Holy Ghost
          Kindles our hearts, which joyously espouse,
          Informed by Him, whate'er delights Him most.

55   This lot, which seems but as a lowly house,
          Is given to us because we did withal
          Neglect and partly disavow our vows."

74

Then I to her: "The features I recall   58
   Are changed by something of a wondrous kind –
   Some divine likeness mirrored in you all;

This made my recognition lag behind;   61
   Now that thy words have helped to make things clear
   I bring thy face more readily to mind.

But tell me, you whose happiness is here,   64
   Have you no hankering to go up higher,
   To win more insight or a love more dear?"

She smiled a little, and the spirit-choir   67
   Smiled too; and when she spoke her looks expressed
   Such joy, she seemed to burn in love's first fire:

"Brother, our love has laid our wills to rest,   70
   Making us long only for what is ours,
   And by no other thirst to be possessed.

If we could wish to bide in loftier bowers,   73
   Our wish would jangle with that will of His
   Which hath assigned our proper place and powers;

And in these gyres thou'lt find no room for this,   76
   If love is here our necessary state,
   And thou bethink thee what love's nature is.

Nay, 'tis the essence of our blissful fate   79
   To dwell in the divine will's radius,
   Wherein our wills themselves are integrate;

Whose being from threshold unto threshold thus   82
   Through all this realm doth all the realm so please,
   And please the King that here in-willeth us

To His own will; and His will is our peace;   85
   This is the sea whereunto all things fare
   That it creates or nature furnishes."

Then I saw plain how Heav'n is everywhere   88
   Paradise, though the grace of the First Good
   Falls differently in different regions there.

But as, when we've enjoyed one kind of food,   91
   We're ready for the second course, and ask
   For that, and for the first show gratitude,

94   So, bringing voice and gesture to the task,
         Did I, and begged her draw the shuttle's thread
         Right through, and all the patterned web unmask.

97   "High merit and perfected love", she said,
         "Ensky aloft a lady, by whose rule
         Maids in your world are veiled and habited

100 To wake and sleep till death, inseparable
         Still from the Bridegroom who doth aye accept
         Every good vow that love has put to school.

103 From the vain world my eager girlhood leapt
         To follow her; I donned her habit, chose
         Her order's rule, and vowed it should be kept;

106 But men more apt for ill than good arose
         To snatch me out from the sweet cloister's fold,
         And what my life thenceforth became, God knows.

109 This other splendour that is here enrolled,
         Who on my right displays herself to thee
         In all the radiance that our sphere can hold,

112 Saith that as I was even so was she –
         A sister also, from whose head they tore
         The sheltering holy wimple, as with me.

115 But though they flung her to the world once more,
         Against her will, in decency's despite,
         Ne'er did her heart put off the veil it wore.

118 Constance the Great her name, and this her light;
         By Swabia's second gale engendering
         She bare the third – the last imperial might."

121 The spirit spake, and straight began to sing
         Ave Maria, vanishing in song
         As through deep water slides some sinking thing.

124 I strained my sight to follow her as long
         As might be, till I lost her; wherefore, yearning
         To an attraction that was still more strong,

127 Toward Beatrice's self I moved me, turning;
         But on mine eyes her light at first so blazed,
         They could not bear the beauty and the burning;

130 And I was slow to question, being amazed.

THE IMAGES. *The Moon.* See under Images to Canto ii.

Piccarda dei Donati, the sister of Corso Donati and of Dante's friend, Forese (cf. *Purg.* xxiii and xxiv), entered the convent of St Clare in Florence while still a young woman. Her brother Corso obliged her to break her vows and marry Rossellino della Tosa, with whom he sought political alliance. Shortly after her marriage, Piccarda fell ill and died. Forese speaks tenderly of her beauty and virtue when questioned about her by Dante on the sixth cornice of Mount Purgatory.

Her gentleness and sweetness of disposition, skilfully conveyed by her words to Dante, make her a fitting image in general of the nature that yields to the pressure of others and lacks the necessary steadfastness to remain constant to the will's resolve. Specifically, both Piccarda and the Empress Constance, whom she names, are symbols of inconstancy to religious vows.

NOTES. l. 1: *The sun* ... etc.: Beatrice, as a woman, had first awakened love in Dante's heart; now, as guide, and in her allegorical significance of revealed theology, she has illumined his mind and revealed truth to him.

l. 3: *by proof and counter-proof*: by demonstrating the truth and refuting error.

l. 18: *The pool-enamoured swain's, but in reverse*: Just as Narcissus, catching sight of his reflection in water, mistook it for an actual person and became enamoured of it, so Dante, seeing the faces in the moon, mistook them for reflections. Thus Dante's error was the reverse of that committed by Narcissus and, just as Narcissus was too credulous, so Dante was too slow to believe what he saw. Beatrice, in ll. 25-7, chides him for his immaturity and lack of trust.

l. 29: *"True substances are these thou dost perceive"*: Beatrice here uses the word "substances" in its scholastic sense. In scholastic philosophy, a "substance" is anything that exists in itself, such as a human being, a dog, a plant, a table. It is opposed to and distinguished from "accident", by which the schoolmen meant something which exists only as an experience or an attribute of a substance, such as love, hunger, greenness, solidity. Beatrice means, therefore, that these are actual souls whom Dante sees, not reflections or images of something else.

l. 30: *"... and so are cloistered here"*: On earth these souls were guilty of inconstancy to vows. They are the first whom Dante meets in Paradise and represent the lowest order in the hierarchy of bliss. Their status is indicated by their presence in the moon, the planet nearest the earth and the symbol of inconstancy. They do not dwell permanently in the moon, for, as we learn in Canto iv, all the blessed are with God in the Empyrean where Dante will behold them. As he mounts through the successive spheres, souls descend to meet him in the planet which during their life on earth was most influential over them. By this means Dante achieves two things: (1) he refutes the Platonic belief that souls returned to the planets after death and remained there; (2) he introduces incident and variety into the narrative of his ascent.

l. 34: *So to the shade that seemed most keenly bent on speech*: This is Piccarda dei Donati. For information concerning her, see above under *Images*.

ll. 40–41: The singular and plural forms of the second person ("thou" and "you") are here used, as in the Italian, to make clear Dante's desire both to learn the condition and status of all the souls in the moon, and, in particular, the name of that soul whom he is addressing.

ll. 43–5: In expressing her readiness to answer Dante's questions, Piccarda associates herself with the love which pervades all the blessed in Heaven and which, like the love of God Himself, cannot but respond to rightful prayer. Such attribute the souls derive from God who wills that all His court shall resemble Him in this.

l. 51: "*the slowest sphere*": i.e. the sphere of the moon, which, being the innermost of the nine concentric spheres of heaven, revolves the most slowly round the earth in its daily revolution from east to west. In its proper motion, from west to east, the moon is, on the contrary, the swiftest planet, in that it has a shorter period than any other. Dante is careful to speak of the moon's *sphere* as being the slowest, for it is that which carries the moon round the earth from east to west (see Appendix, Note A).

ll. 52–4: Piccarda here explains the source of the souls' joy: what God delights in they joyously conform to, or, in other words, they rejoice to have their "form", or essential being, in conformity with the divine order, which is the "form" of the universe (cf. Canto i. 103–5).

ll. 64–9: "*But tell me, you whose happiness is here* . . .": Dante shows by this question how much he has yet to learn concerning Paradise. Since God is the ultimate desire of the soul, and since the more it learns to know God the greater the longing grows to be united with Him, it follows, so Dante reasons, that any lesser degree of nearness to Him must leave the souls unsatisfied. The joyous look of Piccarda and of the other souls as she replies leaves him in no doubt that their joy is perfect and complete.

ll. 70–76: "*Brother, our love has laid our wills to rest*" etc.: The perfecting of the love of the blessed for God has removed any possibility of their wills being in conflict with His.

ll. 78–85: "*and thou bethink thee what love's nature is*" etc.: The nature of love and its operation in the human soul have been the subject of a lengthy analysis and commentary by Virgil in *Purgatory* (Cantos xvii and xviii). This canto itself opens with a recollection of Dante's own first awakening to the personal experience of love. Piccarda's adjuration is, therefore, laden with significance. "Remember", she seems to bid him, "all you have experienced and learned of love, and now know that in Paradise to love is to dwell within the will of God, with which our own wills are made one."

ll. 85-7: ... *"and His will is our peace"* ...: in this famous utterance
Piccarda sums up the very essence and nature of Paradise. In the iden-
tity of the souls' will with the will of God reside the perfection of their
joy and the utter fulfilment of their desire. (The present translation
follows the reading "e la sua volontade è nostra pace" in preference to
"in" or "e'n la sua volontade", on the grounds that it is founded on
Ephes. ii. 15: "Ipse enim est pax nostra". This seems to be supported by
the fact that the end of the verse, "qui fecit utraque unum" is echoed by
Dante four lines earlier, "perch *una fansi* nostre voglie stesse" (*lit.*
"whereby our wills are made one").

l. 87: *"that it creates or nature furnishes"*: i.e. all things, whether created
directly by God (as human souls) or by secondary causes or nature (as
the brute creation and inanimate matter).

ll. 88-90: *Then I saw plain how Heav'n is everywhere Paradise*: Dante
now sheds his earthly hankering after equality and sees clearly that
diversity in the souls' capacity for bliss does not imply any imperfection
in fulfilment.

ll. 95-6: ... *and begged her draw the shuttle's thread right through*:
Dante asks Piccarda to tell him what vow she "neglected and partly
disavowed" (l. 57).

l. 98: *"a lady"*: This is St Clare, the founder of the Franciscan Order
of the Poor Clares. She was a friend and disciple of St Francis of Assisi.

ll. 101-2: *"... the Bridegroom who doth aye accept every good vow that
love has put to school"*: Not every vow is pleasing to God, but only
those which love (charity) renders in accord with His will (cf. Canto v.
64-84).

l. 106: *"but men more apt for ill than good arose"*: Piccarda refers here
particularly to her brother, Corso dei Donati, who compelled her to
leave the convent and marry Rossellino della Tosa, a man of violent
character and political ambition with whom Corso at the time sought
alliance.

l. 109: *"This other splendour ..."*: This is the soul of Constance, the
mother of Frederick II. She was the wife of Henry VI, son of the
Emperor Frederick Barbarossa, whom he succeeded. Constance herself
was the heiress of the Norman house of Tancred which had conquered
Sicily and Southern Italy from the Saracens in the eleventh century. She
was thus also heiress to the crown of Naples and Sicily. Manfred, who
describes himself as her grandson, refers to her as "Empress Constance"
(*Purg.* iv. 113). It was believed in Dante's day that she was at one time a
nun and had been taken from the convent against her will, in order to
be married to Henry VI. The marriage took place in 1185, when Henry
was 22 and Constance about 32. Their son was not born until nine years
later. His enemies, who sought to identify him as the Anti-Christ, seized
on the story that his mother had been in a convent, for according to an
ancient prophecy the Anti-Christ would be born of an elderly nun.
Dante evidently believed that Constance had been a nun before her

marriage and seems intentionally to offset the evil spoken of her and her son by mentioning the great radiance in which she is displayed.

ll. 119–20: "*By Swabia's second gale engendering she bare the third – the last imperial might*": Frederick Barbarossa, his son Henry VI, and his grandson Frederick II are the three "gales" of Swabia. Frederick II is here regarded by Dante as the last true Emperor. (There is an account of the circumstances in which Constance gave birth to Frederick at the age of 41 in Richard Oke's historical novel, *The Boy from Apulia*.)

ll. 128–9: The beauty of Beatrice's eyes and smile increases as they mount heavenwards, and Dante's power to gaze on her is gradually strengthened until he is able to gaze ultimately on God Himself.

CANTO IV

THE STORY. *The words of Piccarda have aroused in Dante two doubts:*
(1) if both she and Constance were forcibly prevented from fulfilling their
vows, how can they be on that account less deserving of beatitude? (2) Pic-
carda spoke of the moon as her allotted sphere; was Plato then right after all
in teaching that souls returned to the stars after death? Beatrice explains that
all the souls of the blessed dwell only in the Empyrean, where all share "one
sweet life, diversified". They have appeared to Dante in the moon not
because they reside there but in order that their less exalted state may thus be
signified to him. His doubt concerning heavenly justice is removed when
Beatrice distinguishes between what we wish to do and what, under pressure,
we consent to do, for "our least acquiescence signs a pact with force."

Dante's mind, now clarified as to his two doubts, conceives yet a third:
can man by good works render satisfaction for unfulfilled vows? To this
Beatrice gives her answer in Canto V.

Between two dishes, equally attractive
   And near to him, a free man, I suppose,
   Would starve to death before his teeth got active;

So would a lamb 'twixt two fierce wolfish foes,   4
   Fearing the fangs both ways, not stir a foot;
   So would a deerhound halt between two does;

So I can't blame myself for standing mute,   7
   Nor praise myself: for I must needs so do,
   Suspended 'twixt two doubts, alike acute.

I held my tongue; but my desire showed through,   10
   With livelier colours painted in my look
   Than speech could lend – so did my questions, too.

So, taking now a leaf from Daniel's book,   13
   When he assuaged Nebuchadnezzar's ire
   Which made him cruel, unjust, and hard to brook,

Beatrice said: "Well know I how desire   16
   Tugs thee two ways, and thy great eagerness
   Can find no vent, being choked in its own wire.

19   Thou arguest: 'If the will to righteousness
        Persists, how is it just that violence wrought
        By other men should make my merit less?'

22   A further puzzle gives thee food for thought:
        These souls which, as it seems, complete their course
        Returning to the stars, as Plato taught;

25   And these two questions with an equal force
        Weigh on thy will; so I'll begin straightway
        With that which has most venom in its jaws.

28   No seraph, not the most in-godded – nay,
        Not Moses, Samuel, nor either John
        (Take which thou wilt), not Mary's self, I say,

31   Is throned in any heaven but in that one
        Where dwell these souls thou hast beheld, nor hath
        Their being more or fewer years to run;

34   But each in the First Circle glittereth,
        And all share one sweet life, diversified
        As each feels more or less the eternal breath.

37   They're shown thee here, not that they here reside,
        Allotted to this sphere; their heavenly mansion,
        Being least exalted, is thus signified.

40   This way of speech best suits your apprehension,
        Which knows but to receive reports from sense
        And fit them for the intellect's attention.

43   So Scripture stoops to your intelligence:
        It talks about God's 'hand' and 'feet', intending
        That you should draw a different inference;

46   And so does holy Church, in pictures lending
        A human face to Michael, Gabriel,
        And him by whom old Tobit found amending.

49   That which Timaeus of the soul doth tell
        Is not like things shown here for thy behoof,
        For what he says he seems to think as well.

52   He says the soul at death returns above
        To its own star, from which it was divided
        (He thinks) when Nature made a form thereof.

Yet he may not have meant men to be guided   55
  By the words' surface sense, and thus might claim
  Another purport, not to be derided.

If it's their influence whose praise or blame   58
  He would refer back to these wheeling stars,
  His bow may not have wholly missed its aim.

Hence almost all the world in former years   61
  Rushed off, misconstruing this theory,
  To call on Jove and Mercury and Mars.

The other question that is troubling thee   64
  Is less envenomed: it breeds no sedition
  To turn thee elsewhere and away from me.

That heavenly justice should to human vision   67
  Appear unjust arises from belief,
  And not from vile heretical misprision;

But since thy mental reach is not too brief   70
  To grasp this truth, neither will I refuse
  To please thee, and to give thy mind relief.

If this is violence: when brute force subdues   73
  A sufferer who does nothing to endorse it,
  Why then, these souls could not plead that excuse;

For if the will won't will, nothing can force it;   76
  But, as fire acts by nature, it will act,
  Though thousand gales of violence beat across it.

But our least acquiescence signs a pact   79
  With force; so did these souls – for to regain
  Their holy house 'twas will, not power, they lacked.

That uncorrupted will which could sustain   82
  Laurence, and hold him steadfast on the grill,
  And harden Mucius to his own hand's pain,

Would, to the road they had been forced from, still   85
  Have thrust them back, the moment they were loosed;
  But it is all too rare, that single will.

These words, if rightly gathered and perused,   88
  Should rid thee of the doubt that otherwise
  Might oft return, and leave thee much abused.

91   But a fresh obstacle now meets thine eyes,
        Of such a sort that scrambling over it
        Unaided were a weary enterprise.

94   Firmly have I impressed upon thy wit
        That souls beatified can tell no lie,
        So near the Primal Truth these spirits sit.

97   Now comes Piccarda: 'Constance ne'er put by
        Devotion to the veil,' she told thee here;
        And thus we seem to differ, she and I.

100 Brother, it oft befalls that to steer clear
        Of danger, men will do things odious
        In their own eyes, constrained to this by fear.

103 Urged by his father's prayer, Alcmaeon thus
        His mother slew and turned unfilial
        Lest piety should make him impious.

106 Mark at this point, I bid thee, mark withal
        How will with force and force with will works in,
        Till the offence has no excuse at all.

109 Absolute will assents not to the sin,
        Yet it assents, at least to the extent
        That it does not refuse lest worse begin.

112 It was the absolute will Piccarda meant,
        And I the other, speaking on this theme,
        So that we both speak truth with one consent."

115 Thus did it ripple forth, the sacred stream
        Sprung from the fount whence every truth doth flow,
        Thus to my two desires sing requiem.

118 "O loved", said I, "of the First Lover! O
        Most heavenly Lady, by whose words I live
        More and yet more, bathed in their quickening glow,

121 My love's whole store is too diminutive,
        Too poor in thanks to give back grace for grace;
        May He that sees, and has the power, so give!

124 That nothing save the light of truth allays
        Our intellect's disquiet I now see plain –
        God's truth, which holds all truth within its rays.

Intellect, like a wild thing in its den,   127
   When it has run and reached it, there can rest,
   As reach it must, else all desire were vain.

Hence, at the foot of truth, the undying quest   130
   Springs like a shoot, and doubt is still the lure
   That speeds us toward the height from crest to crest.

This thought invites and makes me more secure   133
   To ask you, Lady, with all reverence due,
   About a further truth I find obscure.

This would I know: can one atone to you   136
   For broken vows with other merchandise,
   Nor weigh too short upon your balance true?"

Beatrice looked at me, and lo! her eyes   139
   Grew so divine, with sparkling love alight,
   That I was lost in wonder and surprise,

My gaze downcast, my powers all put to flight.   142

THE IMAGES. *The resolving of Dante's dilemma and the allaying of his doubts*: In the *story*, the discourses by Beatrice upon existence in Heaven and upon absolute and qualified will are occasioned by words uttered by Piccarda in the preceding Canto. *Allegorically* the freeing of Dante from the paralysis of his will, and the illuminating of his mind by revealed theology (Beatrice), represents a step forward in the soul's progress towards God. The desire of the mind for knowledge and understanding is in itself a natural image of the desire of the soul to see God; in another sense the two desires may be seen to be identical, since the mind can be satisfied only by the ultimate Truth, which is God. Throughout *Paradise*, Dante's advancement in understanding is a symbol and a measure of his progress towards his ultimate vision in the last canto.

NOTES. l. 1: *Between two dishes*: Piccarda's words have aroused in Dante's mind two doubts which disturb him equally acutely (l. 9). He cannot decide which to mention first and so stands mute. In this he likens himself to one to whom two dishes, equally tempting and accessible, are offered. This imaginary dilemma was a favourite subject in logical exercise in the Middle Ages and can be traced back as far as Aristotle. One form of it, attributed to the French scholastic philosopher, Jean Buridan (who was Rector of the University of Paris soon after Dante's death) is referred to as the dilemma of Buridan's ass which, finding itself between two equal and identical bundles of hay, would, logically, starve to death. St Thomas Aquinas refers to the dilemma of the two dishes as one of the arguments used in support of the thesis that all choice is *de necessitate*, the validity of which St Thomas then proceeds to refute.

l. 2: *a free man*: a man endowed with free will.

ll. 13-15: *So, taking now a leaf from Daniel's book* etc.: Beatrice reads what is passing in Dante's thoughts as easily as Daniel read and interpreted the dream which Nebuchadnezzar had forgotten (*Daniel* ii. 1-46), thus placating the ferocious wrath of the king who had commanded that all the sages of Babylon should be put to death.

l. 19: *"Thou arguest"* etc.: Beatrice tells Dante what his two doubts are. She mentions first his perplexity concerning the case of Piccarda and Constance: if they still desired to adhere to their vows and were prevented from doing so by the violence of others, why have they a lesser degree of merit? Secondly, since Piccarda has said that the allotted place of her companions and herself is the moon (cf. iii. 55-7), Dante wonders how far the Platonic doctrine is true, according to which human souls returned to the stars whence they came.

ll. 25-7: *"And these two questions with an equal force weigh on thy will"*: To Dante his two doubts seem equally pressing and important; hence, his will to choose between them is paralysed. Beatrice, however, perceives that the one she has mentioned second is the more urgent of the two since it contains a pernicious theological error. Dante knew very little of Plato's writings. The dialogue on natural science, the *Timaeus*, was known in his day in an imperfect Latin translation by Chalchidius. Dante may have derived his notion of the Platonic doctrine of souls either from this or from references to it by St Augustine or Albertus Magnus. Plato's doctrine, as Dante understood it, by placing the origin and end of human souls in the stars, ascribed to the influence of heavenly bodies such ineluctable and over-riding power that free-will and, consequently, morality, would logically be ruled out. Dante admitted the influence of the planets and stars on human personalities and events, but insisted that the will was free. He has already discussed this fundamental question in *Purgatory* xvi. 58-81 and xviii. 61-72, first with Marco Lombardo in connection with stellar influence, and then with Virgil in connection with the relation between innate and inherited tendencies and man's will to assent to evil or choose the good. The implications of his second doubt are therefore of greater importance. The two "dishes" were not "equally attractive", they merely seemed so, and Beatrice, with her divine insight, has released Dante from an apparent dilemma.

ll. 28-36: *"No seraph, not the most in-godded"* etc.: Dante's meaning is: "not the sublimest angels, nor the most exalted saints have their abode in any other heaven than that wherein dwell the souls just now encountered in the moon." He mentions first the seraphim (whose function is contemplation and "who have a clearer vision of the first cause than any other angelic nature", as he says in the *Convivio*, II. vi); then Moses, the greatest of all the prophets, coupling him (as Jeremiah did) with Samuel; next the two Johns ("take which thou wilt"), either the Apostle or St John the Baptist, and finally the Virgin Mary; with all these Piccarda and her companions, and all the souls whom Dante will encounter during his ascent, share the abode of the Empyrean (the First Circle, here so-called because it is the nearest to God) and eternity. Yet, although they share, their bliss is diversified "as each feels more or less" the eternal afflatus of God, or, in other words, according to their several capacities to feel the ardour of God's love.

ll. 37-48: "*They're shown thee here*" etc.: The word "signified" (l. 39) is a key to this passage. That which Dante is shown in Paradise is a *sign*, presented to his senses, so that his intellect may grasp the meaning. According to Aristotelian and scholastic psychology, the intellect works upon images which are retained in the mind after the sense impressions that produced them have vanished. Thus the imaginative faculties ("apprehension", l. 40) receive from the faculties of sense the impressions which they present for the intellect to work on. When the intellect has done so, as Virgil explained in *Purgatory* xviii, love is awakened. Thus it is that Holy Scripture presents man with the knowledge of God by means of images which the sense perceptions can imprint on the imagination; this in its operations leads to intellectual understanding and finally to love. It is probable that Dante intends the reader to understand the literal meaning and the imagery of the *Divine Comedy* in the same way. Using means similar to those of scripture and of religious art, Dante renders Paradise intelligible in terms of sense, imagination and intellect.

l. 48: "*And him by whom old Tobit found amending*": the archangel Raphael, who enabled Tobias to cure the blindness of his father, Tobit.

ll. 49-51: "*That which Timaeus of the soul doth tell*" etc.: Plato, in the dialogue of *Timaeus*, appears not to speak in symbols or signs but to mean literally what he says. (It was not known for certain in Dante's day, nor is it yet, how far Plato was to be taken literally concerning his doctrine of the soul; that is why Beatrice allows the possibility that he may have been speaking figuratively, ll. 55-7.)

l. 54: "*When Nature made a form thereof*": In Plato's myth of the creation, he teaches that the soul leaves its native star when, at its birth on earth, nature allows it to *inform* the body, and at death, if it has lived well, it returns again to its star. "Form" is the scholastic term for the essential formative principle which makes a thing what it is. When the soul was joined with a body it became the body's essential and constituent form.

ll. 58-60: If Plato intended merely to convey that the stars influence human life, then his doctrine has been more misunderstood than erroneous. Dante believed that the will was free; having no bodily organ, it was immune from the coercion of nature. Bound up with the notion of stellar influence was the conception of individuality, which, in Dante's philosophical system, is imprinted by the stars (or, as we might express it today, is the outcome of environment, heredity, upbringing, education, climate, in other words, of the whole nexus of conditions into which it is our fate to be born).

ll. 67-9: The second doubt in Dante's mind, as to whether it is just that souls who were coerced into breaking their vows should on that account enjoy less beatitude than others, does not arise from heretical misunderstanding, but from insufficient faith. Both questions are however related to the doctrine of free will.

ll. 76-8: "*For if the will won't will, nothing can force it*" etc.: These three lines contain the substance of Beatrice's reply to Dante's second doubt, and are a magnificent assertion of the freedom of the will.

l. 83: "*Laurence ... steadfast on the grill*": St Laurence, a deacon of the Church of Rome, who suffered martyrdom in the year 258. On being grilled alive on an iron frame he remained steadfast, refusing to reveal where the treasures of the Church were hidden.

l. 84: "*And harden Mucius to his own hand's pain*": Caius Mucius Scaevola, on being ordered by Lars Porsena of Clusium to be burned alive, thrust his right hand into the flame and held it there without flinching. Porsena was so impressed by his fortitude that he spared his life.

ll. 94-6: "*Firmly have I impressed upon thy wit*": Beatrice has told Dante (Canto iii. 31-3) that the souls in Paradise cannot depart from truth.

l. 103: *Alcmaeon*: the son of Amphiaraus the seer and Eriphyle. Amphiaraus, foreseeing that the expedition against Thebes would prove fatal to him, hid himself away so as to avoid joining it, but his wife betrayed him. Before he died, Amphiaraus enjoined his son Alcmaeon to avenge him by slaying his mother. The slaying of Eriphyle is represented in the carvings on the wall of Mt Purgatory on the Cornice of the Proud, where the incident displays the type of vainglory that is called Vanity (*Purg.* xii. 49-51). Here the deed of Alcmaeon is cited as an example of qualified will. Actions that are performed through fear, or to avoid some greater evil, are not really committed against the will of the perpetrator.

ll. 112-14: "*It was the absolute will Piccarda meant*": when Piccarda said that Constance in her heart "ne'er put off the veil she wore", she meant that her absolute will remained unchanged; but the qualified will, which chose marriage rather than death, assented to the broken vow.

l. 118: "*the First Lover*": God.

ll. 124-6: "... *nothing save the light of truth allays our intellect's disquiet*": the mind's appetite for knowledge and understanding can be sated only by the final, ultimate and first Truth that is God. Dante now sees this plainly because despite, or rather, because of, Beatrice's illuminating reply, another doubt has sprung up in his mind.

ll. 127-32: "*Intellect, like a wild thing in its den*" etc.: When the intellect has finally caught the Supreme Truth which it is ever pursuing, it will rest therein content like a wild creature in its den. Until this comes to pass, all truth, however sublime, is incomplete and gives rise to doubt after doubt (that is, increasing desire for knowledge) until the ultimate goal is reached.

CANTO V

THE STORY. *Beatrice rejoices in the progress of Dante's mind towards the light of truth and explains that every vow consists of two conditions: (1) the thing pledged; and (2) the covenant made with God of the abdication of one's own will. The second condition must in every case be fulfilled, but the content of the vow may, under due authority, be substituted by some other pledge, provided that the exchange involves the sacrifice of something of still greater value. In no case, therefore, can vows of self-dedication (e.g. monastic vows) be substituted by anything else. Hence it behoves men not to take vows lightly.*

They now ascend swift as an arrow to the second heaven, where they enter the planet Mercury. Thousands of souls, swathed in light, draw near. One offers converse and, at the urgent bidding of Beatrice, Dante puts to it questions which are answered in the next canto.

"If in the fire of love I flame thus hot
    Upon thee, past all wont of mortal mood,
    Forcing thine eyes' surrender, marvel not;

4   This comes of perfect sight, with power endued
    To apprehend, and foot by foot to move
    Deeper into the apprehended good.

7   Full well I see thine intellect give off
    Splendours already of the eternal light
    Which once to look upon is aye to love;

10   And if aught else your wandering loves invite,
    Still is it nothing but some gleams of this
    Which there shine through, though not yet known aright.

13   Fain wouldst thou learn if any service is
    Enough to offset broken vows, and fend
    The soul against pursuit for damages."

16   Thus did Beatrice to my canto lend
    The prelude; nor paused there, but fluently
    Pursued her sacred theme unto the end.

19   "The greatest gift of God's largesse, when He
    Created all, most prized by Him, and best,
    As most akin to His own quality,

Was the will's freedom, crown of all the rest,   22
  Whereof all creatures made intelligent,
  They all, they only, were and are possessed.

Hence thou may'st well conclude the eminent   25
  Worth of a vow so tendered that in fact
  When thou consentest, so doth God consent;

Since, to confirm 'twixt God and man the pact,   28
  This gift, being such as I describe, is made
  The sacrifice, and that by its own act.

What compensation, therefore, can be paid?   31
  Take back the gift and use it well, think'st thou?
  'Twere to finance good works by thievish trade.

That settles the main point for thee. But now,   34
  Since holy Church seems somewhat to rebuff
  My truth, when she dispenses from a vow,

Thou must sit still at table long enough   37
  To let digestion work, the which would fain
  Have more assistance, for this food is tough.

Open thy mind; take in what I explain   40
  And keep it there; because to understand
  Is not to know, if thou dost not retain.

Two things are requisite: the deodand,   43
  And the vow's self, to make the sacrifice:
  These two essentials all such rites demand.

The latter cannot be in any wise   46
  Discharged, except by the performance; so
  'Twas this I meant when I was thus precise;

Witness the Hebrews, who might not forgo   49
  The act of offering, though the offered thing
  Might sometimes be redeemed, as thou shouldst know.

That part – the *matter* of the offering,   52
  So-called – is sometimes such that it may be
  Changed for new matter without trespassing.

But none may shift by private self-decree   55
  The load on his own back, but must await
  The turn of both the white and yellow key;

58   And all exchange were vain to contemplate
        Unless as four to six you may esteem
        The values of the gift and surrogate.

61   Wherefore, if aught that's weighed upon the beam
        Outweigh all else, the value that so doth
        Is something that no purchase can redeem.

64   Let not men take vows lightly; keep your oath,
        But not with stubborn wall-eyed foolishness,
        As Jephthah pledged his first-met, and kept troth;

67   Whom more behoved to say: *I did amiss,*
        Than keep it and do worse. And the great chief
        Of Greeks, thou'lt find, showed folly like to his,

70   Making Iphigenia wail for grief,
        Too fair to die; whence wise and simple too
        Wail that curst rite while song and story live.

73   Christians, be steadier in what you do,
        Not blown like feathers at the wind's discretion,
        Nor think that every water cleanses you;

76   You have both Testaments in your possession,
        You have the Shepherd of the Church for guide;
        So let these things suffice for your salvation.

79   If you hear nostrums in the market cried,
        Behave like men, and not like witless sheep,
        Lest the Jew dwelling in your midst deride.

82   Don't imitate the lamb that will not keep
        Its mind on milk, but skips away to fight
        Its silly self, with wanton frisk and leap."

85   Thus unto me, even in the words I write,
        Beatrice; and, all desire, she turned her glance
        Then to where most the world is quick with light.

88   Her silence and her altered countenance
        Restrained my busy wits from chattering,
        Primed as they were with questions in advance;

91   And, as the shaft smites home or e'er the string
        Has ceased vibrating, so we found us there,
        Shot to the second realm, untarrying;

And O! such joy I saw my Lady wear   94
    When to that shining heav'n she entered in,
    The planet's self grew brigher yet with her;

And if the star laughed and was changed, what then   97
    Was I, who am but flesh, and ticklish
    To touch of change, and all the moods of men?

As in a fish-pond clear and still, the fish   100
    Draw to some dropped-in morsel as it moves,
    Hoping it may provide a dainty dish,

So I saw splendours draw to us in droves,   103
    Full many a thousand, and from each was heard:
    "Lo, here is one that shall increase our loves!"

And every shade approaching us appeared   106
    Glad through and through, so luminously shone
    Its flooding joy before it as it neared.

Think, Reader, if this tale I have begun   109
    Broke off abruptly here, how thou wouldst fret,
    Wondering and wondering how it should go on,

And judge by this how keen I was to get   112
    News of those beings there and then revealed,
    Of what they were, and in what station set.

"Blest-born! by grace beholding unconcealed   115
    The triumph-thrones of the eternal years,
    While yet a soldier in the battle-field,

The Light whose radiance runs through all the spheres 118
    Illumines us; and if from us thou seek
    Light, take thy will of us and sate thine ears."

Thus unto me one gracious soul; and quick   121
    Beatrice cried: "Ask, ask, nor fear therefor!
    Trust them as though the gods themselves should speak."

"I see thee nestle in thine own light's core;   124
    Thine eyebeams weave the light, and that see I,
    For at each smile they sparkle more and more;

But who thou art I cannot tell, nor why   127
    Thy rank, majestic soul, is this shy star,
    Masked by another's rays from mortal eye."

130 Thus, turning to the bright particular
   Light which had first addressed me, did I say;
   Whereat he beamed more brilliantly by far.

133 E'en as the sun veils him in blinding day
   When heat has nibbled through the thick cloud-haze
   That tempered him, and worn it all away,

136 So that blest form vanished in his own blaze
   Of ever-mounting joy, and straight began,
   All close enclosed in his bright carapace,

139 What next I'll sing as best my canto can.

THE IMAGES. *The resolving of Dante's doubt concerning vows:* see Canto iv, under *Images*.

Mercury: The second planet is the place of meeting between Dante and "full many a thousand souls" whose great gifts had enabled them on earth to assume positions of leadership and responsibility. Their relatively lowly status in the hierarchy of bliss is explained (in the following canto) by the admixture of pride and delight in fame which marred their service to mankind. In the natural universe, and, thus, in the *story*, Mercury is so near the sun that it is seldom visible from earth. *Allegorically* this is seen to be appropriate to the souls who congregate in this planet, since beside the glory of God their own is invisible.

NOTES. l. 2: "*... past all wont of mortal mood ...*": to a degree transcending earthly experience.

l. 4: "*perfect sight*": The earliest commentators understood Beatrice to be referring here to her own power to see God, which is illumining her gaze so brilliantly. The power to see and apprehend the Supreme Good increases and draws the soul nearer to its ultimate desire, and she perceives (ll. 7–9) that Dante's intellect is already illumined by a deeper vision and understanding. Notice that the sequence of this progress is in accordance with the psychology of Dante's day: (1) vision (through the senses), (2) apprehension (through the intellect), (3) love.

ll. 10–12: "*And if aught else your wandering loves invite*": If any earthly good becomes the object of men's love (Beatrice is here addressing mankind, and that is why she says "your", not "thy"), it is because some part of the Supreme Good is contained in it. In *Purgatory* xvi. 85–93, Virgil has explained how men are led astray by false images of good, or by mistaking what partakes of the Supreme Good for the total Good Itself. The rational love, endowed with selective powers, can err in its choice; but natural or instinctive love, though it needs guidance, is susceptible neither of praise nor blame. By "wandering loves" Beatrice evidently means the natural, instinctive impulses in man, undirected by reason.

ll. 13–15: *"Fain wouldst thou learn . . ."*: cf. Canto iv. 136–8.

ll. 23–4: *"Whereof all creatures made intelligent, they all, they only, were and are possessed"*: The only creatures to possess God's greatest gift, free will, are the Angels and men; and all Angels and all men are endowed with it, even after the rebellion of Lucifer and the fall of Adam.

ll. 29–30: *"This gift, being such as I describe, is made the sacrifice"*: When man makes a vow to God (in such terms as are acceptable to Him), he makes an offering of God's greatest gift, free will. From this may be inferred the eminent worth of such a vow.

ll. 31–3: *"What compensation, therefore, can be paid?"* etc.: If the vow is broken, what recompense is possible? A man who has made sacrifice of his free will to God cannot then, on breaking his vow, compensate by good works. That would be as dishonest as giving stolen money to charity.

ll. 43–57: *"Two things are requisite"* etc.: In making a vow to God, man enters into a double agreement: (1) he agrees to keep faith with God ("the vow's self"), (2) he pledges some particular thing ("the deo-dand"). The first is the compact, the abdication or sacrifice of one's own will, and cannot be discharged except by keeping faith. On the other hand, *what* one pledges may be exchanged or replaced by something else, but only by dispensation granted by priestly authority. *"The turn of both the white and yellow key"*: Beatrice here refers to the symbols of absolution, the Silver and the Golden Key (see *Purgatory* ix. 117–29 and *note*). In this context, the silver key symbolizes the discernment by which the priest is enabled to judge of the fitness of the person desiring to be absolved from a vow, the golden key the authority to absolve.

ll. 58–60: *"And all exchange"* etc.: If the thing pledged is replaced by something else, the new offering must be greater than the other in the proportion of six to four. The mathematical manner of expressing this concept is not, of course, to be taken literally.

ll. 61–3: *"Wherefore, if aught that's weighed upon the beam outweigh all else"* etc.: If a man has vowed to renounce something that is of such value that it preponderates over everything else, then nothing can re-place it. Such are the vows of chastity, poverty, and obedience made by members of monastic orders.

l. 66: *Jephthah:* The vow made by Jephthah to sacrifice the first living creature that should come to greet him as he returned home is quoted by Beatrice as an example of a vow wilfully and wrongly adhered to. "And Jephthah vowed a vow unto the Lord, and said, If thou shalt without fail deliver the children of Ammon into mine hands, then it shall be, that whatsoever cometh forth out of the doors of my house to meet me . . . I will offer it up for a burnt offering . . . And behold, his daughter came out to meet him" (*Judges* xi).

ll. 68–9: "*And the great chief of Greeks ...*": Agamemnon, who offered his daughter, Iphigenia, in sacrifice to Diana, to obtain favouring winds for the expedition against Troy.

l. 79: "*If you hear nostrums in the market cried*": It has been suggested by an early commentator (known as the "Postillatore Cassinese" because the MS. of his commentary was found in the monastery at Monte Cassino) that Beatrice (who in the Italian speaks in the abstract of "evil greed calling out other explanations") is referring here to the Friars of St Anthony who undertook to absolve people from vows for a moderate fee. Dante refers to the abuses of the Friars of St Anthony in Canto xxix. 124–6.

l. 87: *... where most the world is quick with light*: Where does Beatrice turn her gaze? To the east, to the heaven of Mercury into which they now ascend, to the Empyrean, towards the equinox or towards the sun? A precise answer is not necessary for, since the sun is near the equinoctial point at the time of the narrative, each of the above answers implies the other.

l. 88: *Her silence and her altered countenance*: The discussion concerning vows and the abuse of them by men and friars is over. Beatrice, transfigured, has moved from argument to contemplation.

l. 93: *the second realm*: the sphere of the second planet, Mercury.

ll. 97–9: *... what then was I* etc.: If the planet, Mercury, of eternal and unchanging form, underwent an increase of radiance as Beatrice drew near, what can Dante, who is mortal and susceptible to change of every kind, say of the alteration wrought in him by the splendour of Beatrice?

l. 117: "*While yet a soldier in the battle-field*": The soul (Justinian) addresses Dante as a member of the Church Militant; though still in the mortal state and not yet, therefore, of the Church Triumphant, Dante is privileged to behold the saints in Heaven.

ll. 124–6: "*I see thee nestle in thine own light's core*" etc.: Dante is able to perceive the elements of human semblance within the radiance which encloses this soul; he can make out the expression of the eyes and the smiles. (The image here is probably that of the silk worm; cf. Canto viii. 54.) In the heaven of the moon, the souls, though pale and faint, were discernible as human countenances. Henceforth the souls will be visible to Dante only as light. The reason for this is conveyed in ll. 133–7.

ll. 128–9: "*... this shy star, masked by another's rays from mortal eye*": Mercury is so near the sun that it is seldom visible from earth.

CANTO VI

THE STORY. *Replying to Dante's questions, the soul reveals himself as Justinian, the Lawgiver and former Emperor of Rome. At first a believer in the divine but not the human nature of Christ, he was converted to the true faith by Bishop Agapetus. From then on, committing military affairs to his general, Belisarius, he dedicated himself to the codifying of Roman Law. Rebuking both the Guelf and Ghibelline factions, he goes on to show the august nature of the Roman Empire, unfolding the panorama of its history from the earliest times down to the Redemption, the fall of Jerusalem and the championship of the Church by Charlemagne.*

Concerning the souls whom Dante has seen in Mercury, Justinian explains that, though they all performed virtuous and noble deeds in the first life, they were at the same time tainted with wordly ambition and desire for good repute. Now freed from envious desire for greater reward, they rejoice in the beatitude assigned to them. Among them is Romèo, minister of Raymond Berengar, Count of Provence.

"When Constantine turned back the eagle's flight
    Against the heavens whose course it kept of yore,
    Following Lavinia's bridegroom and the light,

A hundred and a hundred years and more   4
    The bird of God on Europe's last confine
    Dwelt near the hills that taught it first to soar;

Thence ruled the world, as line succeeded line   7
    Under the sacred wings' o'ershadowing span,
    And passed from hand to hand to light on mine.

Caesar I was, and am Justinian,   10
    Who from the Laws – urged by that Primal Love
    Which now I feel – winnowed the dust and bran.

Before I set me to the toil thereof,   13
    I deemed one nature and no more was in
    Christ's Person, and I thought that creed enough;

But blessed Agapetus, who was then   16
    Chief Pastor, used his eloquence to woo
    My heart unto the perfect faith, and win.

19 Him I believed; and what by faith he knew
    I now see plain as thou dost see how one
    Contradictory must be false, one true.

22 Soon as I walked the way the Church had gone,
    God's grace inspired me to my glorious
    Task, and I gave myself to that alone,

25 My arms unto my Belisarius
    Committing, whom Heav'n's right hand so befriended,
    'Twas token clear I should withdraw me thus.

28 To thy first question there's the answer ended;
    But such its tenor is that, ere I close,
    My speech must be a little more extended.

31 That thou may'st tell how justified are those
    Who with that emblem sacrosanct make free,
    To grab it for themselves, or to oppose,

34 Behold what valours made it reverend, see
    What deeds were done, beginning from the day
    That Pallas died to give it sovereignty.

37 Three hundred years and more, thou know'st, it lay
    In Alba, till by three and three was fought,
    Still for its sake, the fierce and final fray.

40 Under sev'n kings thou know'st the acts it wrought,
    E'en from the Sabine rape to Lucrece' woe;
    What neighbouring nations 'neath the yoke were brought;

43 How, borne by illustrious Romans, it laid low
    The might of Brennus, and made Pyrrhus tame,
    And warred down states and princes, thou dost know;

46 And how Torquatus, Quintius (whom men name
    'The Unkempt'), the Decii and the Fabii, all
    Won thence, what gladly I embalm – their fame.

49 The Arabian powers that passed with Hannibal
    Those Alpine crags whence, Po, thy streams run down,
    It crushed to earth and gave their pride its fall;

52 With it, young Scipio won the triumph-crown,
    Young Pompey too; and bitter to that hill
    It showed itself, which shades thy native town.

Then, near the time ordained, when Heaven would fill 55
  The whole world with its own celestial peace,
  Caesar laid hold upon it by Rome's will;

And then from Var to Rhine, what victories 58
  It won, Isère beheld, and Saone, and Seine,
  And every vale whence Rhône receives increase;

And from Ravenna such a flight was ta'en 61
  When, soaring forth, o'er Rubicon it leapt,
  That tongue and pen toil after it in vain.

On Spain it wheeled, then toward Dyrrachium swept 64
  The host, and at Pharsalia dealt a stroke
  Such that, far off, Nile's burning waters wept.

Antandros, Simois then, whence first it woke, 67
  It saw again, and looked on Hector's grave;
  Then – woe to Ptolemy! – shook its vans; then broke

Forth like the lightning, and on Juba drave; 70
  Whirled on your West its beating pinions flexed,
  And heard the blast the trump Pompeian gave.

For what it wrought with him who bare it next 73
  Brutus and Cassius bellow in Hell's grasp;
  Thence Mòdena and Perugia too were vext;

Still must sad Cleopatra wail and gasp 76
  Because of this that once she fled before
  To snatch death, swift and fearful, from the asp.

With him it ran unto the Red Sea shore; 79
  With him it wrought such world-wide peace as shut
  Janus within his shrine and barred the door.

Yet what this banner that I speak about 82
  Had done and was to do in every land
  That called it lord, the mortal world throughout,

Seems but a dim and paltry thing, if scanned 85
  With a clear eye and with a heart entire,
  To what it did in the third Caesar's hand;

For in that hand, the life which I respire, 88
  The Living Justice, granted it to win
  The glory of wreaking vengeance for His ire.

99

91   Marvel how plea meets counter-plea herein:
       For afterward, in Titus' time, it sprang
       To avenge the vengeance for the ancient sin.

94   And when on Holy Church the Lombard fang
       Had fastened, Charlemagne unto her aid
       Bore the winged triumph through the battle-clang.

97   Now canst thou judge of those I did upbraid
       Erewhile, and of their crimes, whence all that host
       Of troubles came, by which you are dismayed.

100 One to the public standard hath opposed
       The golden lilies; one hath made of it
       A party flag – hard to say which sins most.

103 Let Ghibellines 'neath some other sign more fit
       Go ply their ploys; this brooks no follower
       That between it and justice makes a split;

106 Let with his Guelfs this second Charles strike there
       No blow, but dread the talons that ere this
       Have from a mightier lion stripped hide and hair.

109 Full oft for what the sire has done amiss
       The sons have wept; nor let him flatter him
       God will swap arms against his fleurs-de-lis.

112 Virtuous souls this little star begem,
       Who, busied in good actions, sought the praise
       And honour that should live on after them;

115 And when desire would scale those heights, and strays
       Thus from the path, needs must the true love rise
       To its objective with less lively rays.

118 Yet is this balance 'twixt desert and prize
       Part of our joy; we see it so complete:
       Nothing too much or little, but precise.

121 Herein the Living Justice maketh sweet
       All our affections, which can never be
       Perverted now to vice or lusts unmeet.

124 As different voices down on earth agree
       In one sweet music, so our difference
       Of rank makes in these wheels sweet harmony.

Here, in this self-same pearl, flames forth intense   127
  Romèo's flame; right fair and goodly was
  His work, and shabby was his recompense;

Yet had the Provençals, his envious foes,   130
  Little to laugh at: he that thinks he's been
  Wronged by his neighbour's virtues, wrong he goes.

Daughters four, and every one a queen,   133
  Had Raymond Berengar; one alien
  Wrought this for him – Romèo, poor and mean.

But lying tongues seduced his lord, who then   136
  Called to account this man who was so just,
  And who'd returned him seven and five for ten.

Agèd and penniless, go trudge he must;   139
  Could the world know how brave a heart he bore,
  Begging his daily pittance, crust by crust,

Much as it lauds him now, 'twould laud him more."   142

THE IMAGES. *Mercury*: see under Canto v.

Justinian: surnamed "the Great", Emperor of Constantinople, A.D.
  527–65. He made a valiant effort to hold together the decaying fab-
  ric of the Empire, and by the help of his famous generals, Belisarius
  and Narses, overthrew the Vandals in Africa and the Ostrogoths in
  Italy. He is chiefly renowned for his great codification of the Roman
  Law (see also Notes to this Canto). In the establishment of Justinian's
  government at Ravenna, Dante saw the divinely ordained restora-
  tion of Imperial sovereignty in Western Europe. In his own great-
  ness Justinian symbolizes the greatness of Rome, and to him Dante
  accords the honour of unfolding the scroll of Rome's history from its
  foundation to the time of Charlemagne. Dante's awareness of the
  majesty of Justinian must have been borne in upon him during his
  years of residence in Ravenna and especially by the impressive figure
  of the Emperor in the sixth-century mosaic in the Church of San
  Vitale. His beliefs concerning the divinely ordered destiny of Rome
  (which he set forth also in his treatise on world government, *De
  Monarchia*) have been the subject of many an allusion, discussion and
  discourse throughout the *Divine Comedy*, but here, in the speech of
  Justinian, the theme is raised to sublime proportions in which Roman
  justice is seen as the earthly symbol of the divine.

The Eagle: In this canto it appears as an image within an image, sym-
  bolizing in Justinian's speech the destined might of Rome. (In Cantos
  xviii–xx, it reappears as an image in its own right, symbolizing both
  divine and Roman justice.)

Romèo: Romieu, or Romèe, of Villeneuve (1170–1250), a minister of Raymond Berengar IV, Count of Provence, has been identified as the original of Dante,'s Romèo. He is said to have been a friend of Sordello (cf. *Purg.* vi–viii). Dante, in the words of Justinian, stresses two things concerning him: his faithful service to his lord, and the undeserved disgrace into which he fell. In the *story*, Romèo is seen to be, like Pier delle Vigne (cf. *Hell* xiii), an instance of the loyal but ill-rewarded servant, of which Dante himself was a living example, having faithfully served Florence and having likewise received ill usage in return. *Allegorically* Romèo, like Justinian, symbolizes the nature which serves loyally but with hope of personal advancement; earthly reward was denied him, but in Heaven his recompense is equal to Justinian's.

NOTES. l. 1: "*When Constantine turned back the eagle's flight*": When the Emperor Constantine (who ruled from A.D. 306–37) transferred the seat of the Empire from Rome to Byzantium (from west to east), he turned the eagle, the emblem of the Roman Empire, back upon its course (which it had followed when Aeneas, Lavinia's bridegroom, brought it from Troy to Italy) and against the course of heavens (which revolve from east to west). Dante held that the foundation of the Roman Empire was willed by God and regarded all attempts to weaken its authority as contrary to the divine plan for world order. (He sets forth his arguments in support of this thesis in his treatise on world government, *De Monarchia*; see particularly Book II.) Constantine, by endowing the Papacy with temporal sovereignty over Italy, had encouraged the increase of secular authority and wealth in the Church; to this Dante attributed all the major evils of his time. The transference of power was alleged to be embodied in a document known as the "Donation of Constantine". Dante believed this to be authentic (it has since been shown to be a forgery) but he denied its validity. In *Hell* he condemns the action of Constantine:

> "Ah, Constantine! what ills were gendered there –
> No, not from thy conversion, but the dower
> The first rich Pope received from thee as heir!"
>
> (xix. 115–17)

Constantine himself, however, the first Christian Emperor and convener of the Council of Nicaea, is referred to by Dante as present in the heaven of Jupiter among the Spirits of the Just (xx. 55–7). See also Glossary.

  l. 3: *Lavinia*: daughter of Latinus, King of Latium. She had been betrothed to Turnus, King of the Rutuli, but Latinus gave her in marriage to Aeneas. (See also Glossary.)

  l. 4: "*A hundred and a hundred years and more*": Constantine removed the seat of Empire from Rome to Byzantium (Constantinople) in

A.D. 324. Justinian became Emperor in A.D. 527, that is, 203 years later.

l. 5: *"The bird of God on Europe's last confine"*: The eagle, symbol of Roman authority, ruled from Byzantium through a succession of Emperors until Justinian established his government in Ravenna.

l. 6: *"Dwelt near the hills that taught it first to soar"*: near the mountains of Troas from which arose the destiny of Rome (symbolized by Aeneas, its founder).

l. 10: *"Caesar I was, and am Justinian"*: His individual personality remains, but in Heaven his Imperial office is no more. By this, Dante conveys that after a man's death all earthly dignities are at an end.

ll. 11–12: *"Who from the Laws ... winnowed the dust and bran"*: One of Justinian's first actions, on his succession as Emperor, was to appoint a commission of jurists, under the direction of Tribonian, to gather together all the valid edicts of the Roman Emperors since Hadrian. The result of their labours was the compilation of the Codex Justinianus (529). In 530 another commission was set up to revise all the rulings and precedents of the classical Roman lawyers, and to reject all irrelevancies, contradictions and anachronisms. The result was the *Digesta*, or *Pandectae*, in fifty volumes. The definitive edition of the *Codex* was published in the year 534. The originality of this great compilation lay in its adaptation of Roman law to the conditions of the Christian Empire of the sixth century.

ll. 14–15: *"I deemed one nature and no more was in Christ's Person"*: Justinian says that before his conversion by Pope Agapetus (A.D. 533–6), he adhered to the Eutychian heresy (so called from Eutyches, an abbot of Constantinople) according to which only the divine, not the human, nature existed in Christ. (For a lively discussion of this and other heresies in relation to modern attitudes to religion, see *Creed or Chaos?* by Dorothy L. Sayers.)

l. 16: *Agapetus*: Pope Agapetus is said to have been at Constantinople for the peace negotiations between Justinian and Theodatus, King of the Goths. While there, he discovered the heretical views of the Emperor and persuaded him to embrace the true faith.

ll. 25–6: *"My arms unto my Belisarius committing"*: Belisarius, the great general who served under Justinian, overthrew the Vandal kingdom in Africa and enabled Narses to reconquer the Goths in 552. Justinian was thus enabled to found the exarchate of Ravenna upon the ruins of the Gothic dominions. In the mosaic in the Church of San Vitale in Ravenna it is thought to be Belisarius who is standing beside the Emperor. Gibbon called him "the Africanus of new Rome".

ll. 31–3: *"... those who with that emblem sacrosanct make free ..."*: Justinian here reproves both the Guelfs and Ghibellines, the former for fighting against the Imperial symbol, the latter for appropriating it to themselves.

l. 34: *"Behold what valours made it reverend"*: Justinian now proceeds to unfold the great panorama of Roman history from the time of Aeneas to that of Charlemagne. It was believed in Justinian's time that the Roman Empire participated in the dignity of Christ, transcending every other power, and that it would remain unconquered till the final consummation. "It was Justinian's dream to win back the separated western provinces and to build again the Empire of the Caesars, ruled by one hand, guided by one law and inspired by one faith." (D. M. Nicol "The Emperor Justinian", *History Today*, Aug. 1959, p. 515.)

ll. 35–6: ". . . *the day that Pallas died to give it sovereignty*": Pallas, the Trojan, son of Evander, was killed by Turnus (see also Glossary).

ll. 37–9: "*Three hundred years and more . . .*" etc.: Rome is supposed to have been founded by the inhabitants of Alba Longa, and to have remained under their sway until the three Alban Curiatii were defeated by the three Roman Horatii.

ll. 40–42: "*Under sev'n kings*" etc.: From the rape of the Sabines, in the time of Romulus, the first king, down to the suicide of Lucrece, which led to the expulsion of Tarquin, the seventh king, Rome brought many neighbouring powers beneath her sway.

ll. 43–5: ". . . *it laid low the might of Brennus, and made Pyrrhus tame*": Brennus was the leader of the Senonian Gauls who in 390 B.C. besieged the Capitol, and was defeated by Camillus. Pyrrhus, King of Epirus, in 280 B.C., at the invitation of the Tarentines, crossed over into Italy to help them in their war against the Romans. In this and subsequent attempts he failed and was eventually defeated at Beneventum in 275 B.C. and compelled to leave Italy.

l. 46: *Torquatus*: Titus Manlius Torquatus, who was twice Dictator (353, 349 B.C.) and three times Consul (347, 344, 340 B.C.). In the year 340, he fought a decisive battle against the Latins (see also Glossary). *Quintius*: Lucius Quintius Cincinnatus (his surname means "shaggy-haired") was called from his farm in 458 B.C. to assume the dictatorship in order to deliver the Roman army from the Aequians (see also Glossary).

l. 47: *the Decii*: a famous Roman family, three members of which father, son, and grandson, all bearing the name of Publius Decius Mus, laid down their lives for Rome. *the Fabii*: an ancient family celebrated as having furnished a long line of eminent Romans. Fabius Maximus Cunctator, who was five times Consul (233–209 B.C.), is famous for the delaying tactics (whence his surname) which he employed against Hannibal at the Battle of Lake Trasimene. (This is known as the Fabian policy.)

l. 49: "*The Arabian powers*": i.e. the Carthaginians, led by Hannibal across the Alps in 218 B.C.

l. 52: "*Young Scipio*": Scipio Africanus the Elder, in 218 B.C., when a boy of about seventeen, won fame by saving his father's life at the defeat of Ticinus.

l. 53: "*Young Pompey*": By a leap of 137 years, Dante brings us to the first triumph of Pompey, in 81 B.C.: "*and bitter to that hill*": the hill of

Fiesole which overhangs Florence. According to a legend, Catiline took refuge there and Fiesole was attacked and conquered by the Romans.

l. 55: "*. . . near the time ordained*": i.e. in the fullness of time, the year ordained for the birth of Christ.

l. 57: "*Caesar laid hold upon it by Rome's will*": Julius Caesar took possession of the eagle, i.e. was elected ruler of Rome.

ll. 58–60: These lines refer to the victorious campaigns of Julius Caesar in Gaul. The River Var bounded Gaul on the east, the Rhine on the north. The Isère, the Saône and the Seine flow into the Rhone.

ll. 61–3: These lines refer to Caesar's crossing of the Rubicon (49 B.C.), the river between Ravenna and Rimini, by which action he began the civil war against Pompey.

ll. 64–6: In the same year (49 B.C.), Caesar overcame opposition in Spain; in 48 B.C. he besieged Pompey in Dyrrachium and finally defeated him at Pharsalia in Thessaly. Pompey escaped to Egypt, where he was treacherously slain by Ptolemy.

ll. 67–72: Caesar crossed the Hellespont, visited the Troad (according to Lucan), took Egypt from Ptolemy and gave it to Cleopatra; subdued Juba, King of Numidia (who had protected Caesar's opponents after the Battle of Pharsalia), and returned to Spain, where Pompey's sons ("the trump Pompeian") had raised a new army.

ll. 73–5: "*him who bare it next*" etc.: The nephew of Caesar, Augustus, defeated Mark Antony at Modena (43 B.C.); then, with Mark Antony as his ally, he defeated his uncle's assassins, Brutus and Cassius, at Philippi (42 B.C.) and, later, Antony's brother, Lucius, at Perugia (41 B.C.). It seems that Dante has forgotten that in *Hell* (xxiv. 66) he has said (through the words of Virgil) that Brutus, writhing in Satan's mouth "utters never a word", or perhaps Justinian disbelieves in Brutus's stoicism.

ll. 76–8: In 31 B.C., Augustus finally defeated his rival, Mark Antony, at Aetium. He, and Cleopatra after him, committed suicide, leaving Augustus master of the whole Roman Empire (as far as the Red Sea, the remotest confine of Egypt), and the doors of the temple of Janus, which were always kept open in time of war, were closed (for the third time only in Roman history) in sign of universal peace.

l. 87: "*the third Caesar's hand*": Tiberius Caesar, under whose reign Christ was crucified. It was at this point that the Eagle's glory reached its highest peak, for then divine justice granted it to wreak vengeance upon the Son of Man for the sin of Adam. Dante regarded the Crucifixion as an act made legally valid under Imperial jurisdiction because carried out with the assent of the Imperial legate, Pontius Pilate. Since, in the Crucifixion, the sins of all mankind were redeemed, the Imperial authority which sanctioned it was legitimate and valid over all mankind. If it were not, then the Crucifixion did not redeem all men. This is the crux of the argument in the second book of Dante's treatise, *De Monarchia* (XII–XIII).

l. 91: "*Marvel how plea meets counter-plea herein*": Justinian here speaks in terms of Roman Law, according to which a defendant pleading special circumstances was said to put forward an *exceptio*. If the plaintiff countered this, his reply was called the *replicatio*. In the words of Justinian, the plea (*exceptio*) that the Jews might make was that the Crucifixion was the appointed atonement for the fall of man. The counterplea (*replicatio*) would be that this in no way affected the guilt of the Jews in crucifying an innocent man. Thus, rightly, so Justinian infers, the eagle, in the hand of Titus, avenged "the vengeance for the ancient sin". The theological justification of this legal concept is the subject of Canto vii.

l. 92: "*in Titus' time*": Titus, the son and successor of Vespasian, was Emperor from A.D. 79–81. When his father was proclaimed Emperor in A.D. 70, Titus continued the siege of Jerusalem which Vespasian had been commanding, and destroyed the city in September of that year. The belief that Titus, as the destroyer of Jerusalem, was the avenger of the death of Christ is derived from Orosius.

ll. 94–6: Justinian concludes his recital of Roman history with an epilogue concerning the defence of the Church by Charlemagne against the Lombard, King Desiderius, whom he dethroned in A.D. 774. This great leap of seven centuries is significant: Dante believed that the authority of the Holy Roman Empire (as the Mediaeval Empire dating from Charlemagne was called) was derived from the ancient Roman tradition.

ll. 97–9: Justinian now returns to the subject of the Guelfs and Ghibellines whom he has upbraided previously in ll. 31–3.

ll. 100–1: "*One to the public standard hath opposed the golden lilies*": The one (the Guelf faction) has set up the golden lilies (of France) in opposition to the eagle.

ll. 106–8: "*this second Charles*": Charles II, King of Naples, Count of Anjou and Provence (the father of Charles Martel, the titular King of Hungary and friend of Dante). (See Canto viii and also *Purg.* xx. 79 and *note*.)

ll. 109–10: "*Full oft for what the sire has done amiss the sons have wept*": This may refer to the misfortunes of Charles Martel, the son of Charles II (see Canto viii and Glossary).

l. 128: *Romèo*: a minister of Raymond Berengar IV, Count of Provence. For information concerning him, see above under *Images*.

ll. 131–2: "*he that thinks he's been wronged by his neighbour's virtues, wrong he goes*": that is, he who looks upon other people's good deeds as a kind of personal injury is guilty of the sin of envy (cf. the definition of this sin by Virgil in *Purg.* xvii. 118–20).

CANTO VII

THE STORY. *Justinian, with the other spirits in Mercury, whirls out of sight, singing Hosannah. Dante longs to question Beatrice about the Redemption but is too much overcome by awe to do so. She, reading his mind, goes straight to the heart of his perplexity: if the Crucifixion was a just penalty for the sins of man, how could it be justly avenged by the fall of Jerusalem? By the act of Incarnation, human nature was united with God and by the Crucifixion human nature paid the penalty for sin. Yet the outrage upon the Divine Person remained to be avenged, and was avenged by the destruction of Jerusalem. But why was this means of redemption chosen? Beatrice answers this by proving that no other means would have been adequate. Man himself could not have made just amends; it was necessary for God to renew man's proper life and reinstate him. This He chose to do, not by cancelling the debt, but by His self-giving.*

Beatrice then touches on the mystery of the resurrection of the body. The elements and compounds of the material world, not being made directly by God, but by secondary causes, are subject to decay; but first matter, the Angels themselves, the heavenly spheres and life in man, being direct creations of God, are eternal.

"Hosanna sanctus Deus sabaoth,
  Superi lustrans claritate tua
  Felices ignes horum malacoth!"

Thus as he sang, I saw that substance pure,   4
  Twin-lustred with his two-fold luminance,
  Revolve to his own music, whose allure

Drew with himself the rest into the dance,   7
  And, like to sparks which quickly fly away,
  Suddenly distance hid them from my glance.

Then, much perplexed: "Say, say to her, O say,"   10
  Heart whispered, "Say it to my Lady here,
  Whose honey-dews my deepest drouth allay."

But awe, which still can daunt me with a mere   13
  ICE or BE, again bowed down my head
  As a man's head droops down when sleep is near.

16   Not long Beatrice left me thus, but said,
        With such a smile as would bring happiness
        To one laid on the martyr's burning bed:

19   "My unerring insight sees thee in distress;
        How the just vengeance justly was avenged –
        That is the riddle which thou canst not guess.

22   But I will solve the doubt which hath impinged
        Upon thy mind; mark well! there's much to gain,
        For a great doctrine on my word hangs hinged.

25   Because he would not brook the wholesome rein
        Laid on his will, the man who ne'er had birth
        Damned in his own damnation all his strain,

28   So that, in error sore, mankind on earth
        Lay sick for many an age, till from above
        God's Word came down and, as it pleased His worth,

31   This nature, from its Author thus strayed-off,
        Did in one person with Himself unite,
        By the sole act of His eternal love.

34   On this great argument fix now thy sight:
        That nature, to its Author joined thus-wise,
        Was as He'd made it, single and upright;

37   Itself exiled itself from Paradise,
        Itself deprived itself of life, because
        It left truth's way, wherein its true life lies.

40   Thus was the doom inflicted by the Cross,
        If measured by the nature so assumed,
        The most just penalty that ever was;

43   Yet judgement ne'er so monstrously presumed,
        If we reflect Who bore the punishment,
        Being joined in person with the nature doomed.

46   Single the act, then, and diverse the event:
        God and the Jews were pleased in one same death,
        Whereat Heaven opened and the earth was rent.

49   Henceforth no cause remains why he who saith
        That the just vengeance was by a just court
        Later avenged should take away thy breath.

But now I see thy mind, from thought to thought,   52
    Tangling itself into a knotted band,
    Anxious for aid and panting till it's brought.

'That which I hear', thou say'st, 'I understand;   55
    It is God's choice that seems so difficult –
    Why, to redeem us, just this means was planned'.

Brother, that choice lies buried and occult   58
    From all men's eyes save theirs alone whose wit
    Has ripened in love's warmth and grown adult;

Nevertheless – since, though men gaze at it   61
    Right hard, this mark's not easy of discerning –
    I'll prove no other means to be so fit.

God's excellence, all envy ever spurning,   64
    The eternal beauties everywhere reveals
    By sparkles shot from its own inward burning.

That which immediately thence distils   67
    Thereafter hath no end; God's patternings
    Cannot be moved, once He's impressed the seals.

That which from thence immediately springs   70
    Is wholly free, because it never knows
    Subjection to the secondary things.

God loves His like – the better, the more close,   73
    Because the sacred fire that lights all nature
    Liveliest of all in its own image glows.

All these prerogatives the human creature   76
    Possesses, and if one of them should fail,
    He must diminish from his noble stature.

Sin only can disfranchise him, and veil   79
    His likeness to the Highest Good; whereby
    The light in him is lessened and grows pale.

Ne'er can he win back dignities so high   82
    Till the void made by guilt be all filled in
    With just amends paid for illicit joy.

Now, when your nature as a whole did sin   85
    In its first root, it lost these great awards,
    And lost the Eden of its origin;

88 Nor might they be recovered afterwards
    By any means, as if thou search thou'lt see,
    Except by crossing one of these two fords;

91 Either must God, of His sole courtesy,
    Remit, or man must pay with all that's his,
    The debt of sin in its entirety.

94 Within the Eternal Counsel's deep abyss
    Rivet thine eye, and with a heed as good
    As thou canst give me, do thou follow this.

97 Man from his finite assets never could
    Make satisfaction; ne'er could he abase him
    So low, obey thereafter all he would,

100 As he'd by disobedience sought to raise him;
    And for this cause man might not pay his due
    Himself, nor from the debtor's roll erase him.

103 Needs then must God, by His own ways, renew
    Man's proper life, and reinstate him so;
    His ways, I say – by one, or both of two.

106 And since the doer's actions ever show
    More gracious as the style of them makes plain
    The goodness of the heart from which they flow,

109 That most high Goodness which is God was fain –
    Even God, whose impress Heaven and earth display –
    By all His ways to lift you up again;

112 Nor, between final night and primal day,
    Was e'er proceeding so majestical
    And high, nor shall not be, by either way;

115 For God's self-giving, which made possible
    That man should raise himself, showed more largesse
    Than if by naked power He'd cancelled all;

118 And every other means would have been less
    Than justice, if it had not pleased God's Son
    To be humiliate into fleshliness.

121 But now, that thou and I may see as one
    Therein, and to content thy whole desire,
    There is a point I must go back upon.

Thou sayest: 'I see the water and the fire,   124
  The earth, the air, their compounds manifold;
  They change, they rot – a breath, and they expire;

Yet these are creatures – and if truth was told   127
  Just now, it seems an everlasting bar
  Should fend them from decay and growing old.'

For angels, and for this pure space spread far   130
  About thee, brother, rightly is it claimed
  They were created, whole, and as they are;

But those four elements which thou hast named,   133
  And all the various things which they compound,
  Were by created power informed and framed.

Created was their matter and their ground,   136
  Created were the informing agencies
  Lodged in these stars that circle them around.

The souls of beasts, the souls of plants – all these   139
  Spring from complexions, whence the holy fires'
  Motion and light draw forth the potencies;

But life in *you* the Primal Good inspires   142
  Direct, and makes it of His own perfection
  Enamoured so, that Him it aye desires.

Hence, too, the manner of your resurrection   145
  Thou may'st infer; bring by a little thought
  The two First Parents to thy recollection,

And then remember how man's flesh was wrought."   148

THE IMAGES. *Dante's doubt as to "how the just vengeance justly was avenged"*: In the *story*, Dante's eager desire for clarification on this matter arises from the words of Justinian in Canto vi concerning the just penalty for the sin of Adam (the Crucifixion) and the just penalty for the Crucifixion (the destruction of Jerusalem). In relation to the *allegory* of *Paradise*, Dante's perplexity in the face of this enigma is a type or symbol of mankind's perplexity in the face of the paradoxes of history. The solution, which Beatrice supplies, leads Dante nearer to the realization that justice in heaven is justice on earth, that history, the actual course of world-events, is ultimately and essentially just, until finally (in Canto xix) he sees that divine justice and the will of God are one.

NOTES. ll. 1–3: *"Hosanna sanctus Deus sabaoth"* etc.: These words are sung by the soul of Justinian and mean "Hosannah holy God of Sabaoth, who dost abundantly illumine with thy brightness the blessed fires of these realms!" Dante knew no Hebrew and is believed to have copied the word "malacoth" from the Prologue by St Jerome to the Vulgate. The correct form is "mamlacoth" (i.e. "of these realms"). The combination of Latin and Hebrew in hymns of praise is traditional in Christian liturgy, and the Hebrew word "sabaoth" meaning "of hosts" is perpetuated in the *Te Deum* (cf. the Anglican Prayer Book: "We praise Thee O God . . . Lord God of Sabaoth."). It is fitting that Justinian, "after his survey of the divine working and convergence of events through the ages" . . . and "at the beginning of the canto of the scheme of human redemption . . . should praise God in the languages of Jerusalem and Rome . . . the two sacred tongues of history" (Sinclair).

l. 5: *Twin-lustred with his two-fold luminance*: the two-fold splendour of Justinian may be symbolic of his two-fold glory on earth as Emperor and Lawgiver, or it may signify the illumining by God's light (*claritas*) of the light of the soul (*felix ignis*).

ll. 10–12: Dante longs to ask Beatrice the question which she reads in his mind (cf. ll. 19–21).

l. 14: ICE *or* BE: Dante is awed even by a fragment of the name of Beatrice.

ll. 19–21: This doubt arises in Dante's mind from the words of Justinian (vi. 91–3) which refer to the destruction of Jerusalem by Titus as "avenging the vengeance for the ancient sin". If the Crucifixion was a "just vengeance" on human sin, how could it be "justly avenged"?

l. 26: *"the man who ne'er had birth"*: Adam.

l. 31: *"This nature, from its Author thus strayed-off"*: human nature, which had become separated from God by sin.

l. 36: *"Was as He'd made it"*: The human nature in Christ was, as God had created it in Adam, without sin.

l. 37: *"Itself exiled itself from Paradise"*: The human nature in Adam, which was sinless, was endowed with free will. Hence, of its own accord it exiled itself from the Garden of Eden.

ll. 40–51: The Crucifixion was a "just vengeance" on human nature, borne by Christ, but was, in equal measure, a wrong done to Christ. This was both because He had done no wrong and also (which Beatrice stresses) because of His divine nature. It was monstrous presumption for man to inflict judgement on such an exalted being (cf. ll. 43–5).

l. 47: *"God and the Jews were pleased in one same death"*: Dante (through the mouth of Beatrice) here paraphrases *Acts* ii, 23: "Him, being delivered by the determinate counsel and foreknowledge of God, ye have taken, and by wicked hands have crucified and slain." The doctrine that human nature in its totality was judiciously executed on the Cross is one which Dante stresses also in *De Monarchia*, where the use he makes of it in connection with his theory of government appears to be his own invention (see Book II, ch. xii–xiii). In *Purgatory* (xxi. 82–5), Titus is referred to by Statius in the following words:

> "When the good Titus was avenging bold –
> Having the High King's aid to reckon on –
> The wounds whence gushed the blood that Judas sold."

ll. 52–7: Beatrice now perceives and interprets another question which has arisen in Dante's mind, namely "Why did God choose to redeem man by this particular means?"

l. 64: *"God's excellence, all envy ever spurning"* etc.: In reply to Dante's unspoken question concerning the means of redemption, Beatrice goes back to the act of creation, to which God was moved by love, having no envious reserve in communicating to His creation what He might well have retained as His own.

l. 67–72: *"That which immediately thence distils"* etc.: The immediate creations of God, Angels and men's souls, are immortal; they are also wholly free, not being subject to secondary causes, which are distinguished from the direct operation of God, the First Cause.

l. 75: *"Liveliest of all in its own image glows"*: Compare *Genesis* i. 26 *ff*.

l. 76: *"All these prerogatives the human creature possesses"*: The prerogatives or special privileges which man possesses are immortality (l. 68), freedom (l. 71) and likeness to God (ll. 73–5).

l. 79: *"Sin only can disfranchise him"* etc.: Sin deprives man of his freedom and likeness to God. Compare the words of Christ, *John* viii. 34 "Verily, verily, I say unto you, whosoever committeth sin is the servant of sin."

l. 94: *"the Eternal Counsel's deep abyss"*: the infinite depth of the hidden decrees established by God from the beginning of the world.

ll. 97–100: *"Man from his finite assets never could . . ."* etc.: Expiation of sin is beyond man's ability. Specifically, he can never humiliate himself as much as he had attempted to raise himself (presuming to "be as gods, knowing good and evil").

ll. 103–5: *"Needs then must God, by His own ways . . ."* etc.: Therefore God alone must rehabilitate man, either by mercy alone, by justice alone, or by the combination of mercy and justice.

l. 112: *"between final night and primal day . . ."* etc.: Between the Last Judgement and the Creation, that is, from the first instant of the creation of the world to its extinction, there never was nor ever will be so vast a going forth of the excellence of God's works as was the Redemption.

l. 114: *"by either way"*: either by mercy alone or by justice.

ll. 123–9: *There is a point I must go back upon*: Beatrice has said (ll. 67–8) that what God directly creates is eternal. Yet it is evident that the four elements, of which all material things are created, are subject to decay.

ll. 130–41: Beatrice here distinguishes between the results of an immediate act of creation (e.g. the Angels and the heavens) and the results of intermediate and created agents (or secondary causes). The former are eternal and incorruptible, the latter are subject to change and decay. *Genesis* i speaks of direct creation, however. Dante is on firmer ground, scripturally, when he speaks (through Beatrice) of the resurrection of the body. See following note.

ll. 142–8: The body, Beatrice recalls, was made by God (*Genesis* ii. 7–22); she reasons that therefore it will not finally be lost. God will raise it up (cf. *I Corinthians* xv. 49: "And as we have borne the image of the earthy, we shall also bear the image of the heavenly"; and *II Corinthians* iv. 14: "Knowing that he which raised up the Lord Jesus shall raise up us also by Jesus, and shall present us with you".)

CANTO VIII

THE STORY. *Dante and Beatrice rise from Mercury to the planet Venus. So rapid is their ascent that Dante is aware only of the increased loveliness of Beatrice, which grows ever more radiant as they mount from sphere to sphere. They encounter now the souls of those who, born of amorous temperament and ardent affections, yielded to the love that is a kind of madness. Now, chastened and disciplined, rejoicing in their place in Heaven, they sing a hymn so ravishingly sweet that Dante longs to hear its loveliness renewed. The soul of Charles Martel, a beloved friend, draws near and converses with Dante on the diversity of natural attributes.*

'Twas once believed that the fair Cyprian, whirled
 Radiant in the third epicycle, shed
 Love's madness on the yet unransomed world;

By which old error men of old were led   4
 To honour her; and not for her alone
 The votive cry went up, the victim bled;

But Cupid and Dione too, her son   7
 And mother, they revered, and fabled how
 In Dido's lap he lay, yon Cupidon;

And so from her who heads my proem now   10
 They named the star that gazes amorous-eyed
 Now on the sun's nape, now upon his brow.

Up to that sphere I did not feel us glide,   13
 But that we had arrived I well might know,
 Seeing my Lady still more beautified.

And as through flames a glittering spark will show,   16
 Or voice through voice sounds clear and definite
 When one holds firm and one runs to and fro,

So I saw gleams go circling through that light,   19
 Swift or more swift, according, I suppose,
 Unto the measure of their inward sight.

No visible or viewless blast from floes   22
 Of icy cloud e'er darted but would seem
 Heavily handicapped, lumbering and gross

25   To one who'd seen those heavenly meteors skim
          Our way, quitting their reel that was on high
          Begun amid the exalted seraphim;

28   And from the foremost ranks as they drew nigh
          Rang such Hosannas that the ache to hear
          Those songs again will haunt me till I die.

31   Then one alone approached us, crying clear:
          "We'd have thee glad of us, and to fulfil
          Thy whole desire we all stand ready here.

34   Here, in one thirst, one wheeling, and one wheel
          We whirl with the celestial princes, even
          Those to whom thou on earth didst once appeal,

37   Saying: *You that by your thought move the Third Heaven;*
          And love so fills us that, for thy content,
          Sweet shall short stillness seem, our sport to leaven".

40   Mine eyes, when first they'd made their reverent
          Plea to my Lady, and her own, no less
          Clearly, had certified her full consent,

43   Turned to that light which had with such largesse
          Proferred himself, and: "Tell me, who are you?"
          Said I, in accents fraught with tenderness.

46   How, and how great in brilliance then he grew
          To hear me speak! how wondrously was seen
          Joy upon joy kindling in him anew!

49   And shining thus he said: "The earthly scene
          Held me not long; had more time been allowed
          Much ill that now shall happen had not been.

52   My own bliss hides me from thee in a cloud
          Of dazzling radiance, which it winds and weaves,
          As weaves the worm in its own silken shroud.

55   Well didst thou love me, and my heart conceives
          Thou hadst good cause; for, living, I'd have shown
          More of my love to thee than barren leaves.

58   The leftward river-bank that's washed by Rhone,
          Before he's joined with Sorgue, acknowledged me
          Its lord to come, when time should claim its own.

So did the Ausonian Horn, whose boundary   61
    Bari, Catona, and Gaëta hem,
    Traced from where Tronto and Verde meet the sea.

Already on my brow the diadem   64
    Flashed of those lands which Danube, once he's passed
    His German brinks, runs through to water them;

While, on that gulf most plagued by Eurus' blast,   67
    Between Pachynus and Pelorus set,
    By sulphur, not Typhoeus, overcast,

Lovely Trinacria still had looked to get   70
    Kings born of me, and of blood-kindred with
    Rudolph and Charles, to wear her coronet,

If evil rule, which ever rendereth   73
    A subject people heartsick, had not raised
    Shouts in Palermo: 'Let them die the death!'

And could my brother in good time have faced   76
    The facts, he'd sack those Catalans, all made
    Of needs and greeds, before he is disgraced.

Good heed by him, or some one, should be paid   79
    In sober truth, lest in his vessel's hold,
    Deep-laden now, a heavier load be laid;

His nature, mean, though issued from a mould   82
    More generous, calls for officers whose ambition
    Is not confined to hoarding chests of gold."

"Dear Prince, I well believe that thy keen vision   85
    Sees, in the source and end of every bliss,
    How thy words fill my soul with sweet fruition –

Yea, sees it even as I do; therefore is   88
    My joy the more; and this, too, makes me glad:
    That 'tis in God that thou dost see all this.

Having rejoiced me, teach me; for in sad   91
    Earnest thy words have set me wondering
    How from sweet seed sour harvest can be had."

Thus I to him; and he to me: "I'll bring,   94
    Canst thou but learn one truth, this crux before
    Thine eyes; thou hast thy back turned to the thing.

97   The God which wheels and gladdens evermore
         This whole realm thou dost scale, is pleased to deal
         To these great orbs His providential power;

100 And, in His own self-perfect mind which still
         Provides all kinds of natures, He intends
         Not their existence only, but their weal.

103 Hence, whatso shafts fly forth when this bow bends
         Must, like all missiles to a target sped,
         Alight disposed for their provided ends.

106 Were it not so, this sphere thou now dost thread
         Would make wild work, whereof, as its effects,
         Not artefacts but chaos would be bred;

109 Which may not be, unless the intellects
         That move these stars be faulty – faulty, yea,
         The Primal One who shaped them with defects.

112 Wouldst have me make this truth still clearer?" – "Nay,
         I see no nature can be lacking of
         Essential needs", said I, "in any way."

115 Whence he again: "Say, would man be worse off
         On earth, if he were not a citizen?"
         "Yes," I replied, "and here I ask no proof."

118 "And can this be, unless the earth breed men
         Differing in function and in competence? –
         No, not if one can trust your Master's pen."

121 Thus far deducing, step by step, he thence
         Concluded: "Differing so, your various
         Effects must have their root in difference.

124 One man a Solon, one a Xerxes thus
         Is born, one a Melchisedec, or that sire
         Whose wing'd flight cost him his son Icarus.

127 Right well doth cyclic Nature in her gyre,
         Printing the mortal wax, perfect her art;
         But where it lodge, she stays not to inquire.

130 So we see twin-born Jacob grow apart
         From Esau, and Quirinus men assign
         To Mars, from such base loins he took his start.

> Were't not o'erruled by Providence divine,   133
>   The nature that is gotten would but trace
>   A slavish copy of the getters' line.
>
> What was behind stands now before they face,   136
>   But for sheer joy of thee I'll drape thee round
>   With a corollary for gift and grace.
>
> It cannot be that any nature, found   139
>   At odds with its environment, should thrive;
>   No seed does well in uncongenial ground.
>
> If men on earth would bear in mind, and strive   142
>   To build on the foundation laid by nature,
>   They'd have fine folk, with virtues all alive.
>
> But you distort the pattern of the creature;   145
>   You cloister him that's born to wield the sword,
>   And crown him king who ought to be a preacher;
>
> Thus from the path you wander all abroad."   148

THE IMAGES. *The planet Venus.* In the third planet, Dante encounters souls whose ardent temperament had led them to surrender wantonly to the passion of love. In a Christian context, Venus, whose influence the ancients held to be irresistible, is a symbol or type of the natural propensities with which men are born but which the will is free to resist or use well. Her planet here symbolizes love as Virgil has expounded it in *Purgatory* and which Dante, like the souls he meets, has now set in order in his soul.

Charles Martel, the grandson of Charles I of Anjou, was born in 1271, the eldest son of Charles II and of Mary, the daughter of the King of Hungary. In 1291, he married Clemence of Hapsburg, daughter of Emperor Rudolph I, by whom he had three children, Charles Robert (Carobert), Clemence (who married Louis X of France) and Beatrice. In the Spring of 1294, he visited Florence, where he remained for over three weeks, awaiting the arrival of his father from France. The Florentines were overjoyed to welcome and fête the young royal whose grandfather, Charles I of Anjou, had been so powerful a champion of Guelf interests. Of Dante's friendship with him we have no knowledge apart from the evidence afforded by this canto. The tender words alluding to their love seem to indicate that Dante was held in high regard by Charles, who here quotes the first line of one of Dante's odes (cf. Note to l. 37).

In the *story*, Charles Martel is a link in the narrative between Dante of Paradise and Dante of Florence. At the time of their first meeting, it must have seemed to both young men that they had every reason to look confidently to the future. Dante, at the age of twenty-nine, had an established reputation as the leading poet among a notable group in Florence and was about to embark on a period of distinguished public service. Charles Martel, six years younger, had been crowned King of Hungary at the age of nineteen and was also heir to the Kingdom of Naples and the County of Provence (see Genealogical Tables, Kings of France, p. 398). Yet Dante's destiny was exile and that of Charles Martel premature death from cholera the following year. Though their fates are so different, yet they are linked by friendship, by a shared experience of disappointed hopes, and by a common readiness to surrender to love. (See also note to l. 37.) In the wider implications of the *story*, that is, in *history*, Charles Martel is a representative of the House of Anjou, to whom Dante owed the defeat of his hopes, for not only had the daughter of Charles II married Charles of Valois (who engineered the defeat of the White Guelfs, an event which led to Dante's exile) but the Angevins (especially Robert, King of Naples, the brother of Charles Martel) were strenuous opponents of the Emperor Henry VII. Yet, had Charles Martel lived to succeed his father as King of Naples, he might have followed a different policy. In himself, and in his descendants, the strife of Europe might have been reconciled, for the Emperor Rudolph (the leader of the Ghibellines) was his father-in-law and grandfather to his children, while his own grandfather, Charles I of Anjou, was remembered as the champion of the Guelfs.

In the *allegory*, Charles Martel and the other souls encountered in Venus are symbols of the sensual man whose easy surrender to the temptations of the flesh is accompanied by an affectionate and generous ardour. Now, purged of their sin, they come, swifter than lightning, to meet and converse with Dante, showing a ready eagerness that recalls the response of Paolo and Francesca (cf. *Inf.* v). In himself, as a member of the Angevin dynasty, Charles Martel is an instance also of the diversity of human endowments. It is fitting, therefore, that he should have the task of discoursing to Dante on the operations of Providence.

NOTES. l. 1: *the fair Cyprian*: the goddess Venus, believed to have risen from the sea off the island of Cyprus.

l. 2: *the third epicycle*: the epicycle of the planet Venus. (See Appendix, Note A.)

l. 3: *the yet unransomed world*: the heathen world before the birth of Christ.

ll. 8–9: . . . *and fabled how in Dido's lap he lay, yon Cupidon*: the fable in question is related by Virgil in *Aeneid* I. 657–722. Venus sent Cupid in the guise of Ascanius (the young son of Aeneas) to be received by Dido, who embraced him and received from Cupid the wound which inspired her with her fatal love for Aeneas.

ll. 11–12: *. . . the star that gazes amorous-eyed now on the sun's nape, now upon his brow:* Venus is both the evening star, Hesperus, and the morning star, Lucifer; that is, she is sometimes not visible from earth in the morning because she does not rise until after the sun is above the horizon, but she is seen at evening after the sun is set (i.e. she gazes at his nape, following behind him); at other times she sets before the sun and is not visible in the evening, but rises before him in the morning (i.e. she gazes on his brow).

l. 17–18: *Or voice through voice* etc.: When two voices sing in unison they sound as one voice; but if one holds the note and the other performs a roulade, the one can be distinguished from the other.

l. 22: *No visible or viewless blast*: lightning or wind. Dante's understanding of meteorological phenomena is derived, through Averroës, from Aristotle's work on meteors, in which lightning is defined as wind made visible by ignition.

ll. 26–7: *. . . quitting their reel that was on high begun amid the exalted seraphim*: The souls detach themselves from the circular movement which they began with the Seraphim, and move swifter than lightning or hurricane. The Seraphim govern the movement of the Primum Mobile, the first circle through which they passed on leaving the Empyrean to come to greet Dante in the heaven of Venus. It is significant that these images of circling and whirling (cf. also l. 19, "So I saw gleams go *circling* through that light") so reminiscent of the whirlwind carrying the lovers round remorselessly in Canto v of *Inferno*, should occur in the heaven of Venus (cf. also Appendix, Note A).

l. 35: *"We whirl with the celestial princes"* etc.: They now revolve with the third sphere, which is moved by the third order of angels, the Principalities.

l. 37: *You that by your thought move the Third Heaven*: This is a quotation of the first line of Dante's ode, "Voi che intendendo il terzo ciel movete", which is the subject of a commentary in the second tractate of the *Convivio*. Dante there addresses the angelic intelligences which at that period he called the Thrones, not the Principalities, following the order of the angelic hierarchies found in Brunetto Latini's *Trésor*, not, as he here does, the order set forth by Dionysius (cf. Canto xxviii. 133–5). The ode is an account of the conflict in Dante's heart between his love for the memory of Beatrice and his new love for the "donna gentile", of whom he speaks also in the *Vita Nuova*. From the allusion to it here by Charles Martel, two things may be inferred: (1) that Dante presented it to him on the occasion of his visit to Florence (it seems to have been composed at about that period); (2) that the ode is a confession of Dante's susceptibility to the influence of love, an influence he then believed to be irresistible; addressing the angelic movers of the Heaven of Venus, he says in the ode: "The heaven which doth obey your influence, gentle creatures that ye are, draweth me into my present plight."

ll. 49–50: "*The earthly scene held me not long*" etc.: Charles Martel died at the age of twenty-four. For information concerning him, see above under *Images*.

l. 54: *as weaves the worm in its own silken shroud*: The comparison is to a silk-worm in its cocoon (cf. Appendix, Note C).

ll. 58–9: "*The leftward river-bank that's washed by Rhone, before he's joined with Sorgue, acknowledged me*: The territory thus designated is Provence. The Sorgue flows into the Rhone about five miles north of Avignon and together the two rivers form the western boundary. Charles Martel was heir to Provence as the grandson of Beatrice, daughter of Raymond Berengar (see Genealogical Tables, Kings of France, p. 398).

l. 61: "*So did the Ausonian Horn*" etc.: The southern part of Italy, of which Ausonia is the ancient name. It takes a curve to the south resembling a horn. The region indicated is the Kingdom of Naples and Apulia, which Charles would have inherited from his father.

l. 63: "*Verde*": i.e. the river Garigliano (cf. *Purg.* iii. 131).

ll. 65–6: "*. . . those lands which Danube, once he's passed his German brinks, runs through to water them*": i.e. Hungary. In 1290, when Ladislaus of Hungary died without issue, Charles Martel, his nephew, became King and was duly crowned in Naples at the age of nineteen. He never reigned in Hungary, for his grandfather's cousin, Andrew, seized the throne.

ll. 67–8: "*While, on that gulf most plagued by Eurus' blast, between Pachynus and Pelorus set*": Eurus is the ancient name of the east or southeast wind. The gulf here mentioned is the Gulf of Catania in Sicily, where the prevailing wind is the scirocco, the stormy south-east wind. Pachynus, the promontory at the south-east extremity of Sicily, is now called Cape Passaro. Pelorus, the promontory at the extreme north-east, is now called Cape Faro, and is mentioned by Guido del Duca in *Purg.* xiv. 33 as being divided from the Apennine range by the Strait of Messina.

l. 69: "*By sulphur, not Typhoeus, overcast*": Typhoeus, the hundred-headed monster who attempted to acquire sovereignty over gods and men, was vanquished by Jove with a thunderbolt and (according to Ovid) was buried under Mt Aetna, the eruptions of which were said to be caused by his struggles to regain his freedom. Dante attributes the eruptions to the presence of nascent sulphur, a view which he may have derived from Isidore of Seville, who says that the sulphur is ignited by the current of air driven by the force of the waves through the caves in the mountain.

l. 70: "*Lovely Trinacria*": Trinacria is the ancient name for Sicily.

l. 72: "*Rudolph and Charles*": Charles Martel married Clemence, the daughter of Rudolph of Hapsburg, Emperor from 1272 to 1292.

(Rudolph is among the Negligent Princes in the valley of flowers in Antepurgatory, *Purg.* vii. 94; see also Glossary to this volume.) The Charles referred to is Charles I of Anjou, the grandfather of Charles Martel. (See also Glossary.) Charles Martel here implies that in his descendants the Guelf and Ghibelline factions were reconciled (see above, under Images).

l. 75: "*Shouts in Palermo*": Charles Martel is referring here to the rebellion known as the Sicilian Vespers, but for which his descendants would have succeeded to the throne of Sicily. The uprising took place on the evening of 30 March 1282. The French were massacred by the Sicilians and the sovereignty of Sicily was transferred from the house of Anjou to the house of Aragon.

l. 76: "*my brother*": This is Robert, the younger brother of Charles Martel, and third son of Charles II of Anjou. (He was crowned King of Sicily in 1309.)

ll. 77–8: ". . . *those Catalans, all made of needs and greeds*": These would seem to be the needy and grasping Catalan retainers of Robert, whom he gathered round him when he was held as a hostage in Catalonia for his father, Charles III of Naples, by the King of Aragon. Catalonia, the north-east province of Spain, formed in Dante's time part of the Kingdom of Aragon. After Robert became King of Naples and Sicily in 1309, his Catalan (and Aragonese troops) were employed in Italy against the Emperor Henry VII.

ll. 80–81: ". . . *lest in his vessel's hold, deep-laden now, a heavier load be laid*": lest the avarice of others be added to his own, and the State, already burdened, become even more so. Modern historical opinion has reinstated the figure of Robert of Anjou, exculpating him especially of the charges of greed and avarice.

ll. 82–3: "*His nature, mean, though issued from a mould more generous*": The father of Robert, Charles II, is here referred to as generous, whereas in *Purg.* xx. 79–81, Hugh Capet speaks of his avarice in haggling with Azzo d'Este over the price to be paid for his daughter's hand in marriage. It would appear that Dante thought less well of him than his son did, for he denounces him in the *Convivio* and in *De Vulgari Eloquentia*.

ll. 92–3: ". . . *thy words have set me wondering how from sweet seed sour harvest can be had*": Dante wonders how a mean nature can descend from a generous one.

l. 95: "*Canst thou but learn one truth*": namely, the truth that inborn characteristics are not hereditary but are the direct gift of God, operating through secondary causes.

l. 97–114: "*The Good which wheels and gladdens evermore*" etc.: Charles Martel unfolds to Dante the law of individuality (or differentiation) which, as Beatrice explained in Canto ii, and as is implied in the opening lines of *Paradise*, is everywhere manifested in creation. The natures of individuals are influenced by the heavenly bodies and this is a provision of God's goodness and wisdom for the welfare of man. All the influences of the heavens are directed by God to an infallible end foreseen by Him. Were this not so, the effects of heavenly influence would be not providential but chaotic, issuing not in construction but in destruction; but this would imply a defect in the Intelligences who move the heavens and this in its turn would imply a defect in the Primal Cause who made them.

ll. 115–19: The need for difference in character, temperament, gifts and powers of the mind arises from the necessity for men to live in society for their good.

l. 120: *"No, not if one can trust your Master's pen"*: The Master referred to here is Aristotle, "the Master of the men who know" as Dante called him in *Inf.* iv. 131.

ll. 124–6: *"One man a Solon"* etc.: One man is born to be a lawgiver, another a general, another a priest, or yet another a mechanician.

l. 129: *"But where it lodge, she stays not to inquire"*: i.e. Nature determines a man's disposition without a thought as to his origin.

l. 131: *Quirinus*: the name given to Romulus after his death. So great were his achievements men could not believe him to be basely born.

ll. 137–8: *"I'll drape thee round with a corollary"*: In Latin, *corollarium* (from which Dante's *corollario* is derived) was (a) a garland, (b) a garland bestowed as a prize, (c) a gratuity, (d) a corollary. By using the verb *ammantare*, to cloak or drape, Dante appears to have fused the concrete meaning of a garland with the abstract one of a corollary.

ll. 139–48: *"It cannot be that any nature"* etc.: Charles Martel here adds his corollary, or special, additional conclusion. Providence does all things well, but men too often ignore the disposition implanted by heavenly influences and turn the greatest gifts to mistaken ends, not recognizing their special aptitudes. Thus they turn a born soldier into a priest and make a king of one who has all the marks of the priesthood upon him. (The early commentators saw in these concluding lines an allusion to the natural dispositions of the two brothers of Charles Martel, Louis and Robert. Louis abdicated his princely rights and entered the Frati Minori, later becoming Bishop of Toulouse; Robert, though a king, wrote sermons and was highly esteemed for his knowledge of theology.)

CANTO IX

THE STORY. *Still in the heaven of Venus, Dante speaks first with Cunizza, the mistress of the troubadour poet, Sordello, and sister of the tyrant, Ezzelino da Romano, and secondly with Foulquet of Marseilles, a troubadour poet, renowned as much for his amours as for his poetry. The discourse of both souls is concerned with affairs on earth, Cunizza foretelling the disasters which will befall the inhabitants of the Trevisan territory, and Foulquet deploring the avarice of the Church and her neglect of true religion. Both spirits rejoice in the degree of bliss to which God has destined them; the love in which they erred in their first life is now discerned by them as the power by which the universe is governed.*

Thy Charles, fair Clemence, after he had shown
    Me light, disclosed the plots from first to last
    That should defraud his children of their own.

But, "Hold thy peace and let the years roll past,"   4
    Quoth he; so I can say no more than this:
    That on your wrongs just woes shall follow fast.

Already to the Sun that brims his bliss   7
    The holy flambeau's life had turned again,
    As to the Good which filleth all that is.

Ah, souls deceived! ah, creatures warped in grain,   10
    That from such goodness wrench your hearts awry,
    Setting your minds on impious thoughts and vain!

And lo! another splendour now drew nigh,   13
    Eager to please, and showed me its intent
    Clearly, by growing brighter to the eye.

Beatrice's look, that as before was bent   16
    On me, gave warrant that my longing still
    Might surely count upon her sweet consent.

"Pray, quickly now, blest spirit," said I, "fulfil   19
    My hope, and show me that I am to thee
    A mirror where thou readest all my will."

Whereat this light, as yet unknown to me,   22
    Spoke, as it erst had sung, from its deep heart,
    As one delighted to give generously: –

25   "In sinful Italy, and in that part
      Between Rialto and the mountains whence
      The springs of Brenta and of Piave start,

28   Rises a hill, of no great eminence,
      From which erewhile a dreadful firebrand came
      Swooping to waste the land with violence.

31   One root with him had I, and was by name
      Cunizza; and I glitter here because
      I was o'ermastered by this planet's flame;

34   Yet gaily I forgive myself the cause
      Of this my lot, for here (though minds of clay
      May think this strange) 'tis gain to me, not loss.

37   Of this rich jewel neighbouring me, whose ray
      Adds lustre to our sphere, doth yet survive
      A fame on earth that shall not pass away

40   Before this century has grown to five;
      See if man should not make, by making good,
      A second life to keep the first alive!

43   Little for that care they whose present brood
      Adige moats and Tagliamento pens,
      Nor all their scourgings bate their stubborn mood;

46   But soon shall Padua in the marshy fens
      Pollute the waters of Vicenza's stream,
      So dead to duty are these citizens.

49   Where Silë and Cagnano join their brim,
      One lords it, head in air, though all the time
      The net's a-making for the catching of him.

52   Feltro shall weep her impious pastor's crime,
      Which shall be such that to La Malta's jail
      None was e'er sent stained with a filthier grime.

55   Right broad must be the vat that should avail
      To hold the blood, and weary would he grow
      That ounce by ounce should weigh it on the scale –

58   Ferrara's blood, that largely he'll bestow –
      This courteous priest – his party zeal to prove;
      Well with that country's ways do such gifts go!

Mirrors – you call them Thrones – there are above,   61
  Whence God in judgement shines to us, and there
  Rightly we read these things we tell thee of."

She ceased to speak, and turned her thoughts elsewhere,   64
  Meseemed, for back into the dance she spun,
  And so resumed her wheelings as they were.

The other joy, made known to me as one   67
  Illustrious, now flashed forth in brilliance clad
  Like a fine ruby smitten by the sun;

For lustre grows, up there, when hearts grow glad,   70
  As laughter does on earth; but darkness dyes
  The shades below in measure as they're sad.

"God seëth all", said I, "and in such wise,   73
  Blest spirit, thy sight in-Hims itself, that things
  Hid in my heart lie open to thine eyes.

What stays thy voice, whose song charms Heav'n, and rings   76
  Tuned to those burning quires perpetually
  Who worship, hooded in their six-fold wings?

Why grants it not the longing prayer in me?   79
  I would not wait for thee to make demand,
  Could I in-thee me as thou in-meëst thee."

"The greatest valley where the seas expand",   82
  (Thus he began, and waited not for more),
  "Forth of that ocean girdling all the land,

Runs on so far 'twixt wrangling shore and shore   85
  Against the sun, it makes meridian
  At last where its horizon was before.

Upon that coast dwelt I, at the mid-span   88
  'Twixt Ebro and Macra, whose short banks divide
  The man of Genoa from the Tuscan clan.

Sunset and dawn well-nigh at once bestride   91
  Both Bougia and my city, which long syne
  With her own blood made hot her harbour's tide.

Foulquet men called me, where my name and line   94
  Were known; and on its front this heav'n now bears
  My imprint, as its print was once on mine.

97 Not Belus' daughter burned in fiercer flares,
    Wronging Sichaëus and Creusa too,
    Than I, ere time's rebuke had touched my hairs,

100 Nor Rhodope's fair maid, on her untrue
    Demophoön doting, nor Alcides, while
    He caged Iole in his strong heart's mew.

103 But here there's no repentance; here we smile –
    Not at the sin, which comes no more to mind,
    But at God's ordering touch, His master-style.

106 We contemplate His art, which hath designed
    Great works and fair; His goodness, which draws home
    To this high world the world of lower kind.

109 But now, to satisfy the full round sum
    Of all thy longings gendered by this sphere,
    I must tell on, for thou hast more to come.

112 Fain wouldst thou learn who dwells beside me here
    In yonder light, blazing amongst all these
    As sunbeams blaze from water sparkling clear.

115 Know then that, there-within, Rahab hath peace;
    Joined with our order in the loftiest grade
    She hath impressed on it her seal of bliss.

118 She, by this heaven your earth's cast cone of shade
    Just touches, from the triumph of Christ's arms
    First of all souls was lifted and displayed.

121 'Twas fit some sphere should sing her home with psalms,
    As palm and trophy of the victory gained
    By high emprise of those extended palms;

124 For she promoted that first glory attained
    By Joshua in the Holy Land – alack!
    Now by this Pope forgotten and disdained.

127 The city – sprung from him who turned his back
    First on his Maker, and whose nature, sour
    With envy, brings the wailing world to wrack –

130 Sows and proliferates the cursed flower
    Which makes the sheep and lambs run wild – for lo!
    Their shepherds have turnéd wolves; and hour by hour

Dust gathers on the Gospels, gathers slow 133
  On the great Doctors, while they thumb and scrawl
  O'er the Decretals, as the margins show.

That's the whole lore of pope and cardinal 136
  Alike; to Nazareth that felt the beat
  Of Gabriel's wings they give no thought at all.

Yet Vatican, and every hallowed seat 139
  That marks in Rome some burial-ground where lies
  The soldiery that followed Peter's feet,

Soon shall be freed from those adulteries." 142

THE IMAGES. *The planet Venus*: See Canto viii, under *Images*.
Cunizza: The soul of Cunizza, speaking from her "deep heart, as
one delighted to give generously", tells Dante that she was the sister
of the ferocious Ezzelino da Romano, notorious for his cruelty and
especially for his hideous massacre of the citizens of Padua (cf. *Inf.*
xii. 109–10). In this relationship, Cunizza is a living symbol of the
principle of individual differentiation upon which Charles Martel
has discoursed in the previous Canto. By using this extreme and
striking instance, Dante thrusts upon our notice the limitations of
material causation. Here are two children, he seems to say, born of
the same parents, brought up together in the same hilltop castle –
and lo! one is in Hell and the other in Paradise.

Cunizza's temperament was not, like her brother's, savage and
cruel, but ardent and passionate. A glance at her biography shows
that she was indeed swayed by the planet Venus, for she had no
fewer than two lovers and four husbands. One of the former was
the troubadour, Sordello (cf. *Purg.* vi), with whom she ran away
from her first husband, Da San Bonifacio. On being sent for safe-
keeping to her second brother, Alberico, at his court in Treviso,
Cunizza again made off, this time with a knight named Bonio, with
whom she wandered about Italy. When Bonio was killed in battle
against Ezzelino, she married, as her second husband, the Count of
Breganze. When he, too, died in combat against Ezzelino, she married
a gentleman of Verona (of unknown name) and finally, fourthly,
Salione Buzzacarini of Padua, who was Ezzelino's astrologer. In
about the year 1260, her brothers and husband being dead, she went
to live in Florence and, in 1265, in the house of the Cavalcanti, she
executed a deed granting freedom to the slaves of her father and
brothers. She died soon after 1279, being then over eighty years of age.

The presence in Florence of the notorious sister of the dread
Ezzelino, quietly passing her old age (so the chroniclers tell us) in the
performance of acts of mercy and compassion, must have created

something of a stir. Dante may even have known her, for he was about fifteen years of age when she died; at any event, he would have heard first-hand accounts of her from his friend, Guido Cavalcanti, whose family gave her hospitality. Something authentic of her personality may be reflected in that gay forgiveness of herself which she expresses in one of the most joyous utterances in the whole of *Paradise*. Her words recall Piccarda's "and His will is our peace" (iii. 85). Dwelling now within the will of God, Cunizza is able to see that her place in Heaven is in conformity with her natural capacity for love, which she therefore counts not as loss but as gain.

Foulquet of Marseilles: Foulquet, a famous troubadour, flourished as a poet from 1180 to 1195. According to his Provençal biographer, he was the son of a rich merchant of Genoa who left him a large fortune. Devoting himself to a life of pleasure, Foulquet attached himself to various courts and counted among his patrons Richard Coeur-de-Lion, Alphonso VIII of Castile, Raymond V, Count of Toulouse and Barral, Viscount of Marseilles. Later, he retired from the world and entered a Cistercian monastery, from which he emerged in 1201 to become Abbot of Torronet and, in 1205, Bishop of Toulouse. He died in 1231.

Foulquet, like Cunizza, acknowledges the overmastering influence of love, which caused him, he says, torments equal to those of Dido, Rhodope and Demophoön. This three-fold comparison is thought to be an indirect allusion to his love for three women: Adelais, the wife of his patron, Barral, Laura, Barral's sister, and Eudoxia, the wife of William VIII of Montpellier. Foulquet's role in *Paradise* is not, however, to relate his loves, but to relate human to divine love. Whereas formerly he suffered the pangs of unrequited love, now he and all the souls with him contemplate with ecstasy the wondrous order of God's plan, wherein the love by which they formerly erred is discerned in its highest manifestation as the power by which the universe is governed.

NOTES. l. 1: *Thy Charles, fair Clemence*: The opening lines of this canto are most probably addressed to the widow of Charles Martel, Clemence, the daughter of the Emperor Rudolph. The fact that she died in 1301, many years before Dante wrote *Paradise*, led some of the early commentators to interpret these lines as addressed to the *daughter* of Charles Martel, also called Clemence, who married Louis X of France. The objection to this interpretation is that at the fictitious date of the narrative (usually assumed to be 1300) the younger Clemence was still a small child. Furthermore, the reference to Charles ("Thy Charles"), would be more suitably addressed to his widow than to his daughter. It remains for the reader to imagine that Dante, in addressing Charles's widow, is thinking himself back to the year in which his narrative is set and in which Clemence the elder was still living.

ll. 2–3: *... the plots ... that should defraud his children of their own*:
Charles Robert, the son of Charles Martel, was heir to the kingdom of
Naples. His right was contested by his uncle Robert (see Canto viii),
who appealed to Pope Clement V. The Pope decided in Robert's
favour. His succession had in fact been laid down in 1296 by Charles II
in agreement with Pope Boniface VIII. Dante, as has been seen in Canto
viii, was a staunch supporter of the Martel party and regarded Robert
as a fraudulent usurper. This view was shared by many of Dante's con-
temporaries, among whom it was rumoured that, moved by contrition
and remorse, Robert arranged the marriage between his grand-daughter
(his only heir) and the son of Charles Robert.

l. 6: *... on your wrongs just woes shall follow fast*: In 1315, the brother
and nephew of Robert were killed at the battle of Montecatini.

l. 7: *Already to the Sun*: literally, in the direction of the sphere of the
sun, which is above that of Venus; figuratively, towards God.

l. 8: *The holy flambeau's life*: that is, the vital principle of the light
which is the soul of Charles Martel.

l. 13: *And lo! another splendour now drew nigh*: This is the soul of
Cunizza. For information concerning her, see above, under *Images*.

ll. 20–21: *"... and show me that I am to thee a mirror"* etc.: Dante
entreats Cunizza to read and comply with his request without his
having to express it.

ll. 25–7: *"in that part"*: Cunizza is describing the March of Treviso
which was bordered on the south by the Duchy of Venice (indicated
here by Rialto, its principal island) and on the north by the Alps of the
Trentino, in which the river Brenta rises, and the Alps of the Cadore,
from which the river Piave flows.

l. 28: *"Rises a hill"*: The castle of Romano was on a hill to the north-
east of Bassano; it was the birthplace of Ezzelino (see Glossary).

l. 31: *"One root with him had I"*: that is, I was born of the same
parents as he.

l. 33: *"I was o'ermastered by this planet's flame"*: Cunizza here acknow-
ledges the influence which Venus had over her life and temperament.

l. 37: *"Of this rich jewel neighbouring me"*: Cunizza thus indicates the
soul of Foulquet of Marseilles. For information concerning him, see
above, under *Images*.

l. 40: *"Before this century has grown to five"*: i.e. before 500 years have
passed.

ll. 43–4: *"... they whose present brood Adige moats and Tagliamento
pens"*: The river Adige and the Tagliamento enclose the March of
Treviso.

ll. 46–8: *"But soon shall Padua"* etc.: Paduan blood shall dye the
Bacchiglione red ("Vicenza's stream") because of Paduan resistance to
the Empire. (Can Grande of Verona, representing the Imperial cause,
defeated the Guelf Paduans near Vicenza in 1314.)

ll. 49–51: *"Where Silè and Cagnano join their brim, one lords it"* etc.:

The rivers Sile and Cagnano have their confluence at Treviso. These lines refer to the fate awaiting Riccardo da Cammino, Lord of Treviso, Feltre and Belluno. He was the son of "the good Gerard", to whom Marco Lombardo refers in *Purgatory* xvi. 124 and whom Dante cites as an example of nobility in *Convivio* IV. xiv: "Let us suppose that Gherardo da Cammino was the grandson of the meanest peasant that ever drank of Sile or Cagnano . . . who would have dared to say that Gherardo was a base fellow? Surely nobody . . . for Gherardo was noble, and so will his memory ever be." Notice that in this canto Dante again indicates Treviso by referring to the two rivers, Sile and Cagnano. The baseness of the tyrannical and oppressive grandson, Riccardo, is another instance of the divine law which Charles Martel expounded in Canto viii. Riccardo is connected with another *Purgatory* character, in that he was the husband of Judge Nino's daughter, Giovanna (*Purg.* viii. 71).

ll. 52–60: *"Feltro shall weep her impious pastor's crime"* etc.: The Bishop of Feltre, Alessandro Novello, betrayed thirteen Ghibellines from Ferrara who had taken refuge with him. They were executed in 1314 by the delegate of King Robert. *". . . to La Malta's jail none was e'er sent stained with a filthier grime"*: La Malta was the name of an ecclesiastical prison on Lake Bolsena, or possibly in Viterbo. Dante's meaning is: this pastor of the Church was guilty of a crime more heinous than any for which his brethren of the cloth were imprisoned in La Malta.

ll. 61–3: *"Mirrors – you call them Thrones – there are above"* etc.: Cunizza here refers to the angelic hierarchy which moves the third heaven. Charles Martel (Canto viii. 34–9) has already told Dante that they are the Principalities, whereas Dante, in the *Convivio*, following the order he had found in Brunetto Latini's *Trésor*, had identified them as Thrones. Cunizza seems here to be courteously acknowledging Dante's designation (see also Canto xxviii. 133–5).

l. 74: *"thy sight in-Hims itself"*: thy sight penetrates into and becomes interpenetrated with God. The reflexive verb "in-Hims itself" is a literal translation of Dante's invention, "s'inluia". (See also l. 81.)

ll. 77–8: *". . . those burning quires perpetually who worship hooded in their six-fold wings"*: the Seraphim. Compare *Isaiah*, vi. 2–3: "Above it stood the Seraphims: each one had six wings; with twain he covered his face, and with twain he covered his feet, and with twain he did fly."

l. 81: The reflexive verbs, "in-thee me" and "in-meëst thee", are literal translations of two words which, like the "s'inluia" of l. 73, Dante invented to convey the interpenetration of personalities. Dante's meaning is: "If I could enter thee as thou canst enter me (and read my mind), I would not wait for thee to ask any question thou mightest desire me to answer." Dante is here addressing Foulquet of Marseilles.

l. 82: *"The greatest valley where the seas expand"* etc.: This is the basin of the Mediterranean Sea, into which the ocean pours at Gibraltar.

l. 84: *". . . that ocean girdling all the land"*: According to the mediaeval geographers, the ocean encircled the whole of the dry portion of the globe. Land was thought of as constituting a single continent extending from the equator to the Arctic Circle, between the Columns of Hercules (i.e. the Straits of Gibraltar) on the west and the mouth of the River Ganges on the east. Within this area the Mediterranean is the largest sea.

ll. 85–7: "*. . . 'twixt wrangling shore and shore*": between Europe and Africa, discordant in race and religion. "*Against the sun*": from west to east. "*. . . it makes meridian at last where its horizon was before*": The Mediterranean was believed by mediaeval geographers to cover 90° of longitude; therefore it reaches so far eastward that the celestial horizon from the west is from the eastern end of the Sea the zenith or meridian (and vice versa).

ll. 88–90: "*. . . at the mid-span 'twixt Ebro and Macra, whose short banks divide the man of Genoa from the Tuscan clan*": that is, at Marseilles, which is situated half-way between the mouth of the Ebro and the mouth of the Magra.

ll. 91–2: "*Sunset and dawn well-nigh at once bestride both Bougia and my city*": Marseilles and Bougia (Bougie), on the coast of Africa, are in almost the same longitude.

ll. 92–3: "*which long syne with her own blood made hot her harbour's tide*": During the first year of the Civil War, 49 B.C., Caesar took Marseilles after great slaughter. (See also Canto vi. 61–6 and *notes*.)

l. 97: *Belus' daughter*: Dido, daughter of the King of Tyre.

l. 98: "*Wronging Sichaëus and Creusa too*": Dido had married her uncle Sichaëus, who was murdered by her brother Pygmalion for the sake of his wealth. Dido fled from Tyre to Africa, where she founded Carthage. She had sworn to remain faithful to the memory of her husband, whom her love for Aeneas therefore "wronged". Creusa, a daughter of Priam and Hecuba, was the wife of Aeneas and mother of Ascanius. When Troy was sacked Creusa became separated from Aeneas in the confusion and perished.

l. 100: "*Rhodope's fair maid*": Rhodope is a mountain in Thrace. Phyllis, who loved the faithless Demophoön, son of Theseus and Phaedra, was the daughter of Sithon, King of Thrace.

ll. 101–2: "*. . . Alcides, while he caged Iole in his strong heart's mew*": Hercules, the grandson of Alceus, loved Iole, the daughter of Eurytus, King of Oechalia, in Thessaly, whom he killed, carrying off Iole as a prisoner. All the three lovers mentioned by Foulquet owed their deaths to their fatal passions. Foulquet himself is said to have been in love with three women, and his *canzone*, which Dante quotes in his *De Vulgari Eloquentia*, is addressed to "las tres dompnas" ("the three ladies").

l. 115: *Rahab*: the harlot of Jericho who contributed to Joshua's great victory by receiving and hiding the two spies whom he sent to bring back information from the city. Her position in heaven is explained by the fact that through her marriage with Salmon she became an ancestress of Christ. In *Hebrews* xi. 31 it is said of her: "By faith the harlot Rahab perished not with them that believed not, when she had received the spies with peace." And St James (iii, 25): "Likewise also was not Rahab the harlot justified by works, when she had received the messengers, and had sent them out another way?"

ll. 118–20: *"your earth's cast cone of shade"*: It was formerly calculated that the cone of shadow cast by the earth extended as far as the heaven, or sphere, of Venus (not to the planet itself, the distance of which from the earth was known to vary greatly). It is known now that the earth's shadow extends about 1½ million kilometres, and that the smallest distance between Venus and the earth is about fifty million kilometres.

l. 119: ". . . *the triumph of Christ's arms"*: This is a reference to the victory of Christ over the powers of Hell when He descended to the Limbo and drew forth the souls of patriarchs, etc. (cf. *Inf.* iv. 56–63).

l. 123: ". . . *those extended palms"*: i.e. the hands of Christ outstretched upon the Cross.

l. 126: *"Now by this Pope forgotten and disdained"*: Pope Boniface VIII, preoccupied with strengthening his position in Europe, neglected his duty to liberate the Holy Land from the Infidel. The same reproach, more forcefully expressed, was uttered by Guido da Montefeltro in *Inf.* xxvii. 85–90:

> "But he, the Prince of the modern Pharisees,
> 　　Having a war to wage by Lateran –
> 　　Not against Jews, nor Moslem enemies,
>
> For every foe he had was Christian,
> 　　Not one had marched on Acre, none had bought
> 　　Or sold within the realm of the Soldan – "

Acre, the last stronghold remaining to the Christians in Palestine after the Crusades, was retaken by the Saracens in 1291, and no attempt had been made to regain it.

ll. 127–30: In this terrible indictment against Florence, Foulquet says she is sprung from the Devil, and from such evil plant the florin is produced which, stamped with the fleur-de-lis, became the standard currency of Italy.

l. 135: *"the Decretals"*: These are the Papal decrees of monetary gains, the books of Canon Law, which prove more productive than the Gospels or the writings of the Church fathers.

ll. 136–42: Foulquet's discourse ends on a note of general remonstrance to the Papacy and cardinalate for their greed for wealth and their neglect of the true spirit of Christianity. He reiterates in the last line the prophecy of retribution soon to overtake the Church, a prophecy which occurs at intervals throughout the *Divine Comedy*.

CANTO X

THE STORY. *Dante and Beatrice ascend to the heaven of the Sun, leaving below them the spheres which are tinged with the shadow cast by the earth. Outlined against the brightness of the sun are spirits characterized by the gift of wisdom. Forming a circle of twelve lights and revolving three times round Dante and Beatrice, they utter music so ineffable that it cannot be described on earth. A speaker, identifying himself as St Thomas Aquinas, tells Dante the names of the other eleven souls.*

The uncreated Might which passeth speech,
　　Gazing on His Begotten with the Love
　　That breathes Itself eternally from each,

All things that turn through mind and space made move　　4
　　In such great order that without some feel
　　Of Him none e'er beheld the frame thereof.

Look up with me, then, Reader, to the reel　　7
　　The exalted heavens tread, and scan that part
　　Where one wheel crosses with the other wheel;

There gaze enamoured on the Master's art,　　10
　　Whence never He removes the eye of Him,
　　Such is the love He bears it in His heart.

Observe how, branching off as from a stem,　　13
　　Runs slant the circle that the planets ride,
　　To meet the calls that the world makes on them;

For were their path not tilted thus aside,　　16
　　Much heavenly power would go for naught, and nigh
　　All earthly potencies unborn had died;

While more or less than this if it should lie　　19
　　Out of the straight, 'twould cause a grievous lack
　　Of order in the low world and the high.

Bide on thy bench now, Reader, and think back　　22
　　Upon this foretaste, if the feast in store
　　Thou wouldst enjoy ere relish tire and slack;

25   I've served it up, and I can do no more.
            Pray help thyself; the theme I have to rhyme
            Is one I need my whole attention for.

28   Of Nature's ministers the chief and prime,
            Who sets on earth the seals of heavenly sway,
            And makes his light the measure of our time,

31   Had reached that point we named, and on his way
            Through heav'n was moving up the spiral stair
            Whereon he shows him earlier day by day.

34   And I was with him, but no more aware
            Of my ascent than as a man may know,
            Ere a thought strikes him, that a thought is there.

37   'Tis she, Beatrice, she that wafteth so
            From good to better, with a flight so keen,
            The act is done ere time has time to flow.

40   How bright in its own right must that have been,
            Which light, not colour, outlined on the light
            Of the sun's self, when there I entered in!

43   Call on experience, genius, art, I might,
            But paint imaginable picture, none;
            Yet trust we may, and long to see that sight;

46   And if imagination cannot run
            To heights like these, no wonder: no eye yet
            E'er braved a brilliance that outshone the sun.

49   But such was God's fourth family, there set
            In endless joy, bathed by the Father's rays,
            Which show them how He breathes and doth beget.

52   Beatrice then began: "Give thanks, give praise
            Now to the Sun of Angels, that to this,
            The visible sun, hath raised thee by His grace!"

55   Ne'er was man's heart with such great eagerness
            Devoutly moved to make his whole self over
            To God, with all the will that in him is,

58   Than at those words was I; I grew God's lover
            So wholly, needs must Beatrix' self admit
            Eclipse, and I became oblivious of her.

But this displeased her not; she smiled at it,   61
  So that the splendour of her laughing eyes
  From one to many things recalled my wit.

Lo! many surpassing lights in a bright device,   64
  We at the centre, they as a wreath, were shown,
  And sweeter of voice they were than bright of guise.

So girdled round we now and again have known   67
  Latona's daughter, when the teeming air
  Catches and holds the threads that weave her zone.

Those heavenly courts I've stood in, treasure there   70
  Many rich gems, too precious, being unique,
  To be removed out of the kingdom's care;

Such were those fiery carols – they who seek   73
  To hear them must find wings to reach that goal,
  Or wait for tidings till the dumb shall speak.

So carolling, that ardent aureole   76
  Of suns swung round us thrice their burning train,
  As neighbouring stars swing round the steady pole;

Then seemed like ladies, from the dancing chain   79
  Not loosed, but silent at the measure's close,
  Listening alert to catch the next new strain.

Now from within one fire a voice arose: 82
  "Since grace – whose radiance, wheresoe'er extended,
  Kindles true love, and thus by loving grows,

Still multiplied in thee shines forth so splendid   85
  As up that stair to lead thee, whence none ever,
  Except to re-ascend it, hath descended,

He that should seal his flask up, nor deliver   88
  Wine to assuage thy thirst, were no more free
  Than, from the sea damned back, a running river.

What flowers, thou askest, deck this garlandry   91
  Circling the Lady, and with joy surveying
  Her beauty, who for Heav'n doth strengthen thee.

Lamb of the holy flock was I, obeying   94
  Dominic on that road he led us by,
  Where is good fattening if there be no straying.

97　Brother to me and master, one stands nigh
　　　On my right hand here: Albert of Cologne
　　　Was he, and Thomas of Aquino, I.

100　Wouldst learn the rest? Then let thy sight be thrown
　　　Behind my speech, till right around we've sought
　　　The sacred wreath, and all are named and known.

103　Next flames the light of Gratian's smile, who taught
　　　In either forum, and in both gives pleasure
　　　To Paradise, by the good work he wrought.

106　That Peter next adorns our choir, in measure
　　　Generous as she whose widowed means were small,
　　　On Holy Church bestowing all his treasure.

109　The fifth light yonder, brightest of us all,
　　　So breathes out love that every man on ground
　　　Thirsts for his news; that mind majestical

112　There dwells, in whom such wisdom did abound,
　　　None ever rose in any generation,
　　　If truth speak true, to insight so profound.

115　Next him, that cerge sheds forth illumination
　　　Who in his mortal flesh right well discerned
　　　Angelic natures and their ministration.

118　Laughs in yon flamelet, with his ardour burned,
　　　That pleader for the Christian age, whose learning
　　　Provided lore from which Augustine learned.

121　Now, if thy mind's eye has been duly turning
　　　From light to light, as I pronounced their praises,
　　　'Tis on the eighth thou fixest now thy yearning;

124　There on the total good enraptured gazes
　　　That joy who strips the world's hypocrisies
　　　Bare to whoever heeds his cogent phrases;

127　The flesh they reft him from, Cieldoro sees
　　　At rest in earth; himself came forth from sore
　　　Exile and martyrdom unto this peace.

130　There flames the glowing breath of Isidore,
　　　Bede, and that Richard who was wont to be
　　　In speculation not a man, but more.

138

This fire, from whom thy glance returns to me,   133
  Shines from a spirit grave in thought, who knew
  Sorrow; for him death came too tardily;

That's the eternal light of Sigier, who,   136
  Lecturing down in Straw Street, hammered home
  Invidious truths, as logic taught him to."

Then, like the horloge, calling us to come,   139
  What time the Bride of God doth rise and sing,
  Wooing His love, her mattins to her Groom,

Where part with part will push and pull, and ring,   142
  Ding-ding, upon the bell sweet notes that swell
  With love the soul made apt for worshipping,

E'en so I saw it move, the glorious wheel,   145
  And voice with voice harmonious change and chime
  Sweetness unknown, there only knowable

Where ever-present joy knows naught of time.   148

THE IMAGES. *The Sun*: In the *story*, the sun, which in the Ptolemaic
system was the fourth of the seven planets circling the earth, is the
next stage in the ascent after Venus. In the *allegory*, the sun is the sym-
bol of intellectual illumination and, ultimately, of God Himself,
since the goal of wisdom is knowledge of the Divine Essence.

The Passage beyond Earth's Shadow: In the *story*, the passage of Dante and
Beatrice beyond the heaven which the "earth's cast cone of shade
just touches" (ix. 118–19) marks the completion of the first stage of
their ascent. As in the *Inferno* and *Purgatory*, so now in *Paradise*, the
tenth Canto constitutes the beginning of another section of the poem.
To mark this division, there is a pause in the narrative, and what may
be called a new prologue opens the Canto, recalling to our notice the
ultimate theme of the whole work: the mystery of the Holy Trinity.
In the *allegory*, the ascent beyond sense to the suprasensible symbol-
izes the progress of the soul in its advance towards knowledge of
God, for it is by the illumination of the mind rather than by sense
impressions that Dante comes ultimately to know Him.

The Circle of Twelve Lights: In the *story*, these are the souls of twelve
wise men. With the exception of Solomon, who represents kingly
prudence, they are all exponents or doctors of learning, philosophy
or theology, men through whom the Word of God was mediated in
wisdom to the world. In the *allegory*, the garland of lights, gyrating
in celestial dance and uttering music of a sweetness so ineffable it can-
not be described on earth, symbolizes the order and harmony in
which all the diverse manifestations of God's truth are here conjoined.

NOTES. ll. 1-3: The opening lines of this canto are an expression of the relationship of the Three Persons of the Trinity. The "uncreated Might", God the Father, self-existent, contemplates Himself as manifested, "gazing on His Begotten" in that Love, the Holy Spirit, which in either aspect He breathes forth. The emphasis on "each" is significant, for it faithfully reproduces the prominence Dante gives to the proceeding of the Holy Ghost from the Son as well as from the Father.

ll. 5-6: . . . *that without some feel of Him none e'er beheld the frame thereof*: He who contemplates the order of all that revolves in mind and space cannot but be aware of God.

ll. 7-8: . . . *the reel the exalted heavens tread*: i.e. the revolution of the spheres carrying the planets round the earth.

ll. 8-9: . . . *that part where one wheel crosses with the other wheel*: One wheel is the daily movement of the planets round the earth, and this is parallel to the equator; the other wheel is the annual movement of the sun along the ecliptic (or zodiac) and this is not parallel but oblique to the equator. These two movements cross each other at the first point of Aries (at the spring equinox) and at the first point of Libra (at the autumnal equinox). In its yearly, oblique revolution round the earth, the sun performs a slanting, spiral-like twist or coil, moving from north to south and from south to north, thus bringing about the change of seasons.

l. 14: . . . *runs slant the circle that the planets ride*: The circle that the planets ride is the zodiac, a wide band along which the sun traces its annual path (or ecliptic) and the planets and constellations are seen in constantly changing positions.

l. 16: "*For were their path not tilted thus aside*": If the ecliptic were not inclined to the poles, or if it were tilted *more* or *less*, the warmth of the sun would be limited to a much more restricted area of the globe.

l. 21: *the low world and the high*: i.e. the northern and southern hemispheres. It is interesting to compare Dante's pleasure in the order of the universe with Milton's impassioned and rhetorical lines (*Paradise Lost*, x. 650 ff.) explaining how that same inclination (which Dante considers providential) was part of the Curse brought about by the Fall, whereas if Eve had left the apple alone, the temperate zone (in which Eden was situated) would have enjoyed "Spring perpetual".

ll. 22-7: These lines indicate that Dante was aware of the difficulty his readers would have in understanding the foregoing astronomical passage. Like a teacher conscious of the syllabus, he presses onward with his main theme, advising the reader to think the problem out further for himself.

l. 28: *Of Nature's ministers the chief and prime*: the sun.

l. 31: *Had reached the point we named*: i.e. the point at which the ecliptic meets the equator. See note to ll. 8-9.

ll. 32-3: . . . *was moving up the spiral stair whereon he shows him earlier day by day*: From winter to summer solstice, the sun follows a spiral-like course about the earth, rising (for the northern hemisphere) a little earlier each day. After the summer solstice, he begins his downward spiral, moving from north to south, from the tropic of Cancer to the tropic of Capricorn, rising a little later each day. Since he has reached the point mentioned, he is half-way between the winter and the summer solstice, or at the spring equinox.

l. 34: *And I was with him*: Dante has entered the heaven of the sun.

l. 49: *such was God's fourth family*: The fourth group of souls in Heaven, encountered by Dante in the sun, consists of those endowed with wisdom.

l. 51: *how He breathes and doth beget*: The Father begets the Son and in either aspect breathes forth the Spirit (cf. ll. 1–3).

l. 53: *the Sun of Angels*: i.e. God. In the *Convivio* III. xii, Dante said: "No object of sense in the whole world is more worthy to be made a type of God than the sun, which illumines first himself and then all other celestial and elemental bodies with sensible light. So God illumines with intellectual light first Himself and afterwards the dwellers in heaven and all other intellectual beings."

ll. 62–3: *"the splendour of her laughing eyes from one to many things recalled my wit"*: Dante, in his eager praise and love of God, was drawn up into the One, from which he is recalled by the reflection ("splendour") of His glory in the many.

l. 68: *Latona's daughter*: Diana, the moon. The circle of light girdling Dante and Beatrice is compared to a halo round the moon.

ll. 71–2: *... too precious ... to be removed out of the kingdom's care*: i.e. there are things in Heaven that cannot be described on earth.

l. 78: *as neighbouring stars swing round the steady pole*: This comparison seems to convey that the circle of lights swung horizontally round the central figures (cf. Canto xii. 2).

ll. 79–81: The revolving circle of lights has ceased singing. Dante compares them to a ring of women dancers who, having reached the end of a *ripresa*, continue dancing in silence while their leader sings a stanza, ready to begin singing again when they reach the next *ripresa*.

ll. 94–5: *"Lamb of the holy flock was I, obeying Dominic"*: He now names each member of the circle and from his information the diagram on p. 142 is deduced.

St Thomas Aquinas, the most famous of the scholastic theologians and philosophers, was born of noble family (he was kinsman to Louis VIII) at Rocca Sicca near Aquino in Campania. He received his early education at the neighbouring Benedictine Monastery of Monte Cassino (cf. Canto xxii) and at the University of Naples. He entered the Dominican Order as a young man and went to study at Cologne under Albertus Magnus (whose light is next to his). In 1257, he was created a doctor of theology by the Sorbonne, where he acquired a great reputation. He continued lecturing on theology, in Rome and Bologna and again in Paris, and in 1272 he was sent by his religious superiors to organize the

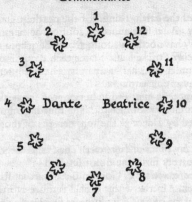

1. St Thomas Aquinas
2. Albertus Magnus
3. Gratian
4. Peter Lombard
5. Solomon
6. Dionysius the Areopagite
7. Orosius
8. Boethius
9. Isidore of Seville
10. Bede
11. Richard of St Victor
12. Sigier of Brabant

Dominican house of studies in Naples and to teach theology there. During these years he was occupied also with the affairs of the Church and in January 1274 he was summoned by Pope Gregory X to attend the Council of Lyons, which had been called in the hope of uniting the Greek and Latin Churches. He fell ill on the journey and died at a Cistercian monastery on the borders between Campania and Latium.

His most important and influential work is the famous *Summa Theologiae*, in which he attempted to present a summary of "all accessible knowledge, arranged according to the best method, and subordinate to the dictates of the Church". It is an exposition of the teachings of the Church in the light of the philosophy of Aristotle and his Arabian commentators. It is divided into three parts of which the third, which was unfinished at his death, was completed by others in accordance with his design for the work. The first part deals with the nature and attributes of God; the second is concerned mainly with ethics; in the third, Aquinas speaks of the person and work of Christ and of the sacraments.

He also wrote a summary of the Christian faith for the refutation of unbelief (the work known briefly as the *Contra Gentiles*); this is several times referred to by Dante. He wrote as well commentaries on Aristotle's works on ethics, physics, metaphysics, the soul, and on various other Aristotelian treatises. He took part in producing a new translation of Aristotle from the Greek (previous translations having been made from Arabic). There is reason to suppose that this is the translation to which Dante refers in the *Convivio*, when he says: "What Aristotle may have said about it (i.e. the galaxy) cannot be accurately known, because the two translations give different accounts of his opinion. And I think that any mistake may have been due to the translators, for in the New Translation (i.e. *probably St Thomas's*) he is made to say that the galaxy is a congregation, under the stars of this part of the heaven, of the vapours which are always being attracted by them, and this opinion does not appear to be right. In the Old Translation he says that the galaxy is nothing but a multitude of fixed stars in that region . . ." [1]

Dante was deeply indebted to the writings of Aquinas, especially to the *Summa Theologiae*, which, although he never quotes it by name, is the source of many of his discussions of ethics and the soul.[2] He was not, however, exclusively dominated by him and in some respects, notably in regard to the question of free will, he seems to owe more to St Thomas's master, Albertus Magnus. Something of the personality and manner of lecturing of St Thomas seems to be reflected in Canto xi in the careful distinctions he draws at the beginning and the end, and later elaborates in Canto xiii. "By the time Dante studied in Paris, probably in the earlier years of his exile, more than thirty years had passed since Aquinas had lectured there; but there would still be many from whom Dante could gather, and would be eager to gather, reminiscences of 'the Ox of Knowledge' who, in his books, was Dante's greatest teacher and had in Dante his greatest pupil." Sinclair. See also Kenelm Foster, *The Life of Saint Thomas Aquinas* (Longmans, Green, 1957).

l. 98: *Albert of Cologne*: This is Albertus Magnus, the Master of Aquinas, who was called the Universal Doctor on account of his vast learning. Born in Swabia towards the end of the twelfth century, he entered the Dominican Order and studied theology at Padua, Paris and Bologna, and later lectured at Cologne and elsewhere in Germany. It was at Cologne, where the Order had a house, that Thomas Aquinas studied under him. Together they went to Paris in 1245, where Albertus received his doctorate, returning together to Cologne three years later. (This companionship is reflected in St Thomas's words, "Brother to me and master".) In 1260, he was appointed Bishop of Ratisbon by Pope Alexander IV. He died at Cologne, on the 15 November 1280, at the age of eighty-seven.

He was an even more voluminous writer than his pupil, Thomas Aquinas. When his collected works were printed in Lyons in 1651, they filled twenty-one folio volumes. Six of these are devoted to commentaries on Aristotle, five to Biblical commentary, two on Dionysius the Areopagite (cf. l. 115), three on the *Liber Sententiarum* by Peter Lombard (cf. l. 106); the remaining five contain his *Summa Theologiae*, his *Summa de Creaturis*, a treatise on the Virgin, and various scientific works, includ-

1. *Convivio* II. xv.
2. See Dorothy L. Sayers, "The Divine Poet and the Angelic Doctor" in *Further Papers on Dante* (Methuen, 1957, pp. 38-52). This was originally a paper read to the Aquinas Society in 1946.

ing one on alchemy. He seems to have been much interested in what might be called – with all due allowance for the difference implied by modern use of the phrase – experimental science. In his writings he distinguishes carefully between what he had only read and what he had personally seen. Having read, for instance, that the eagle laid only one egg, he arranged for a man to be lowered over a cliff on a rope to look at an eagle's nest and count the contents. He qualified statements which he repeated from others by such *caveats* as "I don't think this is true" or confirmed by such corroboration as "my colleagues and I tried this out". When Beatrice (in Canto ii. 95–6) speaks of experiment as "that source whence all your science has to start", she is quoting Albertus Magnus.

l. 103: *the light of Gratian's smile*: Gratian, the founder of the science of Canon Law, was born towards the end of the eleventh century, either at Chiusi in Tuscany or at Carraria, near Orvieto. He is said to have become a Benedictine and to have entered the Camaldulian monastery at Classe, near Ravenna, whence he transferred to that of San Felice at Bologna. His famous work known as the *Decretum Gratiani*, published between 1140 and 1150, is a *concordia*, or reconciliation, between the laws of the ecclesiastical and secular courts. That is why St Thomas says of him: "he taught in either forum (i.e. both the ecclesiastical and the civil courts) and in both gives pleasure to Paradise, by the good work he wrought."

l. 106: *"That Peter next adorns our choir"*: This is Peter Lombard, known as the Master of the Sentences, from the title of his work *Sententiarum Libri Quatuor*. He was born near Novara about the year 1100 and studied first at Bologna and then at Paris, where he held a Chair in theology. In 1159, he was appointed Bishop of Paris, but died shortly afterwards, either in 1160 or 1164. He is said to have been a pupil of Abelard and was also, with Richard of St Victor (cf. l. 131), a pupil of the still more celebrated mystic and theologian, Hugh of St Victor (cf. Canto xii). Peter's book of Sentences is primarily a collection of the sayings of the Fathers. They are arranged, like an anthology, under four headings or subjects, the Godhead, creation, the incarnation, and the sacraments. The ethical principle is predominant and reconciliation of conflicting authorities is the principal criterion of selection. It became a text-book in the schools of theology and the subject of a great many commentaries.

ll. 107–8: *"generous as she whose widowed means were small, On Holy Church bestowing all his treasure"*: At the beginning of his work, Peter Lombard offers it humbly as a modest tribute to the Holy Church, as the poor widow offered her mite (cf. *Luke*, xxi. 1–4). Dante quotes his definition of hope in Canto xxv. 67–9.

l. 109–14: *"The fifth light yonder"* etc.: This is the soul of Solomon. His inclusion in the circle is remarkable on two counts. First, the question as to whether Solomon was saved or damned was in dispute among the theologians; hence, everyone on earth "thirsts for his news" (ll. 110–

11). Tertullian, St Cyprian, St Augustine, and even Dante's friend and master, Brunetto Latini, had said that Solomon was damned, partly on grounds of idolatry, partly also owing to interpretations of the *Song of Songs*. The more modern theologians of Dante's time inclined to the belief that he had repented and been saved, certain leaden tablets (subsequently proved spurious) having been discovered at Granada, with a verse in Arabic characters (attributed to St James) which stated that Solomon turned from his sinfulness and was forgiven. The second, and more difficult, point concerning his presence here is the nature of his wisdom. St Thomas, in ll. 111–14, calls him:

> ...; "that mind majestical,

> ..., in whom such wisdom did abound,
> None ever rose in any generation,
> If truth speak true, to insight so profound."

This is so difficult a saying that almost an entire canto is devoted to its elucidation (cf. Canto xiii. 34–108). St Thomas is here quoting God's words as related in *I Kings*, iii. 5–13: "I have given thee a wise and understanding heart; so that there was none like thee before thee, neither after thee shall any arise (*post te surrectus sit*) like unto thee." St Thomas's later explanation is, in fact, a gloss on this passage (see Canto xiii. 93 ff., and *notes*). For the present, he is content with an indirect reference to its source; "if truth speak true", which is to say, if the Bible does not err, which it cannot, being the truth; any error concerning it arises from our misunderstanding.

There remains the question as to why Solomon is included in the circles of the Doctors of the Active Life. His is the wisdom of kings, not of learning, and it would seem that Dante wished to emphasize the relationship between them. This is characteristic of Dante's preoccupation with justice and government and it is significant that it is a phrase from the *Book of the Wisdom of Solomon* which the souls form in the Heaven of the Just before the transformation of the letter M into the emblem of the Eagle. (See also Canto xiv, under *Images*.)

l. 115: "*that cerge sends forth illumination*": Dionysius the Areopagite, the Athenian who was converted by the preaching of St Paul (*Acts*, xvii. 34) was believed in the Middle Ages to be the author of a work on the Angelic orders (cf. Canto xxviii. 130–32 and *note*.)

l. 119: "*that pleader for the Christian age*": This is Paulus Orosius, whose principal work, *Historiae adversum paganos*, is intended to prove by the evidence of history that the world had not deteriorated since the adoption of Christianity, as the pagans asserted. Dante owed much of his knowledge of ancient history to Orosius, whom he cites on several occasions.

l. 125: "*that joy who strips the world's hypocrisies*": Boethius, the fifth-century Roman statesman and philosopher (A.D. *c.* 475–525), was the author of an allegorical work, *On the Consolation of Philosophy*, which he wrote in prison in Pavia. He had previously held high honour under the Emperor Theodoric, who in his old age allowed himself to be influenced by jealous courtiers and had Boethius cast into prison on suspicion of treason and finally put to death with cruel torture. In his work, Boethius represents philosophy as a gracious and beautiful woman with whom he holds converse and who speaks to him of the mutability of fortune and the insecurity of everything except virtue. Dante was very familiar with this work which, he says, together with Cicero's *De Amicitia*, provided him with his greatest consolation after the death of Beatrice.

In his fate, Boethius is a type, like Pier delle Vigne and like Romèo, of the faithful minister who is unjustly suspected of disloyalty and is shabbily or even cruelly treated by those he has served. It is a type in which Dante recognized something of his own vicissitudes. When his ancestor Cacciaguida speaks to him in the Heaven of Mars, he echoes St Thomas's words about martyrdom and the peace of Heaven to which Boethius escaped from the deception of the world (cf. Canto xv. 145–8).

l. 127: *Cieldoro*: Boethius was buried in the Church of St Peter in Ciel d'Oro at Pavia.

l. 130: *"the glowing breath of Isidore"*: St Isidore of Seville was born about 560 and died in 636. His chief work was a massive encyclopaedia of scientific knowledge, entitled *Origines*, on which Brunetto Latini based much of his *Trésor*.

l. 131: *Bede*: The Venerable Bede (about 673–735) is the author of the *Ecclesiastical History of England*. In one of his Latin epistles, Dante reproaches the Italian cardinals for neglecting the works of Bede, as well as those of Gregory the Great, St Ambrose, St Augustine, Dionysius, John of Damascus, in preference for the works of the Decretalists in their pursuit of temporal interests. The authors they neglect "sought after God as their end and highest good", while the Cardinals "get for themselves riches and benefices".[1]

ll. 131–2: *"that Richard who was wont to be in speculation not a man, but more"*: Richard of St Victor, said to have been a native of Scotland, was a mystic of the twelfth century. With Peter Lombard, he studied in Paris under Hugh of St Victor and was a friend of St Bernard of Clairvaux. His works, which are quoted by St Thomas, consist of commentaries on parts of the Old Testament, St Paul's Epistles and on the Apocalypse, as well as works on mystical contemplation, which earned him the title of "Magnus Contemplator". It has been said that the mystical writings of Richard are a scientific attempt to systematize the facts of the contemplative life. It is interesting to notice that in the original Italian, Dante does not use the verb "contemplare" in connection with Richard, but, instead, the verb "considerare". We have not yet reached the heaven of

1. *The Letters of Dante*, edited and translated by Paget Toynbee, Oxford (Clarendon Press), 1920, No. viii. p. 145.

the contemplatives, and it would seem from this choice of word that Dante did not include Richard among them. The following passage from Dom C. Butler's *Western Mysticism* suggests why: "Contemplation is concerned with the certainty of things, consideration with their investigation. Accordingly, contemplation may be defined as the soul's true and certain intuition of a thing, or as the unhesitating apprehension of truth. Consideration is thought earnestly directed to investigation or the application of the mind searching for the truth (the modern 'meditation')".[1] Consideration, thus defined, is more appropriate than contemplation to the circle of the Doctors. The writings of Richard of St Victor had a considerable influence on Dante, not only in the Leah and Rachel allegory (cf. *Purg.* xxvii, *Images*) but also in the image of the Mountain. "Richard does not ascend to God by the way of negation. His 'dark night of unknowing' occurs at the end of a progressive affirmative system of experimental and acquired spiritual knowledge. . . . It is only in the last stages of contemplation that the soul, according to Richard, is passive and all is received from God." (Clare Kirchberger, Richard of St Victor, *Benjamin Minor*, Faber and Faber.)

ll. 136: "*the eternal light of Sigier*": Sigier of Brabant was a doctor of philosophy in the University of Paris in the thirteenth century. His position beside St Thomas, on his left, is the most striking juxtaposition in the circle. St Thomas and Sigier had been opponents on earth in the dispute that arose in the University of Paris concerning the expounding of Aristotle in the light of the commentary by Averroës. In 1269, St Thomas was sent to Paris for two years to preach against the Averroist doctrine. He found Sigier lecturing (in the Rue du Fouarre, or Straw Street, according to tradition) to the Arts Faculty, members of which, both lecturers and students, were mostly laymen, who asserted their right to study Averroës irrespective of the disapproval of the theologians. In 1270, both Aquinas and Sigier published manifestoes about a particular point in Averroist doctrine, and Aquinas publicly refuted the practice of those who "study philosophy and who say things which are not true according to the Faith; and when it is pointed out to them that this is repugnant to the Faith, they reply that this is what the Philosopher[2] says; they themselves, they say, do not affirm it; they are merely repeating the words of the Philosopher." By 1275 the whole University of Paris was in an uproar and the Papal Legate, Simon de Brion (who later became Pope Martin IV), went so far as to threaten the leaders of the factions with "the sword of justice and of vengeance". Sigier left Paris and retired to Liège, but in 1277 he was summoned to appear before the inspector-general of the faith for France on a charge of heresy. According to one tradition, Sigier was later executed by order of the Court of Rome at Orvieto, not, evidently, for heresy, for which the punishment was death by burning, but for a political offence. It is known that Sigier took an active part in political as

1. p. 148.   2. i.e. Aristotle.

well as religious disputes and controversies. He would probably not have favoured the temporal claims of the Papacy, and may well have incurred the animosity of the Papal Court on this account. According to another tradition, he was murdered by his servant.

Whatever the reasons for his death, there was a well-established tradition that his life was sorrowful. An Italian imitation of the *Roman de la Rose* (*Il Fiore*), written in a series of sonnets towards the end of the thirteenth century by a poet named Durante (who has been by some scholars identified with Dante himself), contains a reference to his suffering and to his death by the sword. Dante, in l. 138, appears to sum up the situation in the phrase "invidious truths", truths, that is, which Sigier taught and which brought him hatred.

That St Thomas should now say that Sigier taught truths, when in the first life he opposed him for propagating falsehoods, is paradoxical indeed. It is impossible that Dante should be making St Thomas eat his words as regards Averroism. The explanation probably lies in the plural use of "truth". It is not the *truth* which Sigier taught, but truths as he saw them and deduced them according to logic. As such, they claimed his intellectual integrity, "that rare and radiant virtue, the scholar's honour".[1]

The overriding and compelling pattern revealed in the choice of souls who form the first circle of the wise is one of reconciliation. Some explicitly (Albertus Magnus, St Thomas Aquinas, Gratian, Peter Lombard), and others implicitly (Dionysius and Boethius), still others by refutation of error and the establishment of verifiable fact (Orosius, Isidore and Bede), and Solomon by the application of his faculty of discernment to the problems of judging between right and wrong, devoted their intellectual powers to the pursuit of the one indivisible Truth of God among the many and various and often conflicting truths of men.

l. 140: *what time the Bride of God doth rise and sing*: i.e. at the hour when Church mattins are sung.

ll. 142–3 : *Where part with part will push and pull, and ring, ding-ding, upon the bell sweet notes*: The movement of the circle of souls (l. 145) is compared to the multiple mechanism of a chiming clock, for as it moves it sings, just as the revolving wheels of a chiming clock release a hammer which plays on a series of bells (cf. Canto xxiv. 13–15 and *note*).

ll. 143–4: *notes that swell with love the soul made apt for worshipping*: The original metaphor, "che il ben disposto spirto d'amor turge" is an erotic one, which an archaic meaning of the word "apt" conveys (cf. *Timon of Athens*:

> . . . she is young and apt:
> Our own precedent passions so instruct us
> What levity's in youth).

1. Channing-Pearce, *The Terrible Crystal*, p. xv. For further discussion of Dante's conception of Sigier of Brabant, see É. Gilson, *Dante the Philosopher*.

CANTO XI

THE STORY. *Still in the Heaven of the Sun, Dante listens again to the voice of St Thomas Aquinas, who explains the meaning of certain words he has used in the preceding canto. His explanation leads him to relate the wondrous love of St Francis for the Lady Poverty.*

O imbecile ambition of mortality!
 What ill-directed reasonings syllogistical
 Weight down thy wings to mundane triviality!

Chasing juridical or aphoristical   4
 Successes, church preferments, domination
 By any methods, brutal or sophistical,

One bent on commerce, one on spoliation,   7
 Another fagging at his carnal pleasure,
 Entoiled, one sprawled in idle dissipation –

There they all were; while I, at blessèd leisure   10
 From all these cares, at Beatrice's side
 Enjoyed Heav'n's welcome in right glorious measure.

When to the point he first had occupied   13
 Each light upon the circle came once more,
 They bode, as candles on their prickets bide;

And from that one which spake to me before   16
 I saw a smile light up within, and blaze
 More radiant yet from out his flaming core:

"Even as I shine, resplendent with His rays,   19
 So, as I contemplate the Light eterne,
 I see what hidden doubts thy mind amaze.

Thou art perplexed, and gladly wouldst thou learn   22
 My meaning, in as explicit and plain
 Terms as thy understanding may discern,

When I said: *Where's good fattening*, and again,   25
 None ever rose – which latter will involve
 A nice distinction, subtle to maintain.

28   The Providence whose rule and sway devolve
         World-wide, and whose unfathomed counsels shroud
         A mystery no created sight can solve,

31   Mindful of her whose Bridegroom, crying loud,
         With His own sacred blood espousèd her –
         That she to her delight might pass endowed

34   With more self-certainty, and livelier
         Faith in her Lord – did at her court instal
         A prince on either hand for counsellor.

37   One of the two was in his ardour all
         Seraphic; one in knowledge was on earth
         A splendour of the light cherubical.

40   Of one I'll speak, for he that lauds the worth
         Of which he will, lauds both in one account,
         Since to one end their labours were brought forth.

43   Between Tupino and the stream whose fount
         Runs from the hill Ubald the Blest selected,
         A fertile slope hangs from a lofty mount

46   Whence heat and cold Perugia feels reflected
         Through Porta Sole; Gualdo and Nocera weep
         Behind it, to their heavy yoke subjected;

49   And bursting from this slope where most the steep
         Is broken, earth saw such a sun's ascent
         As this one makes sometimes from Ganges' deep;

52   Let him who names the place not rest content,
         Then, with *Ascesi* – that's too weak a word;
         Who'd speak aright should say *the Orient*.

55   He'd not long risen when the earth was stirred
         By touches of invigorating power
         From his great strength, as boldly he incurred,

58   Yet young, his father's stern displeasure for
         A Lady's sake, to whom, as unto death,
         No man is eager to unbar the door;

61   And unto her he pledged his wedded faith
         In spiritual court and *coram patre* too,
         And loved her more each day that he drew breath.

150

She, of her first Spouse widowed, had lived through,   64
   Obscure and scorned, twelve centuries, or near,
   With never a lover, till he came to woo.

Nought it availed her that the world should hear   67
   How he whose voice made all men timorous
   Had found her with Amyclas, free from fear;

Nought it availed that she so constant was,   70
   And so courageous, that when Mary stayed
   Below, she leapt with Christ upon the cross.

But, lest too covertly I should proceed,   73
   Know that in all this tale the lovers' parts
   By Francis and by Poverty are played.

Their sweet accord, their gay and amorous arts,   76
   With tender looks, and marvellings, and love
   Roused up such godly motions in men's hearts

That Venerable Bernard first threw off   79
   His shoes and ran, and quick as he went, too slow,
   Running to so great peace, him seemed to move.

O wealth undreamed! O goods that teem and grow!   82
   Sylvester, Giles, they fling off their shoes, they fly
   To follow the groom, the bride delights them so.

Father and master, hence behold him hie,   85
   His lady and his household now beside him,
   Known by the humble cord they're girded by;

And no false shame abashed or mortified him,   88
   Though he was Peter Bernardone's son,
   And though with wondrous scorn the mockers eyed him,

But his fixed purpose, kinglike, he made known   91
   To Innocent, who blessed it, and enrolled
   His Order, setting the first seal thereon.

As that poor following grew, still keeping hold   94
   On him, whose wondrous life would rather merit
   In Heaven's glory to be sung than told,

So came their archimandrite to inherit   97
   A second crown to crown his labours, from
   Honorius, legate to the Holy Spirit.

100   And when, urged on by thirst for martyrdom,
            He had preached Christ and His blest company
            In the Soldàn's proud presence, and had come –

103   Because he found that folk unripe to be
            Converted, and would not stand idle there –
            Homeward to reap his sheaves in Italy,

106   Then he received from Christ, upon the bare
            Ridge between Tiber and Arno, that last seal
            Which two years long his body lived to wear.

109   When He that had ordained him for such weal
            Pleased to exalt unto his guerdon due
            This man made poor and humble by his zeal,

112   He, as unto his lawful heirs, unto
            His brethren did commend his lady dear,
            Bidding them love her and be always true;

115   And from her bosom, with right willing cheer,
            His glorious soul returned to his own realm,
            And for his corse would have no other bier.

118   Think, then, how great was he who at the helm
            Stood as his colleague, holding Peter's bark
            To the right course through the deep waters' whelm:

121   And such a steersman was our patriarch;
            Hence thou wilt see that whoso follows him
            Sails with rich cargo laden to the mark.

124   But now his flock feel such a gluttonous whim
            For fancy foods, they range o'er wood and glen
            Dispersed, and so it needs must be with them.

127   And all the more, the farther from his ken
            The sheep run wild at random through the rough,
            Do they return dry-uddered to the pen.

130   Some, fearing to be lost, cling – true enough –
            Still to their shepherd, but they're few indeed;
            To cut their cowls would take but little stuff.

133   And now, if thou hast heard and paid good heed,
            And if my speech is not ambiguous,
            And if thou dost recall my former rede,

Thy will's half won; for 'twill be obvious   136
  Now, to what kind of tree I have been laying
  The axe, and what rebuke I hinted thus:

Where is good fattening if there be no straying."   139

THE IMAGES. *The Heaven of the Sun*: See Canto x, under *Images*.

St Francis of Assisi: The story of St Francis as related in this canto by
St Thomas Aquinas has features which are significant both for the
literal and the allegorical sense of the poem. In the *story*, the recount-
ing of this great Franciscan epic by a Dominican arises from a need
to clarify a rebuke which St Thomas, himself a Dominican, has
uttered against his own Order. That a Dominican should sing the
praises of the founder of the Franciscans and that a Franciscan should
return the compliment and extol St Dominic (as occurs in Canto
xii) is an instance of the gracious mutuality and harmony of Heaven.
In the *history* of the Church Militant, St Francis is shown to have
been (with St Dominic) divinely ordained as her prince and coun-
sellor. Of St Francis's personality, Dante has chosen to present, with
an epic fervour which leaves unspoken almost every other charac-
teristic of the Saint, that utter renunciation of worldly possessions
which he judged, evidently, to be the most outstanding and efficacious
feature of the Franciscan message. In this, as in the ardour of his love
of God, St Francis is seen by Dante as a new embodiment of the
spirit of Christ on earth.

  (For further information concerning St Francis, see Glossary.)

NOTES. ll. 1–9: This canto opens with an exclamation of scorn and pity
for the pursuit of happiness on earth and the means which men mis-
takenly employ to attain it; among these are the study (for personal
motives of ambition or greed) of law, medicine, theology, statecraft,
and finance, adventuring and plundering, indulgence in the pleasures of
the flesh and, likewise, total idleness. Though all these come under his
contempt, it should not be deduced from this that Dante despised
human activity as such. He is here contrasting the secondary aims of
earthly life with the absolute values of Paradise, for, as he wrote in the
Convivio: "He should not be called a true philosopher who is the friend
of wisdom for gain. as are lawyers, physicians, and almost all in the
religious orders, who do not study for the sake of knowledge but for the
gaining of money or dignities."

  ll. 13–15: The image which Dante has in mind is probably that of a
great circular chandelier, the *corona lucis* which hangs in a cathedral, with
candles all round it, swinging on a central rod. The mediaeval candle
was not set in a socket but on a pricket, as all votive candles are to this
day.

l. 16: *... that one which spake to me before*: St Thomas Aquinas.

ll. 22–6: "*... gladly wouldst thou learn my meaning ... when I said 'Where's good fattening', and again, 'None ever rose'* ": St Thomas knows that Dante is puzzling over two things: (1) the reference (in Canto x. 96) to the "good fattening" to be had on the road along which St Dominic led his flock; and (2) the reference to the wisdom of Solomon (ibid., 113). St Thomas's explanation of this second point will be a gloss on a passage in *I Kings* v–xii. (See Canto xiii. 37–110 and *notes*.)

l. 36: "*A prince on either hand*": The two princes ordained by Providence to guide the Church are St Francis of Assisi and St Dominic.

ll. 37–8: "*One of the two was in his ardour all seraphic*": This is St Francis, inspired by charity. The seraphim are the highest of the angelic orders and symbolical of love. "Seeing more of the First Cause than any other angelic nature", as Dante says of them in *Convivio* II. vi, they therefore love more. For the sources of Dante's information concerning St Francis, see Canto xii. 28–9, *note*. P. H. Wicksteed makes the interesting suggestion that the foregoing account of St Francis may have been written previously as an independent composition and later incorporated in *Paradise*. (From *Vita Nuova to Paradiso*, 1922, p. 151.) It is generally accepted as highly probable that Dante became a tertiary of the Franciscan Order.

ll. 38–9: "*... one in knowledge was on earth a splendour of the light cherubical*": This is St Dominic, characterized especially by his great learning. The cherubim are symbolical of knowledge and the second highest in the angelic hierarchy.

ll. 43–4: "*Between Tupino and the stream whose fount runs from the hill Ubald the Blest selected*": Assisi lies between the river Topino, which runs from the Apennines past Foligno into the Tiber. It rises in a hill near Gubbio which St Ubald selected for his hermitage before he became Bishop of Gubbio. He died in 1160, before he was able to carry out his intention of retiring there.

l. 45: "*a lofty mount*": This is Mt Subasio, from which Perugia receives the rays of the sun reflected back in summer, and the blast of icy winds in winter. (See ll. 46–7.)

ll. 47–8: "*... Gualdo and Nòcera weep*": two small towns in the neighbourhood of Perugia, under whose dominion they were from the end of the thirteenth to the beginning of the fourteenth century. Some commentators understand "the heavy yoke" to be a geographical rather than a historical allusion, in that Mt Subasio offers them no protection from the northerly winds and, on the contrary, robs them of sunlight, whereat they weep.

ll. 49–50: "*... where most the steep is broken*": Assisi is situated on the western side of Mt Subasio where the slope is less steep.

l. 51: "*As this one makes sometimes from Ganges' deep*": It was supposed that the sun rose in the extreme east with a splendour such as was never seen in Europe.

l. 53: "*Ascesi*": This is the old form of the name, Assisi, and is identical with the Italian verb, *I ascended*.

ll. 57–9: "*. . . boldly he incurred . . . his father's stern displeasure for a Lady's sake*": The Lady is Poverty; see below, ll. 61–3.

ll. 61–3: "*And unto her he pledged his wedded faith in spiritual court and 'coram patre' too*": St Francis, before the tribunal of the Bishop of Assisi and in his father's presence, renounced his inheritance and took a vow of poverty, as it were taking Poverty for his bride.

l. 64: "*her first Spouse*": Christ.

l. 68: "*he whose voice made all men timorous*": Julius Caesar.

l. 69: *Amyclas*: a poor fisherman, who transported Caesar in his boat across the Adriatic from Epirus to Italy. Dante had read of the episode in Lucan's *Pharsalia* and refers to it in the *Convivio* (IV. xiii) as an example of the freedom (from care) which poverty bestows.

l. 72: "*she leapt with Christ upon the cross*": Poverty kept company with Christ on the Cross in that He was naked. A prayer, ascribed to St Francis, addressed to Poverty contains the phrase: "when Thy very Mother, because the Cross was so high, could not reach Thee, Lady Poverty embraced Thee more closely."

ll. 79–80: "*That Venerable Bernard first threw off his shoes and ran*": This is Bernard of Quintavalle, surnamed the Venerable, who was the first follower of St Francis. He was a wealthy merchant of Assisi. At first he distrusted St Francis but, on being convinced of his sincerity, he sold his own possessions for the good of the poor and submitted himself to the rule of poverty. After the death of St Francis, he became head of the Franciscan Order. The eager running and the baring of the feet, expressive of the ardour with which the followers of St Francis embraced poverty, are mentioned in the Latin *Life of St Francis* by Tommaso di Celano, whom Dante follows here.

l. 83: "*Sylvester, Giles*": St Sylvester, one of the earliest followers of St Francis, was a priest concerning whom it is related that, having sold St Francis some stone for the repairs of the Church of San Damiano, he felt remorse at having overcharged him and became one of his disciples. St Giles was the third follower (the second, Peter, is not mentioned by Dante). He was a native of Assisi and the author of a book called *Verba Aurea* ("Golden Words"). He died in Perugia in 1272.

ll. 91–2: "*. . . he made known to Innocent*": The reference here is to Pope Innocent III, elected in 1198. He died in Perugia in 1216. It was he who in 1214 formally sanctioned the Order of St Francis.

l. 97: "*archimandrite*": Dante gives to St Francis a title in use in the Greek Church for one who has the supervision of many convents. It corresponds to the title of "Provincial" in the western Church.

ll. 98–9: "*A second crown to crown his labours from Honorius*": Pope Honorius III, elected in succession to Innocent in 1216, solemnly con- ̄...ed the Franciscan Order in 1223.

ll. 100–105: In 1219, at the time of the fifth Crusade, St Francis joined

the Crusading army at Damietta and made his way into the camp of the
Sultan, El-Melik El-Kamil. The Sultan received him courteously and
listened to his preaching, but remained unconverted. He was given a safe
escort back to the Crusaders' camp and from there returned to Italy.

ll. 106–108: "*. . . the bare ridge between Tiber and Arno*": In the year
1224, St Francis was on Mt Alvernia for the purpose of fasting for forty
days. He prayed that he might experience something of Our Lord's
sufferings on the Cross, and received the stigmata on his hands, feet and
side. He was said to bear these wounds for two years, until his death in
1226.

l. 117: "*and for his corse would have no other bier*": It is related that on
dying St Francis requested that his body be stripped naked, laid on the
bare earth and sprinkled with ashes, as a token that even in death he
remained faithful to the Lady Poverty.

ll. 118–20: "*how great was he*": The reference here is to St Dominic
who, like St Francis, had been predestined by God to steer the bark of
the Church.

l. 122: "*whoso follows him*": whoever lives according to the rule of the
Dominican Order.

ll. 124–5: "*But now his flock feel such a gluttonous whim for fancy foods*":
But the Dominicans have grown greedy for honours and preferments.

l. 136: "*Thy will's half won*": St Thomas has now removed the first
of the two sources of perplexity mentioned in ll. 22–6.

CANTO XII

THE STORY. *At the conclusion of St Thomas's discourse, the circle of lights begins once more to revolve and is itself encircled by a second ring of twelve more lights. One of the new arrivals, St Bonaventure, the Franciscan, extols the life and works of St Dominic, just as, in the preceding canto, St Thomas, the Dominican, has extolled St Francis. Finally, St Bonaventure names himself and the other lights that circle with him.*

As the last word fell from the blessèd fire,
    Straightway the heavenly millstone set in train
    Its former motion and melodious gyre;

Nor had it come full circle once again   4
    Before another ringed it all the way,
    Measure with measure matching, strain with strain:

Strains which in those sweet pipes the loveliest lay   7
    Of Muse or Siren here as far outdo
    As a first splendour its reflected ray.

Like as, concentric and of self-same hue,   10
    When Juno has sent forth her handmaiden,
    'Mid filmy clouds the double bow glides through –

The outer iris born of that within,   13
    In fashion of her wistful voice whom love
    Consumed like vapours that the sun drinks in;

Whence men foreknow that never flood shall move   16
    A second time to drown the world beneath –
    Such was God's pledge to Noah, such the proof;

So did those sempiternal roses wreathe   19
    Twofold about us and, antiphonal
    In song, the outer to the inner breathe.

Then, when the dance and the high festival   22
    Made up of singing and of leaping flame,
    Light upon light serene and joyous, all

By one mind moved, and at one moment, came   25
    To rest, as when the will that moves the eyes
    Together shuts or opens both of them,

28   From one new heart of fire was heard to rise
        A voice, that like the needle to the pole
        Turned me to whence it came; and on this wise

31   It spoke: "The love that makes me beautiful
        Bids me proclaim that captain who praised mine
        With such fair words, and him in turn extol;

34   One with the other we must still combine,
        And as they waged their warfare side by side,
        Let side by side their mingled glory shine.

37   Following its banner with uncertain stride,
        Christ's army, once rearmed at such dear cost,
        Was straggling on, thin-ranked and terrified,

40   So that the eternal Emperor was disposed –
        Not by their merit, but by His sole grace –
        To reinforce His gravely threatened host,

43   And for His Bride's relief was pleased to raise
        Two champions, fit (as has been shown to us)
        By word and deed to rally those poor strays.

46   Within that province where sweet Zephyrus
        Swells till the springtide foliage is unfurled,
        Wherewith all Europe is made beauteous,

49   Nor distant from that coastline where the hurled
        Waves beat in which, his longest course pursued,
        The sun at times hides him from all the world,

52   Long time hath happy Calahorra stood,
        Protected by the mighty shield which shows
        The lion by turns subduing and subdued;

55   And in that town was born the amorous
        Sweet leman of the Faith, the wrestler-saint,
        Kind to his friends and ruthless to his foes;

58   A soul created so pre-eminent
        In living might, that a prophetic power
        From her womb's burden through his mother went.

61   And when the sacred font in nuptial hour
        Had wed the Faith to him and him to her,
        With their salvation for their mutual dower,

The lady who stood sponsor for him there   64
  Dreamed of the wondrous fruit that afterward
  He and his heirs should foster by their care;

And there, that name and nature might accord,   67
  Seeing Whose he was, the Spirit going forth
  Named him by the possessive of the Lord.

Dominic was his name, whose work and worth   70
  I publish, as the husbandman whom Christ
  Called to His garden to help till the earth.

Right well the friend and messenger of Christ   73
  He showed him, for the first love he displayed
  Was love for the first counsel given by Christ.

Full many a time his nurse would find him laid   76
  On the bare gound, silent and wide awake,
  As though to say: 'For this end I was made.'

O father, well named Felix for his sake!   79
  O thou his mother, rightly named Joanna
  If name makes meaning, as 'tis said to make!

Not for the world's love, in the modern manner   82
  Of those who pore on him of Ostia, and
  Thaddeus, but for love of the true manna

He grew a mighty doctor soon, who scanned   85
  In every part that vine which, all too sure
  Withers if dressed by an unskilful hand.

And from that See which once, but now no more –   88
  (I blame not it, but him who there doth fix
  His cankered sway) cherished the righteous poor,

No leave to pay out three or two for six,   91
  No tithes *quae pauperum Dei sunt* sought he,
  Nor first cut at fat stalls and bishoprics,

But only licence to fight ceaselessly   94
  Against the erring world for that good seed
  Whence four-and-twenty scions girdle thee.

With Apostolic sanction guaranteed,   97
  Equipped with doctrine and with zeal as well,
  Like some high torrent thundering down at speed

100   On briars and brakes of heresy he fell
           Uprooting them, and still was swift to go
           Where opposition was most formidable.

103   From him, unnumbered rillets took their flow
           To irrigate the Catholic garden-plot
           Thenceforth, whence all its bushes greener grow.

106   If such was one wheel of the chariot
           That Holy Church employed for her defence
           In civil war, and thus her victory got,

109   Thou canst not doubt the other's excellence,
           Whose tale, before my coming here, was told
           By Thomas with such courtly eloquence.

112   Alas! the track that wheel's wide felly rolled
           Is quite abandoned now and out of mind,
           And in the cask the crust has turned to mould.

115   His family, once orderly aligned
           Following his steps, have so turned head to tail
           That those in front collide with those behind.

118   But soon shall come the harvest, with its tale
           Of rank bad farming, and the tares be cast
           Out of the barn and loud shall be their wail.

121   True, if one searched our volume first to last
           Leaf after leaf, he'd find one now and then
           Inscribed, *Where once I stood I still stand fast;*

124   But such will not be found among the men
           Of Aquasparta or Casal, who play
           Now fast, now loose with rule and discipline.

127   Bonaventura's life makes bright my ray,
           Surnamed of Bagnoreggio; temporal ends
           Came second always where I held high sway.

130   Here Austen with Illuminato blends
           His fire; with those poor brethren first to go
           Barefoot, these took the cord to be God's friends.

133   Hugh of St Victor's here with them, and so
           Are Peter Mangiador, Peter of Spain
           Who in twelve books enlightens men below,

Nathan the Prophet, metropolitan   136
    Chrysostom, Anselm, and Donatus, who
    Taught the first art and thought it no disdain.

Here stands Rabanus; here, and last in view,   139
    Calabria's abbot ends where I begin:
    Joachim, spirit-fired, and prophet true.

To emulous praise of that great paladin,   142
    The modest speech and glowing courtesy
    Of Brother Thomas moved me, and therein

Moved all this fellowship to join with me."   145

THE IMAGES. *The Heaven of the Sun:* See Canto x, under *Images.*
The second circle of twelve lights: The second garland of lights, which, at
the conclusion of St Thomas's discourse, encircles the first, consists of
a further twelve spirits, most of whom were followers of St Francis.
By the perfect accord and harmony between the two circles, com-
pared to the co-ordination of two eyes which open and shut in
obedience to a single controlling mind, Dante conveys his concep-
tion of the divine union and inter-relation of love and learning, of
seraphic ardour and cherubic insight, the former being born of the
latter, since, in the Thomist theology, knowledge of God precedes
love. In the lesser, historical, sense, this image, suggesting an ideal
partnership between these and other Orders, rebukes all worldly
rivalry between the ideals of renunciation and of learning.
St Dominic: The founder of the Dominican Order is presented, together
with St Francis, as one of the two champions divinely destined to
rally the straggling army of Christ. His story, as related by the
Franciscan, St Bonaventure, is one of loving self-surrender to the
combat for the Faith, to which he brought the relentless weapons of
his zeal and learning. By his victory over heresy, the Christian faith
was and still continues to be restored and invigorated.

NOTES. l. 2: *the heavenly millstone* etc.: The circle of twelve lights which
had been revolving horizontally round Dante and Beatrice in Canto x
now resumes its gyration and its song.
    l. 11: *When Juno has sent forth her handmaiden:* The handmaiden of
Juno is Iris, the rainbow.
    ll. 13–15: *The outer iris born of that within* etc.: In a double rainbow, the
outer ring is of fainter hue than the inner. For this reason it was believed
that the outer was a *reflection* of the inner, and it is this which Dante seeks
to convey by comparing the reflection to an echo. The one "whom love
consumed" is the nymph, Echo, who wasted away for love of Narcissus.
    ll. 16–18: *Whence men foreknow that never flood shall move* etc.: The

sight of the rainbow in the sky is a reminder to man of God's pact with Noah: "And I will establish my covenant with you; neither shall all flesh be cut off any more by the waters of a flood; neither shall there any more be a flood to destroy the earth. And God said, This is the token of the covenant which I make between me and you and every living creature that is with you, for perpetual generations: I do set my bow in the cloud, and it shall be for a token of a covenant between me and the earth." (*Gen.* ix. 11–13.)

ll. 24–7: *all by one mind moved and, at one moment*: i.e. moving in accordance with a single, unanimous will and with perfect synchronization (cf. Canto xx. 146).

ll. 28–9: *From one new heart of fire was heard to rise a voice*: This is the voice of St Bonaventure (Giovanni Fidanza), who was appointed General of the Franciscans in 1255. He is the author of the official biography of St Francis, the *Legenda Major S. Francisci*, from which Dante's account of St Francis in Canto xi is partly derived. The earlier account of St Francis by Tommaso di Celano laid even more stress than Bonaventure's on the absolute poverty embraced by the first Franciscans. St Bonaventure was concerned to reconcile certain opposing tendencies within the Order and consequently he glosses over or omits the descriptions he found in Tommaso of the hardships endured in the early years. Dante, in stressing the poverty of St Francis, seems to range himself on the side of the Spirituals, or stricter sect of Franciscans. (See John R. H. Moorman, *The Sources for the Life of S. Francis of Assisi*, Manchester University Press, 1940.)

l. 32: "*that captain*": St Bonaventure intends now to extol St Dominic, who is conceived of, ultimately, as the author of the praise which St Thomas has uttered concerning St Francis.

l. 38: "*Christ's army, once rearmed at such dear cost*": i.e. humanity, redeemed by the blood of Christ.

l. 44: "*Two champions*": i.e. St Francis and St Dominic.

l. 46: "*that province*": Spain, where the west wind rises, carrying the Spring into Europe.

l. 49: "*that coastline*": i.e. of the Bay of Biscay.

ll. 50–51: "*in which, his longest course pursued, the sun at times hides him from all the world*": During the summer solstice (i.e. after the longest day of the year) the sun sets in the Atlantic directly opposite the west coast of Spain. By the phrase "from all the world", Dante means "from all inhabitants of the northern hemisphere". The southern hemisphere was believed by mediaeval cosmographers to consist entirely of water. In Dante's cosmography the only land there is the Mountain of Purgatory.

ll. 52–4: "*Long time hath happy Calahorra stood*" etc.: The city of Calahorra was in the dominion of the kings of Old Castile, in whose arms were quartered two castles and two lions, one lion being above one of the castles, and the other lion beneath the other castle; hence the lion is described by Dante as "by turns subduing and subdued".

ll. 58–60: "*A soul created so pre-eminent*" etc.: The human soul is created individually and directly by God and implanted in the foetus as soon as the brain is sufficiently formed to receive and sustain it (cf. *Purg.* xxv). Thus the mother of St Dominic, under the influence of the soul of her unborn son, dreamed her prophetic dream that she would give birth to a dog with a burning torch in its mouth. The Dominicans are called "the dogs of the Lord" (i.e. from the Latin, *Domini canes*).

ll. 61–3: These lines refer to the baptism of St Dominic.

l. 64: *The lady who stood sponsor for him there*: i.e. the godmother of St Dominic, concerning whom it is related that she dreamed of him with a bright star in his brow which illumined the world.

l. 69: "*Named him by the possessive of the Lord*": This is a reference to the name of St Dominic, which means "the Lord's".

l. 75: "*the first counsel given by Christ*": It is not certain which of Christ's counsels is intended here. St Thomas, distinguishing between the precepts and counsels of Christ, said that the counsels could all be reduced to three: poverty, chastity, and obedience. Commentators who believe the line to be an allusion to some passage in the New Testament are divided in their views. Some think it may be a reference to the first beatitude in the Sermon on the Mount: "Blessed are the poor in spirit' (*Matth.* v. 3). If this is so, St Dominic's first love was for humility. Others see in it an allusion to the reply of Christ to the one who asked "What good thing shall I do, that I may have eternal life?" – "If thou wilt be perfect, go and sell that thou hast, and give to the poor, and thou shalt have treasure in heaven: and come and follow me". (*Matth.* xix. 16, 21.)

l. 81: "*If name makes meaning, as 'tis said to make!*": The Platonic doctrine that the inherent quality of things issued in their names, current among mediaeval philosophers and grammarians, is reflected in Dante's *Vita Nuova*, where he quotes the formula "nomina sunt consequentia rerum" ("names are the consequences of things", *V.N.* xiii. 4; see also xxiv. 4). Felix de Guzman, the father of Dominic, was well named, in that he was happy and blessed in his son; likewise, his mother, Giovanna (Joan), whose name means (in Hebrew) "abounding in the grace of Jehovah", is an instance of a similar relationship between name and specific virtue.

ll. 82–5: "*Not for the world's love*" etc.: St Dominic gave himself to a life of learning, not out of personal ambition, but for love of true knowledge and wisdom (cf. the opening lines of Canto xi). Dante here contrasts St Dominic with the theologians who pore over the works of Henry of Susa ("him of Ostia") and with the doctors of medicine who follow the teachings of Thaddeus Alderotti.

Henry of Susa (Enrico Bartolomei) was Archbishop of Embrun and Cardinal of Ostia in 1261. He died in 1271. He is the author of a famous commentary on the Decretals, i.e. the Papal decrees which form the groundwork of a large part of Roman ecclesiastical law. Dante considered that the study of the Gospel and of the early patristic writings was being neglected, and that attention was paid by theologians to the Decretals alone (cf. Canto xi. 133–5). He also held that, though the Decretals were worthy of veneration, they were not to be regarded as of higher authority than Holy Scripture. His disapproval is levelled not at the Decretals, but at the "Decretalists", whom he considers totally lacking in a true knowledge of theology and philosophy. The following passage from his treatise on world government, *De Monarchia*, may be taken as representing his attitude: "The Decretalists [are] ... ignorant in every kind of theology and philosophy, who carp at the empire, laying all their weight upon their Decretals (which, for the matter of that, I hold to be worthy of reverence), and setting their hopes, I take it, on the supremacy of the same. And no wonder; for I have heard one of them declare and volubly maintain that the traditions of the Church are the foundation of the faith; may which impious thought be extirpated from the minds of men."

Thaddeus Alderotti is instanced here as an example of the self-seeking physician, pursuing his profession for love of gain. He wrote commentaries on the works of Hippocrates and Galen.

l. 86: *"that vine"*: i.e. the Church. St Doninic tended the Lord's vineyard, removing the weeds of false doctrine and strengthening it with the reasonings of true theology and Christian faith.

ll. 88–90: *"And from that See"* etc.: Dante draws an important distinction between the Papacy, which is guiltless, and the present Pope, Boniface VIII.

ll. 91–3: *"No leave to pay out three or two for six"*: St Dominic did not apply to the Pope (as did so many ecclesiastics) for a dispensation to be allowed to pay one-third or one-half only of the sum due to the poor, nor for the tithes which belong to God's poor (*quae sunt pauperum Dei*), nor for the first vacant benefice.

ll. 94–6: *"But only licence to fight ceaselessly"* etc.: He applied only for permission to fight against the erring world on behalf of the Truth, twenty-four symbols of which now encircle Dante. By the "erring world" is probably meant the Albigensians, against whom Dominic's Order was authorized to preach.

l. 102: *"where opposition was most formidable"*: i.e. in Provence, where the Albigensian heresy was most tenacious. St Dominic has been regarded as a relentless persecutor of heretics and the founder of the Inquisition. In fact, the inquisitorial functions did not become attached to his Order until some years after his death, nor did he take any considerable part in the persecution of the Albigensians. (A crusade against them was launched in 1209.)

l. 109: *"the other's excellence"*: i.e. the excellence of St Francis.

ll. 112–17: *"Alas! the track that wheel's wide felly rolled"* etc. St. Bonavenure turns now to censure the degenerate state of the Franciscan Order.

ll. 124–5: "*among the men of Aquasparta or Casal*": St Bonaventure is referring here to Matthew of Aquasparta (a village in Umbria), who, on being appointed General of the Franciscan Order in 1287, introduced relaxations of discipline. He was strongly opposed in this by Ubertino of Casale (a town in Piedmont), who with his followers adopted a narrower and more literal interpretation of the Franciscan Rule. Pope Clement V did what he could to reconcile the two factions.

ll. 127–8: "*Bonaventura's life makes bright my ray, surnamed of Bagnoreggio*": Now, for the first time, St Bonaventure announces his identity. Bagnoreggio (now Bagnorea), his birthplace, is a village on the top of a hill, about eight miles south of Orvieto. He was born in 1221 and entered the Franciscan Order at the age of twenty-two, becoming General of it in 1257. He became a Cardinal and was appointed Bishop of Albano in 1272. He died in Lyons in 1274. His life of the founder of his Order, "The Legend of St Francis", a prose narrative in Latin, is closely followed by Dante in the account of St Francis in Canto xi. His philosophic writings were markedly mystical in character (as contrasted with the more intellectual and reasoned works of St Thomas) and earned for him the title of Doctor Seraphicus. He is not here presented as a contemplative, however. As E. Gilson has pointed out: "Obviously such a life is not that of a pure philosopher. It was not given over totally to the contemplation of abstract truths. St Bonaventure is not only the leader of a philosophical school, an extremely fertile writer, a theologian and a mystic; he is likewise a man of action, an administrator of a great religious Order and of the race of the leaders of men" (*Philosophy of St Bonaventure*, p. 35).

ll. 130–45: "*Here Austen with Illuminato blends his fire*" etc.: St Bonaventure now tells Dante the names of the other souls who compose the second circle of lights. (A diagram, incorporating the inner circle, is given for the convenience of the reader on page 166.) *Austen* is Fra Agostino, a Franciscan friar. *Illuminato*, also a Franciscan, accompanied St Francis to the Holy Land and later became head of his Order in the Terra di Lavoro.

l. 133: "*Hugh of St Victor*": He was a Fleming born in Ypres in 1097. He entered the monastery of St Victor in Paris in 1133 and died in 1141. Among his pupils were Richard of St Victor and Peter Lombard, who are present in the inner ring. His theological writings aimed at combating rationalism and are considered by St Thomas Aquinas to be of great authority.

l. 134: "*Peter Mangiador*": Better known by the name of Petrus Comestor, he was born at the beginning of the twelfth century in Troyes, where he became Dean of the Cathedral in 1147. He died in the monastery of St Victor in 1179. His best known work is the *Historia scholastica*, a recompilation of the books of the Bible. Dante follows his estimate of the duration of Adam's stay in Eden (cf. Canto xxvi. 139–42 and *note*). "*Peter of Spain*": He was born in Portugal about 1226, the

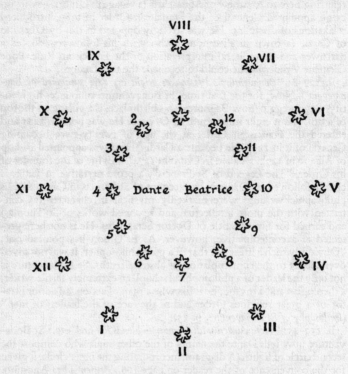

The Double Circle of Souls

1. St Thomas Aquinas	I. St Bonaventure
2. Albertus Magnus	II. Illuminato
3. Gratian	III. Fra Agostino
4. Peter Lombard	IV. Hugh of St Victor
5. Solomon	V. Petrus Comestor
6. Dionysius the Areopagite	VI. Peter of Spain
7. Orosius	VII. Nathan
8. Boethius	VIII. St Chrysostom
9. St Isidore	IX. St Anselm
10. Bede	X. Donatus
11. Richard of St Victor	XI. Rabanus
12. Sigier of Brabant	XII. Joachim of Flora

son of a physician of Lisbon. He became Archbishop of Braga, and in 1276 was elected Pope, taking the title of John XXI. He died in 1277 after a reign of only eight months, his death being caused by the fall of the ceiling of one of his rooms in his palace at Viterbo. His well-known manual of logic, entitled *Summulae Logicales* and divided into twelve books, expanded the logic of the schoolmen by the introduction of new material of a semi-grammatical nature.

ll. 136–7: "*Nathan the Prophet*": The story of Nathan's rebuke to David is told in *II Samuel* xii. 1–15. It is thought that Dante couples him with Chrysostom because they were both outspoken in rebuking the sins of kings. "*St John Chrysostom*" was born in Antioch about 344. He became renowned for his preaching and was made patriarch of Constantinople (397). He publicly rebuked the Empress Theodosia for her life of wanton luxury and was sentenced to be banished. The people rose in revolt against the sentence and he was reinstated, only to be exiled again to the shores of the Black Sea, where he died in Comana in Pontus in 407. "*Anselm*": Archbishop of Canterbury was born in Aosta in Piedmont in 1033. He became a monk in the Abbey of Bec in Normandy and succeeded Lanfranc as prior of the Abbey of Caen. William Rufus appointed him Archbishop of Canterbury. His best known theological writing is the famous *Cur Deus Homo*, a treatise on the Atonement intended to prove the necessity of the Incarnation. His arguments are summarized by Beatrice in Canto vii. "*Donatus*": the Roman grammarian of the fourth century, author of the famous treatise on elementary Latin grammar, *De octo partibus Orationis* ("On the eight parts of speech"). "The first art" is grammar, the first of the quadrivium.

l. 139: "*Here stands Rabanus*": Rabanus Maurus, a learned theologian, was Archbishop of Mayence and the author of many works of theology and Biblical exegesis. His treatise, *De Laudibus Sanctae Crucis* ("On the praise of the Holy Cross"), contains figures in which rows of letters are arranged in stars, crosses, and other similar symbols. It has been suggested that Dante may have borrowed from him the idea of representing the spirits as arranging themselves in the shape of letters to form the words "Diligite iustitiam qui iudicatis terram". (See Canto xviii.)

ll. 140–41: "*Calabria's abbot*": The Abbot Joachim of Flora, preacher and visionary, and for a great part of his life a hermit in the wild hill country of Calabria, was the originator of the doctrine that the dispensation of the Father (Old Testament) and of the Son (New Testament) would be followed by the dispensation of the Holy Ghost, a period of perfection, freedom and peace, the *Sabbatum Fidelium* (Sabbath of the Faithful). Joachim was a Cistercian whose influence extended beyond his own Order, especially among the "Spirituals" of the Franciscans. It is considered by some scholars that Dante himself was much influenced by Joachism. If, as is also held by some, Dante became a member of the Franciscan Order, he would have come into contact with the influence of Joachism in the extreme Spiritual movement among the Franciscans. It is noteworthy that Joachim is called a true prophet by St Bonaventure in Dante's narrative, whereas in life Bonaventure was an opponent of Joachism. This juxtaposition corresponds symmetrically, and significantly, to that of St Thomas and Sigier of Brabant in the inner ring. (See Canto x. 136 and *note*).

l. 142: *"that great paladin"*: i.e. St Dominic.

CANTO XIII

THE STORY. *The double circle, composed of twenty-four lights, again revolves round Dante and Beatrice, singing of the Three Persons in the one nature of God and of the two natures in the one Person of Christ. They pause again and St Thomas resolves the second perplexity to which his previous words (in Canto x) gave rise in Dante's mind. He concludes with a warning against making hasty judgements, whether intellectual or moral.*

Let him imagine who would fully grasp
    What then I saw – and while I speak hold tight,
    Like a firm rock, that image in his clasp –

The fifteen stars that here and there so bright   4
    Enkindle heaven that of their rays take toll
    No densest vapours in the air of night;

Imagine that true Wain, content to roll   7
    Through our own skies, that so, by eve or morn,
    The plough lacks never to its turning pole;

Imagine, too, the bell-mouth of the horn   10
    Whose point springs from the axle's tip on high
    Round which the Primum Mobile is borne;

That all these stars have formed upon the sky   13
    Two signs like that which Minos' daughter traced
    When the chill took her and she came to die;

That like a ring within a ring embraced   16
    They shine, and both together make rotation,
    Each in its pacing by the other paced;

He'll get some shadow of the constellation   19
    And double dance that really circled so
    About the spot whereon I kept my station;

Just a faint shadow – for these things o'ergo   22
    As much our usage as the sphere that runs
    Swiftest of all outspeeds the Chiana's flow.

Bacchus nor Paean made their antiphons,   25
    But the One Nature in the Persons Three,
    And in One Person that and ours at once.

28   Their measure done of dance and melody,
            The sacred fires again gave heed to us,
            Turning from task to task with right good glee.

31   The light who'd told me all that marvellous
            Tale of the Lord's first mendicant, then broke
            The hush of the harmonious hallows thus: –

34   "With one sheaf threshed already" (so he spoke)
            "And the seed stored, love's kindness makes me fain
            To bring the next one to the swingle-stroke.

37   Into that breast, thou thinkest, whence was ta'en
            The rib from which the cheek was fashioned fair
            Whose palate brought about the whole world's bane,

40   And into that which felt the thrusting spear,
            And so for past and future paid the fine
            Which on those scales outweighs all sin soe'er,

43   Such light as may in human nature shine
            Was all infused by Him that did create
            Both one and other with His power divine;

46   Hence thy surprise at what I said of late,
            Namely, that this fifth light of ours doth hold
            An excellence that ne'er had duplicate.

49   Open thine eyes to what I now unfold,
            And see! my word and thy belief have shot
            Alike at truth, and both have hit the gold.

52   All that which dies and all that dieth not
            Is naught but splendour of the Idea that knows
            The Father's Love whereby It is begot;

55   Because the living Luminance that flows
            Forth of Its Luminant, yet parts not thence,
            Nor from the Love that aye in-trines with Those,

58   Doth, of Its grace, converge Its radiance,
            Glassed as it were, in nine subsistences,
            Itself still One, eterne in permanence;

61   Which radiance thence to the last potencies
            Descends, from act to act, becoming even
            Such as to make mere brief contingencies –

An epithet, as I conceive it, given   64
  To things engendered, formed, as requisite,
  From seed, or seedless, by the moving heaven.

Now, more or less of light such things transmit   67
  When stamped with the Idea, so variable
  Are both the wax and that which stampeth it;

Wherefore the tree brings forth good fruit or ill   70
  After its kind, and mortals are born rich
  In various gifts of intellectual skill.

Were the wax always wrought to perfect pitch,   73
  Might at full power the spheres unchanging stand,
  The signet's light would shine complete in each;

But Nature fumbles, with no sure command   76
  Over her tools, like an artificer
  Who knows his trade but has a trembling hand.

Yet, should Love's self on what His fires prepare   79
  Stamp the clear Image of the Primal Worth,
  Total perfection would be compassed there;

Such act it was that dignified dull earth   82
  To mould the noblest animal of all;
  Such act it was begat the Virgin-birth.

Thou judgest well: it never did befall   85
  Man's nature, truly, to be what it was
  In those two persons, and it never shall.

Should I proceed no further, but here pause: 88
  'That other, then, without a peer confest',
  Thou wouldst begin, 'how so? and what the cause?'

That the obscure may now be manifest,   91
  Think who he was, and think with what intent,
  When bidden 'Choose', he proffered his request.

A king he was, so runs my argument,   94
  And wisdom did he crave for his behoof,
  That as a king he might be competent;

Not how to count these movers high aloof,   97
  Or know if e'er contingent and *necesse*
  Could yield *necesse* in the final proof;

100   Not *si est dare primum motum esse,*
      Or if 'triangles in half-circles must
      Be right-angled' states facts with accuracy.

103   Take this along with what we first discussed;
      Then, kingly prudence is that insight true
      My shaft was aimed at, and *unmatched* is just;

106   And if that phrase *none rose* thou rightly view
      Thou'lt see that kings alone are meant by this,
      Whereof are many, but the good ones few.

109   With this distinction take, nor take amiss,
      My words, consistent thus with thy true thought
      Concerning the First Father and Our Bliss;

112   And to thy feet be this a hobble, wrought
      Of lead, to make thee move at sluggard pace
      Toward Yea and Nay where thou perceivest naught,

115   For low among the dunces is his place
      Who hastens to accept or to reject
      With no distinction made 'twixt case and case;

118   Thence come rash judgements, mostly incorrect
      And prejudiced, and stubborn all the more
      That self-conceit shackles the intellect.

121   Worse than in vain does any quit the shore
      To fish for truth, the fisher's art unknowing –
      He'll not return the man he was before;

124   Witness Parmenides' and Bryson's showing
      In the world's eyes, Melissus – school on school
      Who went their way, nor knew where they were going;

127   Sabellius, too, and Arius – every fool
      That e'er distorted Scripture, as a sword
      Distorts straight faces into fanciful.

130   No one should ever be too self-assured
      In judgement, like a farmer reckoning
      His gains before the corn-crop is matured,

133   For I have seen the briar a prickly thing
      And tough the winter through, and on its tip
      Bearing the very rose at close of spring;

And once I saw, her whole long ocean-trip   136
  Safe done, a vessel wrecked upon the bar,
  And down she went, that swift and stately ship.

Let Jack and Jill not think they see so far   139
  That, seeing this man pious, that a thief,
  They see them such as in God's sight they are,

For one may rise, the other come to grief."   142

THE IMAGES. *The Heaven of the Sun*: see Canto x, under *Images*.

The Wisdom of Solomon: In the *story*, St Thomas's discourse on the peerless wisdom of Solomon arises from the need to distinguish between the wisdom of kings and the wisdom of all men. This is preceded by a preliminary discourse on direct and indirect creation, in which the wisdom of Solomon is seen as a reflection of the Word of God. In the *allegory*, God's gift of kingly wisdom to Solomon is an instance of the specific qualities (and limitations) of all men, resulting from the varying dispositions and influences of the heavens at the time of their birth and from the imperfect nature of the material of which they are made. The legend of Solomon's wisdom is divested by St Thomas of all mystery and set coherently within the rational structure of logic and orthodoxy. Yet, in the process, a far greater mystery is seen to emerge: the mystery as to how an imperfect world can be produced from the operations of nature on primal matter, both themselves direct creations of God.

St Thomas Aquinas: In this canto, St Thomas, firmly guiding Dante away from undefined and ambiguous terms along the disciplined path of intellectual deliberation and distinctions, warning him, too, against unreasoned and hasty judgements, is a natural symbol of the influence which his writings had on Dante's mental growth. From no one, as from Aquinas, had Dante learnt intellectual integrity, and, more than any other Christian teacher, he summed up for Dante the doctrine of God. It is fitting, therefore, that for three cantos Aquinas should be his mentor, playing in this capacity the longest role after Beatrice.

NOTES. l. 4: *The fifteen stars*: Dante presumably intends the reader to imagine the fifteen stars of the first magnitude which were visible to the world as it was known in his time. They are the following: Sirius (Canis Major), Capra (Auriga), Arcturus (Boötes), Vega (Lyra), Rigel (Orion), Procion (Canis Minor), Bethelgeuse (Orion), Altair (Aquila), Aldebaran (Taurus), Spica (Virgo), Antares (Scorpio), Pollux (Gemini), Regulus (Leo), Fomalhaut (Piscis australis), Deneb (Cignus).

ll. 7–9: *Imagine that true Wain* etc.: The Great Bear (Ursa Major) never sets in the northern hemisphere.

173

ll. 10–12: *Imagine, too, the bell-mouth of the horn* etc.: The Little Bear (Ursa Minor) is here compared to a horn, the wide mouth of which is formed by the two stars, Beta and Gamma. The narrow end, or tip, consists of the Pole Star and is the axis on which the Primum Mobile revolves. The comparison of Ursa Minor to a horn was well known to Spanish sailors in the sixteenth century, and Richard Eden, in his translation from the Spanish of the *Arte of Navigation* (1561), calls Beta and Gemma of Ursa Minor "the guardians, or the mouth, of the horne". See diagram which follows.

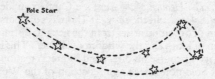

l. 13: *That all these stars*: The fifteen stars of the first magnitude (l. 4), the seven stars of the Great Bear (l. 7), and the two stars at the bell-mouth of the horn of the Little Bear (l. 10) make twenty-four stars in all.

ll. 14–15: *Two signs like that which Minos' daughter traced* etc.: When Ariadne (Minos' daughter) died, the garland she had worn at her marriage with Bacchus was changed into the constellation known as Ariadne's Crown. This is the Corona Borealis, or the Northern Crown, which suggests a circle, though not a perfect one. The reader is to imagine a double circle or crown, composed of lights at least as bright as the twenty-four stars recalled.

ll. 22–4: *Just a faint shadow* etc.: After all the effort of imagination which the reader is called upon to make, conjuring up in his mind stars from the remotest regions of the heavens, visualizing their brightness and arranging them in a new pattern, even then the imagined result will fall far short of the realities of Heaven. The brilliance of the double ring which Dante saw as far exceeds the brightest constellation we can imagine as the speed of the Primum Mobile exceeds the pace of the sluggish river Chiana. (The Chiana, in the territory of Arezzo, was in Dante's day a sluggish stream, almost stagnating in the marshes of Valdichiana.)

l. 25: *Bacchus nor Paean made their antiphons*: Paean was one of the names applied to Apollo. The song the souls sing in Paradise is quite other than the songs of the Bacchanals or of the priests of Delos.

ll. 31–2: *The light who'd told me all that marvellous tale of the Lord's first mendicant*: St Thomas, who had told the story of St Francis.

ll. 34–6: "*With one sheaf threshed already*" etc.: St Thomas refers here to the first explanation he has given (i.e. of the line, "Where is good fattening if there be no straying") and is now about to explain the other, "None ever rose" (cf. Canto x. ll. 96, 109–14).

ll. 37–45: "*Into that breast*" etc.: St Thomas had said (Canto x. 112 *et sqq.*) that in the mind of Solomon such wisdom was implanted that never had a second arisen who had such profound insight. This has (as St Thomas knows) left Dante in some doubt, for was not the wisdom of Adam and of Christ more profound than that of Solomon?

ll. 52–4: "*All that which dies and all that dieth not*" etc.: St Thomas's explanation involves a discourse on creation. All created things, whether mortal or immortal, are reflections of the Word, or Idea, of God.

ll. 55–7: "*Because the living Luminance that flows*" etc.: The living Luminance is God the Son; its Luminant is God the Father. (cf. the Nicene Creed: "God out of God, Light out of Light, *lumen de lumine*, Very God out of Very God begotten.")

l. 59: "*nine subsistences*": i.e. the nine Orders of the Heavenly Hierarchy.

ll. 61–6: "*Which radiance*" etc.: This is the reflected light (the "splendour" referred to in l. 53) and represents the divine energy which operates through secondary causes. God, quâ Godhead, cannot be divided, diminished or distributed, as Dante has carefully pointed out (l. 60); it is His radiance which, reflected from mirror to mirror, descends "to the last potencies" (i.e. enters into the several orders of Being in a constantly diminishing degree, as they are removed in a descending scale from the Divine Source of all Being). Note however that it is still the Divine Energy and does not originate with the Intelligences (the "nine subsistences"). As it descends upon and vivifies the remoter and duller potentialities of things least capable of impression, it becomes so attenuated that it can only produce things corruptible and of short duration ("mere brief contingencies"), such as animals and plants ("formed . . . from seed, or seedless").

ll. 67–9: "*Now, more or less of light such things transmit*" etc.: The corruptible material ("the wax"), like all the primal matter of the universe, is the direct creation of God (cf. Cantos vii, xxix), but Dante here appears to conceive of it as something on which His power acts only imperfectly. The problem here involved is one that is far greater than the question of Solomon's superiority in wisdom, and St Thomas does not solve it. P. H. Wicksteed saw in it "the veiled dualism which may constantly be traced in Dante's conception of the universe", but there is no inference that Dante regarded the material world as inherently evil, only as inherently finite and, therefore, subject to change and difference.

ll. 73–5: "*Were the wax always wrought to perfect pitch*" etc.: If primal matter were always perfect, and if Divine Energy were always at its highest point (instead of being diminished by its gradual descent through the spheres), all created things would show the perfect imprint of the Divine Idea.

l. 76: "*But Nature fumbles*" etc.: Here once again is the problem alluded to in the Note to ll. 67–9. How can Nature, a direct creation of God, produce an imperfect world?

l. 83: *"the noblest animal of all"*: Adam, directly created by God.

l. 93: *"When bidden 'Choose' "* etc.: The story of Solomon's choice is related in *I Kings* iii, 5–13: "In Gibeon the Lord appeared to Solomon in a dream by night: and God said, Ask what I shall give thee. And Solomon said . . . Give therefore an understanding heart to judge thy people, that I may discern between good and bad: for who is able to judge this thy so great a people? . . . And God said unto him, Because thou hast asked this thing, and hast not asked for thyself long life; neither hast asked riches for thyself, nor hast asked the life of thine enemies; but hast asked for thyself understanding to discern judgement; Behold, I have done according to thy words; lo, I have given thee a wise and an understanding heart; so that there was none like thee before thee, *neither after thee shall any arise* like unto thee" (in the *Vulgate*, "post te surrexit sit").

l. 94: *"A king he was, so runs my argument"* etc.: The wisdom of Solomon is to be considered as the wisdom of a king, and as such it is unrivalled. (See also l. 106 and *note*.)

ll. 97–102: *"Not how to count these movers high aloof"* etc.: St Thomas here lists subjects of great learning which Solomon did not ask to understand, preferring the wisdom that should enable him to govern rightly. Solomon did not ask God to reveal to him (1) how many are the Intelligences that move the heavenly spheres; (2) whether, in logic, a limitation occurring in either of the premises can be escaped in the conclusion (a thing which Aristotle affirms, but Plato denies); (3) whether it must be conceded that there is such a thing as first motion; (4) whether the truths of geometry are valid throughout the universe. In other words, Solomon did not ask for philosophic, speculative or scientific wisdom, such as is required for the understanding of metaphysics, logic, physics and geometry, but for practical wisdom.

l. 106: *"And if that phrase 'none rose' thou rightly view"*: Of all who ever *rose* to kingly rule (which Adam and Christ did not), none had such wisdom as Solomon.

ll. 109–10: *"With this distinction take, nor take amiss, my words"*: The distinction is to be drawn between the wisdom of men who rose to regal authority and the wisdom of all men.

l. 111: *"Our Bliss"*: i.e. Christ.

ll. 112–42: The concluding lines of this canto, and of St Thomas's speech, are a warning against jumping to hasty conclusions (such as result from interpreting words out of their context) and not making distinctions between one case and another (cf. Canto xi. 27). Once we are committed to an opinion, vanity prevents us from retreating from it and fortifies us against the truth. Hasty moral judgements, too, are as likely to be false as intellectual ones. (The warning is particularly relevant to the main subject of St Thomas's discourse, for theologians were in some doubt as to whether Solomon was damned or saved.)

ll. 124–5: *"Witness Parmenides' and Bryson's showing in the world's eyes Melissus"*: Parmenides, a Greek philosopher, was born at Elea, in

Italy, in about 513 B.C. He was the founder of the Eleatic school of philosophy, in which he was succeeded by Zeno. Bryson, another Greek philosopher, is mentioned by Aristotle as having tried dishonestly, by non-geometrical methods, to square the circle. Melissus, a philospher of Samos, was a follower of Parmenides. Dante quotes Aristotle's disapproving comment on these two philosophers in *De Monarchia*: ". . . the Philosopher (i.e. Aristotle) objected to Parmenides and Melissus, saying, 'For they lay down what is false, and syllogize wrongly'."

l. 127: "*Sabellius, too, and Arius*": Sabellius, a third-century theologian, rejected the doctrine of the Trinity and maintained that the terms Father, Son and Holy Ghost were merely different names for the One God. Arius was the originator of the Arian heresy, according to which the Father and the Son were not 'one substance', a doctrine which 'split the Church for an iota' and was controverted by the Nicene Creed, formulated at the Council of Nicaea in A.D. 325.

ll. 128–9: " . . . *as a sword distorts straight faces into fanciful*": A sword, if it is slightly curved, gives back a distorted image. To understand what Dante means, the reader may try seeing himself reflected in a tablespoon, if he has not a sword handy.

CANTO XIV

THE STORY. *Beatrice, on Dante's behalf, questions the souls concerning the degree of radiance which will envelop them after the Last Judgement. In reply, Solomon explains the relationship between grace, vision, love and radiance.*

A third circle of light appears, but, before Dante can do more than glimpse it, he finds he has been raised to the Heaven of Mars. Here, two white bands of light, pricked out with ruby splendours, form themselves into the pattern of a cross, and Dante beholds a vision of Christ. The souls sing a hymn of praise, the beauty of which surpasses all that Dante has experienced in the preceding spheres.

    Water in a round bowl makes ripples glide
        Centre to rim, or back from rim to centre,
        As from within 'tis jarred, or from outside.

4   This image dropped into my mind instanter
        When Thomas' glorious life had said his say;
        Like an apt simile it seemed to enter

7   In likeness of the verbal interplay
        'Twixt Beatrice and him; for she, as suited
        Her pleasure, thus took up her cue straightway:

10   "This man has need, though unexpressed – being muted
        Of voice, nor yet in thought articulate –
        To trace another truth to where it's rooted;

13   So tell him if this radiance, floreate
        Thus in your substance, shall as now remain
        Unchanged with you, eternal as your state;

16   And, if it shall, go further and explain,
        How shall your mutual brightness not annoy
        Your sight, when you're restored to sight again?"

19   As carol-dancers in their merry ploy
        Break into music, and so wind and wheel
        With livelier gestures, through access of joy,

22   So, at that prompt and worshipful appeal,
        New pleasure did the circling hallows show,
        In wondrous song exprest and swifter reel.

He that laments because we die below   25
   To live up yonder, sees not how they spring,
   Those showers eternal, freshening where they flow.

The One and Two and Three that there is King,   28
   And lives for ever Three and Two and One,
   By naught contained, containing everything,

Was three times hymned in such melodious tone   31
   By every spirit there, as well might carry
   Praise of a worth past all comparison.

And then, from the divinest luminary   34
   Of the inner ring, I heard a voice arise
   Mild as the Angel's was, belike, to Mary:

"Long as shall last the feast of Paradise,   37
   Even so long," it said, "our love shall lace
   This radiance round us for our festal guise.

Its brightness with our fervour shall keep pace, 40
   Fervour with sight, sight so enlarge the mesh
   Of its own worth as it hath more of grace;

And when we put completeness on afresh,   43
   All the more gracious shall our person be,
   Reclothèd in the holy and glorious flesh;

Whereby shall grow the unearned gift and free   46
   The Highest Good bestows – that gift of light
   By which we are enabled Him to see;

Hence must we ever win to more of sight,   49
   And by more sight more fervour still acquire,
   And by more fervour radiance still more bright.

But, as the living coal which shoots forth fire 52
   Outgoes it in candescence, and is found
   Whole at the heart of it with shape entire,

The lustre which already swathes us round   55
   Shall be outlustred by the flesh, which long
   Day after day now moulders underground;

Nor shall that light have power to do us wrong, 58
   Since for all joys that shall delight us then
   The body's organs will be rendered strong."

61   So swift they were, so keen to cry *Amen*,
        As made me feel the yearning of those choirs
        To welcome their dead bodies back again;

64   Not for themselves alone, but for their sires,
        I take it, and their mothers, and all those
        They loved ere they became eternal fires.

67   And see! all round in level lustre rose
        A shine beyond those shining ones, which grew
        As gathering light on the horizon grows;

70   And as at twilight stealing into view
        Peep forth in heav'n half-guessed appearances,
        So that sight seems a liar and yet true,

73   I now began to glimpse existences
        Newly-arrived, and forming a fresh wreath
        Beyond the other two circumferences.

76   O sparks that from the Holy Breath outbreathe
        Living and true, how swift, how sudden growing,
        The light mine eyes bore not, but sank beneath!

79   But Beatrice appeared all smiles, and glowing
        With beauty such that I must leave it there
        With things outgone by memory in its going.

82   This gave me strength to lift mine eyes up where
        I stood, and find me raised to loftier bliss
        Beside my Lady, and alone with her.

85   That I'd been lifted up I saw by this:
        The warm smile of the star, whose burning ball
        Seemed ruddier to me than his custom is.

88   With my whole heart, and in that tongue which all
        Men share, I made burnt-offering to the Lord,
        Such as to this new grace was suitable,

91   And ere the sacrificial fire had soared
        Forth of my breast, I knew my prayer had sped
        Accepted, and found favourable accord;

94   For such bright splendours, and so ruby-red
        Within two rays appeared, "O Eloi,"
        I cried, "that giv'st them thus the accolade!"

As, white between the two poles of the sky   97
     Gleaming, and decked with great and lesser stars,
     Riddle of sages, shines the Galaxy,

E'en so, constellate in the depth of Mars,   100
     Those rays displayed the venerable sign
     Traced in a circle by the quadrant-bars.

Here memory beats me, and my wits resign   103
     Their office, for that cross so flashed forth Christ
     As beggars all similitude of mine;

But whoso takes his cross and follows Christ   106
     Will pardon me this gap in my narration
     When, lightening through Heav'n's brightening, he sees Christ.

From horn to horn, from top to base their station   109
     Changing, went moving lights, which as they met
     And passed threw out a dazzling coruscation;

Thus we on earth, swift, slow, zig-zag or straight,   112
     Little or large, in this or that direction,
     See particles of bodies disparate

Dance in the shaft of light that carves a section   115
     Sheer sometimes through the shuttered darkness which
     By art and skill men make for their protection.

As harp and viol, with strings of various pitch   118
     Twangling attuned, in dulcet harmony
     Speak to the ear by sounds which have no speech,

So from the lights which there appeared to me   121
     Swelled in the cross a song, obscure to sense,
     Which yet entranced me with its melody;

For some high song of praise I knew it, since   124
     "Arise" and "conquer" caught my ear, although
     I heard it not with full intelligence.

This so enamoured me that well I know,   127
     Nothing I'd seen till then had bound my breast
     With such sweet fetters or enthralled me so.

Maybe this seems too daringly expressed,   130
     As placing second those blest eyes and fair
     Gazing whereon my longings find their rest;

133   Yet, since more power in each more loftier sphere
          The living sigils of all beauty wield,
          And to those eyes I'd not yet turned me there,

136   Think, and to my self-accusation yield
          The excuse which was its pretext; yea, and count
          Me truthful, holy joys being not expelled

139   Those heights, but growing purer as they mount.

THE IMAGES: *Solomon*: In the previous canto, St Thomas made clear to Dante that Solomon did not ask God for speculative but for kingly wisdom; yet in Heaven Solomon so partakes of the wisdom of all the blessed that he is able to solve Dante's doubt as to the splendour of the body after the resurrection. In the *story*, it is a master-touch that Dante should receive from such a source so precious a pearl of wisdom. In the *allegory*, it is as the supposed author of the Song of Songs that Solomon is chosen to pronounce upon the ultimate bliss of union between the body and the soul.

The third circle of lights: There has been much speculation as to what Dante intended to signify by the third circle of radiance, which rises into view like light on the horizon before dawn. Within its lustre he begins to pick out new lights, like stars at twilight. Though he does not stay long enough to accustom himself to their brilliance, he recognizes them as emanations from the Holy Spirit. It would seem, therefore, that they represent some further extension into the infinity of God's truth which ever and infinitely exceeds man's knowledge and understanding of it.

The Heaven of Mars: In the *story*, Mars, the fifth planet in order from the earth, is the next stage in Dante's ascent towards the Empyrean, or abode of God. Traditionally the symbol of war, Mars is the scene of Dante's encounter with the souls of those who have died for the faith. In the *allegory*, the fortitude of the warrior saints and martyrs is shown as issuing in "loftier bliss" than all the knowledge of the wise. Dante's utter surrender of himself in a prayer of gratitude and devotion represents the Christian's sense of indebtedness to the soldiers and martyrs of the Cross.

The Cross of Souls: Two bands of light, white against the redness of Mars and pricked out with glowing rubies, form a Cross, pulsating with the sacrificial love of the Crusader knights and martyrs of the Faith. In the *allegory*, the Cross is the symbol of Christ Himself, and it is in His soldiers and martyrs that He shines forth upon Dante in a momentary and incommunicable vision. A hymn of praise, gathering through the Cross, holds Dante so rapt with its melody that till this moment nothing in Paradise has so sweetly enthralled him. This vision of glory represents Dante's faith in the ultimate victory of the Cross.

NOTES. ll. 1–9: As St Thomas ceases speaking, Beatrice begins. This passing to and fro of heavenly wisdom reminds Dante of the undulating movement of water in a round vessel, from the centre to the rim, or from the rim to the centre, according as the water is struck from outside or from within.

ll. 10–18: *"This man has need, though unexpressed"* etc.: Beatrice reads in Dante's mind and conveys to the spirits his anxiety to know whether, after the Last Judgement, the brightness which enwraps them will be tempered and, if not, whether it will be too brilliant for them to endure when they are reunited with their bodies. The question as to the intensity of radiance which would swathe the souls after the resurrection of the flesh was much debated by theologians, including St Thomas.

l. 28: *The One and Two and Three*: One God, two natures in Christ, three Persons in the Godhead.

l. 34: *. . . from the divinest luminary of the inner ring*: This is Solomon, whom St Thomas has described as the most beautiful of the inner ring (Canto x. 109).

l. 37: *"Long as shall last the feast of Paradise"* etc.: i.e. for all eternity.

ll. 40–42: *"Its brightness with our fervour shall keep pace"* etc.: The brilliancy of their guise of light comes from the fervour of their love and is in proportion to it; their love is in proportion to their vision of God, which is in proportion to the grace vouchsafed to each soul.

l. 43: *"And when we put completeness on afresh"*: Dante has already asked and received an answer to this question in *Hell* vi. 103–8:

> . . . "Master," said I, "this woe –
> Will it grow less, or still more fiercely burning
> With the Great Sentence, or remain just so?"

> "Go to," said he, "hast thou forgot thy learning,
> Which hath it: The more perfect, the more keen,
> Whether for pleasure's or for pain's discerning?"

As in *Hell*, so in *Paradise*, Dante is told that after the Last Judgement the souls will be "more perfect" because they will then be united with their bodies. This doctrine is derived from the philosophy of Aristotle, as incorporated in the theology of St Thomas.

l. 46: *"the unearned gift"*: i.e. grace. As grace is increased, so the amount of vision will grow.

ll. 49–51: *"Hence must we ever win to more of sight"* etc.: As their vision increases, so, in proportion, will their love become more fervent, and this increased fervour will, in proportion, increase the brilliancy of the light which swathes them. The doctrine that love proceeds from vision and knowledge is again stressed in Canto xxviii. 106–11.

ll. 67–8: *And see! all round in level lustre rose a shine beyond those shining ones*: A third circle of light now appears, embracing the first two (cf. above, under *Images*).

ll. 83–4: *. . . and find me raised to loftier bliss beside my Lady, and alone with her*: Dante and Beatrice have been lifted to the sphere of Mars.

ll. 88–9: *. . . and in that tongue which all men share, I made burnt-offering to the Lord*: Dante means that in the language of thought, which is universal, he surrendered himself to God in an act of gratitude and devotion.

l. 90: *this new grace*: i.e. his elevation to the fifth heaven.

ll. 94–5: *For such bright splendours* etc.: These are the spirits of warriors who died in defence of the Faith. They appear to Dante thronging in two bands of light. The name of Eloi for God appears to be a combination of the Greek *helios*, the sun, and the Hebrew, *El*, God. (See also Canto xxvi. 136 and compare the cry of Christ from the Cross "Eloi, Eloi, lama sabachthani".)

ll. 97–9: *As, white between the two poles of the sky* etc.: The crowded lights make Dante think of the Milky Way, with its multitudinous points of light, differing in brightness, although that is white (not ruby-red) and lies in a great circle between the celestial poles. The nature of the Milky Way (or Galaxy) had indeed been a "riddle of sages", as Dante was well aware, for he had read in Albertus Magnus an account of ancient speculations concerning it. These he discusses in *Convivio* II, xv. and comes himself to the correct conclusion.

ll. 101–2: *Those rays displayed the venerable sign traced in a circle by the quadrant-bars*: The venerable sign is the Cross, and is formed of the two rays so arranged that their lines cross as do the quadrants of a circle, *viz*:

This is the Greek cross, familiar from the crossed halo of Christ as depicted in mediaeval art.

ll. 112–17: *"Thus we on earth"* etc.: The movement of the lights along the horizontal arms of the cross ("from horn to horn") and up and down ("from top to base") is compared to the dancing motion of particles of dust caught in a beam of sunlight filtering through the slats of a shutter. Milton uses the same comparison in *Il Penseroso*:

> "As thick and numberless
> As the gay motes that people the sunbeam."

l. 125: *"Arise" and "conquer" caught my ear*: The hymn of praise is addressed to Christ, Conqueror of death and Hell.

l. 134: *The living sigils of all beauty*: i.e. the successive spheres of Heaven, which give their impress to the human soul, growing more efficacious the higher the soul ascends.

ll. 138–9: *... holy joys being not expelled those heights, but growing purer as they mount*: The beauty of Beatrice will become still more glorified, the higher they ascend. The literal sense of the concluding thirteen lines of this canto may conveniently be summarized as follows:

(1) Every kind of beauty and joy increases as Dante ascends from sphere to sphere, including the beauty and joy of Beatrice. (See also Cantos xxi. 4, xxx. 19–27).

(2) The beauty and joy of everything in the sphere of Mars therefore exceed the beauty and joy of anything in any lower sphere (ll. 127–9).

(3) The loveliness of the song of praise which Dante now hears in the heaven of Mars surpasses the beauty and joy of all that he has seen or experienced in preceding spheres. He does not, however, say that it surpasses in loveliness the eyes of Beatrice for he has not yet turned to look on them in this sphere.

(4) Dante's comparison therefore does not imply that the holy joy conveyed by the eyes of Beatrice is excluded from the experience of the higher spheres; on the contrary, it becomes ever more intensified the higher they ascend.

CANTO XV

THE STORY. *The souls of the warriors of God cease their singing in order that Dante may converse with one of them who, like a shooting star, speeds to the foot of the Cross. In answer to Dante's question, the spirit reveals himself as his ancestor and describes the simple virtues of the citizens of twelfth-century Florence.*

The limpid and distilled benevolence
    That from true charity is aye diffused,
    As malice issues from concupiscence,

4   Silenced that lyre's sweet music, and reduced
    To stillness all its sacred strings, whose tension
    By the right hand of Heav'n are drawn and loosed.

7   Think you good prayers shall not receive attention
    From beings who, conspiring thus to move
    My will to pray, waited in hushed suspension?

10   Well may his woe be endless, that for love
    Of fleeting things eternally puts by
    Such love as this, and robs himself thereof.

13   As, through the clear and tranquil evening sky
    Darting sometimes, a sudden conflagration
    Diverts the watcher's erstwhile steady eye,

16   Seeming as though a star had changed location,
    Save that none such is missing in the place
    It flared from, and itself hath brief duration,

19   So did a star detach itself, and race
    From dexter horn to cross-foot, bright between
    The constellated splendours there ablaze;

22   Nor shot the gem from off its band, but clean
    Along the radial line went skimming on,
    Like flame behind an alabaster screen.

25   So did Anchises' shade devoutly run,
    If we give credit to our *major musa*,
    When in Elysium he beheld his son.

"O sanguis meus, O superinfusa   28
    Gratia Dei, sicut tibi, cui
    Bis unquam coeli janua reclusa!"

So spake that light; I marked him eagerly,   31
    Then looked back to my Lady, with surprise
    This side and that dumbfounded equally,

For such a smile was blazing in her eyes,   34
    I thought that mine had plumbed the deepest bound
    Both of my grace and of my paradise.

Then, in appearance joyful as in sound,   37
    The spirit added things to this beginning
    I could not grasp, his speech was too profound;

Not that on purpose he concealed his meaning;   40
    Necessity was cause of this effect,
    His thought so far outsoared all human kenning;

But when the bow of burning love had checked   43
    Its force a little, and his speech descended
    To hit the target of our intellect,

These were the first words that I comprehended: 46
    "Blessèd be Thou, O Three-in-One, for this
    Great courtesy unto my seed extended!"

Then he went on: "A long, sweet eagerness,   49
    Aroused by reading that great book whose white
    And black abide eterne in changelessness,

Thou hast assuaged, my son, within this light   52
    Where I may now address thee, thanks to her
    Who gave thee wings to soar to such a height.

Thy thought flows into mine, thou deemest, clear 55
    From the First Thought, as (once we've grasped it) flow
    The five and six from the first integer;

Hence, who I am thou askest not to know,   58
    Nor why I make thee greater festival
    Than all the rest that here in gladness go.

Rightly thou deemest thus, since, great or small, 61
    We in this life gaze ever on that glass
    Where thought, ere it be thought, is mirrored all.

64 Yet, that the sacred love wherein I pass
  My ceaseless vigil here, the better may
  Slake the sweet thirst and longing which it has,

67 Let thine own voice, assured and bold and gay,
  Ring out, give wish a tongue, give will its word;
  Then will I speak what I'm ordained to say."

70 I turned; but ere I spoke Beatrice had heard,
  Vouchsafing me a sign whereat, immense
  Beyond all wont, my wings of yearning stirred.

73 So I began: "Love and intelligence
  Achieved their equipoise in each of you
  When first you saw the Prime Equivalence;

76 Because that Sun which lit and warmed you through
  With heat and light, maintains preëminent
  A poise no likeness can do justice to.

79 But among mortals, will and argument,
  Unequal winged, no level flight maintain,
  For reasons that to you are evident.

82 Being mortal yet, I feel the unequal strain;
  For welcome that bespeaks a father's heart
  My heart alone can render thanks again.

85 Natheless to thee, bright topaz, living part
  Of this rich jewel, I may yet make suit
  To gladden me by telling who thou art."

88 "Scion of mine, for whom 'twas bliss acute
  Even to wait and on thy coming count",
  Thus his reply began, "I was thy root."

91 Continuing thus: "Thy surname hath its fount
  In one that now some hundred years maybe
  Has circled the First Cornice of the Mount;

94 He was my son, great-grandfather to thee,
  And meet it were thou pray for him, to haste
  This weary toil of his and set him free.

97 Florence, within her ancient walls embraced,
  Whence nones and terce ring still to all the town,
  Abode aforetime, peaceful, temperate, chaste.

No glittering chain she wore, she wore no crown;   100
  There went no dames bedizened, no bright girdle
  To catch the eye and shine the wearer down;

Nor at a daughter's birth did terror curdle   103
  The father's blood, for date and dower between
  Due limits kept both ways, nor leaped the hurdle.

No empty houses in her streets were seen;   106
  Sardanapalus had not come, to show
  What chambering and wantonness might mean;

Neither did your Uccellatoi' outgo   109
  Yet Montemalo, which, as in late days
  It rose above, so shall it fall below.

I've seen Bellincion Berti go his ways   112
  Bone-buckled, leather-girt; his lady quit
  Her mirror with no paint upon her face;

I've seen de' Nerli and del Vecchio sit   115
  In plain buff-coats, their wives in homespun thread
  From their own distaffs, and content with it.

O happy wives! each knowing where her head   118
  Should come to lie at last; not one turned loose,
  Jilted for France, and left alone in bed.

One, watching by the cradle, would amuse   121
  And soothe her infant, crooning o'er and o'er
  The baby-talk young parents love to use;

One, with her spindle dancing on the floor,   124
  Her children round her, would spin yarns enow
  Of Troy and Rome and Fiesole of yore.

How strange had a Cianghella seemed! and how   127
  Monstrous a Lapo Salterello then!
  Like Cincinnatus or Cornelia now.

To this good way of life for decent men,   130
  This dear, this tranquil homestead undefiled,
  Friended with many a loyal citizen,

When the loud crying called her, Mary mild   133
  Gave me; your Baptist'ry of ancient fame
  Made me both Cacciaguida and God's child.

136   Moronto and Elisèo did they name
            My brothers; Vale of Po gave me my bride;
            From her thy family's cognomen came.

139   Later, I rode at Emperor Conrad's side,
            Who belted me among his chosen knights,
            My service left him so well satisfied;

142   And in his train I marched to foreign fights
            Against those Infidels that, through the sin
            Of the Chief Pastors, have usurped your rights.

145   There was I reft by the vile Saracen
            From this deceitful world whose vanities
            Win many souls and ruin all they win;

148   And came from martyrdom unto this peace."

THE IMAGES. *The Heaven of Mars*: see Canto xiv, under *Images*.
Cacciaguida: The existence of this great-great-grandfather of Dante (see
    Genealogical Tables, p. 397) is attested by a document (still pre-
    served in Florence) which refers to his two sons. Apart from this, we
    have no independent testimony concerning him. From Dante we
    learn that he served in the Second Crusade under the Emperor Con-
    rad III, by whom he was knighted, and that he died in battle against
    the Infidel about the year 1147. He was born in Florence about 1090
    of one of the old Florentine families who claimed Roman descent;
    from his wife, who came from the region of the river Po, the sur-
    name of Alighieri was derived.
        In the *story*, this encounter between Dante and his illustrious ances-
    tor is one of the most poignant and climactic moments in the poem.
    Of all the souls with whom he has conversed in Hell, Purgatory and
    Paradise, this is the one from whom his life-blood flows. Caccia-
    guida claims him insistently as his 'blood', his 'seed', his 'son', his
    'branch', and renders thanks to God for the measureless grace
    whereby his descendant has visited Heaven. The link, so intimate
    and personal, between ancestor and scion, is also the link between
    past, present and future which binds all men in an unending chain
    of heritage. From Cacciaguida to Dante flows not only the blood of
    illustrious forbears but also the past events of Florence, the history of
    Christendom, the inheritance of sin and of redemption, the burden
    and the glory of the Cross.
Florence of olden times: The ideal of twelfth-century Florence as a free
    Commune, confined within her ancient walls and peopled by up-
    right and simple-living republicans, is conveyed by Cacciaguida in
    moving and nostalgic terms, mingled with stern reproach for the

immoral influences which have since corrupted the city. In the *allegory*, the decline of morals in Florence is an instance of that widespread increase of evil throughout the world, the causes of which are the subject of *Inferno* and *Purgatory*, the remedy for which Dante believes it to be his mission to proclaim.

NOTES: ll. 4-6: *Silenced that lyre's sweet music* etc.: The two bands of lights (now in the form of a cross) are called a lyre; the lights (i.e. the singing souls) are the strings, and the instrument is played by the hand of God.

ll. 8-9: ... *conspiring thus to move my will to pray*: The souls have hushed their singing in order that Dante may make his wishes known to them.

ll. 10-11: ... *for love of fleeting things*: i.e. by yielding to an ill-directed love for secondary good.

l. 14: *a sudden conflagration*: i.e. a shooting star.

l. 19: *So did a star detach itself*: i.e. a star of the constellation of saints forming the Cross.

l. 24: *Like flame behind an alabaster screen*: Light shining through alabaster sends a diffused glow over all the surface and, if moved, is seen as a concentration of light in the midst of luminosity. Alabaster was sometimes used as a shade for candle-light in the Middle Ages, but, being costly, would be associated in the mind of Dante and his readers with sumptuous or palatial surroundings. Landino (an early commentator) relates having seen in the Vatican in the fifteenth century a vase of alabaster used to increase the intensity of candle-light.

ll. 25-7: *So did Anchises' shade devoutly run* etc.: With this reference to the encounter between Aeneas and his father's soul, related by Virgil in the sixth book of the *Aeneid*, Dante conjures up the presence of the *character* Virgil and recalls to the reader's mind the many occasions on which, with Virgil at his side, in Hell and on the Mountain of Purgatory, Dante had received mysterious and hitherto unexplained hints and warnings relating to his future. Now at last (in Canto xvii) their meaning is to be made clear to him. The reference to Anchises also prepares the reader's mind (1) for the relationship between this soul and Dante, and (2) for the revelation to Dante of his calling in a mighty cause. As Aeneas was called to extend the empire of Rome to the world and her genius to Heaven, so Dante is called to re-establish Rome in men's eyes as the civilizer of the world and the centre of man's divinely ordained destiny.

ll. 28-30: "*O sanguis meus*" etc.: These Latin words mean: "O my own blood! O grace of God poured forth beyond measure! To whom, as to thee, was Heaven's gate ever opened twice?"

l. 32: *Then looked back to my Lady*: For the first time, in the heaven of Mars, Dante turns to look at Beatrice.

l. 50: "*that great book*": i.e. the book of divine fore-knowledge. The souls in Paradise, as in Hell and Purgatory, can foresee the future.

ll. 55–7: *"Thy thought flows into mine"* etc.: Cacciaguida confirms Dante's belief that the spirits see all things in God as the mathematician sees all number in the conception of unity.

ll. 61–3: *"Rightly thou deemest thus"* etc.: Dante has not asked who the spirit is nor why he has so joyfully drawn near, because he believes, rightly, that the spirit can read the unspoken questions in his mind. The spirits, whatever their degree of bliss, gaze upon God as on a mirror in which all thoughts, even before they are formulated, are manifested.

ll. 73–8: "... *Love and intelligence*" etc.: In God all attributes, being infinite, are found in equal measure and proportion. As soon as the blessed behold God in His essence, their love and wisdom achieve a perfect equipoise, so that whatever they wish to do they can perform.

ll. 79–84: *"But among mortals, will and argument"* etc.: The word 'argument' (Italian '*argomento*') seems here to be used in a sense comparable to that in *Para.* xxiv. 65, where it represents the Vulgate *argumentum*, of which the Authorized Version is "the *evidence* of things unseen" (*Hebrews*, xi. 1), where, according to St Thomas (*Summa* II, II ae. Q. 4. Art. 1), "*evidence (argumentum)* is taken for the result of evidence. For evidence induces the intellect to adhere to a truth, and so the firm adhesion of the intellect to the non-apparent truth of faith is called *evidence* here". In this passage, Dante seems to be saying that, whereas in the Blessed love and intellect are equally matched ('*affetto*', '*senno*'), he, being only mortal, has no *evidence* to "induce his intellect to adhere to the truth", so that he can only give thanks with his heart for the spirit's manifest good-will. (The Greek word which the Vulgate *argumentum* represents is ἔλεγχος, proof.)

l. 86: *"this rich jewel"*: i.e. the Cross formed by the spirits, of which Cacciaguida is a gem.

ll. 91–6: "... *Thy surname hath its fount in one that now some hundred years maybe*" etc.: The son of Cacciaguida and great-grandfather of Dante bore the Christian name of Alighiero. He had two sons, Bellincione and Bello. Bellincione's son, Alighiero, was the father of Dante. It is not known on what evidence Dante imputes the sin of pride to his great-grandfather. He does not seem to have been accurately informed as to the date of his death, for there is documentary evidence that Alighiero the son of Cacciaguida was still alive in 1201 (cf. Genealogical Tables, p. 397).

l. 97: *"Florence, within her ancient walls"* etc.: The walls to which Cacciaguida here refers were the first extension of the original circuit begun in 1078. They constituted the second line of walls. A wider circuit was begun in 1284.

l. 98: *"whence nones and terce ring still to all the town"*: The reference is to the bells of the Badia (or Abbey Church) which stands near the second line of walls of which Cacciaguida is speaking.

l. 99: *"abode aforetime, peaceful temperate, chaste"*: The civil dissensions which were so marked a feature of Florentine life had not begun in Cacciaguida's lifetime.

ll. 104–5: "*. . . for date and dower between due limits kept both ways*": Brides were not too young, their dowries were not too high.

l. 106: "*No empty houses*": Opinion seems to be divided as to what Dante has in mind when he makes Cacciaguida refer to the empty houses of Florence. He may be thinking of houses too large and sumptuous for their inhabitants, or of houses devoid of children owing to the wantonness of the inhabitants, or of houses left empty by the absence caused by wars and factions.

l. 107: *Sardanapalus*, the last king of the Assyrian empire, is here cited as a type of luxury and wantonness. Dante may have read of him in a work by Aegidius Romanus, *De Regimine Principum*, in which stress is laid on his "chambering".

ll. 109–11: "*Neither did your Uccellatoi' outgo*" etc.: The traveller from Bologna on arriving at Mount Uccellatoio has his first view of Florence, just as, approaching from the north, the traveller on arriving at Montemario (previously called Montemalo) has his first view of Rome. Florence, in the sumptuous ostentatiousness of her buildings, has become more spectacular than Rome; in her fall, likewise, she will outdo her.

l. 112: "*Bellincion Berti*": This distinguished Florentine citizen was the father of the "good Gualdrada" mentioned in *Inf.* xvi. 37. A member of the honourable and ancient Ravignani family, he lived in the second half of the twelfth century (cf. Canto xvi. 97–9).

l. 115: "*I've seen de' Nerli and del Vecchio sit*" etc.: The Nerli, an ancient and noble Florentine family, received knighthood from the Marquis Hugh of Brandenburg, "that great baron" (cf. Canto xvi. 128). The Del Vecchio family, also known as the Vecchietti, were, like the Nerli, Guelfs, and like them, went into exile in 1248 and again in 1260 after the Battle of Montaperti. To the Del Vecchio family belonged Bono Giamboni, who translated into Italian the *Trésor* of Brunetto Latini; the *Historia* of Orosius, the *De Re Militari* of Vegetius, and other works well known in the Middle Ages.

ll. 118–20: "*O happy wives! each knowing where her head should come to lie at last*" etc.: No wives of twelfth-century Florence went in fear of dying in exile, or of being left alone while their husbands went to France for trading.

ll. 127–8: "*How strange had a Cianghella seemed! and how monstrous a Lapo Salterello then!*": Cianghella, the daughter of Arrigo della Tosa, was notorious for her loose and luxurious way of life. She is reported to have been arrogant in manner and an arbitress of fashion in dress. Such a woman in the Florence of Cacciaguida's time would have been as great a marvel as a Cornelia would be now. Similarly, Lapo Salterello, a corrupt lawyer, known to have taken bribes, would have seemed as great a wonder as a Cicinnatus would seem now.

ll. 133–4: "*When the loud crying called her, Mary mild gave me*": i.e. the

Virgin Mary, invoked by Cacciaguida's mother in labour, granted the safe delivery of the child.

l. 135: "*made me both Cacciaguida and God's child*": Here for the first time, Dante's ancestor reveals his name. For information concerning him, see above under *Images*. (See also Genealogical Tables, p. 397.)

ll. 137–8: ". . . *Vale of Po gave me my bride: from her thy family's cognomen came*": Cacciaguida married Alighiera degli Alighieri; their son was named Alighiero, and his descendants took his Christian name as their surname (cf. ll. 91–6).

CANTO XVI

THE STORY. *In reverence to his ancestor and with a gratified sense of his own derived dignity, Dante addresses the spirit with the ceremonious plural "you" instead of "thou", at which Beatrice smiles. Replying to Dante's eager appeal for news of twelfth-century Florence, Cacciaguida speaks of his own birth and origin and mentions many noble Florentine families illustrious in his day but already in Dante's time extinct or fallen to low estate. He deplores the change that has come over Florence, now enlarged, corrupted, and polluted by the influx of greedy and ambitious newcomers, and laments the feud between the Amidei and the Buondelmonti, the origin of civil strife in Florence.*

O puny glories of our blood and state!
  If ye can swell men's hearts with pride down here,
  Where passion's pulse beats but a languid rate,

Never shall I marvel more; for in that sphere   4
  Where appetite's unwarped I gloried – yea,
  Even in Heav'n I gloried in such gear;

Yet that's a mantle which soon shrinks away,   7
  For round the edge time with his shears will go,
  Unless we add to it from day to day.

So, with the *You* which Rome first sanctioned – though   10
  To-day her children make less use thereof
  Than others, I began my speech; and so

Beatrice smiled, standing a little off,   13
  As Guenevere's good dame, when the queen made
  Her first recorded slip, was moved to cough.

"You are my father; right good hardihead   91
  You give my tongue; thus lifted and elated
  You make me greater than myself," I said.

"So many streams of bliss have inundated   19
  My heart, it joys itself to bear such joy
  Nor burst in sunder, being so dilated.

Tell me then, dear my rootstock, tell – deploy   22
  First your ancestral line, and then say on:
  What years made history when you were a boy?

25   Tell me about the sheepfold of St John –
            How large its ambit was, and who the men
            Worthiest of place in those old days bygone."

28   As glowing charcoal glows the livelier when
            The wind breathes on it, so that lustre's blaze
            Burned in my loving breath as bright again;

31   And while he grew more beauteous to my gaze
            He said, in softer, sweeter idiom,
            Though with an accent not of modern days:

34   "Since *Ave* first was uttered, and therefrom
            Until the day my mother, now in bliss,
            Was lightened of me in her heavy womb,

37   Five hundred, fifty, and thirty times hath this
            Our fiery star come to renew his flame
            Under his Lion's paw, whose lord he is.

40   The house which stands where in your yearly game
            The runners first set foot in the last ward
            My birthplace was; my forebears had the same.

43   Enough of them; we cannot now afford
            To talk of whence they came and who they were;
            Silence with modesty will best accord.

46   Take the whole population fit to bear
            Arms, between Mars and Baptist, as it stood,
            'Twas but a fifth of those now living there;

49   But 'twas a citizenry pure in blood
            To the least workman, still unsullied by
            Campi's, Certaldo's, and Fighine's brood.

52   O were Galluzzo still your boundary,
            Still Trespiano! It were healthier
            To have such folk for neighbours than let lie

55   Within your gates that stinking mongrel cur
            D'Aguglio; and that Signa, swift to find
            Pickings and jobs, the sharp-eyed trafficker!

58   Had but those gentry most corrupt in mind
            Not treated Caesar like a step-child brat,
            But, as a mother to her son, been kind,

One chaffering Florentine, self-made at that,   61
   Would have been bundled back to Simifonti,
   Where once his grandfather sent round the hat.

And Montemurlo then could keep her Conti   64
   Guidi, Acone have her Cerchi still,
   Val di Greve, belike, her Buondelmonti.

Always a mingled strain's a principle   67
   Of civic decadence, as, when men cram
   Meat upon meat, the body is made ill.

Heavier the blind bull falls than the blind lamb,   70
   And with a single blade one cuts more deep
   Oftimes, and sharper, than with five of them.

See Luni and Urbisaglia where they sleep,   73
   Dead cities both; see Chiusi following fast
   With Sinigaglia down the slippery steep;

And then to learn how families have passed   76
   And come to naught will not seem strange to thee,
   Since even cities have an end at last.

Mortal are all your works, yea, even as ye,   79
   Though some conceal this truth, since they endure
   Long, and your lives are short. And as the sea

Unceasingly lays bare and hides the shore   82
   While the moon's sphere revolves its endless ring,
   So fortune doth with Florence evermore.

Think it not then a marvel if I bring   85
   To mind full many a noble Florentine
   Whose fame is hid with time, a vanished thing.

I saw the Ughi, Catellini's line,   88
   Filippi, Greci, Ormanni, Alberic's house
   All puissant yet, though starting to decline;

I saw, as ancient as illustrious,   91
   L'Arca and La Sanella; Soldanieri,
   Bostichi, Ardinghi, still right glorious.

Nigh to that gate, beneath contemporary   94
   And brand-new treasons groaning – such a load
   Of guilt as soon shall make the ship miscarry –

97   The Ravignani had their old abode,
          Whence came Count Guido and all those on whom
          Bellincion's mighty name is self-bestowed.

100   'Well did La Pressa know how to assume
          The reins of rule; and gilded was the glaive,
          Pummel and hilt, in Galigaio's home.

103   Brave showed the pale of vair, the Galli brave,
          Sacchetti, Giuochi, Fifanti and Barucci,
          And they who blush now for the bushel-stave;

106   Then was that stock which nourished the Calfucci
          Already grown; and in the curule seats
          Were set the Sizii and the Arrigucci.

109   How great I saw that house which proud conceits
          Destroyed! and the gold bezants bright as these,
          Flower of a Florence filled with all fair feats.

112   Such fathers too had they who now, when sees
          Fall vacant, sit in consistory sleek,
          Spinning out time and fattening on the fees.

115   That shameless breed, still dragons to the weak
          Who flee them, though to any man who shows
          His teeth – or purse – no lambs could be so meek,

118   Were rising, though from such low roots they rose,
          Hubert Donato took it much to heart
          To be made kin-in-law to such as those.

121   Down out of Fièsole into the mart
          Had Caponsacco come; good burghers too,
          Giuda and Infangato played their part.

124   Now, here's a thing incredible but true!
          From the La Peras was the postern named
          Where traffic to the inner ward goes through.

127   All those who carried the escutcheon famed
          Of that great baron whose renown and pride
          Still on the feast of Thomas are proclaimed

130   Were knighted at his hand and dignified,
          Though he who bears it in an orle today
          Has ranged himself upon the people's side.

The Gualterotti and Importuni – they   133
    Were there; your Borgo were a quieter place
    Had their new neighbours only stayed away.

The house which wrung forth tears from all your race   136
    Through that just wrath it was your death to know,
    And which has wiped the laughter from life's face,

With all its kin was honoured then; and woe   139
    To thee, O Buondelmonte, thus to fly
    Its bed, because a woman willed it so!

Many would laugh who now are forced to cry,   142
    If in the Ema God had let thee drown
    When first the city saw thee riding by.

Yet to that battered stone that guards her town   145
    And bridge, 'twas fit that Florence, in the hour
    She last knew peace, should strike a victim down.

With men like these, and more in ample dower,   148
    Did I see Florence, with no woes accurst
    To weep for, tranquil in her place and power.

With men like these I saw her glorious erst,   151
    A righteous folk and wed to righteous rules;
    Never the lily on the spear reversed,

Nor yet by faction dyed from white to gules."   154

THE IMAGES: see Canto xv.

NOTES. l. 2: *down here*: i.e. in the world.

   l. 3: *where passion's pulse* etc.: i.e. where our love is weak compared with the fervour of heavenly love.

   l. 5: *Where appetite's unwarped*: i.e. where love is rightly directed.

   ll. 7–9: *Yet that's a mantle* etc.: If succeeding generations of noble families do not reinforce their nobility of lineage by valiant deeds, the prowess and glory of their ancestors will soon be forgotten.

   l. 10: *... with the "You" which Rome first sanctioned* etc.: It was commonly believed that the use of the Latin pronoun *vos* as an honorific form of address to one person was introduced by the Romans in adulation of Julius Caesar.

   l. 11: *to-day her children make less use thereof*: i.e. the honorific plural was no longer used in Rome.

   ll. 13–15: *Beatrice smiled* etc.: In using the honorific plural in addressing his ancestor, Dante reveals his pride in his descent. Beatrice smiles at his foible, even as the Lady of Malehaut, on perceiving Guinevere's familiarity with Lancelot, coughed to warn her (cf. *Inferno* x, in which Dante is moved by reverence for Farinata degli Uberti to address him similarly as "voi").

ll. 22–3: "*. . . deploy first your ancestral line*": These words recall, perhaps deliberately, the question of Farinata degli Uberti, "What's thy name and race?" (*Inf.* x. 42).

l. 25: "*the sheepfold of St John*": i.e. Florence, so named from its patron saint, St John the Baptist.

l. 32–3: *in softer, sweeter idiom* etc.: i.e. not in Latin, but in archaic Florentine. (Some commentators are of the opinion, however, that Dante's original lines mean that Cacciaguida was speaking Latin. The passage is, in fact, susceptible of more than one interpretation.)

ll. 34–9: "*Since 'Ave' first was uttered*" etc.: From the time of the Annunciation until the birth of Cacciaguida, the planet Mars had completed 580 revolutions, returning to its conjunction with the constellation of Leo. Each revolution of Mars was calculated as taking 687 days, and this number multiplied by 580 leads to the conclusion that Cacciaguida was born in the year 1091. On the other hand, some MSS and editions read *three* for *thirty*, making the number of Mars's revolutions 553. Calculating each revolution of the planet as lasting two years, this reading would give 1106 as the year of Cacciaguida's birth. Either is possible.

l. 39: "*his Lion's paw, whose lord he is*": The association of the Lion with Mars is metaphorical, as well as astronomical, in that the attribute of courage belongs to them both.

ll. 40–42: The annual horse race in Florence was run along the Corso; at the beginning of the "last ward", the quarter of St Peter, stood the houses of the Elisei, one of the ancient Florentine families who boasted Roman descent.

ll. 46–8: "*Take the whole population fit to bear arms*" etc.: The fighting population of Florence at the time of Cacciaguida was one-fifth of what it was in 1300. It has been calculated that the population of Florence in 1300 was about 70,000, of whom 30,000 were fit to bear arms. Consequently, in Cacciaguida's day, the fighting population of Florence was about 6,000 and the total number of inhabitants about 14,000. ". . . *between Mars and Baptist*": The baptistery of St John was situated on the northern boundary of ancient Florence, and the statue of Mars (at the head of the Ponte Vecchio on its north side) was its southern extremity. In Cacciaguida's time, Florence was contained within a semicircle on the north side of the river.

ll. 50–51: "*. . . still unsullied by Campi's, Certaldo's and Fighine's brood*": Campi, Certaldo, and Fighine (now Figline) are nearby villages, whose inhabitants, immigrating to Florence, are considered by Dante to have debased the blood of the Florentines.

ll. 52-3: "*O were Galluzzo still your boundary, still Trespiano!*": i.e.
How much better it would have been if Galluzzo and Trespiano had
remained neighbouring boroughs instead of being incorporated in the
city of Florence! (Galluzzo is on the Siena road, about two miles from
Florence; Trespiano is on the Bologna road, about three miles from
Florence.)

ll. 55-6: "*. . . that stinking mongrel cur D'Aguglio; and that Signa*":
Baldo D'Aguglio and Fazio de' Mori Ubaldini da Signa, two lawyers,
deserted from the White to the Black Guelf faction in 1302 (the year
of Dante's exile). In 1311, D'Aguglio, as prior, drew up a decree re-
calling many of the exiles but expressly excluding Dante. Signa was a
bitter opponent of the White Guelfs and also of the Emperor Henry VII.

ll. 58-60: "*Had but those gentry most corrupt in mind*" etc.: i.e. if the
Church had not opposed the Emperor, but instead had supported secu-
lar authority in Italy.

ll. 61-3: "*One chaffering Florentine*": It is not known who this Floren-
tine is. He would appear to have been an undesirable upstart, grandson
of a beggar, originating from Simifonti.

ll. 64-5: "*And Montemurlo then could keep her Conti Guidi*": Monte-
murlo, a castle on a hill between Prato and Pistoia, formerly belonged
to the Conti Guidi, a great Lombard family. They were obliged to sell
it to Florence as they could not hold it against the Pistoians. Dante men-
tions several of the Conti Guidi in the *Inferno*.

"*. . . Acone have her Cerchi still*": Yet a further result of the feud between
Church and Emperor was to bring the Cerchi, the leaders of the White
Guelf faction, from their original home in Acone to settle in Florence.

l. 66: "*Val di Greve, belike, her Buondelmonti*": The destruction of the
castle of the Buondelmonti family, which occurred in the course of the
expansion of the city of Florence, led to the transference of the Buondel-
monti to Florence and to their taking up residence there.

ll. 67-8: "*Always a mingled strain's a principle of civic decadence*" etc.:
Cacciaguida is here repeating sentiments and opinions already uttered
by Dante himself in *Inferno* xvi. 73-5.

ll. 70-72: "*Heavier the blind bull falls than the blind lamb*" etc.: Increase
in the size of a population does not necessarily mean increase in strength.

l. 73: "*See Luni and Urbisaglia . . .*": Luni, an ancient Etruscan city
(formerly Luna, cf. *Inf.* xx. 46-50), situated on the borders of Liguria
and Tuscany, fell into decay under the Romans and was eventually
destroyed. The district of Lunigiana derives its name from it. Urbisaglia
(Urbs Salvia), once an important town, was in Dante's day, as now, a
collection of ruins, consisting of an amphitheatre, baths and walls.

ll. 74-5: "*. . . see Chiusi following fast with Sinigaglia down the slippery
steep*": Chiusi, the ancient Clusium, one of the twelve great Etruscan
cities, is situated on the borders of Umbria and Tuscany, about half-way
between Florence and Rome. Sinigaglia (now Senigallia), the ancient
Sena Gallica, is situated on the Adriatic about seventeen miles north-

west of Ancona. It had been devastated by the wars of the Guelfs and Ghibellines and especially by the ravages of Guido da Montefeltro (cf. *Inferno* xxvii).

l. 84: *"so fortune doth with Florence evermore"*: Compare with this Virgil's discourse on Fortune in *Inferno*, vii. 73–96. In the *De Monarchia* (xii. 70) Dante terms fortune the "agency which we better and more rightly call divine providence".

ll. 88–93: *"I saw the Ughi"* etc.: Cacciaguida here names a number of ancient Florentine families concerning whom little is known save that they were dying out or had already become extinct in Dante's day.

ll. 94–9: *"Nigh to that gate"* etc.: Near the old gateway, in the quarter of St Peter, were the houses of the Cerchi, which had been sold to them in 1280 by the Conti Guidi, who had inherited them from the Ravignani, by the marriage of Count Guido Guerra with the "good Gualdrada", daughter of Bellincione Berti (cf. *Inf*. xvi. 37 and *Para*. xv. 112). The Cerchi were the leaders of the White Guelfs.

ll. 100–101: *"Well did La Pressa know how to assume the reins of rule"*: The Della Pressa, an ancient Ghibelline family, were among those exiled from Florence in 1258.

ll. 101–2: *". . . and gilded was the glaive, pummel and hilt, in Galigaio's home"*: The gilded hilt and pommel of the sword are the symbols of knighthood. The family declined in status and one member, Puccio, is mentioned by Dante as being among the thieves in Hell (see *Inf*. xxv. 148).

l. 103: *"the pale of vair"*: The arms of the Pigli family were gules, a pale, vair (i.e. a red shield divided longitudinally by a stripe of the heraldic representation of the fur called vair).

"the Galli brave": Villani says the Galli were Ghibellines living in the Mercato Nuovo. Their houses, like those of the Galigai (cf. ll. 101–102), were demolished in 1293.

l. 104: *"Sacchetti, Giuochi, Fifanti and Barucci"*: The Sacchetti were Guelfs, and were among those who fled from Florence after the Ghibelline victory at Montaperti in 1260. According to some early commentators, the first cousin of Dante's father, Geri del Bello, sowed discord among the Sacchetti, one of whom killed him (cf. *Inf*. xxix. 18–36). Franco Sacchetti, the author, was a member of this family and relates various anecdotes concerning Dante. The Giuochi, a Ghibelline family, had held office in Florence in the twelfth century. They were excluded from the magistracy in 1293 and again in 1311 and gradually declined in status. The Fifanti, who were Ghibellines, were expelled from Florence in 1258. A member of their family, Oderigo Fifanti, who took part in the murder of Buondelmonte, has been identified by some commentators as the Arrigo mentioned in *Inf*. vi. 80. The Barucci, said by Villani to have been a very ancient Ghibelline family, were extinct in Dante's day.

l. 105: *"and they who blush now for the bushel-stave"*: Durante de'

Chiarmontesi, when at the head of the Salt Import Department in Florence, reduced the size of the bushel-measure by one stave, and appropriated the balance of the salt. This fraud has already been referred to in *Purg.* xii. 105. Chiar montesi was eventually found out and executed for his dishonesty; hence the remembrance of his misdeed is a perpetual shame to his descendants.

l. 106: *"that stock which nourished the Calfucci"*: The Calfucci, an ancient Guelf family, extinct in Dante's time, were descended from the Donati.

ll. 107–8: *". . . and in the curule seats were set the Sizii and the Arrigucci"*: These two families, who held office in Cacciaguida's time, were among those who fled from Florence to Lucca after the Ghibelline victory at Montaperti in 1260.

ll. 109–10: *"How great I saw that house which proud conceits destroyed!"*: Cacciaguida refers here to the powerful Ghibelline family of the Uberti. Like the Lamberti referred to in ll. 110–11, they were said to be of Germanic origin and to have come to Florence in the tenth century with the Emperor Otho I. The famous leader of the Uberti, Farinata, is among the heretics in Hell (see Canto x. 32 *et sqq.*). When banished from Florence in 1250, they allied themselves to the Siennese and in 1260 lured the Florentine Guelfs into an ambush and defeated them with great slaughter at Montaperti, near the river Arbia. The Guelfs, among whom were Dante's ancestors, fled from Florence. They never forgave Farinata and when they returned to power they razed the Uberti palaces to the ground and pronounced relentless decrees of exile against the whole family.

ll. 110–11: *". . . and the gold bezants bright as these"* etc.: The Lamberti are here referred to by their arms (golden balls on a field azure). To this family belonged the notorious Mosca (cf. *Inf.* xxviii. 106), who urged on the Amidei to murder Buondelmonte, who had jilted one of their kinswomen. From this family quarrel flared up the great Guelf-Ghibelline feud in Florence.

ll. 112–14: *"Such fathers too had they who now"* etc.: Two Guelf families, the Visdomini and the Tosinghi, members of the Black faction, had the privilege of enjoying the episcopal revenues whenever the Bishopric of Florence fell vacant. Though their twelfth-century ancestors behaved honourably, the descendants of Dante's day are accused here of deferring the appointment of a new Bishop in order to prolong their enjoyment of the revenue.

ll. 115–20: *"That shameless breed"* etc.: Cacciaguida, at the climax of his accusations, reproaches the Adimari, a powerful Florentine family which was divided into three branches, the Argenti, the Aldobrandi and the Cavicciuli. They were Dante's near neighbours and notoriously hostile to him. One member of the Cavicciuli branch, which, unlike the rest of the family, joined the Black faction of the Guelfs, took possession of Dante's property when he was exiled and was always actively opposed to his being recalled. Filippo Argenti, another member of the Adimari family, tries to attack Dante as he crosses the Styx (cf. *Inf.* viii. 11–63). Cacciaguida alleges that they were of such low extraction that Hubert Donato (Ubertino Donati), who had married a daughter of Bellincione Berti, of the Ravignani family, was much displeased when his wife's sister married one of them.

ll. 121–2: *"Down out of Fièsole into the mart had Caponsacco come"*: The Caponsacchi, who came originally from Fiesole, were one of the most ancient Ghibelline families of Florence. They took part in the expulsion of the Florentine Guelfs in 1244 and were among the Ghibellines who were themselves banished in 1258. After their return from exile they joined the White Guelfs and were among those expelled in 1302. It is said that the mother of Beatrice was a member of the Caponsacchi family.

"into the mart": Cacciaguida means that in his day the Caponsacchi had already settled in the quarter of the Mercato Vecchio.

ll. 122–3: *". . . good burghers too, Giuda and Infangato played their part"*: The Giudi family held consular office in Florence in the twelfth century and at the beginning of the thirteenth. As Ghibellines they shared the fortunes of their party in 1258 and 1260. They were excluded from the magistracy in 1293 and eventually declined in status. The Infangati, also Ghibellines, suffered a similar series of vicissitudes.

ll. 124–6: *"Now, here's a thing incredible but true! From the La Peras was the postern named"* etc.: The Della Pera family, who were quite unimportant in Dante's time, had once been so prominent that one of the gates of Florence was named after them. The gate in question is said to have been the Porta Peruzza, which was not one of the four principal gates, but a postern.

ll. 127–32: *"All those who carried the escutcheon"* etc.: Cacciaguida now groups five families together. Though he does not mention them by name, they have been identified as the Pulci, the Nerli, the Gangalandi, the Giandonati and the Della Bella. They are listed by Villani as having been knighted by "that great baron" (the Marquess Hugh of Brandenburg), the Imperial Vicar of Otho III. They were granted leave to quarter his arms with their own. The Marquess died on St Thomas's Day, in the year 1006, and was buried in the Badia of Florence, which his mother had founded and which he himself had richly endowed. The anniversary of his death was commemorated with great honour. *"he who bears it in an orle today"*: i.e., he who bears the arms of the Marquess in a border of gold (Giano della Bella) has ranged himself with the commons of Florence against the nobles. Giano it was who in 1293 enacted the famous Ordinances of Justice to check the power of the nobles.

ll. 133–5: *"The Gualterotti and Importuni"* etc.: These are two Guelf families of some importance in Cacciaguida's time. When the Castle of Montebuono was destroyed, the Buondelmonti (who are the "new neighbours" referred to in l. 135) came to inhabit Borgo Santi Apostoli, where the Gualterotti and Importuni had been residing peacefully till then. The Borgo mentioned is in the very centre of Florence.

ll. 136–41: *"The house which wrung forth tears from all your race"* etc.: From the vengeance wrought by the Amidei family for the insult to a daughter of their house arose all the civil discord of Florence. The lines are addressed to Buondelmonte de' Buondelmonti, who owed his death to the wrath of the Amidei (l. 137). It was an evil hour for Florence when Buondelmonte broke his betrothal with the Amidei family, owing to the persuasions of the mother of the Donati girl whom he married instead.

ll. 142–4: *"Many would laugh who now are forced to cry"* etc.: How much happier many would be if Buondelmonte had been drowned while fording the river Ema on his way to Florence from his castle of Montebuono!

ll. 145–7: *"Yet to that battered stone that guards her town and bridge . . ."* etc.: The "battered stone" is the statue of Mars which stood at the head of the Ponte Vecchio at the north end. At the foot of the statue Buondelmonte was struck down by the Amidei and murdered. Cacciaguida says that it was appropriate that Florence should sacrifice to the god of war on the eve of a period of civil discord.

ll. 153–4: *"Never the lily on the spear reversed"* etc.: Cacciaguida refers here to two customs which prevailed during the subsequent conflicts: (1) the victorious power used to dishonour the standard of the defeated party or State by dragging it in the dust; and (2) the Guelfs, after the expulsion of the Ghibellines, had altered the arms of Florence from a white lily on a red field to a red lily on a white field.

CANTO XVII

THE STORY. *Still in the heaven of Mars, Dante appeals to his ancestor for an explanation of the mysterious and ominous hints concerning his future which he has heard in Hell and Purgatory. Speaking in plain, undisguised language, Cacciaguida tells him the truth: he will be exiled from Florence. Leaving behind all things that are dear to him, he will experience the bitterness of penury. His first refuge will be the court of the Scaligers, and there he will return a second time, when Can Grande shall be Lord of Verona. In him Dante is to repose his trust and hopes for the future. In reply to Dante's timid suggestion of prudence, Cacciaguida bids him reveal boldly all that he has seen and heard in his journey through the three realms.*

    As, hearing ill things said of him, came once
      To Clymenè for confirmation, he
      Who still makes fathers chary with their sons,

4   Even such was I, and such was felt to be
      By Beatrice and by the sacred lamp
      Which had already altered place for me.

7   Wherefore: "Speak on", my Lady said, "nor damp
      Thy ardent wish, but bring it out o'door,
      Perfectly minted with the inward stamp;

10   Not that thy words can make our knowledge more;
      Yet learn to tell thy longing, that the cruse
      May pour thee out the drink thou thirstest for."

13   "Dear native soil, whom such high grace endues
      That, as men see no triangle can hold
      Amid its angles more than one obtuse,

16   So you, before they come to be, behold
      Contingent things, on that point gazing still
      That in one Now doth all our times enfold;

19   While I at Virgil's side climbed up the hill
      That has the cure of souls, and while we went
      Through the dead world descending sill by sill,

22   Ominous words were said to me, anent
      My future; though beneath the shrewdest knock
      Fortune may deal, I trust to stand unbent.

Keen is my will to hear, then, what ill luck   25
    Shall come to me, that I may know the worst:
    Forewarned, forearmed, retards the arrow's shock."

Thus to the flame who had addressed me first   28
    I now addressed myself and, even as willed
    Beatrice, all my wish I thus rehearsed.

In no dark oracle, like those that filled   31
    Men's foolish minds with error once, ere yet
    The Lamb, who taketh away sins, was killed,

But forthright speech, plain as the alphabet,   34
    Replied the love paternal, in that light
    Hid and displayed which heavenly smiles beget:

"Contingence, which doth exercise no right   37
    Beyond that frame of matter where you lie,
    Stands all depicted in the Eternal Sight,

Though suffering thence no more necessity   40
    Than doth the vessel down the river gliding
    From its reflection in the watcher's eye;

Thence, as sweet music to the ear comes sliding   43
    Through the piped organ, comes into my mind
    The vision of thy life and times betiding.

As, through his stepdame's treacherous lust unkind,   46
    Hippolytus from Athens had to go,
    So thou must needs leave Florence town behind;

So willed, it is so planned, and soon will so   49
    Be done by him who sits and plots that same.
    Where Christ is daily huckstered to and fro.

The injured side will bear the common blame   52
    As ever; but the day of reckoning,
    By truth appointed, shall the truth proclaim.

Thou shalt abandon each and every thing   55
    Most dear to thee: that shaft's the first that e'er
    The bow of exile looses from the string;

Thou shalt by sharp experience be aware   58
    How salt the bread of strangers is, how hard
    The up and down of someone else's stair;

61   And heaviest on thy shoulders afterward
  Shall the companions of thy ruin weigh,
  All with one brush of vice and violence tarred;

64   For with a savage fury shall they play
  The ingrate, and defame thee; yet anon
  Not thou shalt feel thy forehead burn, but they –

67   Fools all, and proved so by their goings-on;
  Well shall it be for thee to have preferred
  Making a party of thyself alone.

70   Thy first abode, thy refuge first assured,
  Shall be the mighty Lombard's courtesy,
  Who on the ladder bears the sacred bird;

73   For with such kind regard he'll look on thee,
  It shall be Ask and Have between you, and
  The one most men put second, first shall be.

76   With him thou'lt see that youth on whom the hand
  Of this strong star so set its native sign,
  His deeds shall be right famous in the land;

79   Him the world knows not yet, nor can divine,
  For he is still too young to make his mark,
  Of these wheels' circlings having seen but nine;

82   But ere great Henry by the Gascon's dark
  Deceits is trapped, his scorn of pelf and pence,
  His scorn of toils, shall show his mettle's spark.

85   Time shall proclaim his vast munificence
  So wide, his very foes shall not abate
  Their tongues, with such good cause for eloquence.

88   Look thou to him and on his bounties wait;
  For many men shall he make mutable,
  Rich men and beggars changing their estate;

91   Write in thy mind of him, but do not tell,
  This – " Here he spoke of matters that shall seem
  To those who see them, quite incredible,

94   Adding: "My son, I comment thus the theme
  Of what was told thee; a few circling seasons
  Hide, as thou seest, full many a treacherous scheme;

Yet I'd by no means have thee, for these reasons,   97
    Envy thy neighbours; grace shalt thou receive
    Long to outlive God's judgement on their treasons."

Soon as his silence led me to believe   100
    That the blest soul had shuttled all the woof
    Across the warp I'd set for him to weave,

I said, as one perplexed which way to move,   103
    Seeking advice from some wise counsellor
    Who can discern, and rightly will, and love:

"Father, too well I see how time doth spur   106
    Hard on me, with such blows as on the breast
    That shrinks from them fall but the heavier;

I'd better arm myself with prudence, lest,   109
    When from that dearest place of all I'm torn
    Away, my songs should lose me all the rest.

Down in the world whose bitter knows no bourne,   112
    All the way up the hill from whose bright tip
    I've mounted, by my Lady's eyebeams drawn,

And after, while from light to light we slip   115
    Through Heav'n, I've learned things, such that, if retold,
    They'd leave an acrid taste on many a lip;

Yet, if I am truth's friend, and am not bold,   118
    My name, I fear, will live but a brief measure
    With those who'll call these days the days of old."

The light wherein he laughed, my new-found treasure,   121
    Like to a golden mirror in the track
    Of the sun's rays, sparkled at first for pleasure,

Then said: "Indeed, the conscience that is black   124
    With shame for deeds itself or others hatch.
    Will feel thy words a sore upon its back;

Nevertheless, give lies the quick despatch;   127
    Make thy whole vision freely manifested,
    And where men feel the itch, there let them scratch!

Sour as thy speech may seem at first, when tasted,   130
    'Twill leave behind it much good, wholesome stuff,
    Very nutritious, once it's been digested.

133   Thy cry shall beat as beats the wind, most rough
            Against the loftiest tops; this shall redound
            Much to thine honour, and is cause enough

136   Why, in these wheels, and on the mount, and round
            About the dolorous vale, thou hast been shown
            Only those souls whose fame has made some sound;

139   Because the hearer's mind is never prone
            To dwell on, or put faith in, illustrations
            Derived from the obscure or the unknown,

142   Or other unimpressive demonstrations."

THE IMAGES. *The Heaven of Mars, Cacciaguida*: see Canto xv, under
Images.

The prophesy of Dante's exile: In the *story*, Cacciaguida's words, fore-
telling to Dante the blow of exile that is to fall on him, are the cul-
mination, and clarification, of all the dark and sinister hints he has
heard from other souls in the course of his journey. In the *allegory*,
the foretelling of Dante's future is an instance of contingency which,
though foreseeable by the souls in the mind of God, is not a pre-
determined fate.

Cacciaguida's charge to Dante: Dante's hesitancy as to his duty to relate
in the world all he has heard and seen recall the misgivings he
expressed to Virgil at the outset of his journey: "I am not Aeneas,
I am not St Paul." Virgil reassured him, and with that reassurance
implied that, like Aeneas and like St Paul, Dante was by grace
selected for a divinely ordained mission for the benefit of mankind.
Now once again, and for the last time, Dante seeks confirmation of
his calling. Is he to speak out and boldly rebuke vice? His ancestor's
reply leaves him in no doubt as to this or as to the purpose of his
high privilege.

NOTES. ll. 1–3: *As, hearing ill things said of him* etc.: Phaëthon, hearing
that he was not really Apollo's son, went to his mother Climenè to
hear the truth. Climenè swore that he was truly the son of the god and
urged him to go and ask Apollo in person. Phaëthon did so and induced
his father to let him drive the chariot of the sun. This story still makes
fathers chary of granting requests to their sons.

   l. 4: *Even such was I*: Like Phaëthon, Dante, journeying through Hell
and Purgatory, has heard ominous rumours and hints concerning him-
self and now asks his ancestor for a true explanation of them.

   l. 17: "*. . . on that point gazing still*": In the Primum Mobile (the ninth
sphere) God is perceived by Dante as an infinitesimal point of light.

Commentaries

l. 18: *"that in one Now doth all our times enfold"*: All times are present to God. The souls in Heaven read in the mind of God, as in a mirror, the knowledge of things to come (cf. Canto xxix. 10–12).

ll. 19–20: *". . . the hill that has the cure of souls"*: the Mountain of Purgatory.

ll. 37–42: *"Contingence, which doth exercise no right"* etc.: All contingent beings and events (i.e. all things derived from secondary causes) which (contingency having no place in eternity) do not extend beyond the material world, are depicted in the vision of God. Yet, although God foresees and predisposes all things, man's will remains free. God's foreknowledge of events no more necessitates them than the image on a spectator's retina of a ship going downstream causes the motion of the ship.

ll. 46–8: *"As, through his stepdame's treacherous lust unkind"* etc.: Now, for the first time, clearly and plainly, Dante hears that he will suffer exile. The stepdame of Hippolytus was Phaedra. The unfounded charges of fraudulent conversion of funds which were brought against Dante are compared by Cacciaguida to the false accusations brought by Phaedra against her innocent stepson, Hippolytus. As Hippolytus was driven from Athens, so Dante will be driven from Florence, which figures in this comparison as a step-mother.

ll. 50–51: *". . . him who sits and plots that same"* etc.: The reference is to Corso Donati at whose instigation Boniface VIII was induced to summon Charles of Valois to Florence, in consequence of whose intervention the White Guelfs were driven from Florence.

Where Christ is daily huckstered to and fro: i.e. in Rome, where the things of God are bought and sold. Dante has solemnly rebuked the Church for its avarice in Canto xix of *Inferno* and in particular the simony of Pope Nicholas III, Boniface VIII and Clement V.

l. 53: *"the day of reckoning"*: As far as Dante's cherished hope of reinstatement in Florence is concerned, the day of reckoning never came. Yet retribution fell on Corso Donati, who, when the Black Guelfs were left in possession of Florence, tried to get the supreme power into his own hands. He was charged by the Priors of conspiring against the liberties of the Florentines and summoned to appear before the Podestà. On refusing to do so, he was condemned to death as a traitor, and besieged in his own house, from which he escaped. In attempting to flee from Florence he was overtaken, threw himself down from his horse and was speared in the throat by one of his captors (6 October 1308). Dante appears to have heard that he was dragged at the tail of the horse and so battered to death; such, at any rate, is the fate his brother, Forese, foretells for him in *Purg.* xxiv. 82–4.

l. 62: *"the companions of thy ruin"*: i.e. the exiled White Guelfs. They made at least three attempts to march on Florence: (1) in the summer of 1302, (2) in the spring of 1303, (3) in the summer of 1304. Dante is known to have participated in the first and may also have associated himself with the second. After that there is no record of his being connected with the political or military activities of his fellow-exiles, and, from the words of Cacciaguida, it appears that he broke from them in anger, having suffered calumny of some kind. The early commentator known as Ottimo relates that Dante had advised his party to put off until the spring an expedition they wished to make in the winter. They took his advice and more, for they waited till the summer (1304), and when the expedition failed they turned on Dante and accused him of being in league with the Blacks.

ll. 68–9: "*Well shall it be for thee to have preferred making a party of thy-self alone*": It appears that after his breach with the exiled White Guelfs, Dante did not ally himself with any political party, although he wrote in favour of Imperial authority.

ll. 70–72: "*Thy first abode*" etc.: Dante first received hospitality in Verona at the court of Bartolommeo della Scala, "the great Lombard", whose arms were a golden ladder on a red field surmounted by a black eagle. The ladder was the cognizance of the Scaligers (or Della Scala family) and the eagle was the cognizance of the Imperial party. In 1291 Bartolommeo married Constance of Suabia, the daughter of Conrad of Antioch.

ll. 76–7: ". . . *that youth on whom the hand of this strong star so set its native sign*": The youth is Can Grande Della Scala, the younger brother of Bartolommeo, who was born in March 1291. When Dante first saw him he was in his twelfth year. In 1311 he was associated in the government of Verona with his brother Alboino and they jointly received from Henry VII the title of Imperial Vicars. After the death of Alboino in 1312, Can Grande became sole Lord of Verona, a position he maintained until his death in 1329.

ll. 82–3: "*But ere great Henry by the Gascon's dark deceits is trapped*": The Gascon is the French Pope, Clement V (Bertrand de Goth); having supported the Emperor, Henry VII, and invited him to come to Italy, he yielded to the menaces of the French king and gradually withdrew his support, leaving Henry to carry out his task unaided, if not actually opposed, by Papal influence. Can Grande afforded great assistance to the Imperial cause, suppressing the Guelfs of Lombardy while Henry was passing through on the way to Rome.

l. 88: "*Look thou to him and on his bounties wait*": This line probably refers to Dante's personal indebtedness to Can Grande, at whose court he stayed for some time, during his second period at Verona (cf. Introduction, pp. 40–41). Dante placed great hopes in him as the champion of Imperial authority.

ll. 89–90: "*For many men shall he make mutable*" etc.: These lines recall *Luke* i. 52–3: "He hath put down the mighty from their seats and exalted them of low degree. He hath filled the hungry with good things; and the rich he hath sent empty away."

l. 112: ". . . *the world whose bitter knows no bourne*": i.e. Hell.

Commentaries

l. 128: "*Make thy whole vision freely manifested*": Compare with this: "He [the angel] said, 'Yet again follow me and I will show thee that which thou must relate and tell openly'." (*Apocalypse of St Paul*, M. R. James's translation, pp. 526 ff.).

l. 134: "*the loftiest tops*": i.e. the most eminent personages and dignitaries.

CANTO XVIII

THE STORY. *Dante, pondering the prophecy of Cacciaguida, is roused by the consoling words and beauty of Beatrice, who bids him turn his gaze once more upon the warrior-saints. Having called on eight of these to display their radiance before Dante, Cacciaguida moves among the lights and mingles his voice with their song. Ascending with Beatrice to the heaven of Jupiter, Dante beholds the spirits of the Just who form themselves into letters which spell out the words "Diligite iustitiam qui iudicatis terram". The spirits then transform the final letter into the symbol of justice, the Imperial Eagle.*

Now, while that mirror blest rejoiced once more
 In his own thoughts, and I with mine abode,
 Chewing the sweetness mingled with the sour,

4 The Lady who was leading me to God
 Said: "Change thy thoughts; bethink thee, I am near
 To Him who lightens every sinful load."

7 So at my Comfort's voice I turned – that dear,
 Dear sound – and O, what love I then descried
 In her blest eyes I dare not speak of here;

10 Not only language plays me false; beside,
 There's memory, which is powerless to retrace
 Its course so far, save One should be my guide.

13 This much I may report upon the case:
 My heart from every other longing went
 Completely free while I perused her face,

16 For the Eternal Joy, its radiance bent
 Direct on Beatrice and from her eyes
 Reflected, held me in entire content.

19 She, with a smile that left my faculties
 Quite vanquished, said to me: "Turn and give heed;
 Not in my eyes alone is Paradise."

22 As in men's faces here we sometimes read
 Their feelings plain, when they're so deep concerned
 That all their minds to one sole thought are keyed,

So, in the sacred fire to which I turned,   25
   His wish to tell me more I plainly read
   In the whole look of him, so bright he burned.

"In this, the fifth whorl of the tree," he said,   28
   "That's nourished from its summit, and bears fruit
   All seasons, and whose leaves are never shed,

Are blessèd souls, of whom the mighty bruit   31
   Sent forth on earth, or e'er to Heav'n they came,
   Is rich in themes for every poet's lute;

Watch, then, the cross's horns, and as I name   34
   Each spirit there, lo! he shall move thereon
   As in a cloud moves swift the levin-flame."

He spoke: I saw a flashing lustre run,   37
   At Joshua's name, athwart the cross and stop;
   Nor was it sooner said than it was done;

Great Maccabee was named; I saw him drop,   40
   Spinning as he went, along his fiery lane,
   And gladness was the whip unto the top;

Then Roland on the track of Charlemayne   43
   Sped, and my keen eye following – as it does
   The flight of one's own falcon – watched the twain;

After, my sight was drawn along the cross   46
   By William, Reynald, and Duke Godfrey – three
   Fires, and a fourth, which Robert Guiscard was;

Whereon the soul that had discoursed with me,   49
   Moving and mingling with those myriads bright,
   Showed me his art of heavenly minstrelsy.

I turned to Beatrice upon my right,   52
   Hoping to learn what next I ought to do,
   Even as her word or gesture should invite,

And saw her eyes so clear, so lit all through   55
   With rapture, that her loveliness outshined
   All earlier wont, yea and her latest too;

And as a man, feeling more peace of mind   58
   In doing well, perceives he's gained some ground
   Daily, and is to virtue more inclined,

61 So I, perceiving as we circled round,
 Borne with the spheres, this miracle increase
 Her beauty, knew our gyre had spread its bound;

64 And such an instant change as when release
 From some embarrassment transforms a fair-
 complexioned lady, and her blushes cease,

67 Greeted me when I looked around, for there
 Shone the sixth planet, temperate, and of sheen
 Pure white, which had received me in its care.

70 Before mine eyes the love that dwelt within
 That Jovial torch, with lustre upon lustre,
 In our own tongue spelt signals clearly seen;

73 And as from off a bank birds rise and muster,
 Conjubilant, as 'twere, to have fed so well,
 Now in a long skein, now in a round cluster,

76 So did those winging hallows raise a swell
 Of song among the lights, and in their winging
 Formed themselves into D, then I, then L.

79 First, moving to the strain that they were singing,
 They made the sign, and after it was made
 Awhile hung silent, to their stations clinging.

82 O goddess Pegasean, that dost lade
 Genius with glory, and make it live long years,
 As it makes lands and cities, by thine aid,

85 Be thou my light, to show these characters,
 As I deciphered them, distinctly graven;
 Make manifest thy power in my brief verse!

88 In consonants and vowels five times seven
 Those signs displayed themselves; I noted down
 Each several letter with the meaning given.

91 DILIGITE IUSTITIAM; verb and noun,
 These words came first, and following afterward:
 QUI IUDICATIS TERRAM last were shown.

94 Then, in the final M of the fifth word
 They stood, so that the silver orb of Jove
 Showed in that place all golden-diapered.

And other lights I saw drop from above   97
  On the M's peak and rest there, to that Good
  Chanting, I think, who draws them with His love.

Then, as unnumbered sparks from burning wood   100
  Fly up when it is smitten – and are deemed
  Auguries by the foolish multitude –

So flew aloft a thousand lights, meseemed,   103
  Moved by the Sun that kindles them, to less
  Or greater height mounting in order schemed.

When each had found its place in quietness,   106
  There I beheld an eagle's neck and crest
  Limned out in fire by all these brightnesses;

Their limner needs no model; His own best   109
  Model is He; we know Him, implicit
  As power and form, in every sparrow's nest.

The other joys, content at first to sit   112
  Shaping a lily-pattern on the M,
  With a slight shift made the design complete.

Loved star! what jewels, and how many of them   115
  Showed me 'twas Justice whose terrestrial course
  Is governed by the heaven thou dost begem!

Therefore I pray the Mind which is thy source   118
  Of might and motion, that It mark whence comes
  The smoke that dims thy rays and dulls their force;

That wrath rekindle soon to purge these scums   121
  Of mart and sale within the temple wall
  Built once with miracles and martyrdoms.

O soldiers of that host celestial   124
  On whom I gaze, pray for a whole world run
  Astray after ill example! Pray for all!

Wars, that the sword once waged, are waged and won   127
  By banning now, wherever men think fit,
  That Bread the Father's love locks up from none.

And thou, who writest but to annul the writ,   130
  Take heed! for Peter and Paul, who died to save
  The vineyard thou play'st havoc with, live yet.

133   But thou wilt answer: "I who only crave
          For him who chose to dwell alone, and then
          Was danced away into a martyr's grave,

136   Know naught of all your Pauls and Fishermen!"

THE IMAGES. *The Heaven of Jupiter*: In the *story*, Jupiter is the sixth of
   the seven planets visited by Dante in his ascent to the Empyrean, or
   abode of God. In the *allegory*, the temperate, pure white planet is
   the symbol of public justice in peace, the cause, ultimately, for
   which the warrior-saints have striven and died in battle. As he
   passes from the ruddy glow of Mars to the silvery serenity of Jupiter,
   Dante becomes aware of the increased beauty of the eyes of Bea-
   trice: the concept of justice and world peace is loftier even than victory
   over the Infidel and the establishment of God's word by the sword.
Diligite iustitiam qui iudicatis terram: In the *story*, Dante sees the souls in
   Jupiter spell out in a pattern of lights the letters of this text from the
   Book of Wisdom, "Love justice, ye that judge the earth." Since
   this work was attributed to Solomon, his kingly wisdom is here
   linked with perfect justice. In the *allegory*, this gradual forming of
   the message and Dante's apprehension of it, letter by letter, signify
   the approach of mankind, by trial and error, to the establishment of
   justice in the world. As the series of letters becomes intelligible only
   when it has all been spelled out, so the sequence of world events
   forms a pattern which will be comprehensible only when it is com-
   plete. In the meantime, all endeavour to establish just government
   on earth is a step towards the realization of God's plan for mankind.
The final letter M: In the *story*, the sentence patterned by the lights ends
   with the word "terram", "the earth". The final letter M, while con-
   veying the natural suggestion of the cipher 1,000, together with all
   the associative ideas of a millenium, here specifically symbolizes
   Monarchy, that is, world government, or the concept of all peoples
   united under a universal ruler.
The Eagle: In the *story*, the final letter M is transformed gradually into
   the shape of an eagle. This beautiful and impressive image signifies
   the ancient supremacy of Rome, ordained by God for the peace and
   unity of the world. That the Roman emblem should emerge from
   the meaning spelled out by the souls of the Just is an indication of
   Dante's own gradual comprehension of the meaning of history and
   the divine pattern of justice. In the systems of law of the Italian
   commonwealths, Dante recognized the Roman principles. It is the
   enforcing of these which he has in mind when he speaks and dreams
   of a universal authority guarding all men's peace and freedom.

NOTES. l. 1: "*that mirror blest*": i.e. the soul of Cacciaguida, who, like
a mirror, reflects the light of God.

ll. 5–6: "*. . . bethink thee, I am near to Him who lightens every sinful load*": Beatrice means that she will pray for Dante in his trials to come.

l. 7: *So at my Comfort's voice I turned*: Dante here applies to Beatrice the term he has twice used of Virgil (cf. *Purg.* iii. 22, ix. 43).

ll. 14–18: "*My heart from every longing went completely free*" etc.: As Dante gazes on Beatrice, all thoughts of what he has heard are effaced from his mind.

l. 21: "*Not in my eyes alone is Paradise*": Dante, gazing in the eyes of Beatrice, has experienced the perfection and fulfilment of all desire, and no wonder, for in her he has beheld the reflection of God. In Canto iii, Piccarda has shown that the joy of the souls derives from the identity of their wills with that of God, and her words have enabled Dante to see "how Heav'n is everywhere Paradise" (l. 88). The words of Beatrice, "Not in my eyes alone is Paradise", are a gentle reminder that the light of God is likewise to be seen reflected in all that has yet to be manifested. They may also be intended to convey allegorically that the contemplation of theology is not the only way to attain beatitude; the warrior-saints who died for the Faith are also mirrors of the divine joy.

ll. 28–30: "*In this, the fifth whorl of the tree . . . that's nourished from its Summit*": The tree is the ten heavens; the fifth whorl is the heaven of Mars. Unlike trees on earth which are nourished from the roots, this ten-fold tree takes its nurture from God. The image is reminiscent of *Revelations* xxii. 2: ". . . the tree of life, which bare twelve manner of fruits, and yielded her fruits every month; and the leaves of the tree were for the healing of the nations."

l. 36: "*As in a cloud moves swift the levin-flame*": i.e. as swift as lightning. Lightning was believed to be caused by the explosion of fire from within a cloud (cf. Canto xxiii. 40–42).

l. 37: *He spoke*: Cacciaguida now calls out the names of eight warrior-saints, each of whom in turn goes spinning across, down, up or along the cross so that Dante may identify it.

l. 38: *Joshua*: the conqueror of the land of Canaan and successor of Moses.

l. 40: *Great Maccabee*: Judas Maccabaeus, who successfully resisted the attempts of the King of Syria to destroy the Jewish religion. After restoring and purifying the Temple at Jerusalem (163 B.C.), he was defeated and slain by the Syrians at Eleasa two years later. As his name is called, the light in which his soul is manifested spins along and down the cross like a top kept whirling by a whip.

l. 43: *Then Roland on the track of Charlemayne*: The Emperor of the Franks and his nephew Roland have been mentioned in *Inferno* xxxi. 16–18, in connection with the sound of Roland's horn at the rout of Roncesvalles. Here the souls of the two champions of Christendom ascend the cross and Dante fixes his gaze on them as the falconer follows the flight of his own falcon. A gradation of swiftness seems to be indicated: Joshua moves like lightning, Judas Maccabaeus like a top whirled on by a whip, Roland and Charlemagne soar like falcons.

l. 47: *William, Reynald and Duke Godfrey*: William, Count of Orange, known also as Guillaume au Curb Nes (later Court Nes) is the central figure of a group of Old French chansons-de-geste in the *Geste de Garin de Monglane* which celebrate his defence of Christendom against the Saracens. Reynald or Reneward, called "Rainouart au tinel" from the huge club which he carried, is the half-comic, half-heroic folklore giant of the Old French *Chanson de Guillaume* who reappears in the later epic, *Aliscans*. By birth a Saracen, he was companion and brother-in-law to Guillaume who had married his sister Orable. Two statues flanking the main entrance to the cathedral of Verona (usually said to represent Roland and Oliver) are believed by Catalano to be effigies of Guillaume and Rainouart. If so this may account for Dante's coupling them together here, for he would have been familiar with these statutes which were sculpted by Niccolò of Emilia about the year 1147. This identification has, however, been refuted by Luigi Suttina and, more recently, by Rita Lejeune, who reverts to the traditional theory that the statues represent Roland and Oliver. If so, the association in Dante's mind of William and Reynald can sufficiently well be attributed to his knowledge of the chansons-de-geste. What is remarkable is that Oliver is not mentioned here. Duke Godfrey is Godefroi de Bouillon, the commander-in-chief of the Christian armies in the First Crusade who was crowned King of Jerusalem.

l. 48: *a fourth, which Robert Guiscard was*: Robert Guiscard, Duke of Apulia and Calabria, was one of the twelve sons of Tancred de Hauteville. He succeeded to the command of the Norman troops in Italy and earned glory in his victories over the Saracens and Greeks in Sicily and the South of Italy.

l. 49: *the soul that had discoursed with me*: i.e. Cacciaguida, who, having stayed at the foot of the cross to converse with Dante, now mingles with the other souls and gives proof of his artistry in song.

ll. 61–3: *So I, perceiving as we circled round, borne with the spheres* etc.: Dante and Beatrice not only ascend, they also travel westwards with the spheres. The beauty of Beatrice's eyes has surpassed even that which he beheld when he last looked on her. The reason is that they are mounting from the sphere of Mars to that of Jupiter.

l. 64: *And such an instant change*: Dante now moves out of the ruddy glow of Mars into the white sheen of the sixth planet. In the *Convivio* (II. xiv) Dante quotes Ptolemy as saying "that Jupiter is a star of temperate constitution, midway between the coldness of Saturn and the heat of Mars. The second property is that it shows white among the rest of the stars as if silvered over."

l. 70: *the love that dwelt within*: i.e. the spirits radiant with love.

l. 71: *that Jovial torch*: i.e. the radiance of the planet Jupiter, which was believed to have an influence of joviality.

l. 72: *in our own tongue*: i.e. in Latin.

l. 74: *Conjubilant*: This word was introduced into English by Neale in his translation of Bernard of Cluny's *eonjubilantia* in the hymn "Jerusalem the Golden". Like the Italian "congratulando" which it here translates it conveys the co-inherence of the blessed.

l. 78: *Formed themselves into D, then I, then L*: These are the first three letters of the phrase *Diligite iustitiam qui iudicatis terram*, which is spelt out in its entirety, letter by letter, by the lights (cf. ll. 91–3). The words constitute the first sentence of the *Book of the Wisdom of Solomon* in the Apocrypha ("Love justice, ye that judge the earth").

ll. 82–7: *O goddess Pegasean* etc.: This invocation is probably addressed to Poetry in general rather than to any one Muse in particular, though some commentators have understood a reference either to Calliope or to Urania. Pegasus, the winged horse, with a stroke of his hoof, brought forth the fountain of Hippocrene on Mt Helicon. Dante is therefore saying, "O goddess of the fountain sacred to the Muses".

l. 88: *In consonants and vowels five times seven*: There are thirty-five letters in the sentence which the lights display.

l. 94: *Then, in the final M*: The reader is to visualize a gothic M as follows:

l. 98: *On the M's peak*: The souls, alighting from above on the top of the M, change it as follows:

l. 107: *There I beheld an eagle's neck and crest*: The design has now undergone a further change, as follows:

ll. 112–13: *The other joys ... shaping a lily-pattern on the M*: The other souls, who had formed neither the neck nor the head of the eagle, had been transforming the down-strokes of the M to resemble part of an heraldic lily:

l. 114: *With a slight shift made the design complete*: The souls not forming the neck and head now shift position so as to shape the wings and body of the eagle, as follows:

l. 115: *what jewels, and how many of them* etc.: i.e. how many and what radiant spirits made plain to me that our justice on earth is governed by the sphere which Jupiter adorns!

ll. 119–20: *whence comes the smoke that dims thy rays and dulls their force*: The beneficent influence of the planet Jupiter is prevented from having its full effect upon men by the Pope who, out of avarice and ambition, opposes the establishment of Imperial authority in Italy.

ll. 121–3: *... these scums of mart and sale within the temple wall built once with miracles and martyrdoms*: This rebuke is aimed at the sale of sacraments or ecclesiastical offices and all trafficking in holy things (cf. *Inf.* xix). The "temple wall" indicates the Papacy or the Church ("built once with miracles and martyrdoms") and also recalls the wrath of Christ when He turned out the money-lenders from the Temple of Jerusalem.

ll. 125–6: *a whole world run astray after an ill example*: Once again Dante accuses the Papacy of leading the world astray by the evil example of avarice (cf. *Purg.* xvi. 100–105).

ll. 128–9: *By banning now, wherever men think fit, that Bread the Father's love locks up from none*: i.e. the weapons of excommunication and interdict.

ll. 130–31: *And thou, who writest but to annul the writ, take heed!*: This particular warning is probably addressed to Pope John XXII, who excommunicated Can Grande in 1317. His pontificate was remarkable for a series of excommunications, followed by recommunications, of which the chief object was to extort money, since the cancelling of excommunication was a source of Papal revenue.

ll. 133–5: "*I who only crave for him who chose to dwell alone*" etc.: The image of St John the Baptist, who chose to dwell in the desert and who died a martyr's death in consequence of the dancing of Salome, was imprinted on the florin, which is all the Pope desires.

l. 136: "*know naught of all your Pauls and Fishermen*": The indictment brought by Dante against the Pope is that he is so occupied in accumulating wealth that he cares for nothing else and does not even know of the Apostles.

CANTO XIX

THE STORY. *The Just Rulers composing the sign of the Eagle now speak as one voice, the voice of justice. Dante is emboldened to hope that he may at last learn the solution to a problem which has long troubled him, namely the exclusion from Heaven of virtuous heathens who have never heard of Christ. The Eagle replies that human intellect cannot explore the depths of divine justice; man cannot ask whether the judgements of God are just but only whether they are in accordance with the will of God. If so, they are just, for the will of God is the perfect standard of justice, of which our own is but a reflection. The Eagle then denounces the unjust rulers of contemporary Europe.*

    Grandly before me, with its wings displayed,
        The image shone, which, in their sweet fruition
        Exultant, all those weaving spirits made;

4   Each seemed a ruby, that the ebullition
        Of the sun's fires smote with its burning link,
        So that the splendour blazed upon my vision.

7   What I must now relate was ne'er with ink
        Written, nor told in speech, nor by the powers
        Of mind e'er grasped, to imagine it or think;

10   For I beheld and heard the beak discourse,
        And utter with its voice both *Mine* and *Me*,
        When in conception still 'twas *Us* and *Ours*.

13   Thus it began: "Justice and piety
        Raised me up here, where no desire of glory
        Can e'er outrun the great reality.

16   'Twas mine to leave, in every territory,
        Such a memorial as base men are bound
        To praise, though they continue not the story."

19   As many coals are felt to shed all round
        One glow of heat, so from that image went,
        Blended of many loves, a single sound.

22   Whence I straightway: "O you, the permanent
        Flowers of immortal joy, who waft me forth
        Your mingled odours all in one sweet scent,

Now, with your breathing airs allay the dearth   25
   I've suffered long, by hunger hard assailed
   Because I found no food for it on earth.

Well know I, if God's justice is beheld   28
   Among these spheres in any mirror glassed,
   Yours above all must gaze on it unveiled.

How eagerly I wait the truth at last,   31
   And what it is I ne'er have understood,
   Ye know, with all the cause of my long fast."

Then, as the falcon, issuing from the hood,   34
   Stretches her neck, and claps her wings rejoicing,
   And preens herself, and shows her ready mood,

So, and with songs, I saw that ensign poising,   37
   With praises of God's graces wov'n all through;
   Who there is blest knows best what strain 'twas voicing.

It spake: "He that with turning compass drew   40
   The world's confines, and traced there such largesse
   Of things, all different, seen or hid from view,

Could not on all that universe impress   43
   His worth so wholly but that His word's might
   Must still remain in infinite excess;

Witness that first proud being, made so bright   46
   He topped creation; yet he fell anon,
   Unripe, because he would not wait for light;

Showing that lesser natures, all and one,   49
   Are too strait vessels for that Good which stays
   Boundless, and measured by Itself alone.

Our sight, which must be one among the rays   52
   Of that great Mind which fills all creatures full,
   Can never, then, by nature of the case,

Possess such power but that its Principle   55
   Must penetrate beyond it, and perceive
   Far more than to your eyes is visible.

Such vision, then, as you on earth receive   58
   Drowns in eternal Justice evermore,
   Like sight in ocean, whelmed beyond retrieve;

61   For while it sees the bottom near the shore;
         In the great main no bottom's to be seen,
         Though it is there; the deep has sealed it o'er.

64   There is no light, unless from that serene
         Which ne'er is troubled; darkness is the rest,
         Shadow of flesh, or its black atropine.

67   Now is sufficiently made manifest
         The maze wherein that living Justice hid
         For which thou madest such persistent quest;

70   For 'Here's a man', thou saidst, 'born of some breed
         On Indus' bank, where there is none to tell
         Of Christ, and none to write, and none to read;

73   He lives, so far as we can see, quite well,
         Rightly disposed, in conduct not amiss,
         Blameless in word and deed; yet infidel

76   And unbaptised he dies; come, tell me this:
         Where is the justice that condemns the man
         For unbelief? What fault is it of his?'

79   Now, who art thou to be a judge, and scan
         Truth from thy bench a thousand miles away,
         With thy short sight that carries but a span?

82   Had ye no rule of Scripture, well-a-day!
         He'd find, who subtly went to work with me,
         Fine puzzles there to keep his wits in play.

85   O minds of earth! O clods! it ne'er could be
         That Primal Will, good in Itself, should quit
         Its very Self, of Good the *A per se.*

88   Right's right so far as this with That doth fit;
         No finite good draws That to its own measure,
         But That, by raying forth, gives rise to it."

91   As the stork circles o'er her nest at leisure
         When she has fed her brood, and as the chick
         Fed by her care looks up to her with pleasure,

94   Thus (and thus too my grateful glance was quick)
         Did that blest image, thus it plied its vans,
         Moved by the counsels swarming there so quick;

Wheeling it sang and spake: "My song outspans   97
  Thy mortal wit, surpassing all thou know'st;
  So doth the eternal judgement matched with man's."

When these bright ardours of the Holy Ghost   100
  Resettled, and that standard's form restored,
  Which once made Rome revered from coast to coast,

The voice began again: "None ever soared   103
  To this high realm that had not faith in Christ,
  Ere He was nailed on tree, or afterward;

But see! full many shall cry aloud: *Christ! Christ!*   106
  Who in the Last Day shall be sent to lodge
  Farther from Him than they who know not Christ.

Christians like these, the Ethiop shall judge,   109
  When part the flocks, to taste the wealth that springs
  Eterne, or chew the eternal empty grudge.

What will the Persians say then to your kings,   112
  When the Book's opened and they see uncased
  The chronicle of all these shameful things?

They'll read therein, where Albert's acts are traced,   115
  That deed – already trembling on the pen –
  Which shall lay Prague and all her kingdom waste.

They'll read how he that's fated to be slain   118
  By the wild sanglier's thrust, hath falsified
  The coinage, and pulled ruin down on Seine.

They'll read with what insensate greed and pride   121
  England and Scotland make their raids so many,
  And neither keeps to his own Borderside.

Lo there, the kings of Spain and of Bohenny,   124
  Lechers and sluggards both! – and one of them
  That ne'er knew honour yet, nor wished for any.

Lo there, the Cripple of Jerusalem!   127
  To reckon up his virtue will require
  Only an I, his crimes will need an M.

Lo there, the guardian of the Isle of Fire   130
  Where old Anchises died! – a flagrant case
  Of coward heart and covetous desire;

133 And his record, to show his paltriness,
  Close-writ with cramped contractions, shall confine
  Much crowded matter in a narrow space;

136 And all shall witness by what schemes malign
  Uncle and brother set the brand of shame
  Upon two crowns, and on a princely line.

139 And Portugal shall be held up to blame
  With Norway, and the Rascian who laid eyes
  On Venice coin and forged his own ill-fame.

142 O blest is Hungary, if she now defies
  Further ill-usage! Blest Navarre, if now
  She girds her with her mountain fortalice!

145 In pledge whereof, let all the world allow
  That Nicosia and Famagusta speak,
  Who for their beast, that hard as he knows how

148 Runs with the pack, already wail and shriek."

THE IMAGES. *The Heaven of Jupiter*: see Canto xviii, under *Images*.
The collective voice of the just rulers: In the sphere of Jupiter no one of the
 souls speaks singly, but all speak together in a voice which is both one
 and many. In the *allegory*, this blending of many utterances to form
 a single sound signifies the contributions of just men in the course of
 history towards the establishment of earthly justice.
The Eagle: In this canto, the Eagle represents Divine Justice, of which
 the concept of world peace under imperial authority is but an imper-
 fect image. In its historical operations, Divine Justice is also Grace
 and, as such, lies beyond the reach of human comprehension.

NOTES. l. 2: *The image*: i.e. the Eagle.
 l. 7–9: *What I must now relate was ne'er with ink written, nor told in
speech* etc.: These lines seem to echo the words of St Paul (*I Cor.* ii. 9):
"Eye hath not seen, nor ear heard, neither have entered into the heart of
man, the things which God hath prepared for them that love him."
 l. 11–12: *And utter with its voice both "Mine" and "Me"* etc.: The
voice that issued from the Eagle's beak was the utterance of all the
spirits composing the sacred image; and such was the harmony of their
wills that a single voice expressed them all, and "I" and "Mine" con-
veyed "We" and "Ours". The just rulers both symbolize and constitute
justice.
 ll. 13–14: *"Justice and piety raised me up here"*: The Eagle means that
the souls of the just rulers, who form the image, enjoy the degree of

bliss to which their justice and mercy have raised them, and that the mercy and righteousness of just rulers have exalted the image of justice.

ll. 14–15: "*. . . where no desire of glory can e'er outrun the great reality*": The glory of Heaven surpasses all earthly desires.

ll. 25–6: "*. . . the dearth I've suffered long*": Dante entreats an explanation of a problem which has long troubled him. The problem, which he leaves the souls to read in his mind, is this: many men live and die without having heard of Christ and, consequently, without having the opportunity of embracing the Faith and receiving baptism. Are such men damned? If so, wherein does the justice of their damnation reside?

ll. 28–30: "*Well know I, if God's justice is beheld*" etc.: The order of angels who deliver divine judgements (the Thrones) are associated, not with the heaven of Jupiter, but with that of Saturn. Dante appears to mean: "If elsewhere in Heaven Divine Justice is mirrored, it is *beheld* by the souls of the Just more clearly than by any others."

ll. 37–9: *So, and with songs, I saw that ensign poising* etc.: The Eagle, before replying, utters hymns in praise of divine grace.

ll. 40–45: "*He that with turning compass drew the world's confines*" etc.: God could not create anything greater than, or similar to, Himself, nor transmit His virtue to any created thing to such a degree that His own almighty power did not infinitely exceed all other.

l 46: "*. . . that first proud being*": i.e. Lucifer.

ll. 47–8: "*. . . yet he fell anon, unripe, because he would not wait for light*": Lucifer (and Adam and Eve) sinned not only by desiring what was withheld but also by desiring to possess it before the appointed time.

ll. 49–51: "*Showing that lesser natures*" etc.: God creates nothing equal to His Word. Lucifer was the summit of all creation, the most superb thing that God ever created; and the fact that he fell testifies that God makes nothing equal to Himself. It follows, therefore, that human intellect cannot explore the depths of divine justice (ll. 52–60).

l. 70: "*For 'Here's a man', thou saidst, 'born of some breed on Indus' bank'*" etc.: The Eagle now gives expression to the problem which has perplexed Dante so long. (India was thought of as the country furthest removed from the centre of Christianity, Rome.)

ll. 82–4: "*Had ye no rule of Scripture, well-a-day! He'd find, who subtly went to work with me*" etc.: If Holy Scripture were not there, with its authority, to enjoin men to believe in the infallible justice of God, anyone who attempted to investigate the problem would find matter for doubting to a marvellous degree.

ll. 85–8: "*. . . it ne'er could be that Primal Will, good in Itself*" etc.: The will of God, being just, cannot depart from justice; therefore man cannot ask whether the judgements of God are just but only whether a judgement is in conformity with the will of God; if it is, it is just.

ll. 89–90: "*No finite good draws That to its own measure*" etc.: Our idea of justice is but a reflection of divine justice.

ll. 91–5: *As the stork circles o'er her nest* etc.: The explanation of the relationship between human and divine justice and between justice and the will of God has entirely removed the doubt which has been troubling Dante. St Thomas Aquinas discusses the question of the salvation of the untaught savage in *De Vero* (XIV, ii. I) and concludes: "It is certain that God will impart to him the necessary truths of faith, either through interior illumination, or through a preacher of the faith."

l. 101: *... and that standard's form restored* etc.: The souls again disposed themselves so as to form the pattern of the Eagle. Note that Dante here explicitly states that it is the *Roman* eagle they form.

ll. 103–5: "*None ever soared to this high realm*" etc.: The distinction indicated is between those who believed in Christ to come and those who believed in Him after His coming.

l. 106: "*... full many shall cry aloud: 'Christ! Christ!'*" etc.: Compare *Matt.* vii. 21–23: "Not every one that saith unto Me, Lord, Lord, shall enter into the kingdom of heaven", etc.

l. 108: "*Farther from Him than they who know not Christ*": i.e. deeper down in Hell than the Limbo.

ll. 110–11: "*... to taste the wealth that springs eterne, or chew the eternal empty grudge*": i.e. the sheep and the goats, the souls in Heaven and the souls in Hell.

l. 112: "*the Persians*": here intended as representing all non-Christians (cf. "the Ethiop", l. 109).

l. 113: "*When the Book's opened*": i.e. the Book of Judgement. Compare *Revelations* xx. 12: "The books were opened; ... and the dead were judged out of those things which were written in the books, according to their works."

l. 115: "*They'll read therein*" etc.: From here on until the end of the canto, Dante represents the Eagle as uttering a condemnation of contemporary monarchs. The passage recalls the comments of Sordello in the Valley of the Princes (*Purg.* vi. 91–136).

ll. 116–17: "*That deed – already trembling on the pen – which shall lay Prague and all her kingdom waste*": Albert of Austria, the son of Rudolf of Hapsburg, was elected Emperor (though never crowned) in 1298. In 1304, jealous of the growing power of Wenceslas IV, he invaded and devastated his kingdom of Bohemia.

ll. 118–19: "*... he that's fated to be slain by the wild sanglier's thrust*" etc.: This is Philip IV of France, who died in 1314 while out hunting when his horse was overthrown by the charge of a wild boar. In all the references to him in the *Divine Comedy* he is not once mentioned by name. The issue of base coinage at nominal value (to pay the expenses of his war against Flanders) had a serious effect on the economy of France.

ll. 121–3: "*They'll read with what insensate greed and pride*": Dante is thought to be alluding here to the wars between Edward I and Wallace.

l. 124: "*the kings of Spain and of Bohenny*": The king of Spain is thought to be Ferdinand IV of Castile; the king of Bohemia is Wenceslas IV.

Commentaries

l. 127: *"the Cripple of Jerusalem"*: Charles II, King of Naples, son of Charles of Anjou, was surnamed "Le Boiteux". The title of Jerusalem was attached to the Crown of Naples when Mary of Antioch ceded her claim to Charles I. His virtues may be indicated by the figure 1, but for his crimes the figure M (1,000) is required. The solitary virtue here alluded to is thought to be his liberality.

ll. 130–31: *"the guardian of the Isle of Fire where old Anchises died"*: Anchises, the father of Aeneas, died soon after the arrival of the Trojans in Sicily ("the Isle of Fire", so named from its volcano, Etna). The "guardian" of Sicily is Frederick, son of Pedro of Aragon, whose crime was to have first espoused the cause of the Imperialists and then to abandon it on the death of Henry VII.

l. 134: *"Close-writ with cramped contractions"*: The record of Frederick is so paltry that the old scribal contractions will suffice to record the account of his evil deeds which are not worthy to be written out in an unabbreviated hand.

ll. 137–8: *"Uncle and brother set the brand of shame upon two crowns, and on a princely line"*: The uncle of Frederick is James, King of the Balearic Islands; the brother is James, King of Aragon.

ll. 139–41: *"And Portugal shall be held up to blame"* etc.: In these three lines, the Eagle mentions together Dionysius, King of Portugal (1279–1325), Haakon, King of Norway (1299–1319) and Stephen Ouros, King of Rascia (Dalmatia), who in 1307 struck coins which counterfeited the Venetian ducat.

ll. 142–3: *"O blest is Hungary, if she now defies further ill-usage"*: In 1301 the son of Charles Martel, Carobert, succeeded to the throne of Hungary (cf. Canto viii and Genealogical Tables, p. 398).

Blest Navarre etc.: Navarre was an independent kingdom until 1314, when it was united to the French crown on the accession of Louis X. The "mountain fortalice" of Navarre is the Western Pyrenees.

ll. 145–8: *"In pledge whereof, let all the world allow that Nicosia and Famagusta speak"* etc.: Nicosia and Famagusta, two towns in Cyprus, may serve as a warning of what Navarre may expect if she falls under French rule, for Cyprus now suffers under the misrule of the Frenchman, Henry II of Lusignan, here referred to as the "beast, that hard as he knows how, runs with the pack", i.e. who in his dissolute life keeps pace with the evil monarchs already mentioned.

CANTO XX

THE STORY. *As the Eagle falls silent, the multiple voices burst into heavenly song; this is followed by a murmuring which, rising up through the neck of the sacred ensign, is converted once more into a single utterance. The Eagle bids Dante fix his gaze upon the six lights which compose its pupil and the curve above its eye; these it identifies as David, Trajan, Hezekiah, Constantine, William II of Sicily and Rhipeus the Trojan. Dante expresses his amazement at the presence of Trajan and Rhipeus, who are declared by the Eagle to have died in the true faith.*

When from this hemisphere of ours descending
    The universal lamp so far has gone
    That on all sides the daylight hath its ending,

4   The sky, lit heretofore by him alone,
    Straight reappears, with myriad lights made quick,
    And all reflected splendours of the one.

7   As the world's ensign and the sacred beak
    Which held its leaders paused, it brought to mind
    This act of heaven; for, when it ceased to speak,

10   Out broke those living lights, the while they shined
    Brighter by far, in songs – alas! which slide,
    Slip out of memory and are left behind.

13   Sweet, smiling love! How fervently did glide
    Thy warblings through the vents of that sweet flute
    Breathed on by holy thoughts and naught beside!

16   When those rare gems, precious beyond compute,
    Wherewith I saw the sixth of heav'ns a-gleam,
    Bade silence, and the angelic chimes were mute,

19   I heard a murmuring, as of some clear stream
    Dropping from rock to rock, whose din denotes
    How thick with springs its mountain-sources teem;

22   And, as the music's sound forms into notes
    In the lute's neck, or in the pipes that swallow
    Wind and expel it through their unstopped throats,

So did the murmuring of the eagle follow 25
 That pause of expectation, and it floated
 Up through the neck, as though it had been hollow.

There it took form and voice, to pour full-throated 28
 Out of the beak in words, which in my heart,
 Being there expected, were devoutly noted.

"Fix firm thy gaze on me, and view that part 31
 Which in your earthly eagles", thus it said,
 "Sees and endures the sun's most fiery smart;

For of the fires wherewith I've architected 34
 My figured shape, the chief of rank and mark
 Are those with whom the eye shines in my head.

Midmost, as 'twere the pupil, burns that spark 37
 Which was the minstrel of the Holy Spirit,
 And once from town to town bare forth the ark;

And now he knows how much his own songs merit, 40
 So far as 'twas his art that shaped the strain,
 For even as he deserved, he doth inherit.

Five in the eyebrow's arch – mark these again! 43
 The one that nearest to the beak doth sit
 Consoled the widow when her son was slain;

And now he knows how dear they pay for it 46
 Who serve not Christ, by his experience
 Of this sweet life and of the opposite.

He that lies next on the circumference, 49
 Where springs that arch which now is my concern,
 Delayed his death by his true penitence;

And now he knows that the decrees eterne 52
 Alter not, though good prayer should get today's
 Portion postponed to serve tomorrow's turn.

Next, he that with high purpose – though but base 55
 Its fruit – going eastward with the laws and me,
 Turned Greek, to let the Pastor take his place;

And now he knows that all the iniquity 58
 Springing from his good action hurts not him,
 Though it should make the world in flinders flee.

61   And he thou see'st where downward slopes the rim
           Was William, mourned in his own land, which grieves
           That Charles and Frederick live, and groans for them;

64   And now he knows how warmly Heaven receives
           And loves a righteous king; his sparklings show
           The deathless glory that he here achieves.

67   Who'd credit, in the erring world below,
           That Trojan Rhipeus is the fifth of these
           Most holy lights that in the circle glow?

70   And now he knows the grace of God, and sees
           Much that the world is powerless to descry,
           Though sounding not its last profundities."

73   Like to the lark which soars into the sky
           Singing at first, and then, with utter bliss
           Filled to the full, falls silent by and by,

76   So seemed to me yon image of the impress
           Of that eternal Will by love whereto
           Each thing becomes that which it really is;

79   And though, as through stained glass the stain shows through,
           Amazement showed through me as clear as clear,
           To hold my peace was more than I could do;

82   So that a cry burst forth, "What's this I hear?"
           As though its own weight forced my lips asunder.
           This roused great sparkling and much joyous cheer;

85   And with an eye yet brighter and jocunder
           The blessed emblem answered me straightway,
           As loth to keep me thus suspense in wonder:

88   "I see thou dost believe, because I say,
           That these things are; the *How* escapes thy sight;
           So, though believed, they're hid, and thou dost stay

91   Like one who knows a thing by name aright,
           Yet of its quiddity makes no pretence
           To knowledge, till some other give him light.

94   *Regnum coelorum* suffereth violence
           From ardent love and living hope, which still
           Conquer God's will and beat down His defence –

Not as man beats down man; Himself doth will　　　　97
　　To suffer conquest, who by His own love
　　Conquered, comes conquering and unconquerable.

The brow's first life, yea, and the fifth thereof　　100
　　Make thee amazed to see them deck the seat
　　Of angels. Know, these put the body off,

Not gentiles, as thou deemest, but complete　　　103
　　In Christian faith, clinging – as each had scope –
　　To the passion-pierced, to the yet-to-be-passible Feet.

For one from Hell (where spirits never grope　　106
　　Back to right will), into his flesh and bone
　　Returned; this was the guerdon of living hope,

The living hope that nerved the orison　　　　109
　　Made unto God to raise him up, and dower
　　His will once more with motions of its own;

Which glorious soul, when for a little hour　　112
　　It thus resumed the body whence it came,
　　Believed on Him that hath the saving power,

And, so believing, loved, with ardent flame　　115
　　So bright, that at the second death 'twas found
　　Worthy to join our high celestial game.

The other, by a grace from such deep ground　　118
　　Gushing that no created eye can plumb
　　Its hidden well-springs where they run profound,

On righteousness spent all his earthly sum　　121
　　Of love; whence God from grace to grace unsealed
　　His eyes to the redemption yet to come.

Then he, believing in the truth revealed,　　124
　　The stench of pagan filth no more could bear,
　　And scourged the vice with which the land was filled.

Ere ever baptism was, a thousand year,　　　127
　　He was baptised; thou, at the car's right wheel,
　　Saw'st those three ladies who his proxies were.

Predestination! what far depths conceal　　130
　　From feeble sight, unable to detect
　　The First Cause whole, thy root of woe and weal!

133   And, mortals, keep your judgement straitly checked,
           For here we see God face to face, and still
           We know not all the roll of His elect;

136   Yet sweet to us appears our lack of skill,
           Since this good doth our good the more refine,
           That what God willeth, that we also will."

139   On this wise did that image all-divine
           Medicine to me a sweet and delicate
           Balsam to clear this clouded sight of mine.

142   And even as the good lutanist will wait
           On the good singer with his thrilling wires
           Plucked right, for more delight, nor soon nor late,

145   Just so I mind me how, with twin desires
           Moved, as two winking eyelids move the same,
           The while it spake, I saw those two blest fires

148   Accompany the words with flicks of flame.

THE IMAGES. *The Heaven of Jupiter*: see Canto xviii, under *Images*.
   The Eye of the Eagle: The six lights forming the pupil and the curve
   above the eye of the eagle are recognized by the body as the greatest
   representatives of justice on earth. David, the pupil of the eye, was
   the first true king of the chosen people. Of him Dante writes in the
   Convivio: "It was in the very same age that David was born and
   Rome was born, that is, that Aeneas came from Troy to Italy,
   which was the origin of the most noble city of Rome, as the records
   testify; so that the divine choice of the Roman Empire is manifest
   from the birth of the holy city being contemporaneous with the root
   of Mary's race." David represents a combination of spiritual and
   temporal authority on earth; he is the psalmist who sang of the
   Holy Ghost, he brought the ark, the tabernacle of the divine pre-
   sence, to his city, and his kingdom was founded on worship. In
   Trajan, Hezekiah, and Constantine, Dante presents three instances of
   the wonder of God's grace; for Trajan was restored to life and con-
   verted by the prayers of Pope Gregory the Great; to Hezekiah was
   granted a further lease of life in response to prayer and repentance;
   and Constantine's bliss is shown to be undiminished by the iniquity
   which sprang from his good action. The only modern ruler,
   William II of Sicily, is a striking image in his isolation, at once a
   rebuke and an inspiration to the contemporary world.
       Climax of the six is Rhipeus the pagan, at mention of whom an
   expression of amazement bursts from Dante's lips. The presence in

Heaven of both Rhipeus and Trajan at last provides Dante with the answer for which his soul has yearned for so long. Redemption is not, of necessity, denied to those who knew, or know, not Christ. The divine will, operating by grace in ways which man's mind cannot fathom, grants salvation to the righteous. It would appear from this that Dante's faith had broadened and deepened during his later years and that he came to know, and to rejoice in the knowledge, that Christian truth was not bounded by his understanding.

NOTES. l. 2: *the universal lamp*: i.e. the sun.

l. 10: *Out broke those living lights*: The multiple song of the lights which bursts forth when the beak is silent is compared to the shining forth of starlight which occurs when the sky is dark. (The lights of the souls are not said to increase visibly in radiance.)

l. 18: *the angelic chimes were mute*: The singing, of which the beauty surpasses all mortal melody, is described as angelic, or heavenly (i.e. Dante does not intend to convey that it was uttered by any of the angelic orders).

ll. 22–30: *And, as the music's sound forms into notes* etc.: This is not the first time that Dante has described the transformation of sound into articulated speech. In *Inf.* xxvi. 85–90, he has described "how the words the spirit speaks down at the root of the flame are first translated into 'fire's native speech' – an inarticulate roaring – and then re-translated into words when they reach the tip: much on the principle of the telephone, by which the sound-waves are transmitted as electric vibrations and turned back into sound-waves when they reach the receiver." (D. L. Sayers, *Further Papers on Dante*, p. 113.) In *Inferno* xiii. 40–45, the voice of Pier delle Vigne issuing from the broken splint of the thorn-tree is compared to the issuing of sound from a green branch:

> "As, when you burn one end of a green brand,
>   Sap at the other oozes from the wood,
>   Sizzling as the imprisoned airs expand."

ll. 31–3: "*. . . that part which in your earthly eagles . . . sees and endures the sun's most fiery smart*": i.e. Dante is to fix his gaze upon the eagle's eye. The legend that eagles trained their young to gaze at the sun was current in Dante's time. He has referred to their power of enduring the sunlight in Canto i (l. 48), a power which Beatrice surpasses. Compare Milton's eagle, "Kindling her undazzled eyes at the full midday beam".

ll. 35–6: "*. . . the chief of rank and mark are those with whom the eye shines in my head*": The six souls here alluded to make up the Eagle's eye. (Cf. diagram on p. 238.)

ll. 37–9: "*. . . that spark which was the minstrel of the Holy Spirit*" etc.: David, the psalmist, who fetched the ark (the sign of the divine presence) from Gabba to Geth and from Geth to Jerusalem (cf. *Purg.* x. 57–64 and *II Sam.* vi. 6–18).

ll. 40–42: *"And now he knows how much his own songs merit"* etc.: Although David as the psalmist was "the minstrel of the Holy Spirit", yet David's own art, in as much as it proceeded from his own free will, entitled him to reward in Heaven. Inspiration, being vouchsafed to him by grace, did not constitute merit.

ll. 44–5: *"The one that nearest to the beak doth sit consoled the widow"* etc.: It is related of Trajan (Roman Emperor from A.D. 98–117) that as he was setting out for the wars, on being stopped by a poor widow who asked him for redress for the death of her son, he acceded to her request. The episode is mentioned in *Purgatory* as being sculpted among the examples of humility in the first Cornice (*Purg.* x. 73–96). According to another legend, St Gregory brought the dead Emperor back from Hell by his prayers and baptized him to salvation. A. P. Stanley says of Gregory before he became Pope, "His heart yearned towards those old Pagan heroes or sages who had been gathered to their fathers without hearing the name of Christ. He could not bear to think, with the belief that prevailed at the time, that they had been consigned to destruction. One especially there was, of whom he was constantly reminded in his walks through Rome – the great Emperor Trajan, whose statue he always saw rising above him at the top of the tall column which stood in the market-place, called from him the Forum of Trajan. It is said that he was so impressed with the thought of the justice and goodness of this heathen sovereign, that he earnestly prayed in St Peter's Church that God would even now give him grace to know the name of Christ and be converted. And it is believed that from the veneration which he entertained for Trajan's memory, this column remained when all around it was shattered to pieces; and so it still remains, a monument both of the goodness of Trajan, and the true Christian charity of Gregory" (*Historical Memorials of Canterbury*, Dent, n.d., p. 13).

ll. 47–8: *". . . by his experience of this sweet life and of the opposite"*:

Trajan has already experienced the "opposite" of heavenly existence, namely, the hopeless sadness of Limbo.

ll. 49–54: *"He that comes next on the circumference . . . delayed his death by his true penitence"* etc.: Hezekiah, King of Judah, being "sick unto death" prayed that God would remember his faithful service; and God healed Hezekiah and added fifteen years to his life. Later, Hezekiah fell into the sin of pride, of which he subsequently repented; the consequence of his penitence was not the prolonging of his life, but the averting of the wrath of God. (See *II Kings* xx. 1–6 and *II Chron.* xxxii. 26.) It would appear that Dante has here combined the two episodes.

ll. 55–7: *"Next, he that with high purpose – though but base its fruit –"*: The next is the soul of the Emperor Constantine who "with high purpose" ceded Rome to Pope Sylvester I, withdrawing eastward with the Roman laws and the Imperial standard, and becoming Emperor of Byzantium. (Compare the opening words of the speech of Justinian in Canto vi.)

ll. 58–60: *"And now he knows that all the iniquity"* etc.: The action of Constantine, though its consequences were evil, was good in itself. Here Dante follows St Thomas Aquinas who said: "A consequence cannot make evil an action that was good nor good an action that was evil."

ll. 61–3: *"And he thou see'st where downward slopes the rim was William"* etc.: Next to Constantine on the curve of the Eagle's eye comes William II, the Norman King of Naples and Apulia. His subjects not only mourn his death but groan and lament under the sufferings inflicted on them by Charles "le Boiteux", King of Apulia, and Frederick, King of Aragon. (These last two monarchs have already been denounced by the Eagle in Canto xix. ll. 127, 130.) William II, surnamed "the Good", reigned from 1166 to 1189. The early commentators write in praise of his just and righteous rule. His tomb in the Cathedral of Monreale, near Palermo, bears the simple legend: *Hic situs est bonus rex Gulielmus*. Dying without issue, he bequeathed his dominions of Naples and Apulia to his aunt, the Empress Constance.

l. 68: *"Trojan Rhipeus"*: Rhipeus, a Trojan hero who was slain during the sack of Troy, is described by Virgil as being "the one man amongst the Trojans most just and observant of the right" (*Aen.* II, 426–7). The presence of Rhipeus in Heaven is a further answer to Dante's doubt concerning the virtuous heathen (cf. Canto xix).

ll. 76–8: *". . . the impress of that eternal Will by love whereto each thing becomes that which it really is"*: The imprint of the eternal will is here interpreted as meaning justice. By loving justice (i.e. by conforming to the will of God) each thing becomes its true self.

l. 80: *amazement showed through me as clear as clear*: i.e. amazement at the presence of Rhipeus in Heaven.

ll. 91–3: *"Like one who knows a thing by name aright, yet of its quiddity makes no pretence to knowledge"*: The "quiddity" of anything (a scholastic term) is its essence, that which makes it what it is. Dante knows and believes (because the Eagle has told him) that Rhipeus has been granted salvation; but what the nature of such granting was he does not yet know (in other words, he does not understand how he came to be saved).

ll. 94–6: " *'Regnum coelorum' suffereth violence*" etc.: Fervent love and vivid hope avail to bring a soul to Heaven. The prevailing force of intercession (as in the case of Trajan) and of righteousness (as in the case of Rhipeus) is not a victory over the divine will but a victory of it or by means of it.

l. 100: "*The brow's first life*": i.e. the soul of Trajan; "*and the fifth thereof*": i.e. the soul of Rhipeus.

ll. 101–2: "*the seat of Angels*": i.e. Heaven, the abode of Angels.

ll. 104–5: "*clinging – as each had scope – to the passion-pierced, to the yet-to-be-passible Feet*": Trajan believed in Christ Who had already died on the Cross, Rhipeus in Christ Who had not yet so died.

ll. 109–10: "*. . . the orison made unto God to raise him up*": i.e. the prayers of St Gregory.

ll. 128–9: "*. . . thou, at the car's right wheel, saw'st those three ladies who his proxies were*": The three ladies who took the place of baptism for Rhipeus are those whom Dante saw dancing at the right wheel of the triumphal car in the Terrestrial Paradise (*Purg.* xxix. 121 *et sqq.*). They represented Faith (in white), Hope (in green), and Charity (in red), the three theological virtues.

ll. 130–33: "*Predestination! what far depths conceal . . . thy root of woe and weal!*": Predestination is a mystery of grace deeper even than the vision of saints who see God.

ll. 137–8: "*Since this good doth our good the more refine, that what God willeth, that we also will*": The good which perfects their bliss is the conformity of their wills to the will of God.

l. 146: *as two winking eyelids*: cf. Canto xii. 26–7.

l. 147: *tnose two blest fires*: i.e. the souls of Trajan and Rhipeus.

CANTO XXI

THE STORY. *Dante and Beatrice have risen to the heaven of Saturn where the souls of the contemplatives, manifested as lights, are seen thronging upon the rungs of a golden ladder stretching into the heavens far beyond Dante's sight. A soul draws near and, in answer to Dante's question as to why God has assigned him to be his interlocutor, indicates the unfathomable depths of the mystery of predestination. Revealing himself as Peter Damian, he deplores the present degeneracy of his monastery at Fonte Avellana and rebukes the self-indulgence of modern prelates. Other souls, massing round him, utter so loud a cry of execration that Dante's understanding is overwhelmed.*

My eyes once more had sought my lady's face
    And, with my mind, were fixed on her, the while
    All other thoughts to her had yielded place.

She was unsmiling, but, "Were I to smile",   4
    Her words began, "thou wouldst become the same
    As Semelè, burned to an ashy pile.

For, as thou knowest, with a brighter flame   7
    As we ascend the eternal mansion's stair
    My beauty's splendour glows; if, as we came,

Its radiance were untempered, it would sear   10
    Thy mortal power, as a thunderbolt will smite
    The foliage from a branch and leave it bare.

We have been lifted to the seventh light   13
    Which underneath the burning Lion's breast
    Sends down its beams now mingled with his might.

Behind thine eyes keep now thy mind close pressed;   16
    Thine eyes as mirrors to the figures raise
    Which in this mirror will be manifest."

Whoever knew how it regaled my gaze   19
    To pasture in her blessèd countenance,
    From my transferring it could well appraise

The sweet content wherewith obedience   22
    To my celestial guide my pleasure fed,
    Since one delight the other did enhance.

25   Within that crystal, to the name still wed
         Of its belovèd regent 'neath whose might
         All evil in the world it rings lay dead,

28   Coloured like gold which flashes back the light,
         I saw a ladder raised aloft so far
         It soared beyond the compass of my sight.

31   Thereon I saw descend from bar to bar
         Splendours so numerous I thought the sky
         Had poured from heaven the light of every star.

34   And as at break of day one may espy
         The daws in flocks, as is their natural way,
         To warm their feathers setting out to fly,

37   Some winging far for ever and a day,
         And others wheeling back to where they started,
         Yet others circling where they make a stay,

40   Such mode, it seemed to me, was there imparted
         To all that sparkling, which in clusters flew
         And from the rung it lighted on departed.

43   One splendour, which the nearest to us drew,
         So brilliant showed itself, my thought was then:
         "Plainly the signal of thy love I view,

46   But she whose sign I heed, of how and when
         To speak and to keep silent, now is still;
         Rightly, therefore, from asking I refrain."

49   Then she, my silence being visible
         Within the sight of Him who sees all things,
         Spoke thus to me: "Thy burning wish fulfil."

52   And I began: "No claim my merit brings,
         And wholly undeserving though I be
         To hear thy answer to these questionings,

55   Yet for her sake who bid me speak with thee,
         Blessed life, whom thine own gladness doth conceal,
         What cause has placed thee here so close to me?;

58   And say why in the region of this wheel
         No strains of heavenly symphony arise
         As through the other spheres devoutly peal?"

"Thou hast but mortal ears, even as thine eyes," 61
 The answer came, "hence we forbear to sing,
 As Beatrice forbears to smile likewise.

Down by the holy ladder's steps I wing 64
 My way thus far solely to pleasure thee
 With converse and my soul's bright mantling;

Nor may my swift descent the measure be 67
 Of greater love; equal and more, above,
 Thou seest love sparkle in this treasury.

But the deep charity which bids us move 70
 To serve the Counsel governing mankind
 Assigns our office as thine eyes can prove."

"O sacred lantern, clearly do I find 73
 Love is no bondsman in this court, but guide
 To paths eternal providence designed.

Yet this I am unable to decide: 76
 Why thou alone wert chosen for this part
 From all the souls like-fated here beside."

I'd scarce concluded than about the heart 79
 Of his own luminance the spirit flew
 And like a whirling millstone was his art.

The love that dwelt therein replied anew: 82
 "Bearing directly on me is God's light,
 Piercing the bowel of my being through.

Its power being then conjoinèd to my sight 85
 Lifts me above myself until I gaze
 Upon His essence whence is milked such might.

Thence comes the joyfulness wherewith I blaze; 88
 My sight's intensity these sparklings show,
 Thus flame with vision in the balance weighs.

And yet that soul who doth most brightly glow, 91
 That Seraph fixed on God with peerless might,
 Could not discern the answer thou wouldst know,

The thing thou ask'st is plunged so deep in the night 94
 Of the eternal statute's dark abyss
 It is cut off from all created sight.

97 And to the mortal world take thou back this:
Let men aim lower and no more presume
To encroach on these exalted mysteries.

100 The mind, which here is light, on earth is fume;
How can it there discern what even now
Is hid, though Heaven it to itself assume?"

103 Before the bourne his words prescribe I bow;
Myself withdraw and let my question lie.
Humbly I ask him: "Tell me, who art thou?"

106 " 'Twixt two Italian shores are lifted high
Tall crags, and near thy home so far they rise
The thunder peals below them distantly.

109 And where they shape their skyline humpback-wise
Is Catria; below, a hermitage,
Once to God's service consecrated, lies."

112 These details did the opening words presage
Of his third discourse; now the rest I give.
"There, ever constant in God's vassalage,

115 Through heat and cold serenely did I live
On meagre food, seasoned with olive-oil,
Dwelling content in thoughts contèmplative.

118 Our cloister yielded from its fertile soil
Souls to these heavens; but now 'tis sterile grown.
Soon will men see what sins its fruit despoil.

121 Therein as Peter Damian I was known,
And Peter Sinner was the name I bore
Where Adria's shores Our Lady's house enthrone.

124 My mortal span of life was almost o'er
When I was called and dragged unto the Hat
Which passing downwards ever sinketh lower.

127 Barefoot and lean came Cephas, came the great
Vessel of the Holy Ghost; and they would sup
At whatsoever house they halted at.

130 Pastors today require to be propped up
On either side, one man their horse to lead
(So great their weight!) and one their train to loop.

> Over their mounts their mantles fall, full-spread;   133
> Two beasts beneath one hide behold them go!
> O patience, is thy meekness not yet fled?"

> Upon these words, more lights appeared below;   136
> From rung to rung I saw them whirl and spin,
> And every circling made their beauty grow.

> Clustered about this light, they uttered then   139
> A cry so loud I can relate no more;
> So greatly it surpassed all mortal din,

> My understanding swooned amid the roar.   142

THE IMAGES. *The Heaven of Saturn*: In the *story*, Saturn is the last of the seven planets on Dante's journey into Heaven. In the *allegory*, Saturn figures the life of contemplation and ascetic abstraction from material things. In accordance with the teaching of the Church, Dante represents the contemplative life as higher than the life of action. It should not, however, be imagined that Dante advocated a withdrawal from worldly activity. The cause of God on earth has still to be furthered by the endeavour of men. In Canto xvii, when Dante becomes absorbed in the heavenly truth which he reads in the eyes of Beatrice she bids him turn and look upon the souls of Crusaders, moving, with the swift energy which characterized them, along the pattern of the Cross, for "not in her eyes alone is Paradise". On the spiritual level, the ascent of Dante to the higher sphere of the contemplatives signifies the passing of the soul from active endeavour to a closer insight of the vision of God.

The Golden Ladder: The golden stair which Dante sees rising from Saturn into the infinite spaces above him is a traditional symbol of the life of contemplation or spiritual vision. Jacob's ladder was quoted by preachers as a figure of monastic life and the angels of God "ascending and descending on it" were interpreted as signifying the monks who climbed by contemplation up to God and descended by compassion among men.

NOTES. l. 3: *all other thoughts to her had yielded place*: In the heaven of the contemplatives, Dante's mind is at first wholly given up to contemplating the wonder and beauty of divine science (revealed theology).

l. 4: *She was unsmiling*: If Beatrice smiled, her smile would express the truth of God as He is known to the contemplatives; and that is as yet beyond the capacity of Dante.

l. 6: *Semelè*: the Princess of Thebes, who at the instigation of Juno, persuaded Jupiter to come to her in the full blaze of his unveiled divinity;

whereupon she was instantly consumed to ashes. The story is told in Ovid's *Metamorphoses*, Book III.

l. 13: *"the seventh light"*: i.e. the seventh planet, Saturn.

ll. 14–15: *"Which underneath the burning Lion's breast"* etc.: In March 1300, Saturn was in the constellation of Leo.

ll. 16–18: *"Behind thine eyes keep now thy mind close pressed"* etc.: Dante is now to mirror in his eyes the golden ladder which will be reflected in the mirror which is Saturn, the ladder itself being only a figure of the life that is beyond his sight.

ll. 19–24: *Whoever knew how it regaled my gaze* etc.: The pleasure of contemplation is weighed against the pleasure of obedience to Beatrice. Since Dante transferred his gaze in obedience to her, anyone knowing how sweet was his joy in contemplation of her might judge from that how sweet was the joy of obeying, which compensated for the loss of the other.

ll. 25–6: *Within the crystal, to the name still wed of its belovèd regent* etc.: The "crystal" is the planet Saturn (still named after the father of Jupiter) whose reign was the Golden Age.

l. 43: *One splendour, which the nearest to us drew*: This is the soul of St Peter Damian. Born of a humble family in Ravenna towards the beginning of the eleventh century, he entered the Benedictine monastery of Fonte Avellana on the slopes of Monte Catria in Umbria, of which, in 1041, he became Abbot. Much against his will, he was created Cardinal and Bishop of Ostia in 1058. He was zealous in his efforts to reform Church discipline and became celebrated as a teacher and preacher. According to an early and not improbable tradition, Dante stayed for a time in the monastery on Mount Catria; if this is so, he would there have had access to the writings of Peter Damian, many of which are forthright and unsparing in their criticism of the corrupt morals of prelates. Early commentators quote, for instance, a letter addressed to certain cardinals whom he reproaches for their preoccupation with rare and costly clothing, fine horses and armed escorts. In Ravenna Dante no doubt found the memory of Peter Damian still vividly cherished and his fellow-citizens may well have recognized in the words of rebuke, with which the canto ends, something of the personality and style of the old Benedictine abbot.

ll. 58–63: *"And say why in the region of this wheel no strains of heavenly symphony arise"* etc.: The sound of music has ceased. The reason is that the song of the souls in this heaven, like the smile of Beatrice, would convey a vision of God for which Dante is not yet prepared.

ll. 67–9: *"Nor may my swift descent the measure be of greater love"* etc.: The spirit disclaims for himself any love greater than that of his fellow-contemplatives. All are imbued with equal if not greater love, as Dante may see by their equal or greater radiance. On the literal level, the reply may be taken as indicating that the swift descent of this soul to the foot of the ladder (recalling the swift descent of the soul of Cacciaguida to the foot of the cross) does not in this case signify a personal relationship.

ll. 75–8: "*Love is no bondsman in this court, but guide to paths eternal providence designed*": Dante now reverts to the question of predestination, which, implicit in the predicting of his future by Cacciaguida, was also the subject of the Eagle's discourse in Canto xx. 130–48. Dante has grasped that it is God's love which has predestined Peter Damian to draw near to him; and he understands that love is not coerced, but, being left free, suffices to fulfil the decrees of Providence. What he has not yet comprehended is why Peter Damian, more than any of the other spirits (in all of whom love is sufficient inducement to obey God's will), was chosen for this specific divine command. (The answer to this question would far exceed not only Dante's but all creation's capacity of comprehension. It is the measure of his limitations that he does not realize this.)

ll. 79–81: "*I'd scarce concluded*" etc.: The spirit, by its increased exultation, shows its readiness to respond, though, as will be seen, it cannot answer Dante's question.

ll. 83–7: "*Bearing directly on me is God's light*" etc.: The radiance of the soul of Peter Damian (as of all souls in Heaven) is the reflected splendour of the light of God, the power of which enhances his vision until he is able to see God in His essence, whence comes the power which enables him to do so.

ll. 88–90: "*Thence comes the joyfulness wherewith I blaze*" etc.: St Peter Damian here repeats, in a more condensed form, the explanation given by Solomon of the proportionate relationship between grace, vision, love and radiance (see Canto xiv. 40–51 and *note*).

ll. 91–3: "*And yet that soul who doth most brightly glow*" etc.: The soul in Heaven whose radiance surpasses all others (possibly the Virgin Mary) has, by definition, the clearest vision and the deepest love of God. Yet, not even that soul, nor yet even the most rapt and ecstatic of all the Seraphim (who, as Dante says in the *Convivio* II. vi, "have a clearer vision of the First Cause than any other angelic nature") could answer Dante's question.

ll. 94–5: "*The thing thou ask'st is plunged so deep*" etc.: The mysteries of predestination are beyond the understanding of both angels and men and are known, therefore, only to God.

ll. 97–9: "*And to the mortal world take thou back this*" etc.: The warning to men not to presume to penetrate the mysteries of predestination has already been given in Canto xiii. 112–14, with reference to the unwisdom of forming rash moral judgements.

l. 105: "*Tell me, who art thou?*": In all this converse on the reason as to why this individual soul has been destined to greet Dante, his identity has so far remained undisclosed.

ll. 106–7: "'*Twixt two Italian shores are lifted high tall crags*": i.e. the Apennines, between the Adriatic and the Tyrrhenian Sea. "*. . . and near thy home so far they rise*": The allusion here is to the Tuscan–Emilian region of the Apennines, containing peaks over 2,000 metres high. One of these, the Cimone, is not far from Florence.

ll. 109–10: "*And where they shape their skyline humpback-wise is Catria*": The hog-backed ridge, named Catria, is in the Umbrian region of the mountain range. On its north-eastern slope was the Benedictine hermitage of Fonte Avellana.

ll. 121–3: "*Therein as Peter Damian I was known*" etc.: This is a vexed passage and some commentators have believed that two different persons are referred to here. Peter Damian was in the habit of signing himself Peter the Sinner ("Petrus Peccator"), but there was another Peter (Pietro degli Onesti), a contemporary of Peter Damian, who also called himself Peter the Sinner. He founded the church of Santa Maria del Porto, near Ravenna, where his tomb may be seen with its legend "Petrus Peccans". On the other hand, Peter Damian is said to have spent two years at the monastery of Pomposa (on a small island at the mouth of the river Po), which was known as the convent of Santa Maria. It is to this, probably, (rather than to the church of Santa Maria del Porto) that ll. 122–3 refer.

ll. 125–6: "... *the Hat which passing downwards ever sinketh lower*": Peter Damian refers here to his appointment as Cardinal in 1057. He died in 1072. (The Cardinal's hat was not instituted until 1252.)

ll. 127–9: "*Barefoot and lean came Cephas, came the great Vessel of the Holy Ghost*" etc.: Peter Damian recalls the simplicity of life of St Peter and St Paul as they went about preaching (cf. the commands of Christ, *Luke* x. 5–8). The contrast between the extravagant luxury of prelates and the simple lives of the Apostles was a frequent theme in mediaeval polemical writing directed against clerical abuses.

CANTO XXII

THE STORY. *Dante turns in terror to Beatrice who reassures him and bids him look round again towards the souls in Saturn. One who draws close reveals himself to be St Benedict, the founder of the monastery at Monte Cassino. Like St Peter Damian, he too rebukes the laxity and corruption of monastic life, and predicts the coming of a time of regeneration. Rising to the heaven of the fixed stars, Dante finds he has entered his native sign of Gemini. Bending his gaze downwards, he is able to contemplate all seven planets beneath him and to discern the inhabited portion of the globe. Filled with a serene sense of the latter's insignificance, he turns once more to gaze into the lovely eyes of Beatrice.*

O'erwhelmed with awe and terror, to my guide
   I turned, just as a little boy will run
   Seeking protection at his mother's side.

Swiftly, as though she comforted a son,   4
   Pallid, aghast and gasping in his fear,
   Yet ever by her voice to reason won,

She said: "Thou knowest thou art in Heaven here,   7
   Thou knowest in Heaven all is holiness,
   And zeal the source of every deed soe'er.

How singing had transformed thee, thou mayst guess;   10
   Or, had I smiled, couldst thou have borne it, say,
   Moved as thou art by sound of righteousness?

Hadst thou but heard the boon for which they pray,   13
   The vengeance yet to come thou now wouldst know –
   Thou wilt behold it ere thy dying day.

The sword of God falls neither swift nor slow   16
   Save to those eager to see justice done,
   Or who in guilt and fear await the blow.

Now turn aside and over others run   19
   Thy glance; souls of great lustre thou wilt see,
   If thou but let thy will and mine be one."

So I looked back as she directed me,   22
   And saw a hundred little spheres, whose rays
   Gave beauty to each other mutually.

25   I was as one who in his heart gainsays
             The thrust of his desire, fearing the shame
             Of being importunate, and silent stays.

28   Moving towards me, from those pearls there came
             The largest and most lucent, to fulfil
             My silent longing to enquire its name.

31   From deep within it, this was audible:
             "If thou, as I, our burning love didst know,
             Thy inmost thoughts would be expressible.

34   But, lest by tarrying thou shouldst prove slow
             To reach thy lofty goal, I will reply
             Before thou ask, to what concerns thee so.

37   Cassino on a spur of hill doth lie,
             About whose summit, once, there dwelt a herd
             Of people pagan and perverse. There I,

40   The first, bore up the tidings of the Word
             Which came on earth that truth might be revealed
             And power to rise above on man conferred.

43   Such was the grace illuminating me
             That I reclaimed the neighbouring villages
             From wrongful worship and impiety.

46   These other flames were all contèmplatives,
             Warmed by the sun that kindles bounteously
             The flowers and the fruits of holiness.

49   Here Romualdus, here Maccarius see,
             And here my brothers who, in cloisters pent,
             From every worldly taint kept their hearts free."

52   I answered him: "Thy words' fond sentiment
             And the bright radiance which yonder glows,
             Of favours yet to come seem argument;

55   Whereat, as to their full extent a rose
             Unfolds its petals, warmed beneath the sun,
             So now my confidence dilates and grows.

58   Father, I pray thee, reassure thy son:
             Can I behold thee as thou truly art,
             With face uncovered? May such grace be won?"

yearning, brother," thus he did impart,   61
 In the last sphere will be vouchsafed, even as
 Mine own will be, with those of every heart.

There and there only every longing has   64
 Final attainment, perfect, ripe and whole,
 And there each part is where it always was,

For it is not in space and has no pole;   67
 Wherefore our ladder, at its full extent,
 Steals from thy view, since yonder is its goal.

But Jacob, in the vision which was sent   70
 Of angel figures moving up and down,
 Saw where the ladder's loftiest section went.

No foot stirs now to reach the rungs; to crown   73
 Iniquity, there in my house men sit
 Smirching with wasted ink my Rule's renown.

Dens are the buildings, once for abbots fit;   76
 Rancid the meal, and the cowls in which they dress
 Are like so many sacks stuffed full with it.

Gross usury bears lighter the impress   79
 Of God's displeasure than the well-filled purse
 Which monkish hearts now covet to excess.

Whatever wealth the Church is called to nurse   82
 Belongs to those who ask it in God's name,
 Not to the families of monks, or worse.

The yielding flesh of man is much to blame: 85
 More than a good beginning was required
 Ere ever acorn from an oaktree came.

Peter, to found his house, no wealth desired,   88
 Nor I, by fasting and by prayer made rich,
 Nor Francis, by humility inspired.

If thou wouldst contemplate the point from which   91
 Each one set out, and where their followers are,
 Thou wilt perceive how white has changed to pitch.

Jordan turned back, the waters fled; by far   94
 The greater marvels these, which God once willed,
 Than 'twere these evil doings to debar."

97   Thus he concluded and the voice was stilled.
          Collegiate to *collegium* withdrew,
          Which like a whirlwind sped, its task fulfilled.

100   After them, my sweet Lady, as they flew,
          Impelled me by one sign along the stair,
          My nature vanquished by her power anew.

103   On earth, where Nature speeds men everywhere,
          Aloft and down, no race or swiftest heat
          Comparison with my ascent could bear.

106   Reader, I tell thee, as I hope to meet
          The triumph of God's holy ones again,
          Whence, weeping for my sins, my breast I beat,

109   Thrust thou thy finger in the flame – for pain
          Thou'lt snatch it out, but not so fast as I
          Saw and was in the Heaven of the Twain.

112   O stars of glory, from whose light on high
          A mighty virtue poureth forth, to you
          I owe such genius as doth in me lie;

115   With you there rose and sank again from view
          He who is father of all life below
          When my first breath in Tuscany I drew;

118   And when grace was vouchsafed to me to go
          Within the heavenly circle of your course,
          Your region I was granted then to know.

121   To you my soul devoutly breathes, her source
          Of strength and power for the hardest phase
          Of all her journey towards which now she draws.

124   Beatrice began: "Before long thou wilt raise
          Thine eyes and the Supreme Good thou wilt see;
          Hence thou must sharpen and make clear thy gaze.

127   Before thou nearer to that Presence be,
          Cast thy look downward and consider there
          How vast a world I have set under thee,

130   So that thy heart, taking its utmost share
          Of joy, may greet the host which triumphing
          Exultant comes through this ethereal sphere."

with my vision I went traversing   133
 The seven planets till this globe I saw,
 Whereat I smiled, it seemed so poor a thing.

Highly I rate that judgement that doth low 136
 Esteem the world; him do I deem upright
 Whose thoughts are fixed on things of greater awe.

I saw Latona's daughter all in light,   139
 Without those markings I did once expound
 As matter rare and dense, as I thought right.

Thy child's aspect, Hyperion, I found   142
 I could endure, and saw how, moving near,
 Thine, Maia, and thine, Dione, ringed him round.

Above them I beheld the tempering sphere 145
 Of Jove, between his offspring and his sire;
 How their positions changed, to me was clear.

All seven being displayed, I could admire 148
 How vast they are, how swiftly they are spun,
 And how remote they dwell. I saw entire

The threshing-floor, whereon fierce deeds are done; 151
 Wheeling with the eternal Gemini,
 Down hills I traced the course the rivers run,

Then gazed upon her beauty, eye to eye. 154

THE IMAGES. *The Heaven of Saturn*: see Canto xxi, under *Images*.

Dante's bewilderment at the great cry of the contemplatives: At the conclusion of St Peter Damian's words, a great cry of wrath goes forth from all the other souls. Dante, bewildered and terrified, turns to Beatrice for reassurance. Allegorically, his bewilderment signifies his (and possibly our) misunderstanding of the contemplative life. He had not expected that these souls would voice such vehement concern about the corruption of the monastic ideal on earth; but absorption in the vision of God does not detach the soul from zealous care for the life of the Church Militant.

The Heaven of the Fixed Stars: In the *story*, as Dante and Beatrice rise beyond the seventh and outermost of the planets, they enter the firmament or heaven of the fixed stars. This is the eighth and last of the astronomical spheres. The part of it which Dante enters is, appropriately, that which is constellated by Gemini, the stars under whose sign he was born. At this point, he retraces with his gaze (for it is endowed with supernatural acuity and power) the course he has taken through the seven planetary spheres, until it rests at last upon

the puny semblance of our little globe. Allegorically, it is
sing through a period of spiritual contemplation (the Hea
Saturn) that man can see the world in its true proportions.

NOTES. l. 9: "*And zeal the source of every deed soe'er*": The life of contemplation does not detach the souls' interest from the life of the Church on earth; "righteous zeal is itself a mark of true spiritual contemplation" (Sinclair).

ll. 13–15: "*Hadst thou but heard the boon for which they pray*" etc.: The great cry of the contemplatives which startled Dante was a prayer for retribution upon the evil-living monks and prelates.

l. 15: "*Thou wilt behold it ere thy dying day*": The vengeance referred to may be the attack upon Pope Boniface VIII at Anagni, or the humiliation of the Roman Curia by the transfer of the Papal Court to Avignon; or it may be the coming retribution for which Dante longed and which he still hoped to see realized by the power of the "Five-hundred-ten and-five God-sent" (see *Purg.* xxxiii. 43–4 and *note*).

ll. 25–7: *I was as one who in his heart gainsays* etc.: Dante, as if by instinct, behaves fittingly in the presence of St Benedict, for it was part of the Benedictine Rule that "a monk restrain his tongue from speaking, and, keeping silence, do not speak until he is spoken to".

l. 29: "*The largest and most lucent*": This is the soul of St Benedict, the founder of monasticism in the Western Church. He was born of a noble family in Umbria in the year 480. On being sent to school in Rome, he fled in horror from the undisciplined life of his companions and lived for three years in a cave in the Abruzzi. The monks of a neighbouring monastery elected him as their abbot but, on growing restive under his severe rule, they tried to poison him. He left them and in 528 went to Monte Cassino, where he founded his famous monastery on the site of an ancient temple of Apollo. He died at Monte Cassino in 543.

l. 49: *Romualdus*: St Romualdus (960–1027) founded the Order of Camaldoli or Reformed Benedictines. After a vision of monks climbing a ladder to heaven all dressed in white garments, he changed the Camaldolese Benedictine habit from traditional black to white. His monastery is mentioned in *Purg.* v. 96.

Maccarius: of the several saints called by the name of Maccarius, the one to whom Dante is most probably alluding here is St Maccarius the Younger, of Alexandria, who is said to be the founder of monasticism in the East, as St Benedict was in the West.

ll. 59–60: "*Can I behold thee as thou truly art, with face uncovered?*": Dante, in the heaven of the contemplatives, asks whether he may behold a soul in its essence. The question is one which belongs to the contemplative life.

l. 62: "*In the last sphere*": i.e. in the Empyrean, the abode of God. There Dante will behold all the saints in that aspect which they will have after the Last Judgement (see Cantos xxx–xxxiii).

"There and there only every longing has final attainment, perfect, ~~whole~~" etc.: In the Empyrean, all longing is fulfilled, because ~~of~~ the souls is in accord with the will of God; every part of the Empyrean, which is motionless, is where it has always been from eternity, for it does not exist in space (but in the mind of God) and does not revolve (as do the other nine heavens).

ll. 70-72: *"But Jacob, in the vision which was sent"* etc.: Compare *Gen.* xxviii. 12: "And he dreamed, and behold a ladder set up on the earth, and the top of it reached to heaven: and, behold, the angels of God ascending and descending on it. And behold, the Lord stood above it."

l. 75: *"... my Rule's renown"*: St Benedict's *Rule of Monks (Regula Monachorum)*. It is interesting that Dante here makes St Benedict connect the image of Jacob's ladder with the discipline of his Order, for that is exactly what St Benedict himself does in the preamble to the central chapter of his Rule, No. 7, *De Humilitate*. (I am indebted to Father Alberic Stacpoole, O.S.B., for this observation.)

ll. 79-81: *"Gross usury bears lighter the impress"* etc.: We have seen in *Hell* how Dante rates the sin of usury (cf. Canto xvii. 37-78). It is a sin against Nature and against the labour that should have cultivated its resources; yet even that is less displeasing to God than the avarice of priests and friars who appropriate to themselves the revenues of the Church (the tithes *quae sunt pauperum Dei*, cf. Canto xii. 91-3 and *note*).

ll. 85-7: *"The yielding flesh of man is much to blame"*: etc.: i.e. man is easily corrupted. It is not enough to start him off on the right road; much more is needed if he is not to stray. Many oak-trees are planted in good soil which succumb to bad weather before they bear acorns.

ll. 88-90: *"Peter, to found his house, no wealth desired"*: The reference here may be to St Peter Damian and not to the Apostle as is generally believed.

l. 98: *Collegiate to "collegium" withdrew*: The soul of St Benedict withdrew to the great company of contemplative spirits, which returned upwards whence it had descended.

l. 111: *the Heaven of the Twain*: i.e. the Constellation of Gemini. Dante and Beatrice have risen to the eighth sphere, the heaven of the fixed stars.

ll. 115-17: *With you there rose and sank again from view* etc.: Dante was born under the sign of Gemini, that is, between 21 May and 21 June.

l. 135: *Whereat I smiled, it seemed so poor a thing*: Dante is probably recalling the appearance of the earth as it seemed to Scipio as he looked down on it from the Galaxy, in Cicero's *Somnium Scipionis*. He may also have in mind the following passage from the *Apocalypse of St Paul* (fourth century): "And I looked down from heaven upon the earth and beheld the whole world as it was as nothing in my sight" (M.R. James, translation from the Latin text, p. 525).

l. 139: *Latona's daughter*: Dante now sees the other side of the moon on which he assumes there are no markings. He is partly right, as we

are at last able to confirm, in that there are fewer markings ⟨ ⟩
than on the one with which we are familiar.

l. 142: *Thy child*: i.e. the Sun, Apollo was the son of Hyperion ⟨ ⟩

l. 144: *Thine, Maia*: i.e. Mercury. Maia, the daughter of Atlas, became by Jupiter the mother of Mercury.

l. 144: *thine, Dione*: i.e. Venus.

ll. 145-6: *the tempering sphere of Jove, between his offspring and his sire*: i.e. the planet Jupiter, between Mars, his offspring, and Saturn, his father. He "tempers" the cold of his father with the heat of his son. (Cf. *Convivio*, II. xiv: ". . . Jupiter is a star of temperate constitution, midway between the coldness of Saturn and the heat of Mars.")

l. 147: *How their positions changed, to me was clear*: The movements of the planets Mars, Jupiter and Saturn, which now draw near each other, and now draw apart, were clearly observed and understood. (The reader may have the same satisfying experience on visiting a planetarium.)

l. 148: *All seven being displayed* etc.: Dante is able to observe from above the position, movement and relative size of the seven planets, Saturn, Jupiter, Mars, the Sun, Venus, Mercury and the Moon.

l. 151: *The threshing-floor* etc.: This metaphor, applied to the inhabited portion of the globe, was not unusual in mediaeval writings. Dante uses it twice in *Paradise* (cf. Canto xxvii. 86) and once in the *De Monarchia* III. xvi.

l. 154: *Then gazed upon her beauty, eye to eye*: The canto begins and ends with Dante's gaze fixed on Beatrice, at first in fear, and finally in serenity. The unworthiness of the world no longer alarms him.

CANTO XXIII

THE STORY. *As Beatrice fixes her gaze in the direction of the zenith, Dante's eager expectancy is awakened. Before long he sees the heaven brightened by an increased radiance, the light of the saints of the Church Triumphant, among whom, outshining all, is Christ. Glimpsing for an instant the shining substance of Christ's person, which pierces the swathings of His glory, Dante is at first dazzled and then able to endure the radiance of the smile of Beatrice. His vision thus strengthened, he beholds the lights of the Virgin and the Apostles, the angel who descends to accompany the Virgin on her return to the Empyrean, and the brilliant white radiance of all the other saints assembled before him.*

A bird within the bower of her delight,
  Quiet upon the nest with her sweet brood
  Throughout the dark concealment of the night,

Anxious to look on them and gather food –   4
  No weary task for her, for as at play
  Blithely she toils to seek her fledglings' good –

Before the time, upon the topmost spray   7
  Eager awaits the sun and on the East
  Fixes her wakeful eye till break of day.

Even so my Lady stood, intent to feast   10
  Her gaze upon that region where the sun,
  Climbing at noon, appears to hasten least.

I, seeing her poised in longing, was as one   13
  Who in his heart doth something more desire
  And by his hopes is to quiescence won;

But swiftly did the space of time transpire   16
  Between my waiting and beholding how
  The heaven was lit with ever brighter fire.

Then she: "Behold Christ's hosts in triumph! Thou   19
  Mayst see the fruit all garnered here above
  Which 'neath these circling stars matured ere now."

To me her face seemed all aglow with love;   22
  And in her eyes such joyousness was seen
  I cannot tell of it, but onward move.

257

25   As, when the moon is full, the night serene,
          Trivia smiles mid nymphs eternal, who
          Silver all heaven, to its last demesne,

28   Outshining myriad lamps, One Sun I knew
          Which kindled all the rest, even as our sun
          Lights the celestial pageantry we view.

31   And through the living radiance there shone
          The shining Substance, bright, and to such end
          Full in my face, my vision was undone.

34   O Beatrice! belovèd guide, sweet friend!
          She said: "That which now overmasters thee
          Is might which nothing can evade or fend.

37   Herein the wisdom and the power see
          That opened between Heaven and earth the road
          Long yearned for and awaited ardently."

40   As fire from a cloud must soon explode,
          If it dilate and prove untenable,
          And downward flies, against its natural mode,

43   My soul, grown heady with high festival,
          Gushed and o'erbrimmed itself; and what strange style
          It then assumed, remembers not at all.

46   "Lift up thine eyes and look on me awhile;
          See what I am; thou hast beheld such things
          As make thee mighty to endure my smile."

49   I was as one that out of dreaming brings
          Nothing to mind, though fruitlessly he cast
          About, in search of hints and vanishings,

52   When thus I heard her speak; and to the last
          Her sweet self-offering will never fade
          From the recorded pages of the past.

55   If all the tongues by muses nourishèd
          On sweetest milk of sacred poetry
          Were now to sound in concert, lending aid,

58   Not to one thousandth in their chant would they
          The sacred beauty of her smile comprise,
          Nor how it changed her holy aspect say.

ring of Paradise,   61
song a leaping-place must find,
obstruction in the highway lies.

Think of the theme's great weight, and bear in mind   64
   The mortal shoulder that must take the strain.
   If it then tremble, must it be maligned?

No sea for cockle-boats is this great main   67
   Through which my prow carves out adventurous ways,
   Nor may the steersman stint of toil and pain.

"Why art thou so enamoured of my face   70
   Thou wilt not turn thee to the garden bright
   Shone on by Christ, and flowering in his rays?

There blooms the rose wherein God's Word was dight   73
   With flesh, and there the lilies blow whose scent
   Wooed man to take the road that runs aright."

Thus Beatrice spoke. I, eager to consent,   76
   Unto her counsels, once again did yield,
   And my frail vision to the contest lent.

As when the sky, o'ershadowed, formed a shield,   79
   'Neath which the unsullied sunlight once I spied
   Streaming through cloud-rifts on a flowery field,

So countless thronging splendours I descried,   82
   Ablaze with shafts of lightning from on high,
   Yet saw no founthead to this blazing tide.

O power benign, whose seal on them doth lie   85
   So clearly, thou, to enlarge my vision, didst raise
   Thyself aloft, sparing these eyes thereby.

The sound of that sweet flower's name, whose praise   88
   Morning and eve I sing, my whole soul drew,
   And on that fire of fires led me to gaze.

When, imaged upon both mine eyes, I knew   91
   The size and brilliance of that living star,
   Who, as on Earth, in Heaven rules anew,

Sped from beyond that sphere, a flammifer   94
   Ringed her about, spinning itself around,
   Weaving a circle like a crown for her.

97   The sweetest melody that e'er did sound
          In mortal ears, stealing the soul away,
          Like thunder bursting from a cloud were fou

100   If matched beside that lyre's roundelay
          Ringing the sapphire, whence, ensapphirined,
          The brightest sphere of heaven was made more gay.

103   "Of the angelic loves am I, and wind
          Circling the joy sublime breathed from the womb
          Where once abode our hope for all mankind.

106   Still circling, heavenly Lady, will I come,
          Till with thy holy presence thou hast filled,
          In thy Son's wake, the sphere which is thy home."

109   Thus the entwining melody was sealed.
          All other lights together cried aloud
          And through the sphere the name of Mary pealed.

112   The regal mantle which on high doth shroud
          The world's revolving layers and, nearest Him,
          Is by God's breath with liveliest love endowed,

115   So distant was, so far its nearest rim
          Above us that, for all my scrutiny,
          Its aspect to my vision still was dim;

118   Wherefore my gaze could not accompany
          The crownèd flame which rising from below
          To Heaven returned, following her progeny.

121   As motherwards a baby's arms will go
          When she has fed him at her breast, by love
          His soul being kindled to this outward show,

124   So I saw those white radiances move
          And reaching upwards, after Mary clinging,
          How deep their love towards her to me prove.

127   Then still within my sight they lingered, singing
          Regina coeli with such dulcet sound
          Within me still the joy of it is ringing.

130   O what a fertile yield doth there abound,
          O'erflowing from rich coffers which of old
          On earth were acres of good seeding ground!

...they have, and on that wealth take hold   133
...Babylonian exile dearly won,
...n tears and sorrow, caring naught for gold.

There too, victorious, beneath the Son   136
Of God and Mary, amid the consistory
Of Councils new and ancient, triumphs one

...holds the keys of such celestial glory.   139

THE IMAGES. *The Heaven of the Fixed Stars*: See Canto xxii, under *Images*.

The Church Triumphant: In the Earthly Paradise (*Purg.* xxix-xxx), Dante beholds the Pageant of the Church Militant, imaged forth in symbols in the very scene of man's fall. So now, in the Firmament, the highest visible region of the celestial world, he beholds the Church Triumphant, shining in myriad lights all kindled by one Sun. By a rich and lovely image, the redeemed of the Old and New Covenant are called the fruits of the circling spheres. This extends our understanding of the stellar sphere and, indeed, of all the planetary heavens, since all eight circles, operating as the instruments of God, influence men's souls by the vital powers which are diffused through the stars and planets. (See also Canto ii. 136-8.)

The Vision of Christ: For the second time in *Paradise* (the first was in the Heaven of Mars; cf. Canto xiv) Dante beholds Christ. On this occasion, he glimpses for an instant the unbearable brightness of the shining substance of the Divine Sun who here appears as the means of redemption, the source of glory and Head of the Church Triumphant. Dante's strengthened vision, which can now sustain the smile of Beatrice, signifies his growing power to apprehend the teaching of the Church concerning man's redemption through Christ. Her words bidding him turn again to the vision are yet a further reminder (cf. Canto xviii and xxi) that the soul progresses towards God not only through absorption in the ideal and abstract, but also through the facts of history and the reality of life.

The Virgin Mary: This is Dante's first vision of the Virgin, whom he will later see again, together with all the saints, in her bodily form in the Empyrean (see Cantos xxxii-xxxiii). Here represented as a light of sapphire hue, she signifies the Incarnation, or embodiment of grace.

NOTES. ll. 11-12: ... *that region where the sun, climbing at noon, appears to hasten least*: Beatrice is looking towards the meridian (i.e. eastwards from Gemini), where at midday the sun appears to be moving at its slowest pace.

l. 19: *"Behold Christ's hosts in triumph!"*: The vision of the Church Triumphant now begins.

ll. 20-21: ". . . *the fruit all garnered here above which 'neath stars matured ere now*": In the seven planetary spheres, Dante has understood the differing degrees of bliss enjoyed by the soul Empyrean. Now in the eighth heaven, he is to see the whole fruit of redemption, typifying the "one home", as against the "many mansions". The stars of the eighth heaven receive from above and disperse to the spheres below the vital powers or very stuff of life, which they div (cf. Canto ii. 64-72).

l. 26: *Trivia smiles mid nymphs eternal*: i.e Diana, the Moon, among her stars.

l. 28: *One Sun*: i.e. Christ.

l. 32-3: *the shining Substance* etc.: i.e. Christ in His essence (as a human person) shone so brightly upon Dante's eyes that he was unable to behold Him for more than a brief instant.

l. 34: "*O Beatrice! belovèd guide*" etc.: In his extremity Dante can do no more than utter an exclamation, an appeal for the assistance of theo-logy, an appeal for the human consolation and support of Beatrice who is both guide and belovèd.

l. 37: "*Herein the wisdom and the power see*": In *I Cor.* i. 24, Christ is called "the power of God, and the wisdom of God".

l. 38: "*That opened between Heaven and earth the road*": By His death Christ opened to man the way to Heaven.

ll. 40-42: *As fire within a cloud must soon explode* etc.: Dante here fol-lows Aristotle's theory concerning the laws governing lightning. accord-ing to which compressed air, contained in a cloud, expands, and, on escaping, explodes with the reverberation that we know as thunder; if the exploding air ignites, there is also lightning.

l. 42: *And downward flies, against its natural mode*: It is in the nature of fire to burn upwards; in the case of lightning, it strikes downwards.

ll. 43-5: *My soul, grown heady with high festival* etc.: In the feasts and delights of Heaven, Dante's soul has, like the fire within a cloud, become so enlarged as almost to have changed its nature. Now, on earth, he can no longer recall the experience, let alone recount it.

ll. 46-7: "*Lift up thine eyes and look on me awhile*" etc.: Having looked, even if only for an instant, on Christ, Dante is now able to withstand the radiance of the smile of Beatrice.

ll. 49-51: *I was as one that out of dreaming brings nothing to mind* etc.: The vision of Christ has been effaced from his conscious awareness and he is in the state of mind of one who awakens from a dream, the memory of which just eludes him. This comparison of the forgotten dream is used again by Dante to convey his inability to recall his vision of God in the Empyrean (see Canto xxxiii. 58-60).

ll. 55-60: *If all the tongues by muses nourishèd* etc.: The beauty of the smile of Beatrice is such that no human words can describe it; even if all the poets nurtured by Polyhymnia (the Muse of sacred poetry) and by all the other eight Muses were to come to his assistance, their

capture a thousandth part of the beauty of that smile
ance it gave to her countenance. By this rhetorical means,
mpts to convey the ineffableness of the ineffable.

: *So, in its picturing of Paradise* etc.: Dante here states that some
ly things are so far beyond human expression that he will be
ged to omit them. Dante's power of vision is limited; so, too, is ours.

7-9: *No sea for cockle-boats is this great main* etc.: Compare the
given at the beginning of Canto ii. 1-7. Not only are some
Heaven inexpressible, but many things which are described
e from the reader close attention and an informed understanding.

ll. 70-72: "*Why art thou so enamoured of my face*" etc.: Dante, absorbed
in contemplating the divine beauty of the smile of Beatrice, is gently
reminded by her that he must also turn and look at the souls assembled
before him. In Canto xviii. 20-21, Dante is similarly reminded that he
must turn from gazing in the eyes of Beatrice to look at the heroes of
the Cross; again, on his arrival in the sphere of Saturn, she bids him turn
from her to see the contemplatives on the golden ladder (xxi. 16-24);
and when he takes refuge in her presence like a frightened child (xxii.
1-6), she bids him once again turn back from her and contemplate the
souls (ll. 19-21). Likewise, in the Garden of Eden, the Graces warn
Dante against too intense and exclusive a concentration on Beatrice
(*Purg.* xxxii. 7-9). The meaning intended may be that not in abstract
truth alone is the truth of God to be found.

l. 73: "*. . . the rose wherein God's Word was dight with flesh*": i.e. the
Virgin Mary.

l. 74: "*. . . and there the lilies blow*" etc.: i.e. the Apostles. (Cf. *II Cor.*
ii. 15: "We are unto God a sweet savour of Christ".)

ll. 86-7: *. . . thou . . . didst raise thyself aloft*: Christ has ascended be-
yond the range of Dante's vision, but His light still illumines the souls.
By His withdrawal, Dante is enabled to look on them.

l. 88: *The sound of that sweet flower's name* etc.: i.e. the Rose, which
Beatrice has mentioned in l. 73 (the Virgin Mary, known in the Roman
litany as "the Mystic Rose").

l. 90: *. . . that fire of fires*: The light of the Virgin Mary is the greatest
he beholds, now that Christ has withdrawn from sight.

l. 91: *When, imaged upon both mine eyes*: The eyes of Dante are again
conceived of as mirrors (cf. Canto xxi. 17-18). The emphasis placed on
the imprinting of the image on *both* eyes may perhaps signify not only
his intense outward gaze but also the inward vision of contemplation.

l. 92: *that living star:* The Virgin Mary is known also as "the star of
morning" and "the star of the sea".

l. 94: *a flammifer*: i.e. a torch. This is the brilliant light of an angel
(cf. l. 103).

ll. 103-5: "*Of the angelic loves am I*" etc.: It is usually assumed that
this is the Archangel Gabriel, but a modern commentator, Manfredi
Porena, adduces convincing arguments in favour of the interpretation

that is followed here, namely, that the light represents s[...]
angels. Since he announces himself as being of the angelic l[...]
love is represented specifically by the order of the Seraphim, [...]
that Dante intends us to understand that an angel of the seraphic [...]
indicated. On the other hand, when speaking to Dante of the cr[...]
of all the angels (Canto xxix. 46), Beatrice refers to them collectively [...]
"loves". The chief argument against the traditional interpretatio[...]
that this is the Archangel Gabriel) is that, in Canto xxxii [...]
descends before the Virgin, singing "Ave Maria". Dante asks S[...]
who the angel is and, in his reply, St Bernard makes no mentic[...]
Dante's having previously seen him.

l. 108: ". . . *the sphere which is thy home*": i.e. the Empyrean. The Virgin Mary, escorted by the angel, will return, with all the other souls, to the tenth heaven, where her Son has already ascended.

ll. 112–14: *The regal mantle* etc.: The Primum Mobile encloses and encircles all the revolving spheres, and, being nearest God, is the most fervent in love for Him. In the desire of all its parts to be joined with Him, it spins faster than any other sphere, imparting motion to all the rest.

l. 124: . . . *those white radiances*: i.e. the lights of all the other souls gathered in the eighth heaven.

l. 128: "*Regina coeli*": These are the first words of the Antiphon sung in praise of the Virgin after the Office in Easter week. Compare the lingering memory of this hymn of praise with that of the song which Casella sings in *Purgatory* ii. 112–14:

> "Love in my mind his conversation making,"
>   Thus he began, so sweetly that I find
>   Within me still the dulcet echoes waking.

ll. 130–2: *O what a fertile yield* etc.: On earth these saints were the "good soil" in which the Word multiplied; now they represent so great a harvest that they seem to be overflowing from richly laden treasure-chests.

l. 134: *In Babylonian exile*: i.e. in the first life, on earth, the Babylon in relation to which Heaven is the Promised Land.

l. 135: *In tears and sorrow*: i.e. suffering the many tribulations of life on earth. *caring naught for gold*: i.e. leaving their material possessions behind when they died.

ll. 136–9: *There too, victorious* etc.: In the Celestial Rose, St Peter is seen sitting on the right hand of the Virgin (Canto xxxii. 124–6), amid the saints from the Old and New Dispensation.

CANTO XXIV

*...TORY. Beatrice entreats the souls assembled in the eighth Heaven to
...Dante to partake of their joy. In response to her appeal, St Peter
...hes and examines Dante in the Christian faith.*

"...llowship of the elect who sup
 With Christ the Lamb, Who doth so nourish you
 That full to overflowing is your cup,

If God by grace admits this man unto   **4**
 The broken meats that from your table fall,
 Before the hour prescribed by death is due,

The boundless measure of his love recall.   **7**
 Bedew him with some drops! *your* fountainhead,
 Whence comes what *he* thinks, is perpetual."

So Beatrice spoke. Those happy spirits sped,   **10**
 Whirling about fixed centres circle-wise,
 Each brightly blazing like a comet's head.

As in a clock the movements synchronize   **13**
 So that the lowest wheel appears to sleep,
 To an onlooker, while the topmost flies,

So did those dancers different measures keep,   **16**
 Bidding me judge how great their riches were,
 As they did swiftly whirl or slowly creep.

From out the costliest ring I looked on there,   **19**
 I saw a fire draw nigh, so full of bliss
 No brighter star remained in all that sphere.

Once, twice and thrice it circled Beatrice,   **22**
 Chanting the while a song so heavenly
 My memory cannot recapture this;

And so my pen moves on and I let be.   **25**
 Shades delicate as these, not words alone,
 Our merest fancy paints too vividly.

"O holy sister mine, who dost intone   **28**
 Thy prayer so devoutly, thy love's glow
 Brings me to thee, released from my fair zone."

31   The blessed fire breathed to my Lady, so
            Soon as it had ceased moving, words which ran
            The way I've stated and were answered now

34   By her: "Eternal light of that great man,
            To whom Our Lord on earth bequeathed the keys,
            Which, from this wondrous joy, below were ta'en,

37   Lightly and searchingly, as thou dost please,
        ·   This person test and try concerning faith,
            By which thou once didst walk upon the seas.

40   If love and hope and faith he truly hath
            Thou knowest, for thine eyes are fixed upon
            The centre which all visions mirroreth.

43   Yet since this realm its citizens have won
            By the true faith, 'tis fitting he should seek
            To glorify it, answering thereon."

46   As a Bachelor prepares and does not speak
            Till the Master the question has propounded,
            For argument, not for conclusion's sake,

49   So I prepared, with reasonings well founded,
            While Beatrice spoke, that I in such profession,
            To such a questioner, might prove well grounded.

52   "Speak, as thou art a Christian, make confession:
            What is faith?" To that light I looked which so
            Breathed forth to me the first words of the session,

55   Then looked to Beatrice, who was not slow
            To signify to me that I should make
            The fount of eloquence within me flow.

58   "Since grace is granted me, for my creed's sake
            To speak before the Chief Centurion,
            So may my thoughts their due expression take.

61   As truly wrote the pen," so I went on,
            "Of thy belovèd brother, who with thee
            Set Rome upon the way to union,

64   The substance of things hoped for faith must be,
            And argument of things invisible,
            And this I take to be its quiddity."

266

The three eternal persons next I quote   139
   As tenet of my faith; so One and Trine
   That *are* and *is* their nature both denote.

And on my intellect, of this divine   142
   Profound tri-union, of which I talk,
   The Gospel more than once imprints its sign.

This the beginning is and this the spark   145
   Which, like a living flame, doth now dilate,
   Shining within me like a star at dark."

As when a Lord has heard his page relate   148
   Tidings so pleasing he doth kiss his cheek,
   Embracing him, his joy to celebrate,

So, singing blessings then for my soul's sake,   151
   As I was silent, round me thrice did go
   The apostolic light which bid me speak,

By all I said I did delight it so.   154

THE IMAGES. *The Heaven of the Fixed Stars*: see Canto xxii, under *Images*.

Dante's Examination in Faith, Hope, and Love: According to the teaching of Aquinas, three qualifications are essential before the soul can attain to participation in the Beatific Vision, namely, faith, hope, and love. These are the three theological principles or virtues which direct the soul aright to God. They cannot be acquired by human acts but only by grace operating through revelation. In the *story*, Dante actually undergoes examination in these three virtues and, on satisfying his examiners, is allowed to proceed on his journey. On the mystical level of the *allegory*, man's soul cannot progress by understanding and knowledge alone. In the *De Monarchia*, III, xvi, 43–63, Dante has already expressed in abstract terms the teaching which he here presents in allegorical form. Man by his proper power may not ascend to the blessedness of eternal life unless assisted by the divine light. This light is mediated to us by spiritual teachings which transcend human reason, as we follow them by acting according to the theological virtues, faith, hope, and charity.

It is interesting to consider also the personal implications of the allegory. There is an early tradition that Dante was at one time brought under suspicion and enquiry by the Inquisition for heresy. If this is so, or if the tradition merely represents misgivings as to Dante's orthodoxy, the examination in faith may have been intended as an apologia. It is said that Dante had had personal experience of such formal examinations as he here undergoes during his time as a student at the University of Paris, some commentators even going so far as to maintain that he underwent the preparation for a doctorate in theology.

NOTES. ll. 1–2: *"O fellowship of the elect who sup with Christ the Lamb"*: Compare *Rev.* xix. 9: "Blessed are they which are called unto the marriage supper of the Lamb."

l. 5: *"The broken meats that from your table fall"* etc.: The marriage supper of the Lamb is the bliss which the saints enjoy in their knowledge of God. The Biblical image of the table is used also by Dante in the *Convivio*, not only in the title itself, which means "banquet", but also in the first chapter, in which he expresses his regret that he has not fully attained to membership of the elect (philosophers and theologians), and his desire to share with others less fortunate than himself what little he has gathered up: "I who am not seated at the table of the blest, but am fed from the pasture of the common herd, and at the feet of those who sit at that table am gathering up of that which falls from them, perceive how wretched is the life of those whom I have left behind by the sweetness which I taste in that which little by little I gather up."

l. 10: *Those happy spirits*: These are the souls who remain after the departure of Christ and the Virgin and who now form themselves into several adjacent circles, revolving together but at differing velocity (see ll. 13–15) and manifesting varying degrees of radiance (see l. 19).

ll. 13–15: *As in a clock* etc.: This reference to a train of wheels implies that Dante had seen a striking clock, which in the early fourteenth century would be a novelty. The arrangement of the wheels is vertical. At the top is a two-bladed fan which revolves at speed, to act as a regulator. When the clock strikes, the lowest wheel revolves imperceptibly, and the intermediate wheels go faster, while the fan "flies" round. Galvano Fiamma mentions a striking clock as being a novelty to him in 1335. Dante therefore anticipates him by fifteen years; he may have seen a chamber clock, which would not be generally known to the public. At any rate, it is apparent that Dante is here drawing on the latest contemporary advancement in mechanical science for his comparison. (For an interesting description, with illustrations, of fourteenth-century clock-making, see H. Alan Lloyd, *Giovanni De Dondi's Horological Masterpiece*, Hookwood, Limpsfield, Oxted, Surrey.) (cf. Canto x. 139–48.)

l. 34: *"Eternal light of that great man"* etc.: This is the soul of St Peter.

l. 38: *"This person test and try concerning faith"*: Beatrice here presents Dante to St Peter for oral examination in faith (cf. ll. 46–8). According to an early and not improbable tradition, Dante was at one rime suspected of heresy; if this is so, this interview with St Peter may be intended to bear witness to the orthodoxy of his faith (cf. also his subsequent examination in hope and love in Canto xxv and xxvi). Apart, however, from this biographical significance which the examination-scenes may have, their allegorical meaning is probably that before a man can be admitted to the joy of the saints he must be proved sufficient in the three theological virtues, faith, hope, and charity, for only by the exercise of these can he behold God (see also under *Images*).

l. 39: "*by which thou once didst walk upon the seas*": Compare *Matt*. xiv. 29: "Peter walked on the water, to go to Jesus". Although afterwards he lost faith and "began to sink", the initial act was prompted by faith.

l. 42: "*The centre which all visions mirroreth*": i.e. God, in Whom, as it were depicted, the saints discern all things.

ll. 46–8: *As a Bachelor prepares and does not speak* etc.: The comparison recalls the procedure in mediaeval Universities and may even be a personal reminiscence of scenes which Dante had witnessed (or even taken part in). The Master would propound from the chair questions which were answered by the candidate and then discussed among the scholars present. After the discussion, the Master concluded (cf. l. 48).

l. 62: "*thy belovèd brother*": i.e. St Paul, whom St Peter in *II Pet*. iii. 15 calls "our belovèd brother Paul".

ll. 64–5: "*The substance of things hoped for faith must be*" etc.: Dante is here quoting the *Epistle to the Hebrews* (attributed to St Paul), xi. 1: "Now faith is the substance of things hoped for, the evidence of things not seen." In the Vulgate, the word "evidence" is represented by "argumentum".

l. 66: "*And this I take to be its quiddity*": In scholastic philosophy, *quiddity* is another word for "substantial form" and both terms signify the distinguishing nature of a thing, that which makes it what it is and not another.

ll. 74–5: "*And hope's foundation thus doth represent, wherefore the name of 'substance' it receives*": The mysteries of Heaven, in which man's hope of beatitude lies, are concealed from mortal sight, for they cannot be observed by the senses, nor can they be deduced from first principles; therefore they exist in us only by the assent of faith. On that faith our hope of future bliss is based; therefore faith, being the support, basis, or fundamental principle of hope, was rightly named a *sub-stance*, or that which stands below. Dante here uses the word "substance" in a different sense from that in which it is generally used in scholastic philosophy (i.e. something which exists in itself, as opposed to "accident", which is a quality in a substance). St Thomas Aquinas, in his discussion of the definition of faith in *Hebrews*, objects that faith, being a quality, is not a substance; but he continues: "substance is not to be understood here in the sense of *genus* . . . distinguished from other *genera*, but in the sense that in every *genus* we can find something similar to substance, i.e. that the primary factor in any *genus* contains the rest virtually and so may be called their substance" Dante's explanation may be seen, therefore, to be no mere quibble: a "substance", in the scholastic sense, bears an underlying relationship to an "accident", for an "accident" resides in a "substance". Since hope arises from faith, it may be said that it bears to faith a relationship not dissimilar from that of an "accident" to a "substance".

ll. 76-9: *"And from this faith ... why it is designated argument"*: St Thomas Aquinas, commenting on the passage from the *Epistle to the Hebrews* quoted above (see ll. 64-5 and *note*), interpreted "argumentum" as signifying the adhesion of the *intellect* to the unseen truths of faith. Dante's explanation, then, amounts to this: "faith includes what is meant by *substance* and also what is meant by *argument*, and in the order that is given by St Paul". See also Note to Canto xv. 79-84.

ll. 83-4: *"Thy discourse rightly defines the coin's alloy and weight"*: i.e. Dante has rightly defined *the* faith. He is now to be examined in the orthodoxy of *his* faith (i. 85).

l. 89: *"This precious stone"*: i.e. faith.

l. 90: *"Whereon all virtue founded is by right"*: Compare *Rom.* xiv. 23: "Whatsoever is not of faith is sin."

ll. 91-3: *"The texts ... of scriptures old and new"*: i.e. the Old and New Testaments (cf. Canto xxv. and *note*).

ll. 97-9: *"These prèmises thou dost submit"* etc.: St Peter asks: "What is your reason for believing that the Scriptures are inspired by God?"

ll. 101-2: *"works which knew not Nature's hand"* etc.: i.e. the miracles related in the Bible, which is thereby authenticated.

ll. 103-4: *". . . what else doth stand as guarantor?"*: St Peter continues: "What proves to you that those miracles really occurred? If the miracles prove that the Scriptures are divinely inspired, the Scriptures cannot themselves be cited as proof that the miracles occurred."

ll. 106-8: *"If without miracles the world did bide by Christ"* etc.: i.e. the spread of Christianity is proof that the miracles really occurred. (This famous argument in support of the Christian faith, said to have originated with St Augustine, was later amplified by Bossuet in his *Histoire Universelle*.)

ll. 109-10: *"For, poor and fasting, thou didst come"* etc.: St Peter (and the other Apostles) had no great power or influence (in a material sense) when they preached the gospel; thus the spread of the Christian faith was due solely to its truth.

l. 111: *"where now but thorns and bramble-bushes grow"*: The vineyard of the Lord has been allowed by a degenerate priesthood to become choked and overgrown. Unlike Peter, contemporary prelates are not poor, and do not fast.

ll. 112-13: *When I had done, the Court of Heaven rang with the "Te Deum"*: Dante's answers have proclaimed him a true believer, and the saints sing the great hymn, "We praise thee, O God", which was written by St Ambrose on the occasion of St Augustine's conversion. Dante had already heard it sung when he passed through the gateway to Purgatory (cf. *Purg.* ix. 139-42), as though the souls there rejoiced that a new soul had entered on its way of purgation. Similarly, the souls in Heaven rejoice in accepting Dante as a true believer.

l. 115: *The Baron*: i.e. St Peter. The title of baron was applied to Christ and the more eminent of the saints (cf. Canto xxv. 16, 40–42 and *note*).

ll. 121–2: "*Now thou must say what thy creed is*": Dante has satisfied the examiner concerning the following questions: (1) what is faith? (2) have you that faith? (3) whence do you derive that faith? (4) on what foundation does your faith rest? St Peter now wishes to hear the content of Dante's faith and the specific warrant for it.

ll. 124–6: "*. . . soul who now dost see*" etc.: Dante refers here to the incident related in St John's Gospel, xx. 3–6: "Peter therefore went forth, and that other disciple, and came to the sepulchre. So they ran both together; and the other disciple did outrun Peter, and came first to the sepulchre. And he stooped down, and looking in, saw the linen clothes lying; yet went he not in. Then cometh Simon Peter following him, and went into the sepulchre, and seeth the linen clothes lie", etc. Dante regards Peter's entering the tomb before John as a sign of Peter's stronger faith.

l. 132: *Loving, desiring Him, around they go:* The Primum Mobile is moved by the desire of every part of it to be conjoined with the Empyrean. Its movement is imparted to all the lower heavens (cf. *Convivio*, II, iv and Canto xxiii. 112–14).

ll. 133–5: "*And of such faith the articles are proved by physics, metaphysics and that same truth*" etc.: Dante first declares his faith in God the unmoved Mover, as defined by Aristotle. For this belief, proofs are drawn from physics and metaphysics as well as from Scripture.

l. 136: "*Through Moses*" etc.: Compare *St Luke* xxiv. 44: "And he said unto them, These are the words which I spake unto you, while I was yet with you, that all things must be fulfilled, which were written in the law of Moses, and in the prophets, and in the psalms, concerning me."

l. 138: "*When you were hallowed by the tongues of flame*": i.e. after the first Pentecost. (Cf. *Acts* ii. 1–4.)

ll. 139–40: "*The three eternal persons*" etc.: Dante next declares his faith in God as three Persons in one Essence. For this belief, proofs are drawn from Scripture alone (ll. 142–4).

ll. 140–41: "*so One and Trine that 'are' and 'is' their nature both denote*": i.e. the Holy Trinity can be spoken of as much in the singular as in the plural.

ll. 145–7: "*This the beginning is and this the spark*" etc.: This profession of faith in the Trinity is the source from which all the other articles of Christian faith derive, and is the light which illumines all its teachings.

CANTO XXV

THE STORY. *The soul of St James joins that of St Peter and, at Beatrice's entreaty, questions Dante concerning hope. Beatrice herself proclaims that Dante possesses this virtue to the fullest degree; it is by reason of this that he has been granted grace to behold the joy of the elect. Dante defines hope and states what he looks for in the life to come. The soul of St John now draws near and Dante, gazing eagerly into its brilliant depths, is temporarily blinded.*

If it should chance that e'er the sacred song
   To which both Heaven and Earth have set their hand,
   Whence I am lean with labouring so long,

4   Should touch the cruel hearts by which I'm banned
   From my fair fold where as a lamb I lay,
   Foe to the wolves which leagued against it stand,

7   With altered voice, with altered fleece to-day
   I shall return, a poet, at my font
   Of baptism to take the crown of bay.

10   For unto faith, whereby the Lord is wont
   To know them that are his, I entered there;
   And Peter for that faith now wreathed my front.

13   To us then moved a light, leaving that sphere
   Whence, answering my Lady's prayer, had sped
   The very first of Christ's own vicars here.

16   And Beatrice, with joyous rapture, said:
   "Behold! see now the Baron for whose sake
   Galicia's shrine on earth is visited."

19   As when a dove doth by its fellow take
   Its place and to each other both do coo
   And circle as display of love they make,

22   Even so did I behold those glorious two
   Great princes meet and greet and chant their praise
   Of the repast the Bridegroom bids them to.

25   When mutual bliss had run through every phase,
   Silent before me each was motionless,
   Their fiery brilliance vanquishing my gaze.

Then Beatrice said, smiling in happiness,   28
  "Illustrious Life, who in the world didst write
  Of our High Court and of its bounteousness,

Make sound the name of hope throughout this height,   31
  For oft thou wert her symbol when of yore
  Upon His three Our Lord shed greater light."

"Lift up thy head and thyself reassure,   34
  For whatsoever riseth from the world
  Must here within our radiance mature – "

This comfort from the second light unfurled.   37
  Emboldened then, I raised unto the hills
  My eyelids which, o'erwhelmed, had downwards curled.

"Since by His grace our heavenly Emperor wills   40
  That with His noble lords thou shouldst consort
  In His most privy chamber, ere death stills

Thy voice, so that, remembering our Court,   43
  To hope, whence comes true love in humankind,
  Thou mayst thyself and other men exhort,

Say what hope is, how it adorns thy mind,   46
  And thirdly say whence unto thee hope came."
  This newly from the second light untwined.

And Beatrice, compassionate, the same   49
  Who led my pinions soaring thus on high,
  A prelude to my answer so did frame:

"No child of the Church Militant can vie   52
  With him in hope; this blazoned in the Sun,
  The light of all our host, thou mayst descry.

Hence, leave to come from Egypt he has won,   55
  To see Jerusalem, though many a year
  His soldiering on earth has yet to run.

The two remaining points which thou wouldst hear,   58
  Not to increase thy knowledge, but to train him
  To tell on earth how thou dost hold hope dear,

I leave to him, for they will not o'erstrain him,   61
  Nor by self-praise cause modesty disaster.
  So let him speak, and may God's grace sustain him."

64   Just as a pupil answering a master,
         In eagerness to show his expertise,
         The readier he is, replies the faster,

67   "Hope", I began, "is certainty of bliss
         To come, which God by grace to us concedes
         And for our previous merit promises.

70   From many stars this light to me proceeds,
         But he who first instilled it in my heart
         In praising God all songs of praise exceeds.

73   '*Sperent in te*', so sings he in one part
         Of his great psalmody, 'who thy name know,' –
         (Who of my faith can know not Who Thou art?).

76   Next, in thine own epistle thou didst so
         Instill me with his dew that evermore,
         Brimmed with your rain, on others I o'erflow."

79   While I thus spoke, within the living core
         Of fire, a flare, vibrating, flashing, came
         And went, like lightning blazing o'er and o'er.

28   I heard: "The love with which e'en yet I flame
         For hope, which ne'er forsook me till I earned
         Release from battle and a martyr's palm,

85   Bids me now breathe again to thee who hast learned
         To love this virtue, for I next would know
         What promise in thy hope thou hast discerned."

88   And I: "The scriptures, new and ancient, show
         The sign – and this the promise points to me –
         That God His friendship will on some bestow.

91   Each, saith Isaiah, shall enrobèd be
         In two-fold robe, each in his promised land
         Which is this life of sweet felicity.

94   This revelation by thy brother's hand,
         Where he makes manifest the robes of white,
         Set forth still more explicitly doth stand."

97   And when my answer was concluded quite,
         At first I heard on high '*Sperent in te*',
         And in response the choir of souls unite.

276

And next appeared so bright one light's display,   100
    If such a crystal in the Crab were found
    One winter's month would be unbroken day.

As a maiden rises, joining in the round   103
    Of dancing, joyful, honouring the bride,
    Ne'er thinking how it to herself redound,

So did I see that shining splendour glide,   106
    Joining the circles woven by the twain,
    Wheeling as love within them signified.

Of words and song its voice took up the strain.   109
    Gazing upon them, silent and at rest,
    My Lady seemed a bride among her train.

"This light is he who leant upon the breast   112
    Of Christ our Pelican, and from the Cross
    Was chosen to fulfil the great request."

Although she spoke, no less enraptured was   115
    Her gaze, nor did it interruption brook,
    Nor yet in its intentness suffer loss.

As one who squinnies and by hook or crook   118
    Will strain his eyes to see the sun's eclipse,
    And, looking long, can then no longer look,

So I became, probing those fiery deeps,   121
    The while I heard: "Why treatest thou so ill
    Thy sight, seeking in me what thy world keeps?

Earth in the earth my body lies, and will   124
    So lie with others till our total count
    Be equal God's great purpose to fulfil.

Two only who straightway to Heaven did mount   127
    In our bless'd cloister in both robes are clad.
    This truth unto the world shalt thou recount."

His voice the fiery reeling ended had,   130
    And silenced the sweet mingled melody
    Which with their three-fold breath the trio made,

As, to forestall fatigue or jeopardy,   133
    At the shrill sounding of the whistle's blast
    The flying oars fall idle instantly.

136   Ah! how the soul within me was aghast,
                When next I turned to look on Beatrice,
                To find myself from sight of her outcast,

139   Though I was near her in the realm of bliss

THE IMAGES. *The Heaven of the Fixed Stars*: See Canto xxii, under *Images*.

Dante's Examination in Faith, Hope and Love: See Canto xxiv, under *Images*.

Dante's temporary blindness: See Canto xxvi, under *Images*.

NOTES. l. 4: *the cruel hearts*: i.e. the Florentines, who have exiled him from Florence, his "fair fold".

l. 6: *Foe to the wolves which leagued against it stand*: By this image of the lamb and the wolves, Dante asserts his innocence and lays the charge of cupidity against his enemies, whom he regards also as the enemies of Florence.

l. 7: *With altered voice, with altered fleece* etc.: Dante is no longer a poet of love-songs but of a solemn work on a sacred and sublime theme; he is no longer young, but grey-haired and mature.

l. 8: *I shall return*: Note that he uses the future tense, although his return is dependent upon the condition of his poem's touching the cruel hearts of those who have not recalled him. This conveys the unquenchable hope in his heart that he will one day be honoured with the crown of laurel at his baptismal font in his "own beautiful St John" (*Hell* xix. 17. See also Introduction, p. 38).

ll. 13–15: *that sphere whence . . . sped the very first of Christ's own vicars*: i.e. the circle of lights, the "costliest one" (*Para*. xxiv. 19) from which St Peter had come forth.

ll. 17–18: ". . . *the Baron for whose sake Galicia's shrine on earth is visited*": This is the soul of St James, the Apostle, the son of Zebedee and brother of St John the Evangelist. He is believed to have preached the gospel in Spain and after his death his body was taken to Compostella in Galicia. The shrine containing his relics was visited by pilgrims from all parts of Christendom. (For the title of Baron as a term of respect derived from feudal usage, see Canto xxiv. 115 and *note*.)

l. 22: *those glorious two*: i.e. St Peter and St James.

l. 24: . . . *the repast the Bridegroom bids them to*: i.e. the joy of beholding God. For this image, see Canto xxiv. 1–6 and *note*.

l. 29: ". . . *who in the world didst write*" etc.: Dante evidently confused James bar-Zebedee (St James the Great), whose shrine is at Compostella, with James the brother of Jesus, who is traditionally believed to be the author of the *General Epistle* here intended (cf. l. 76).

l. 32: "*For oft thou wert her symbol*": According (to a traditional allegorical interpretation of the New Testament, St Peter, St James, and

St John stand respectively for faith, hope, and charity. (It is interesting to notice that Dante gave these names to his three sons.)

l. 33: *"Upon His three Our Lord shed greater light"*: Christ chose Peter, James, and John as His special companions on the occasion of the raising of the daughter of Jairus and of the transfiguration, and in the Garden of Gethsemane (cf. *Introduction*, pp. 44–5).

ll. 34–6: *"Lift up thy head and thyself reassure"* etc.: Dante, unable to endure the fiery brilliance of the souls of St Peter and St James, has lowered his gaze (l. 27). St James now encourages him to raise his eyes, promising that his earthly vision will increase in power as it contemplates the radiance of the saints.

ll. 38–9: *I raised unto the hills* etc.: Compare *Psalm* cxxi. 1: "I will lift up mine eyes unto the hills, from whence cometh my help." The image of the hills here stands for the brilliant light of the Apostles.

l. 42: *"In His most privy chamber"*: i.e. in the Empyrean, where it is God's will that Dante shall ascend. Some commentators, however, take the phrase as alluding to Paradise generally.

l. 44: *". . . hope, whence comes true love in humankind"*: As hope arises from faith, so love arises from hope.

l. 46: *". . . how it adorns thy mind"*: This, the second of the three questions which St James puts to Dante, concerns the degree to which Dante possesses hope. It is answered for him by Beatrice (ll. 52–7).

ll. 52–3: *"No child of the Church Militant can vie with him in hope"*: Dante's hope was undying, hope for mankind, for the Empire, for Italy, for Florence, for the regeneration of the Church, for the coming of a political leader, and hope, in the face of bitter disappointments, of his own honourable reinstatement in Florence. Above all, the Christian hope, arising from faith in God, was so strong in him that this great vision and mission had been granted him by grace that he might inspire others likewise to believe, hope, and love.

ll. 53–4: *". . . this blazoned in the Sun . . . thou mayst descry"*: i.e. St James may read the truth of what Beatrice has said in the mind of God.

ll. 55–6: *"Egypt . . . Jerusalem"*: Egypt in Scripture is symbolical of life on earth, Jerusalem of eternal life in Heaven.

l. 58: *"The two remaining points"*: i.e. the other two questions which St James has put to Dante – "what is hope?" – and "whence came it unto thee?" (cf. ll. 46–7).

l. 60 *"To tell on earth how thou dost hold hope dear"*: This purpose has already been indicated by St James (cf. ll. 43–5).

l. 62: *"Nor by self-praise cause modesty disaster"*: For Dante to have said how greatly he possessed the virtue of hope would have involved him in self-praise. That is why Beatrice has answered this question on his behalf.

l. 64: *Just as a pupil answering a master*: Compare Canto xxiv. 46–8, where Dante, about to answer the questions of St Peter, compares himself to a candidate for a doctorate in a University.

ll. 67–9: *"Hope . . . is certainty of bliss to come"* etc.: Dante here follows the definition of hope by Peter Lombard in his *Libri Sententiarum* (a collection of the sayings of the Fathers of the Church). In Book III, which deals mainly with the Incarnation and Redemption, there is a section entitled *De Spe, quid sit* (" On Hope, what it is"), in which the author gives the following definition: "Hope is the certain expectation of future bliss, coming from the grace of God and from preceding merits." Peter Lombard has been seen by Dante in the Heaven of the Sun (cf. Canto x. 106–8 and *note*).

l. 70: *"From many stars"*: i.e. from many minds illuminated by wisdom.

ll. 70–78: The image which Dante uses of *instilling, dew, brimming, rain* and *overflowing* is found in both the Old and the New Testament in connection with the outpouring of the Spirit. In *St John* vii. 37–9, especially, the words of Jesus convey the idea of living water received from Him and then poured forth on to others (cf. *Isaiah* lviii. 11). In the present context, Dante indicates a link between the *Psalms* and the *Epistle* of St James, namely the hope, or trust, which both convey. The dominant mood of the *Psalms* is, indeed, one of hope, hope of a future divine manifestation, hope of life after death, hope despite temporal injustice. Yet the Psalmist can do no more than glimpse afar off the promise that will be fulfilled. Combined, however, with the words of St James, the dew he instilled in Dante becomes rain which brims and overflows.

ll. 71–2: *"But he who first instilled it in my heart"* etc.: Dante thus refers to David, the Psalmist.

l. 73: " '*Sperent in te* ' ": This is a quotation from *Psalm* ix. verse 10. The Authorized translation reads: "And they that know thy name will put their trust in thee." In the Vulgate, the words mean: "Let them that know thy name put their trust in thee."

l. 76: *"in thine own epistle"*: In the *General Epistle* of St James the Less (whom Dante identifies with St James the Great, cf. *note* to l. 29), hope, or trust in God's promise, is several times conveyed (cf. i. 12, ii. 5, iv. 10, v. 7–8).

l. 78: *". . . brimmed with your rain"*: i.e. with the teaching of David and of St James.

l. 84: *". . . a martyr's palm"*: St James the Great was martyred by Herod Agrippa in the year 44 (cf. *Acts* xii. 2).

l. 87: *"What promise in thy hope thou hast discerned"*: As St Peter asked Dante to state the content of his faith (Canto xxiv. 121–2), so now St James asks him to state what it is he hopes for in the life to come.

l. 90: *"That God His friendship will on some bestow"*: This is the promise Dante has read in the Scriptures, that some will know God. The twofold joy of the elect is indicated in the following six lines.

ll. 91–3: *"Each, saith Isaiah, shall enrobèd be in two-fold robe"*: Compare *Isaiah* lxi. 7, 10: ". . . in their land they shall possess the double: everlasting joy shall be unto them . . . he hath clothed me with the garments of salvation." This was understood to mean that in Heaven man would possess the double clothing of both soul and body.

ll. 94–6: "*This revelation by thy brother's hand*" etc.: The allusion is to the passage in *Revelations* vii. 9: "After this I beheld, and, lo, a great multitude, which no man could number, of all nations, and kindreds, and people, and tongues, stood before the throne, and before the Lamb, clothed with white robes, and palms in their hands." The content of Dante's hope is, then, of unbroken immortality of the soul and the resurrection to immortality of the body. It is surprising that Dante did not refer to *I Cor.* xv, which provides an explicit argument for the resurrection. Perhaps, because it is *hope* rather than *reasoning* on which he is being questioned by St James, he preferred to cite instances of imagery rather than argument. (Dante identifies St John the Divine with St John the Apostle.)

l. 98: *at first I heard on high "Sperent in te"*: At first one voice is heard singing the psalm of hope which Dante has already quoted (l. 73). It is thought that the voice may be intended to be understood as that of David; it is joined (l. 99) in response by the whole choir of souls.

ll. 101–2: *If such a crystal in the Crab were found* etc.: Dante means if the constellation of Cancer contained a star as bright as the light which now appears, there would be a month's unbroken daylight between 21 December and 21 January, when Cancer dominates the night sky (the sun being then in Capricorn). This seems equivalent to saying that the new light was equal in radiance to the sun itself. It is, of course, the soul of St John.

l. 107: *the twain*: i.e. St Peter and St James.

ll. 112–13: "*This light is he who leant upon the breast of Christ our Pelican*": Compare *John* xiii. 23: "There was leaning on Jesus' bosom one of his disciples, whom Jesus loved."

ll. 113–14: ". . . *and from the Cross was chosen to fulfil the great request*": St John was entrusted by Christ on the Cross with the care of the Virgin Mary (cf *John* xix. 26–7).

l. 123: ". . . *seeking in me what thy world keeps*": There was a legend that St John had been taken up into Heaven in the body after his death. That is why Dante peers so eagerly into the depth of the light. St John denies the belief that he has not died as other men and bids Dante take back to earth the truth, namely, that only Christ and the Virgin are already in the body in Heaven. Note that it is the *doubt* concerning St John which prompts Dante to seek the truth. There is no doubt in his mind concerning the Virgin Mary; hence no such curiosity prompts him to peer into the depths of her light in order to behold her body (cf. Canto xxiii). The fresco by Giotto in the Church of Santa Croce in Florence of the Assumption of St John may have been commissioned in direct refutal of Dante's recounting of 'this truth unto the world'.

ll. 125–6: ". . . *till our total count be equal God's great purpose to fulfil*": The resurrection will not come until God has "accomplished the number of His elect"

l. 138: *To find myself from sight of her outcast*: i.e. Dante is blind.

CANTO XXVI

THE STORY. *To Dante, bewildered and alarmed by his sudden blindness, come the reassuring words of St John: his sight will be restored to him by the healing gaze of Beatrice. Meanwhile the Apostle questions him concerning love. Dante declares that God is the beginning and end of all his loves and, in response to further questioning, indicates the sources whence he has derived the knowledge that God is the ultimate good, and hence the supreme object of love. Replying still further, he enumerates the blessings by which God manifests His goodness to man. As he concludes, a hymn of praise is sung by all the assembled saints and Dante's vision is restored.*

The soul of Adam joins the three Apostles and replies to Dante's unspoken questions concerning the Fall, the duration of his stay in Eden and of his life on earth, and the language which he spoke.

Fearing and doubting for my blinded eyes,
  From out the brilliance which had blinded me
  I heard an utterance issuing in this guise:

4   "Until thy sight shall be restored to thee,
  Which, focusing in me, consumed thou hast,
  See thou make recompense in colloquy.

7   Begin then: say to what thy soul clings fast.
  Be reassured and rid thee of fear's bias;
  Thy vision is not dead but overcast.

10   She who escorts thee through this bless'd and pious
  Region, holds in her gaze such power to heal
  As once was in the hand of Ananias."

13   I answered: "Swiftly or slowly, as she will,
  May she restore these eyes, that were the gates
  She entered with the fire that burns me still.

16   The Good which in this Court all longing sates
  Alpha and Omega is of every text
  Which love in accents soft or loud dictates."

19   The self-same voice which from my soul perplexed
  Had banished fear, for discourse once again
  Made me attentive as it breathed forth next:

"Now through a finer sieve thou needs must strain   22
  Thy words. Who guided, then, thy shaft to fly
  At such a target? This must thou explain."

"By philosophic arguments and by   25
  Authority which from this realm descended,
  Such love of good imprints me with its die.

For good, as good, as far as apprehended,   28
  Enkindles love so far, and as much more,
  As good within itself is comprehended.

Hence, towards that essence, where abides such store   31
  Of goodness, that all goodness elsewhere found
  Derives its splendour from that radiant core,

The loving mind is, as it must be, bound   34
  To move, more than to all else, if it know
  The truth which is this demonstration's ground.

Such truth, he who the primal love doth show   37
  Of sempiternal substances, to me
  Makes plain, and plain doth utter it also

The voice of that true Author, even He   40
  Who speaking of Himself to Moses said:
  '*Ego ostendam omne bonum tibi.*'

And plainly in thy prelude it is read,   43
  Which cries the mystery of God to man
  Louder than ever news was trumpeted."

"By human reasoning", the answer ran,   46
  "And revelation which concurs with it,
  The highest of thy loves to God doth span.

But are there other cords which pull thee tight   49
  To Him? Show by thy words how many are
  The teeth whereby this love of thine doth bite."

The sacred purpose of Christ's *aquila*   52
  Beneath his questioning was plain to me.
  I knew where he would lead me and how far.

I said: "All ratchets which can severally   55
  Revolve the heart towards God co-operate
  And are indented with my charity:

58   The being of the world and my own state,
          The death He died that I might live the more,
          The hope in which I, by faith, participate,

61   The living truth which I conveyed before,
          Have dredged me from the sea of wrongful love,
          And of the right have set me on the shore.

64   And through the garden of the world I rove,
          Enamoured of its leaves in measure solely
          As God the Gardener nurtures them above."

67   When I had done, then was the heaven wholly
          Filled with sweet song, as with the others there
          My Lady chanted: "Holy, holy, holy."

70   As a sleeper wakens to a piercing glare,
          The visual spirit leaping to the light,
          Which penetrates through layer after layer,

73   And as his startled senses shrink in fright
          From what he sees, for so his mind beguiles
          Him, till discernment comes to aid his sight,

76   So, from my eyes, all matter that defiles
          Was dissipated by her radiant gaze,
          Whose splendour shone more than a thousand miles;

79   New clarity was mine and in amaze
          Of the new light I begged to know the state,
          For where there had been three, now four did blaze.

82   Beatrice replied: "Therein doth radiate,
          In worship of his Maker, the first soul
          That ever Primal Virtue did create."

85   As, tossing in the wind, the tree-tops roll
          Then upright spring again as at one stroke
          Of the resilience within their bole,

88   So did I bend, awe-stricken as she spoke;
          Then confidence returning, at her side
          I drew erect, as from my lips words broke.

91   "O thou, the one and only fruit", I cried,
          "That wast created ripe, First Ancestor,
          Father and father-in-law of every bride,

Vouchsafe, I beg devoutly and implore,   94
　　To speak with me; thou read'st my heart right through;
　　To hear the sooner then, I'll say no more."

Sometimes an animal concealed from view   97
　　Inside a sack vibrates, so that we see
　　Its every movement as the sack moves too;

Thus that primaeval soul transparently   100
　　Showed through the stirring veil wherein it stirred
　　How gladly it was moved to pleasure me.

"Though of thy wish thou utterest no word,   103
　　Yet my discernment of it doth surpass
　　All certainty of which thou'rt most assured.

For I behold it truly in the glass   106
　　In which all things their perfect image show,
　　Yet which in naught its perfect image has.

This is thy wish: to learn how long ago   109
　　God set me in the earthly paradise
　　Where apt for this ascent thy soul did grow.

How long such loveliness rejoiced my eyes,   112
　　The true occasion of the mighty wrath,
　　The language which I spoke and formed, likewise.

'Twas not the tasting of the fruit that hath,   115
　　My son, earned of itself such banishment,
　　But solely the transgression from the path.

From where thy Lady to thee Virgil sent   118
　　I longed for this assembly while the sun
　　Forty-three hundred and two circles went.

Nine hundred times and thirty had he run   121
　　The course of all his stars, when I awoke
　　To find my time of life on earth was done.

Long was extinct the language which I spoke   124
　　Ere work on the unfinishable tower
　　First contemplated was by Nimrod's folk.

No work of reason lasts beyond its hour,   127
　　For usage, as fate wills, doth ever seek
　　To recreate according to its power.

130   Nature so fashioned man that he should speak,
           But how, she leaves to you, as seemeth well
           According to your choice or fancy's freak.

133   Ere I descended to the pains of Hell
           Jah was the name men called the highest Good
           Which swathes me in this joy. Thereafter *El*

136   His title was on earth; for as they should,
           Like leaves upon the branches of a tree,
           The words of mortals die and are renewed.

139   Upon that mount the highest from the sea
           I dwelt, in innocence and in disgrace,
           From first to seventh of the sun's hours, when he

142   Into another quadrant changes place."

THE IMAGES. *The Heaven of the Fixed Stars*: See Canto xxii, under *Images*.

Dante's temporary blindness: Before being examined in the third theological virtue, love, Dante, peering with inquisitive eagerness into the burning depths of the light that is St John, goes blind. There was a legend that St John, of whom Our Lord said "He shall not die", was taken up bodily into Heaven, and it is to satisfy his curiosity as to this that Dante strains his vision in the blinding radiance of the saint. The allegorical meaning of this incident has been much disputed. The general significance seems to be that irrelevant and superstitious curiosity can blind one, temporarily, to the truth of God. Whether there is any more specific, personal significance to be attached to the image is not certain. In the story, Dante experiences a setback; does it correspond to a setback in his spiritual progress? It may, perhaps, signify a period of discouragement or imperception. Faith he has, and hope, but the wells of his love have run dry. Response to St John's questioning as to the object and nature of love precede the restoration of his sight. The mystical significance which seems to be adumbrated here is that vision and love of God are interrelated in a way that the soul cannot apprehend without experience. Vision, in the Thomist system, precedes love, but without love there cannot be vision.

Adam: When Dante's sight is restored to him, he sees the soul of Adam, who has joined St Peter, St James, and St John. Within the image of the Church Triumphant, Adam, who brought sin into the world, is the universal type of redeemed humanity.

NOTES. l. 2: *the brilliance which had blinded me*: i.e. the soul of St John.
l. 7: "*. . . say to what thy soul clings fast*": St John now examines Dante

in charity (love), as St Peter (Canto xxiv) examined him in faith and St James (Canto xxv) examined him in hope.

ll. 11–12: "... *such power to heal as once was in the hand of Ananias*": Dante's sight will be restored by the gaze of Beatrice as St Paul's sight was restored by the hand of Ananias (cf. *Acts* ix. 17).

ll. 14–15: "... *that were the gates she entered with the fire that burns me still*": i.e. love was first awakened in Dante's heart by the sight of Beatrice. The conception of beauty's entering through the eyes of the beholder is one which the Sicilian poets preceding Dante had much elaborated in their lyrics. A detailed description of the operation of the image of beauty upon the apprehensive faculty, and the subsequent awakening of love in the beholder's heart, is contained in a sonnet in the *Vita Nuova*, beginning "L'amor e il cor gentil sono una cosa". The whole process is described by Virgil in *Purg*. xviii. 19–33, this time within the context of ethics. Here, the reminder of the first vision of the beauty of Beatrice takes us back to the source of all Dante's experience of love, an experience he does not reject or consider replaced in any way, but now at last followed aright to where it first directed him.

l. 16: "*The Good which in this Court all longing sates*": i.e. God, the Ultimate Goodness.

ll. 17–18: "*Alpha and Omega is of every text which love ... dictates*": i.e. God is the beginning and end of all my love. (Cf. *Rev*. i. 8: "I am Alpha and Omega, the beginning and the ending, saith the Lord, which is, and which was, and which is to come, the Almighty.")

ll. 23–4: "*Who guided, then, thy shaft to fly at such a target?*": St John now wishes to sift Dante's love more closely and asks what led him to aim at making God the ultimate object of all his love; and this is not inappropriate, for Dante had not always aimed so well (cf. *Purg*. xxx, xxxi).

ll. 25–6: "*By philosophic arguments and by authority*" etc.: i.e. by reason and by revelation, Dante has been led to recognize God as the end and be-all of his love.

ll. 28–30: "*For good, as good, as far as apprehended*" etc.: Goodness, as soon and as far as it is apprehended by the intellect, enkindles love for itself, and the greater the good, the greater the love.

ll. 31–3: "... *towards that essence, where abides such store of goodness*" etc.: Supreme excellence (God) is the source of all other good. Compare the words of St Thomas in Canto xiii. 52–4, to the effect that all created things, whether mortal or immortal, are but reflections of the Word or Idea of God.

l. 36: "*The truth which is this demonstration's ground*": Dante (ll. 28–35) has shown by philosophic and logical argument that God, being the chief Good, must be the highest object of man's love. The foundation of this proof is revelation.

ll. 37–8: "... *he who the primal love doth show of sempiternal substances*": Dante refers here to Aristotle, who has shown God to be the unmoved

Mover for love of Whom the heavens are moved. (Cf. Canto xxiv. 130–34.)

ll. 40–42: "*The voice of that true Author*" etc.: Dante here quotes the authority of God who "said unto Moses ... I will make all my goodness pass before thee". (*Ex.* xxxiii. 17–19; in the Vulgate: "ego ostendam omne bonum tibi".)

ll. 43–5: "*And plainly in thy prelude it is read*" etc.: Dante is probably referring here to *John* i. 1–18: "In the beginning was the word", etc., by which great heralding the mystery of the nature of God is proclaimed to man.

l. 51: "*The teeth whereby*" etc.: see *note* to ll. 55–7.

l. 52: *Christ's "aquila"*: The eagle was the symbol of St John the Evangelist in mediaeval art. It was said to indicate his more fervent insight into the divine mysteries. St Augustine wrote of him "Aquila ipse est Johannes sublimium praedicator" ("John, the preacher of sublime things, is a very eagle").

ll. 55–7: "*All ratchets which can severally*" etc.: Dante begins to answer the question which St John has implied in ll. 50–51, namely: what are the secondary loves which have led and still lead you to direct your highest love to God? The image is here interpreted as that of machinery operated by cogged wheel and ratchet, which has at last "dredged him from the sea of wrongful love" (l. 62).

ll. 58–61: "*The being of the world and my own state*" etc.: Dante here enumerates all the blessings or gifts that have wrought together to set his love in order: the existence of the world, his own existence (l. 58), the Redemption and Dante's own awareness that Christ died for *him* (l. 59), the Christian hope which he holds by reason of his faith (l. 60), the living truth (derived from reason and Revelation) that God is the source of all goodness (l. 61).

ll. 62–3: "*Have dredged me from the sea of wrongful love*" etc.: All Dante's spiritual progress, from the *Vita Nuova* to the *Paradiso*, has consisted of setting his love in order. How love can require guidance was explained to him by Virgil on the Mountain of Purgatory (see *Purg.* Cantos xvii and xviii). Now, at last, the right choice of objects for his love (as listed in ll. 58–61) has led him to make the full commital of his soul to God.

ll. 65–6: "*Enamoured of its leaves in measure solely*" etc.: Now that his love is rightly ordered, Dante loves the things of this life only in so far, and in proportion, as they reflect the glory of God, the Gardener of the "garden of the world".

l. 69: "*Holy, holy, holy*": The chant which Dante hears is probably the hymn of praise in the Apocalypse of St John. (Cf. *Rev.* iv. 8: "And the four beasts had each of them six wings about him, and they were full of eyes within: and they rest not day and night, saying, Holy, holy, holy, Lord God Almighty, which was, and is, and is to come.")

l. 71: *The visual spirit*: According to mediaeval principles of physiology, each sensory organ was governed by a "spirit", or vital power, by the functioning of which the external world was apprehended by the senses.

l. 72: *layer after layer*: i.e. the successive layers of membrane covering the closed eyes of the sleeper.

ll. 76–8: *So, from my eyes, all matter that defiles was dissipated by her radiant gaze* etc.: Dante's sight is now restored to him by the power of the gaze of Beatrice.

l. 80: *"the new light"*: i.e. the soul of Adam, who has joined St Peter, St James, and St John.

ll. 106–8: *"For I behold it truly in the glass"* etc.: i.e. in the mind of God. All created things are perfectly reflected in God, but no created thing is sufficient to be a perfect reflection of God (cf. Canto xix. 49–51).

l. 110: *the earthly paradise*: i.e. the Garden of Eden, on the summit of Mount Purgatory.

ll. 115–17: *" 'Twas not the tasting of the fruit that hath, my son"* etc.: Adam here states the nature of the Fall. It consisted of disobedience ("transgression from the path"), in that a limit had been set beyond which Man should not go. Yet it was not the "tasting of the fruit" which in itself incurred exile. Had not Eve been in such presumptuous haste to know good and evil "as the gods", this knowledge would have been revealed to Man in due course, when his nature was sufficiently developed to know evil, as God knows it, by understanding and not by participation. But her disobedience to the divine warning meant that she and Adam fell into the knowledge while their nature was still such that they could know it only by experience. Lucifer also fell by his haste (cf. Canto xix. 46–8).

l. 118: *"From where thy Lady to thee Virgil sent"*: i.e. in the Limbo.

l. 120: *"Forty-three hundred and two circles"*: i.e. Adam spent 4302 years in Limbo before Christ came to rescue him (cf. *Inf.* iv. 52–5).

ll. 121–3: *"Nine hundred times and thirty"* etc.: Adam says that he was 930 years old when he died (cf. *Gen.* v. 5: "And all the days that Adam lived were nine hundred and thirty years, and he died."). This puts the birth of Christ 5198 years, and His crucifixion 5232 years, after the Creation. (Dante is here following the chronology of Eusebius more exactly than he does in *Purg.* xxxiii. 61–3, where he says of Adam:

> "Yea, for one bite, in grief and longing pent,
>   Five thousand years on Him the first soul yearned
>   Who on Himself imposed the punishment.")

The chronology, as now exactly indicated by Dante, is as follows:

The creation of Adam	5198 B.C.
Adam's death and descent into Limbo	4268 B.C.
Christ's descent into Hell	A.D. 34

l. 124: *"Long was extinct the language which I spoke"*: In his treatise on language and prosody, *De Vulgari Eloquentia* (I. vi), Dante says that the language spoken by Adam was Hebrew, and that this language was spoken by all Adam's descendants until the building of the tower of Babel. When language was "confounded" (*Gen.* xi. 6–9), the sons of Heber inherited the speech of Adam, and after him were called Hebrews. "With them alone", says Dante, "did it remain after the confusion, in order that our Redeemer (who was, as to his humanity, to spring from them) might use, not the language of confusion, but of grace." Dante's opinion had evidently undergone a change by the time he came to write this canto, for he here conveys that Adam's language was not a divine creation (as he formerly believed) but the result of human reason (l. 127) and, as such, susceptible of change and decay.

l. 125: ". . . *the unfinishable tower*": i.e. the tower of Babel.

l. 126: ". . . *Nimrod's folk*": i.e. the people of Babylon, under the guidance of Nimrod.

ll. 134–6: " *'Jah' was the name men called the highest Good*" etc.: Compare *Psalm* lxviii. 4: "Sing unto God, sing praises to his name: extol him that rideth upon the heavens by his name Jah, and rejoice before him." I or J (pronounced Jah) was the initial letter of the sacred name of Jehovah, which was held in such deep veneration by the Jews that it was uttered in full only on certain solemn occasions. The form "Jah" still survives as the final syllable of "Hallelujah". *El*, signifying "the mighty", is an ancient and general name for the Deity. Dante had previously stated (*De Vulgari Eloquentia* I. iv) that this was the first word uttered by Adam: "Now I have no doubt that it is obvious to a man of sound mind that the first thing the voice of the first speaker uttered was the equivalent of God, namely *El*, whether in the way of a question or in the way of an answer." Now, in his revised view of the language of Adam, he considers that this form of the name of God was subsequent to "Jah".

l. 137: "*Like leaves upon the branches of a tree*": The image is taken from the *Ars Poetica* of Horace (ll. 60–62).

ll. 139–42: "*Upon that mount . . . I dwelt*" etc.: Adam now answers the second question: how long did he reside in Eden? The answer is six hours, from the first hour to the seventh, when the sun, having run through a quarter, or 90°, of his circle, moves into his second quadrant. Of the many views put forward by mediaeval theologians concerning the duration of Adam's stay in Eden, Dante chooses that of Petrus Comestor (cf. Canto xii. 134). The hour of the Fall is thus made to coincide with the hour of Christ's death. (cf. *Convivio* IV. xxiii, where Dante quotes St Luke as saying that "it was about the sixth hour when he died".) Since all three synoptists put the last cry from the Cross at the ninth hour, Dante must mean that Christ entered into death at the sixth hour (noon), whereas at the ninth hour the act was completed. Six hours is also the length of time spent by Dante in the Earthly Paradise, and in the eighth heaven.

CANTO XXVII

THE STORY. *For a brief space of time, Dante participates in the exultation of the saints who rejoice in his progress. St Peter then resumes, and turning fiery red, denounces the present occupant of the Papal see, which he declares vacant in his sight. The saints of the Church Triumphant return to the Empyrean and, after looking down once more on earth, Dante ascends with Beatrice into the Primum Mobile.*

"To Father and to Son and Holy Ghost,"
    All Heaven broke forth, "Be glory!" – such sweet din,
    My sense was drunken to the uttermost;

And all I saw, meseemed to see therein   4
    A smile of all creation; thus through eye
    And ear I drew the inebriate rapture in.

O joy no tongue can tell! O ecstasy!   7
    O perfect life fulfilled of love and peace!
    O wealth past want, that ne'er shall fade nor fly!

And those four flamboys blazed without surcease   10
    Full in my sight, and as I looked, the glow
    Of that which first drew near began to increase;

And as in aspect Jupiter would show   13
    If Mars and he were birds, and quill for quill
    Exchanged their plumage, such it seemed to grow.

Then, when that Providence whose sovran will   16
    Each office there assigns and function due
    Had hushed the blissful choirs and all was still,

I heard: "If I change colour as I do,   19
    Marvel not thou, for thou shalt see apace,
    While I shall speak, all these change colour too.

He that on earth has dared usurp that place   22
    Of mine, that place of mine, that place of mine,
    Which now stands vacant before God's Son's face,

Has made my burial-ground a running rhine   25
    Of filth and blood, which to the Renegade
    Down there, who fell from here, is anodyne."

28   That colour, by the sun obliquely rayed,
    Which paints the clouds at morning and at eve,
    All Heaven suffusing then I saw displayed.

31   And as a modest woman, who doth live
    Serene in her own virtue, suffers shame
    The mere report of evil to receive,

34   So Beatrice changed colour, and the same
    Was the eclipse in Heaven, or so I deem,
    When the Almighty to His passion came.

37   And now his words once more took up the theme,
    In voice so altered from its former self,
    No greater change had I observed in him.

40   "The blood of Cletus, Linus, and myself
    Was shed to foster her who is Christ's bride,
    Not that she should be used for gain of pelf;

43   Rather, to gain this life beatified,
    Urban, Calixtus, Pius, Sixtus spilled
    Their blood and in long torment, weeping, died.

46   Never by our intention was it willed
    That Christendom should sit on either hand
    Of those who after us our office held;

49   Nor that the keys bequeathed to me should stand
    As emblem on a banner waging war
    Against the baptized in a Christian land;

52   Nor that a signet which my features bore
    Should seal the lying privileges sold,
    Whence, coruscating, I blush red the more.

55   Rapacious wolves in shepherds' garb behold
    In every pasture! Lord, why dost Thou blink
    Such slaughter of the lambs within Thy fold?

58   Gascons and Cahorsines prepare to drink
    Our blood. Beginning that so fair didst show,
    To what vile ending wast thou doomed to sink!

61   But Providence, which once through Scipio
    The glory of the world and Rome's renown
    Secured, will swift lend aid, as I foreknow.

And thou my son, whose weight must draw thee down 64
    To earth once more, open thy mouth and speak.
    The things that I hide not, see thou make known."

As through our air the frozen vapours leak, 67
    In flakes down-drifting, when the heavenly Goat
    To butt his horns against the sun doth seek,

So upward there I saw those vapours float, 70
    Their triumph spangling heaven with the light
    Of saints who sojourned with us, as I wrote.

My look, pursuing their departing flight, 73
    Lingered until the space had grown so vast
    I could no longer span it with my sight.

My Lady then, who saw me freed at last 76
    From gazing upwards, said to me, "Now bend
    Thy look below; see how thou circled hast."

Since the first glance which downward I did send, 79
    I saw that I had moved through the degrees
    Which the first climate measures mid to end.

Beyond Cadiz I saw to Ulysses' 82
    Mad course and, eastward, to Europa's shore,
    Where she became a burden of sweet ease.

More widely had I viewed this threshing-floor, 85
    Had not the westering sun beneath my feet
    Been distant from me by a sign and more.

My mind in love, which never once did quit 88
    Its dalliance with my Lady, as her wooer
    Longed still more ardently her eyes to meet.

Whatever art or nature made as lure 91
    To take the eye, whereby the mind is caught,
    Of fleshly beauty, or of portraiture,

If all assembled, would appear as naught 94
    Beside the beauty which divinely glowed,
    When her sweet joyous countenance I sought.

The virtue which her gaze on me bestowed 97
    Uprooted me from Leda's lovely nest,
    Till in the swiftest circle we abode.

100   This heaven, the liveliest and loftiest,
        So equal is, which part I cannot say
        My Lady for my sojourn there deemed best.

103   But she, who knew my wish, began straightway.
        Such gladness was reflected in her smiles,
        Meseemed the joy of God therein did play.

106   "The nature of the universe which stills
        The centre and revolves all else, from here,
        As from its starting-point, all movement wills.

109   This heaven it is which has no other 'where'
        Than the Divine Mind; 'tis but in that Mind
        That love, its spur, and the power it rains inhere.

112   The light and love which round this circle wind,
        As it enfolds the rest, He comprehends
        By Whom alone such girdle is confined.

115   This circle's motion takes no measurements
        From other spheres beneath, but theirs computes,
        As two and five of ten are dividends.

118   As in a plant-pot, then, time has its roots
        Herein, and where the other heavens trace
        Their course, thou mayst behold its shoots.

121   Cupidity! thou dost engulf the race
        Of mortal men so deep, not one may then
        Above the o'erwhelming waters raise his face.

124   Fair is the blossom of the will of men,
        But the true fruit is swollen and made weak
        By drenchings of interminable rain.

127   In little children only mayst thou seek
        True innocence and faith, and both are flown
        Before the down has grown upon the cheek.

130   He who the fast-days as a child has known,
        Will every dish in every season have
        Ere out of baby-talk he scarce has grown;

133   Or who affection to his mother gave
        In lisping childhood, learning at her knee,
        In manhood longs to see her in her grave.

Thus the white skin of the fair progeny   136
  Of him who brings the morn and leaves the night
  Darkens upon exposure instantly.

And thou, lest thou shouldst marvel at such plight,   139
  Reflect: since there be none to govern you,
  How can the human household run aright?

Ere January be unwintered, through   142
  The hundredth of a day which men neglect,
  These lofty circles shall give vent unto

Such roaring, that the storm we long expect   145
  Shall whirl the vessels round upon their route,
  Setting the fleet to sail a course direct;

And from the blossom shall come forth true fruit."   148

THE IMAGES. *The Heaven of the Fixed Stars*: See Canto xxii, under
   Images.
St Peter's Denunciation: While St Peter utters his tremendous denuncia-
   tion of Pope Boniface VIII, the light of his soul undergoes so fiery a
   transformation that Dante is moved to imagine, in comparison, the
   silvery sheen of Jupiter transfigured by the ruddy glow of Mars.
   Allegorically, this would seem to indicate that St Peter's zeal is com-
   pounded of the righteousness of the just rulers and the fiery wrath of
   warriors who fought and died for the Faith. Further, the unworthi-
   ness of the Pope is a betrayal both of the Christian martyrs and of
   man's endeavours to establish justice and peace throughout the
   world. The whole of Heaven flushes red in sympathy, and Beatrice,
   the truth of God, likewise changes colour for very shame. St Peter
   bids Dante look forward in faith to the speedy deliverance which
   shall come, and Beatrice, at the end of the Canto, also assures him of
   the coming of a messiah who shall restore order to Church and
   Empire.
The Ascent to the Primum Mobile: After looking downwards once again,
   that he may know how far he has circled with the stellar heaven,
   Dante is raised aloft to the Primum Mobile. This is the ninth circle,
   bearing no stars, but directing with its movement the daily revolu-
   tions of the other eight heavens round the earth. From its invisible
   motion, communicated throughout the cosmos, time is measured.
   Beyond it, there is no space, or time. Allegorically, the perfect order-
   ing of the movements of the spheres represents the operating of the
   divine power which, through the angelic orders, influences the lives
   of men. Thus, time is seen to be "infinitely more than a mere succes-
   sion of corporeal movements. It is a procession of the Light and Love

of Eternity into the temporal life of man" (Carroll). (See also Glossary.)

Beatrice's outburst against covetousness: Beatrice's outburst against covetousness and man's ensuing degeneracy arises out of the context of the sublime concept of time as a consequence of the divinely co-ordinated movements of the universe. Men have become degenerate as a result of their abuse of time, so that progress is turned to regress, the innocence of childhood being quickly lost with the passing of the years. Allegorically, Beatrice's words signify that theology, while enlightening man as to the unimportance of the world in relation to the universe, can also awaken him to a recognition of the purpose of creation.

NOTES. ll. 1–9: "*To Father and to Son and Holy Ghost*" etc.: The request which Beatrice made on Dante's behalf, that the saints should "bedew" him with their joy (cf. Canto xxiv. 1–9), is now granted. His three tests are concluded and he is eligible to proceed beyond the eighth heaven, through the Primum Mobile and into the Empyrean, there to behold God. In recognition of this the saints burst into a hymn of praise to the Three-in-One and Dante, through his sight and hearing, becomes aware of the joy of Heaven.

l. 10: . . . *those four flamboys*: i.e. St Peter, St James, St John, and Adam.

ll. 11–12: . . . *the glow of that which first drew near*: i.e. the radiance of the soul of St Peter.

ll. 13–15: *And as in aspect Jupiter would show* etc.: Dante means if the planet Jupiter exchanged its white light for the ruddy hue of Mars (but retained its present size), it would resemble the increasingly fiery radiance of St Peter. His change of colour is explained in ll. 19–21 and following.

ll. 22–4: "*He that on earth has dared usurp that place of mine*" etc.: These words usher in the culminating denunciation of Boniface VIII, by St Peter himself, before the assembled saints in Heaven.

l. 26: ". . . *the Renegade*": i.e. Satan.

ll. 28–9: *That colour, by the sun obliquely rayed* etc.: The whole of the eighth heaven is seen by Dante to be suffused with the colour which tinges clouds at sunrise or at sunset. The image is taken from Ovid's *Metamorphoses* III. 183–4, and it is clear that in both contexts a rosy flush is intended. The problem is: how does Dante (or Ovid, for that matter) visualize the sun in relation to the clouds? The words in the original Italian mean literally: "with that colour which, the sun being *opposite* ("avverso), paints the clouds at evening or at dawn . . ." Dante's use of "avverso" is taken from Ovid ("qui color infectis *adversi* solis", etc.). Now, when the sun is rising or setting, the rosy hue is chiefly to be observed in the quarter where the sun is; and it is when the sun is *below* the horizon (just before it rises above or sinks below) that the sky becomes rosy. What then, does Dante (or Ovid) mean by the sun's being "opposite" the clouds? The passage has here been interpreted in a different sense from that in which other commentators understand it. It seems likely that Dante is thinking of the position of the sun below the horizon in relation to clouds which are above. A diagram will make this clear:

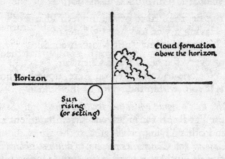

While the sun is below the horizon, only the red of the spectrum will strike the clouds which are diagonally opposite to it. As soon as the sun rises level with the clouds (or, in the evening, while it is still level with them) the colour it sheds on them is gold, not red. That is why Dante particularizes concerning the position of the sun. It is the rays striking up *obliquely* on to the clouds which turn them red. (Other commentators hold that Dante – and presumably, also Ovid – is referring to the rosy hue which is sometimes reflected westwards from the rising, and eastwards from the setting sun, which is thus *opposite* the clouds which it colours red. This phenomenon is, however, less frequent and less vivid.)

It is interesting to notice that in Ovid's context the blush of shame which mantles the features of Diana is occasioned by Actaeon's inadvertently coming upon her as she is bathing; in revenge she turns him into a stag and he is torn to pieces by his dogs. Dante has converted the blush of Diana into the blush of Beatrice, which is occasioned by the mere report of evil.

ll. 34–6: *. . . and the same was the eclipse in Heaven* etc.: That is, it was not an eclipse in the ordinary sense of the word (cf. Canto xxix. 97–102 and *note*).

l. 40: *"The blood of Cletus, Linus"*: Cletus, or Anacletus, Bishop of Rome from A.D. 76 to 88 (or 78–90) was the successor of Linus, who is held to have been the immediate successor of St Peter. Cletus and Linus were both martyred for their faith.

l. 44: *"Urban, Calixtus, Pius, Sixtus"*: These were all Bishops of Rome: Sixtus I (119–27), Pius I (140), Calixtus I (217–22), and Urban I (222–30); they were all martyred.

ll. 46–8: *"Never by our intention was it willed"* etc.: It had never been the intention of the Early Church that Christian people should be divided into pro- and anti-papal factions. (Boniface kept the Guelfs on the right hand and the Ghibellines on the left, almost as though in parody of the parable of the sheep and the goats.)

ll. 49–51: *"Nor that the keys . . . should stand as emblem"* etc.: Boniface, waging war against the Colonna family, displayed the keys of St Peter on the Papal standard. (Cf. *Inf.* xxvii. 85–90:

> "But he, the Prince of the modern Pharisees,
> Having a war to wage by Lateran –
> Not against Jews, nor Moslem enemies,
>
> For every foe he had was Christian,
> Not one had marched on Acre, none had bought
> Or sold within the realm of the Soldàn – ")

ll. 52–4: *"Nor that a signet which my features bore"* etc.: St Peter's head appeared on the Papal seal for indulgences, reinstatement after excommunication, and other "lying privileges".

ll. 58–9: *"Gascons and Cahorsines prepare to drink our blood"*: Pope Clement V (Betrand de Goth) was born in Gascony. During his pontificate, the Papacy was transferred to Avignon. Pope John XXII (Jacques Duèse) was born at Cahors in Guienne. Both Clement and John were guilty of avarice and extortion.

ll. 61–3: *"But Providence, which once through Scipio"* etc.: In the *Convivio* (IV. v), Dante quotes the success of Scipio in Africa as a sign of the intervention of God to secure Roman supremacy. (The defeat of Hannibal by Scipio Africanus took place in 202 B.C.)

ll. 65–6: *". . . open thy mouth and speak"* etc.: Compare the command given by Cacciaguida in Canto xvii. 127–29.

ll. 68–9: *. . . when the heavenly Goat to butt his horns against the sun doth seek*: The sun is in Capricorn from 21 December to 21 January.

l. 70: *So upward there I saw those vapours float*: The whole assembly of the Church Triumphant, assembled in the eighth heaven, now ascends to the Empyrean.

l. 79: *Since the first glance which downward I did send*: On rising to the eighth heaven, Dante was instructed by Beatrice to look down at the planets and the earth beneath him (cf. Canto xxii. 127–54).

ll. 80–81: *I saw that I had moved through the degrees* etc.: The mediaeval cartographers divided the habitable part of the globe (i.e. the northern hemisphere) into seven "climates" or zones. These were marked off on maps by circles drawn parallel with the equator. The constellation of Gemini (in which Dante has been revolving with the eighth heaven) is in the zone of the heavens corresponding to the first climate, which extended twenty degrees north of the equator. Each climate extended 180° longitudinally; therefore, "the degrees which the first climate measures mid to end" equal ninety. Since this represents one quarter of the entire revolution of the heavens round the earth (which occurs once every twenty-four hours), Dante has spent six hours in the eighth heaven.

ll. 82-7: *Beyond Cadiz I saw to Ulysses' mad course*: Dante now indicates the extreme western and eastern limits of his view of earth. Westwards he sees as far as the Straits of Gibraltar (which were the extreme western limits of the inhabited part of the globe); eastwards his view extends almost to the coast of Phoenicia, where Jupiter in the form of a bull carried off Europa on his back to Crete (ll. 83-4). He cannot see any further east (the extreme easterly limit was the mouth of the Ganges) because the sun had set over Phoenicia, and all beyond the extreme edge of the coast was darkness. The sun, in the constellation of Aries, is to the east of him (two signs removed), though it is "westering" in the sense that it is setting. Had he, like the sun, been in the constellation of Aries instead of in Gemini, he could have seen further east, but not so far west.

Note the reference to "Ulysses' mad course" (ll. 82-3). Coming as it does so soon after the declaration by Adam of the nature of the Fall (cf. Canto xxvi. 115-17), which he defines as a "going beyond the mark", it sets the journey of Ulysses in a new and significant context. Ulysses, like Adam, went beyond the boundary which marked the limit of man's legitimate exploration. Ulysses' "mad flight" is thus seen as a type of the Fall.

ll. 88-9: *My mind in love, which never once did quit* etc.: Although he looks downwards and away from Beatrice, Dante's mind is still occupied with thoughts of her; and when he turns once more to look on her, he finds her beauty has grown still more divinely radiant.

l. 98: . . . *Leda's lovely nest*: i.e. the constellation of Gemini. Leda, the mother of Castor and Pollux, was wooed by Jupiter in the form of a swan.

l. 99: *"the swiftest circle"*: i.e. the Primum Mobile.

ll. 109-11: *"This heaven it is"* etc.: Only the Empyrean, no other *material* heaven, lies outside (contains) the Primum Mobile; and the Empyrean is indwelt by God's Mind only. It is thence that that derives the love by which the Seraphim, who are the Intelligence of the Primum Mobile, move it and which they transmit to the lower heavens.

ll. 112-14: *"The light and love which round this circle wind"* etc.: The heaven enclosing the Primum Mobile is the Empyrean, which exists in God. (Cf. the words of St Benedict in Canto xxii concerning the Empyrean, ll. 64-7.)

ll. 117: *"As two and five of ten are dividends"*: The eight heavens below take the measure of their revolutions from the speed of the Primum Mobile, just as the number ten is measured exactly by its half (five) and its fifth (two), which, multiplied together, produce ten.

ll. 118-20: *"As in a plant-pot, then, time has its roots herein"* etc.: Time has its starting-point in the motion of the Primum Mobile, which cannot be perceived by man, as it has no pointer or planet; but the movement of the other heavens is marked for us by the planets or stars which they carry round, and so time is rendered visible to man, as the shoots of a plant may be seen, though its roots are concealed.

ll. 121 to end: *"Cupidity! thou dost engulf the race of mortal men"* etc.:
From here until the end of the canto, Beatrice, filled with righteous
wrath at the shortcomings of the inhabitants of the globe, round which
these stupendous circles of the heavens revolve, upbraids mankind as
though for their unworthiness to dwell in so marvellous and ordered a
universe.

ll. 136–7: *". . . the fair progeny of him who brings the morn and leaves the
night"*: i.e. the human race, the progeny of the sun (here, the symbol of
God).

l. 140: *". . . since there be none to govern you"* etc.: There is no Emperor
to govern the world as it should be governed. (Cf. *Purg.* vi. 88–90.)

ll. 142–3: *"Ere January be unwintered, through the hundredth of a day
which men neglect"*: The "hundredth of a day" is the error in the Julian
Calendar, according to which the length of a year was 365¼ days. This
was too long by eleven minutes and fourteen seconds, roughly one
hundredth of a day. The error was put right in the Gregorian calendar
in 1582 (which was not adopted in England until 1752). In Dante's day,
January had advanced more than eight days nearer the end of winter
since the time when the Julian Calendar was adopted. Eventually, Jan-
uary would have been "unwintered", i.e. become a spring month, if
the correction had not been made. Beatrice does not mean that retri-
bution would be many thousands of years in coming. The substitution
of an immense period for a short one is a rhetorical figure, whereby
irony is conveyed. The inference is: retribution is at hand: has not St
Peter just now foretold that Providence "will swift lend aid"? (ll. 61–3).

l. 148: *"And from the blossom shall come forth true fruit"*: i.e. the blos-
som of the will of men (cf. ll. 124–6), the fruit of which is spoilt at
present by the flood of avarice in the world.

CANTO XXVIII

THE STORY. *Dante, gazing into the eyes of Beatrice, becomes aware of a light reflected in them. He looks behind and sees the light of God as an infinitely small but dazzlingly brilliant point, encircled by nine radiant rings. Beatrice explains the relationship of these circles to the movement of the heavens and identifies them as the three hierarchies or nine orders of angels.*

When life as lived by wretched humankind
   In all its adverse truth to light was brought
   By her who fills with Paradise my mind,

As in a looking-glass a flame is caught,   4
   A waxen torch behind us being lit,
   Anticipating thus our sight and thought,

And, glancing round to test the truth of it,   7
   We find that glass and flame as well agree
   As notes and melody together fit,

So, I remember, did it prove to be,   10
   While I was gazing in the lovely eyes
   Wherewith Love made a noose to capture me;

For, as I turned, there greeted mine likewise   13
   What all behold who contemplate aright
   That heaven's revolution through the skies.

One Point I saw, so radiantly bright,   16
   So searing to the eyes it strikes upon,
   They needs must close before such piercing light.

Of all the stars we see, the smallest one,   19
   Forming a double star with this, would seem
   A moon beside it in comparison.

Perhaps as closely as a halo's gleam   22
   About its source of luminance is curled,
   When a thick haze of mist refracts the beam,

About this Point a fiery circle whirled,   25
   With such rapidity it had outraced
   The swiftest sphere revolving round the world.

28   This by another circle was embraced,
    This by a third, which yet a fourth enclosed;
    Round this a fifth, round that a sixth I traced.

31   Beyond, the seventh was so wide disclosed
    That Iris, to enfold it, were too small,
    Her rainbow a full circle being supposed.

34   So too the eighth and ninth; and each and all
    More slowly turned as they were more removed
    Numerically from the integral.

37   Purest in flame the inmost circle proved.
    Being nearest the Pure Spark, or so I venture,
    Most clearly with Its truth it is engrooved.

40   Observing wonder in my every feature,
    My Lady told me what I set below:
    "From this Point hang the heavens and all nature.

43   Behold the circle nearest it and know
    It owes its rapid movement to the spur
    Of burning love which keeps it whirling so."

46   "If manifested in these circles were
    The cosmic order of the universe,
    I should be well content," I answered her;

49   "But in the world below it's the reverse,
    Each sphere with God's own love being more instilled
    The further from its centre it appears;

52   Whence, if my longing is to be fulfilled,
    Here in this wondrous and angelic fane,
    Where love and light alone the confines build,

55   I must entreat thee further to explain
    Why copy from its pattern goes awry,
    For on my own I ponder it in vain."

58   "There's naught to marvel at, if to untie
    This tangled knot thy fingers are unfit,
    So tight 'tis grown for lack of will to try."

61   Then she went on: "This is no meagre bit
    I'll give to thee. Wouldst thou be filled? Then take,
    And round its còntent ply thy subtle wit.

Material circles in the heavens make 64
   Their courses, wide or small, as more or less,
   Through all their parts, of virtue they partake.

The greater good makes greater blessedness; 67
   More blessedness more matter must enclose,
   If all its parts have equal perfectness.

It follows that the sphere, which as it goes 70
   Turns all the world along, must correspond
   To this, the inmost, which most loves and knows.

Hence, if thou wilt but cast thy measure round 73
   The angels' *power*, not their circumference
   As it appears to thee, it will be found

That wondrous is the perfect congruence 76
   Which every heaven with every mover shows
   Between their corresponding measurements."

As when the dome of air more lovely grows, 79
   By Boreas serene and shining made,
   When from his milder cheek he softly blows,

Purging and scattering the murky shade 82
   Wherewith the sky was stained until, made clean,
   It smiles, with all its pageantry displayed,

So did my understanding there grow keen 85
   Soon as I heard her luminous reply,
   And, like a star in heaven, the truth was seen.

Her words, when they had ceased, were greeted by 88
   A sparkling of scintillas in the spheres,
   As showers of sparks from molten metal fly.

Tracing each fiery circle that was theirs, 91
   They numbered myriads more than the entire
   Progressive doubling of the chess-board squares.

I heard them sing Hosanna, choir on choir, 94
   Unto the Point which holds them in the place,
   And ever will, there where they ever were.

Reading my mind's confusion in my face, 97
   She said: "The Seraphim and Cherubim
   The first ring, and the next, to thee displays.

100   In eagerness to grow the more like Him,
          Their path they follow, and succeed so far
          In measure as their vision is sublime.

103   Those other loves which circle round them are,
          Since they declare God's judgement, called the Thrones;
          They brought the first three to an integer.

106   The bliss of all – set this among thy knowns –
          Abounds in measure as, with sight, they plumb
          The depths of Truth where all disquiet drowns.

109   Their blessedness, therefore, is shown to come
          From seeing, if thou reasonest aright,
          Not loving, which is subsequent. Their sum

112   Of merit is the measure of their sight –
          Merit, which grace and righteousness beget;
          So does their bliss proceed from height to height.

115   The second Triad which is flowering yet
          In this eternal never-fading Spring,
          Ne'er by the Ram in his night-raids beset,

118   With its perpetual Hosanna-ing
          Sings winter out in triple melody,
          In three-fold bliss within its treble ring.

121   The divine beings who form this heirarchy
          Are Dominations, Virtues, one and two,
          And, last, the Powers, whose order makes them three.

124   The dances which remain display to view
          Princedoms, Archangels, and one circle more
          With Angels' jubilation is filled through.

127   And all these orders upwards gaze with awe,
          As downwards each prevails upon the rest,
          Whence all are drawn to God and to Him draw.

130   When Dionysius with ardent zest
          Pondered these orders of angelic bliss,
          He named them in this way, the true and best;

133   But Gregory then differed over this,
          And when his eyes were opened on this scene
          He smiled to see how he had gone amiss.

And that a mortal man on earth could glean   135
    Such secret truth need not astonish thee:
    Paul who in Paradise such things had seen

Gave him full tidings of the mystery."   139

THE IMAGES. *The Primum Mobile*: See Canto xxvii, under *Images*.
The Point of Light: The light of God and of the angelic rings which circle
it are first seen by Dante reflected in the eyes of Beatrice, just as, in
the Pageant of the Church in the Garden of Eden (*Purg.* xxxi) he saw
"mirrored in their range" the double nature of the Incarnate Love,
"now in the one, now in the other guise", that is, now as wholly div-
ine, now as wholly human. He could not then see the two as one;
now, in a prelude to the Beatific Vision, he beholds the immateriality
and indivisible unity of God. The allegorical relationship of Beatrice
to the Trinity had been intuitively apprehended by Dante as long
ago as the time of the *Vita Nuova*, when he wrote ... "this Lady was
accompanied to the end by the number nine, that men might clearly
perceive her to be a nine, that is, a miracle, whose only root is the
Holy Trinity". Now, reflecting the supreme unity of the Trinity,
her eyes image the theological demonstrations of the Church con-
cerning the unity of God.
The Nine Orders of Angels: The concept of the existence of celestial beings
superior to man in power and intelligence, to which tradition has
given the name of "angels", is derived from the apocalyptic writings
of Jewish literature and, before that, from Persian and Babylonian
personifications. Christian teaching early associated them with the
functioning of the heavenly spheres, thereby combining the two
notions of celestial and astrological influence. Dante accepts the trad-
itional division of the angels into nine orders, corresponding to the
nine spheres of Heaven, though he seems to have hesitated for a time
as to the sequence of their nomenclature. Allegorically, the angels
represent the operations of divine Providence, their varied and co-
ordinated power imaging the whole spiritual order of the universe
quickened and sustained by love. Literally, they are God's agents in
the system of secondary causes.

NOTES. l. 10: *So, I remember, did it prove to be*: Dante has seen reflected
in the eyes of Beatrice the light of God and of the angelic circles, shining
through the transparent Primum Mobile from the Empyrean beyond.
God is first glimpsed by Dante as an infinitesimal point of light, follow-
ing the image in Aristotle: "... the Divine Being has no magnitude,
but is without parts and is indivisible."
   l. 25: *About this Point a fiery circle whirled* etc.: From here until l. 36,
Dante enumerates the nine concentric circles which rotate round the

central point of light. They represent the nine angelic orders, "movers" of the nine heavens. For the name of each order see ll. 98–126.

l. 42: "*From this Point hang the heavens and all nature*": Cf. Aristotle: ". . . from such a principle heaven and earth depend." The principle here referred to is the first mover, which, Aristotle says, "is a necessary being. . . . Though locomotion is a primary kind of change, as circular motion is the primary kind of locomotion, it is induced by a first mover" (*Metaphysics*, Book xii. 7, 1072 b).

ll. 43–5: "*Behold the circle nearest it and know*" etc.: The inmost circle represents the angelic order of the Seraphim.

ll. 46–51: "*If manifested in these circles were*" etc.: Beatrice has confirmed (ll. 43–5) what Dante's own vision has perceived (ll. 26–7, 34–6), that the inmost circle is the fastest moving of the nine, and that the speed of each successively decreases. Dante is perplexed by this because the heavenly spheres present a reverse order of speed, the Primum Mobile being the swiftest, the heaven of the moon the slowest.

ll. 53–4: ". . . *this wondrous and angelic fane*" etc.: i.e. the Primum Mobile, bounded only by God.

l. 56: *Why copy from its pattern goes awry*: i.e. why the material world deviates from the supra-sensible world. Compare the *De Monarchia* ii, 2: ". . . nature exists, first, in the mind of the First Agent, who is God; then in heaven; as in an instrument, by means of which the likeness of the eternal Goodness unfolds itself on shapeless matter."

ll. 64–6: "*Material circles in the heavens make their courses*" etc.: The wider the heaven, the greater the divine power with which it is invested in all its parts.

ll. 67–9: "*The greater good makes greater blessedness*" etc.: The larger the heaven, the greater its beneficial influence; the greater the beneficial influence, the greater the sphere which encloses it, since the substance of the heavens is uniform, and excellence is equally distributed in all their parts.

ll. 70–71: ". . . *the sphere, which as it goes turns all the world along*": i.e. the Primum Mobile, which imparts motion to all the other heavens.

l. 72: ". . . *the inmost, which most loves and knows*": i.e. the Seraphim, the angelic order which is nearest God and therefore possesses most love and knowledge of Him.

ll. 76–8: ". . . *wondrous is the perfect congruence*" etc.: If Dante will consider the power of each angelic order (instead of the apparent circumference of each angelic circle), he will see that each heaven is controlled by the angelic order most suited to it: the Seraphim move the Primum Mobile, the Cherubim the eighth heaven, and so on down to the angels who move the heaven of the moon. Hence, swiftness and brightness being the measure of the excellence of the angelic circles, and size the measure of the excellence of the heavenly spheres, the correspondence between the two spatial presentations is complete. There is implicit here a relativity of speed-size-excellence. Compare also Wicksteed:

"God may be conceived of as the spaceless centre of the universe as well as the all-embracer."

ll. 80–81: *"By Boreas . . . when from his milder cheek he softly blows"*: The north-east wind, as opposed to the north-west, clears the skies of Italy.

ll. 89–93: *A sparkling of scintillas in the spheres* etc.: The number of angels in each circle now increases to such a vast extent that they exceed by thousands the total figure arrived at by the progressive doubling of sixty-four figures. According to an ancient Eastern legend, a Brahmin once brought to a king the game of chess, which he had invented. The king was so delighted that he offered the Brahmin in return anything that he might ask. The Brahmin said he would take only a grain of wheat, doubled as many times as there are squares on a chessboard. By geometrical progression (i.e. $1 + 2 + 4 + 8$, etc.) the total figure goes into many millions. The concept of the innumerableness of angels is referred to again in Canto xxix. 130–32.

The Italian commentator, Manfredi Porena, has made the interesting suggestion that there is a distinction to be drawn between the circles of light which Dante first sees, and the innumerable myriads of scintillas which appear when Beatrice has spoken. In the *Convivio* (II. v), Dante refers to Plato's theory of "ideas" in the following terms: "There were others, like Plato . . . who assumed not only that there are as many Intelligences as there are movements of the heavens, but also as many as there are species of things . . . and they would have it that as the Intelligences of the heavens are producers of these movements, each one of its own, so these other Intelligences are producers of everything else, and exemplars each one of its own species; and Plato called them 'ideas'." Dante then proceeds to demonstrate by argument that the number of Intelligences "who live only in contemplation" are much greater in number than those who produce the effects which man can apprehend. Porena is accordingly of the opinion that the angels first beheld by Dante are the movers of the heavens; the myriad countless sparks which secondly appear are the contemplative angels of each order. When both kinds of each order have manifested themselves, Beatrice proceeds to name them.

l. 106: *"The bliss of all"*: i.e. the bliss of all the angels of the nine orders.

ll. 109–11: *"Their blessedness, therefore, is shown to come from seeing"* etc.: In these lines Beatrice formulates a concept which is stated or implied at various points throughout the *Comedy*. The question which she settles here is this: does love of God spring from knowledge of Him, or does knowledge of God arise from love of Him? It is a matter which was debated by theologians and Dante has come down firmly on the side of St Thomas Aquinas, who says: "Ultimate and perfect bliss can only be in the vision of God in His essence."

ll. 111–14: *"Their sum of merit is the measure of their sight"* etc.: The power to see God is greater or less in proportion to the greater or less merit of the soul; and merit itself is grace-given and fostered by the will. The bliss of the souls is in proportion to their power to see God; and their degree of bliss is manifested by their radiance. (Cf. Canto xxi. 88–90.)

l. 115: "*The second Triad*": i.e. the second group of three angelic orders consisting of Dominations, or Dominions, Virtues, and Powers).

ll. 127–9: "*And all these orders upwards gaze with awe*" etc.: The functions of the angelic orders are co-ordinated. Though of different ranks, they are all mirrors of one light.

ll. 130–32: "*When Dionysius with ardent zest*" etc.: Dionysius the Areopagite, who is mentioned in the *Acts of the Apostles* (xvii. 34) as having been converted by St Paul, is said to have been the first Bishop of Athens, and to have suffered martyrdom there in the year 95. In the Middle Ages he was believed to be the author of various theological writings, including the famous work, "On Celestial Hierarchy", which are now known to be the productions of fifth-and sixth-century Neo-Platonists. The doctrine of the hierarchy of angels was derived partly from the definitions of St Paul (*Ephes.* i. 21, *Coloss.* i. 16, *Rom.* viii. 38) and from Jewish apocalyptic writings. Dionysius (or the author of the work accredited to him) distinguishes nine orders, subdivided into three groups or hierarchies, exactly as Beatrice enumerates them.

ll. 133–5: "*But Gregory then differed over this*" etc.: Pope Gregory I, surnamed the Great (590–604), treats of the subject of the angelic orders in his *Homilies on the Gospel*. He differs from Dionysius in the order he attributes to the Dominions, Principalities, Powers, and Virtues. Otherwise their systems are identical. In the *Convivio* (II. vi), Dante follows yet a third system, that suggested by Brunetto Latini. The distinctions between the three systems can best be seen if they are set out in tabular form:

Dionysius	*Gregory*	*Dante in* Convivio
Seraphim	Seraphim	Seraphim
Cherubim	Cherubim	Cherubim
Thrones	Thrones	Powers
Dominions	Dominions	Principalities
Virtues	Principalities	Virtues
Powers	Powers	Dominions
Principalities	Virtues	Thrones
Archangels	Archangels	Archangels
Angels	Angels	Angels

The subject is discussed at length by St Thomas in the *Contra Gentiles* and in the *Summa* (Part I, Question 108), where he compares the different systems of Dionysius and Gregory.

l. 136: ". . . *a mortal man*": i.e. Dionysius.

CANTO XXIX

THE STORY. *For an immeasurably brief instant (in terms of time), Beatrice gazes on the infinitesimal Point which is God (here manifested as spaceless and indivisible). Reading Dante's desire therein, she unfolds to him the mysteries of the Creation, the relationship of the angels to the universe, and to God, since the fall of Lucifer. Although Dante is now fit to contemplate Heaven, Beatrice adds further clarification concerning the endowments of angelic nature, and goes on to denounce the vain and pretentious habits of present-day preachers who prefer to elaborate fables of their own rather than abide by the Scriptures. Finally, returning to the subject of the angels, she bids Dante reflect upon their innumerableness, their individual diversity, and the immeasurable indivisibility of God.*

As, when Latona's son and daughter share
   The belt of the horizon and for crown
   The stars of Aries and Libra wear,

The zenith holds them balanced, till anon,   4
   Freed from their girdle, one moves onwards to
   The hemisphere above, the other down,

So long from converse Beatrice withdrew,   7
   To gaze, with rapturous and smiling mien,
   Full on the Point which pierced my vision through.

"I'll tell, not ask," she said, resuming then,   10
   "What thou would'st know, for thy desire I see
   Where centres every *where* and every *when*.

Not to increase His good, which cannot be,   13
   But that His splendour, shining back, might say:
   Behold, I am, in His eternity,

Beyond the measurement of night and day,   16
   Beyond all boundary, as He did please,
   New loves Eternal Love shed from His ray.

Nor did He lie before this as at ease,   19
   For neither first nor after did proceed
   The moving of the Spirit o'er the seas.

22   Pure form, pure matter, form and matter wed,
        Came forth to being without blemish as
        Three arrows from a three-stringed bow are sped.

25   And as through crystal, amber, or plain glass
        A sunbeam floods its all-pervading fire,
        Not gradual, but instantaneous,

28   So the three-fold creation of the Sire,
        From its beginning without sequences,
        Rayed into being, instant and entire.

31   Order, created with the Substances,
        Distinguishing Pure Act from Potency,
        As summit of the world established these.

34   Pure Potency was lowest in degree;
        Midway came Potency with Act entwisted
        By withy that shall ne'er unwithied be.

37   Though in his writings Saint Jerome insisted
        Ere the remaining universe was known
        Through countless aeons Angels had existed,

40   The truth I tell in many texts is shown
        Inscribed by prophets of the Holy Ghost.
        Read well, 'tis there for thee to come upon.

43   And even Reason fathoms it almost:
        How could the movers for so long remain
        Short of perfection, their fulfilment lost?

46   So now I've taught thee where and how and when
        Such loves were formed, and thy desire to know
        With these three fires will never burn again.

49   Count up to twenty; thou wilt be too slow –
        Even faster did one Angel band rebel
        And bring convulsion to the earth below.

52   The other band remained to ply their skill,
        Weaving their circles with such eager thirst,
        They of their joy can never have their fill.

55   The fall's beginning was the pride accursed
        Of one whom thou hast seen deep in the pit;
        The world with all its weight holds him coerced.

These other Angels humbly did admit   58
  The Goodness whence they have their provenance
  And understanding, for this joy made fit.

Merit and grace their vision so enhance   61
  That now their will, steadfast and perfect grown,
  From its objective knows no severance.

Lest thy belief should waver, be it known   64
  That merit dwells in the receipt of grace
  In measure as the heart to it is prone.

Henceforward, as concerns this sacred place,   67
  Thou mayst unaided contemplate thy fill,
  If garnered are my words for future days.

Yet, since on earth your schoolmen argue still   70
  That mid endowments of angelic nature
  Are understanding, memory, and will,

I'll tell thee more, that purged of all conjecture,   73
  The truth thou'llt see, of which men speak amiss,
  Confounding here two senses when they lecture.

Since first these Substances enjoyed the bliss   76
  Of gazing on God's face, wherein are seen
  All things, ne'er have they turned their eyes from this.

Hence, as no sight unknown can intervene   79
  To cleave their vision, or their concepts break,
  · No thoughts need they recall of what has been.

On earth men dream, therefore, while they're awake,   82
  Some in good faith, and some deceitfully;
  Of guilt and shame the greater share these take.

Ye on the earth, in your philosophy,   85
  Are not for long content to tread one path,
  Enamoured of vain show and subtlety.

Yet even this in Heaven stirs less wrath   88
  Than when God's holy Word is misconstrued,
  Or when supremacy it no more hath.

Ye little think how great the cost in blood   91
  To sow it through the world, how pleasing he
  Who humbly bides by Scripture as he should.

94   All men, to show their ingenuity,
            Contrive their own inventions – these they preach;
            The Gospel is passed over silently.

97   The moon, at our Lord's Passion, so some teach,
            Turned back along her journey and intruded,
            So that no sunlight to the earth could reach,

100   (Denying that the light was self-occluded),
            So that the man of Spain and him of Ind
            Saw the eclipse as clearly as the Jew did.

103   And all such fables from the pulpits dinned,
            Innumerable as Lapi and Bindi are
            In Florence, yearly fly to every wind.

106   So that the silly sheep, all unaware,
            Come home from pasture fed on emptiness;
            No harm they see, no less of guilt they bear.

109   Christ His Apostles did not thus address:
            Go forth, preach idle stories to all men,
            But taught them His true doctrine to profess.

112   Forth with His shield the Apostles sally then,
            None other than His word their lips escapes,
            This only is the sword they wield amain.

115   But nowadays men preach with jokes and japes,
            And if they raise a laugh, their cowls all swell
            With pride – they ask no more, the jackanapes.

118   Yet if the bird, which nestles in the tail
            Of all such hoods, the foolish crowd could see,
            What pardons they confide in they'd know well.

121   So gross has grown the world's credulity,
            No need is there the slightest proof to rig,
            At any promise men will rush with glee.

124   That's how St Anthony doth feed his pig,
            And many others too, more pig-like still,
            Paying with currency not worth a fig.

127   Since of digression we have ta'en our fill,
            Henceforth along the straight road let us wend;
            As time grows short, our way must we curtail.

The angelic nature in number doth extend 130
   So far beyond the range of mortal mind,
   No tongue or thought has ever reached the end.

And in the Book of Daniel thou wilt find, 133
   For all the thousand thousands he there states,
   No fixed and final figure is assigned.

The Primal Light the whole irradiates, 136
   And is received therein as many ways
   As there are splendours wherewithal it mates.

Since, then, affection waits upon the gaze 139
   And its intensity, diversely bright
   Therein the sweets of love now glow, now blaze.

Consider well the breadth, behold the height 142
   Of His eternal Goodness, seeing that o'er
   So many mirrors It doth shed Its light,

Yet One abideth as It was before." 145

THE IMAGES. *The Primum Mobile*: See Canto xxvii, under *Images*.
The Angels: see Canto xxviii, under *Images*.

NOTES. ll. 1–6: *Latona's son and daughter*: i.e. Apollo and Diana, the
sun and the moon.

   . . . *and for crown the stars of Aries and Libra wear*: i.e. when the sun is
in Aries and the moon is in Libra.

   The zenith holds them balanced: i.e. the sun and moon are on opposite
horizons and appear to hang poised as though from a balance:

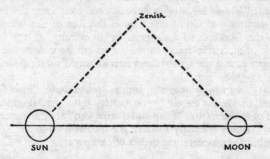

The conditions described concur only when a full moon occurs at the
equinox, and when it lies on the level of the ecliptic. When, in fact, all
these conditions are present, there is a total eclipse of the moon. The

celestial scene, therefore, which Dante wishes to evoke has never been witnessed by human eyes. Consequently the comparison is to be imagined as an abstract hypothesis.

l. 5: Freed *from their girdle*: i.e. moving onward from the horizon, either up or down, according as the planet is rising or setting.

l. 7: *So long from converse Beatrice withdrew*: The length of time during which the sun and moon, in the conditions described above (ll. 1–6), are perfectly equidistant from the zenith, having reached the horizon at opposite points at the same instant, cannot be measured, for, since both planets are moving, it constitutes an infinitesimal point of time. During that immeasurable point of time, Beatrice has been gazing at the infinitesimal point of light, which is God. There seems to be suggested here an infinity of time as well as of space. The story of the *Comedy*, since it is told to mortals living in the space-time continuum, is constructed in accordance with the conventions of sequence and duration; but, just as God is here conceived of as a spaceless, indivisible being, so now Beatrice's contemplation of Him is conceived of as taking place in eternity, or in a point of time as little susceptible of measurement as the Point of light Itself. This would seem to be the whole point of the comparison, for which Dante has evoked a hypothetical series of astronomical phenomena. This interpretation seems further to be confirmed by the statement by Beatrice that in the infinitesimal Point of light all *time* and *space* are centred (l. 12), that is, present.

l. 11: *"What thou would'st know"*: i.e. the reason for the Creation and ts proceeding.

ll. 13–15: *"Not to increase His good, which cannot be"* etc.: The act of creation and the things created could not add to God's goodness, which is infinite. His motive in creating was that His reflected light ("splendour") should shine back to Him in self-awareness.

l. 18: *"New loves Eternal Love shed from His ray"*: The new loves are the angels, the first things created by God.

ll. 19–21: *"Nor did He lie before this as at ease"* etc.: Time did not exist before "the spirit of God moved upon the face of the waters" and created light. God created the angels "in His eternity" (l. 15). Nor can one speak of successive stages in the act of creation, since the angels, primal matter, and the material heavens all issued simultaneously into being (ll. 22–30).

ll. 22–4: *"Pure form, pure matter, form and matter wed"*: "Pure form" is pure mind, that is, the angels; "pure matter" is the primal undifferentiated stuff of the elements; "form and matter wed" are the material heavens. Here, Dante is closely following Aristotle who in *De Anima* (II. ii) distinguishes between three orders of existence:

1. form	2. matter	3. form and
or	or	matter
act	potency	combined

The difference between "act" and "potency" may perhaps be better understood by considering the difference between the two adjectives "actual" and "potential": man's intellect is potential, that of the angels is actual, that is, all the potentialities of an angel's existence are continuously actualized. Primal matter is potential; the material heavens are both potential and actual, they are potency and act held together; that is, the perfectly actualized power of the angels controls the heavens, but the heavenly bodies remain material and subject to the natural laws governing primal matter.

ll. 25–7: *"And as through crystal, amber, or plain glass"* etc.: According to Aristotelian physics, light was instantaneously diffused through a translucent medium.

ll. 31–3: *"Order, created with the Substances"* etc.: Order was created simultaneously with the Angels (the "Substances") and established them as the highest created beings, for they constituted "pure act" or form, distinguished from "potency" or primal matter.

ll. 35–6: *"Midway came Potency with Act entwisted"* etc.: The material heavens, i.e. the spheres, planets, and stars, were produced by a union between the "pure act", which is the state of being of the angels, and "pure potency", which is the state of being of primal matter.

ll. 37–9: *"Though in his writings Saint Jerome insisted"* etc.: St Jerome (A.D. 340–420) was the author of a Latin version of the Old Testament which is known as the Vulgate (though the present text is corrupt). His belief that the angels were created long before the remainder of the universe was contested by St Thomas Aquinas, whose view Dante here follows, maintaining that it is supported by Scripture.

ll. 44–5: *"How could the movers for so long remain short of perfection"* etc.: It is the activity of the angelic movers to move the heavens. If they had been created long before the heavens they would have been like organs without a function.

ll. 46–7: *"So now I've taught thee where and how and when such loves were formed"*: Beatrice has explained that the angels were created:

(where) in the Empyrean,

(how) as beings of perfect goodness,

(when) contemporaneously with the creation of time and of the universe.

ll. 49–51: *"Count up to twenty; thou wilt be too slow"* etc.: The angels who rebelled did so in an immeasurably short space of time. It would seem that Dante implies that the rebellion occurred before time, in eternity. In the *Convivio* (II. iv) he is even more explicit: ". . . of all these [angelic] orders, a certain number were lost *as soon as they were created*, to the amount perhaps of one-tenth, and in order to replace these mankind was afterwards created."

"And bring convulsion to the earth below": Satan and the angels who fell with him convulsed the earth in their fall. (Cf. *Inf.* xxxiii. 121–6.)

l. 52: *"The other band"*: Dante has simply distinguished between the angels who fell and the angels who did not, thus avoiding the vexed question as to whether some angels fell from each of the orders. In the passage already quoted from the *Convivio* (see above under *note* to ll. 49–51), he expressly states that some were lost from each order. Since writing the *Inferno*, Dante has evidently altered his views concerning the neutral angels who are in the Vestibule of the Futile in Hell:

> "They're mingled with the caitiff angel-crew
>   Who against God rebelled not, nor to Him
>   Were faithful, but to self alone were true;
>
> Heaven cast them forth – their presence there would dim
>   The light; deep Hell rejects so base a herd," . . .
>
> (Canto iii. 37–41)

"The caitiff angel-crew" are not mentioned by Beatrice, and Dante seems to have dropped them from the scheme of the universe.

ll. 58–60: "*These other Angels humbly did admit*" etc.: God had created the angels with an understanding fit for their vision of Him, which vision is their joy.

ll. 61–6: "*Merit and grace their vision so enhance*" etc.: Their vision of God is enhanced by grace, the reception of which is in itself a merit.

ll. 70–72: "*Yet, since on earth your schoolmen argue still*" etc.: Beatrice has spoken of the *understanding* and *will* of the angels; but to speak of *memory* in their connection is ambiguous (cf. l. 75). It is the soul of man which possesses all three faculties and retains them after death. Compare *Purg.* xxv. 79–84:

> "When Lachesis has no more flax to twine
>   It quits the flesh, but bears essentially
>   Away with it the human and divine –
>
> Each lower power in dumb passivity,
>   *But memory, intelligence, and will*
>   Active and keener than they used to be."

Among the "schoolmen" who attributed memory to angels was St Thomas.

ll. 85*ff*: In all ages (our own no less than others) it is the constant temptation of the preacher to substitute his own cleverness for the word of God. Beatrice, in a blistering denunciation, brings out the seriousness of trifling with eternal truths.

ll. 97–102: "*The moon, at our Lord's Passion, so some teach*" etc.: The darkness which occurred during the Crucifixion is referred to by St Matthew (xxvii. 45) as follows: "Now from the sixth hour there was darkness over all the land unto the ninth hour." St Luke (xxiii. 44) says: "And it was about the sixth hour, and there was a darkness over all the earth until the ninth hour." The preachers whom Beatrice rebukes elaborate the Gospel and explain the darkness by supposing the moon (which was full, since it was the time of the Passover) to have turned back along her course and intruded between the sun and the earth; or they say that the darkness was extended over the whole of the northern hemisphere and was seen as well in Spain or in India as in Jerusalem. The orthodox interpretation of the references in the Gospel ("darkness over the whole land", etc.) limits the effect of the miraculous obscuring of the sun to the land of Judaea.

"*so that the man of Spain and him of Ind saw the eclipse as clearly as the Jew did*": Jerusalem was thought to be the centre of the northern hemisphere, Spain and India its western and eastern confines.

ll. 104–5: "*Innumerable as Lapi and Bindi are in Florence*": Lapo and Bindo (short for Iacopo and Ildobrando) were common names for boys in Florence.

l. 106: "*the silly sheep*": i.e. the congregations.

ll. 112–14: "*Forth with His shield*" etc.: The Apostles are armed with the "shield of faith" and "the sword of the Spirit, which is the word of God" (cf. *Ephesians* vi. 16–17).

ll. 118–19: "*Yet if the bird, which nestles in the tail*": i.e. the Devil. (The fallen angels are winged.)

l. 120: "*What pardons they confide in*": i.e. indulgences.

l. 124: "*That's how St Anthony doth feed his pig*": St Anthony of Egypt, the hermit (not to be confused with his more famous namesake, St Anthony of Padua), lived from A.D. 251–356. He is regarded as the founder of monasticism. His emblem is a hog, which is represented in effigies as lying at his feet. The monks of the Order of St Anthony are said to have kept herds of swine, which they fattened on the proceeds from the sale of pardons.

l. 127: "*Since of digression we have ta'en our fill*": Beatrice now returns to the subject of angels. She will offer two points for Dante's reflection: (1) the innumerableness of angels; (2) the immeasurableness and indivisibility of God displayed in the angels' individual diversity.

ll. 133–5: "*And in the book of Daniel thou wilt find*" etc.: Compare *Daniel* vii. 9–10: ". . . the Ancient of days did sit . . . a fiery stream issued and came forth from before him: thousand thousands ministered unto him, and ten thousand times ten thousand stood before him."

l. 136: ". . . *the whole*": i.e. all the angels, a total innumerable by the mind of man.

ll. 137–8: "*And is received therein as many ways as there are splendours wherewithal it mates*": According to Thomist philosophy, in things incorruptible there is only one individual of each single species; hence it is impossible that there should be two angels of one species, just as it is impossible that there should be two humanities. The reception of God's light varies, then, in every one of the angels.

l. 141: "*Therein*": i.e. in all the angels, some of whom glow more ardently in as much as they behold God more intensely.

l. 144: "*mirrors*": i.e. angels.

CANTO XXX

THE STORY. *The angelic circles fade one by one from sight, and Dante, turning once more to look on Beatrice, finds her beauty so transfigured as to defeat all his power to describe it. She tells him they have entered the Empyrean and that he will behold the angels and, in the guise of the flesh, the souls of the blessed. A flash of light enwraps him, first blinding him, and then leaving his sight so strengthened that nothing now can vanquish it. He sees first a river of light, in which he bathes his eyes, and straightway beholds the saints in heaven seated on thrones rising in tiers which form the petals of a snow-white rose. Beatrice points to the vacant throne awaiting the Emperor Henry VII and foretells the fate of the soul of Clement V.*

Perchance six thousand miles away high noon
   Is blazing, and earth's shadow, where we are,
   Already lowered, will fall level soon,

4   When in the deep of heaven, beyond us far,
     A gradual alteration has begun,
     Stealing first one, and then another star;

7   And as the brightest handmaid of the sun
     Comes ever nearer, so the starlight wanes,
     Closing its fairest casements one by one.

10   E'en so the triumph-dance whose circling chains
     Aye ring that point which did my sense subdue,
     Seeming contained by that which it contains,

13   Little by little out of sight withdrew,
     Whence I to Beatrice must needs transfer
     My gaze, for love, and lack of aught to view.

16   Were everything I've ever said of her
     Rolled up into a single jubilee,
     Too slight a hymn for this new task were there.

19   Beauty past knowledge was displayed to me –
     Not only ours: the joy of it complete
     Her Maker knows, I think, and only He.

22   From this point on I must admit defeat
     Sounder than poet wrestling with his theme,
     Comic or tragic, e'er was doomed to meet;

For her sweet smile remembered, as the beam   25
  Of sunlight blinds the weakest eyes that gaze,
  Bewilders all my wits and scatters them.

From the first hour I looked upon her face   28
  In this life, till that vision, I could trust
  The poet in me to pursue her praise;

Now in her beauty's wake my song can thrust   31
  Its following flight no farther; I give o'er
  As, at his art's end, every artist must.

Being such, then, as I here relinquish for   34
  A mightier trump to blazon than mine own
  (Of whose hard theme remains but little more),

She, with achievement in her mien and tone,   37
  Resumed: "We have won beyond the worlds, and move
  Within that heaven which is pure light alone:

Pure intellectual light, fulfilled with love,   40
  Love of the true Good, filled with all delight,
  Transcending sweet delight, all sweets above.

And two-fold is the host of heavenly might   43
  Thou'lt here behold, and one in that same guise
  Which on the Judgement Day will greet thy sight."

As lightning startles vision from the eyes,   46
  So robbing them of their capacity
  Objects appear too strong to visualize,

So now a living light encompassed me;   49
  In veil so luminous I was enwrapt
  That naught, swathed in such glory, could I see.

"Love, which in stillness holds this heaven rapt,   52
  Such salutation here doth make alway;
  So is the candle for its flame made apt."

Soon as these words, so brief, had won their way   55
  Within to me, my sense became aware
  Of mounting o'er such power as in me lay.

And a new sight so keen I kindled there,   58
  No brilliancy unmasked that ever glowed
  Had found mine eyes unequal to the glare.

61   Light I beheld which as a river flowed,
         Fulgid with splendour; and on either shore
         The colours of a wondrous springtime showed.

64   And from the stream arose a glittering store
         Of living sparks which, winging mid the blooms,
         To rubies set in gold resemblance bore.

67   Then, as though drunken on the sweet perfumes,
         They plunge anew amid the wondrous deeps,
         And as one enters, lo! another comes.

70   "The deep desire, which in thee flames and leaps,
         Of tidings of this scene thy fill to take
         The more delights me as it tumescent keeps.

73   But of these waters thou must drink," so spake
         Mine eyes' own sun, whose light their solace is,
         "Before so great a thirst as thine thou slake.

76   The stream," she added then, "the topazes
         Which glitter in and out, the smiling shore
         Are of their truth but shadow-prefaces.

79   Not that these in themselves are immature,
         For the deficiency doth lie in thee
         Whose sight as yet beyond them cannot soar."

82   No little infant mouthes as readily
         Towards his mother's breast, if he awake
         Much later than his hour is wont to be,

85   As mirrors of mine eyes I then did make,
         In eagerness inclining o'er the stream,
         Which flows that man his good therein may seek.

88   And as these eyelids drank unto their brim,
         Beneath my gaze the river's contours swayed,
         Spreading and curving to a circle's rim.

91   As people sporting in a masquerade,
         When they put off disguising semblances,
         Altered, yet as they are, then stand displayed,

94   So, as I looked, to greater joyances
         The gems and flowers were changed, and I beheld
         Both courts of Heaven in true appearances.

Splendour of God, whereby these eyes beheld   97
  Thy true realm's triumph, grant me power to say
  How that exalted triumph I beheld.

In yonder heaven the *lumen gloriae*   100
  Reveals the Maker to created mind
  Which in His sight alone finds peace for aye.

In figure of a circle it doth wind   103
  So wide and far that its circumference
  About the sun itself would loosely bind.

The whole is fashioned from a radiance   106
  Shone from above the *Primum mobile*,
  Which draws vitality and virtue hence.

As water by a mountain's foot may be   109
  A glass wherein it sees itself so fair,
  Decked out in grass and flowers luxuriantly,

So, mirrored in that light, tier upon tier,   112
  On myriad thrones, rising on every side,
  Those who from here returned I gazed on there.

If in its inmost petals can reside   115
  So vast a light, in such a rose as this
  What width immense must in the rim abide?

My sight, being undismayed, ne'er went amiss   118
  In all that amplitude and height, but knew
  The full extent and nature of such bliss.

For "near" and "far" no reckoning is due,   121
  Since nothing by the law of nature goes
  Where God no agents needs His will to do.

Amid the gold of the eternal rose,   124
  Whose gradual leaves, unfolding, fragrantly
  Extol that Sun which spring for aye bestows,

Longing to speak, I followed silently   127
  In Beatrice's wake; and there she said:
  "Behold how great the white-robed company!

Look on our city, see its gyres full-spread!   130
  Behold our thrones, that are so nigh complete
  Few souls they lack for whom they're covenanted.

133   There, where thou gazest, on that mighty seat,
         (As from the crown above thou may'st infer),
         Ere at these nuptials thou be called to eat,

136   Shall sit the soul (predestined emperor)
         Of that great Henry who will rise one day
         To straighten Italy before her hour.

139   Bewitched by greed and blinded 'neath its sway,
         Ye are become like babes who've almost died
         For lack of food, yet push their nurse away.

142   Then o'er the sacred forum will preside
         One whose allegiance will be proved infirm,
         Feigning support, but stepping then aside.

145   Him in the Holy Office no long term
         Will God endure, but thrust him down below
         Where Simon Magus pays his score, to squirm

148   Behind the Anagni man, who'll deeper go."

THE IMAGES. *The Primum Mobile:* see Canto xxvii, under *Images.*
  The transcendant and inexpressible beauty of Beatrice: When the light of
    God and of the angels has vanished from his view, Dante turns to
    look once more at Beatrice. He finds her so transfigured that all he
    has ever said till now in praise of her would be inadequate to express
    her beauty at this moment. In this solemn and deeply moving image,
    Dante conveys, in the *allegory,* that only God can fully know and
    fully comprehend the beauty and truth of the most sublime doctrines
    of theology. In the *story,* Beatrice is about to return to her throne in
    the Empyrean and no mortal can express the glory of a blessed spirit,
    for it is derived from the vision of God.
  The Empyrean: Beyond the nine spheres which circle the earth, contained
    within no space, and beyond time, is the Empyrean, the abode of
    God, the angels, and the saints. To this place, or state of being, Dante
    has now come. But first his eyes are dazzled by the light which
    swathes him. Once again he is blinded and this second temporary
    death of the eyesight, giving birth to the final vision of Paradise, is
    taken by some commentators to be an allegory of death itself. No
    living being can see God; therefore, if the vision is to be made cred-
    ible, something analagous to the separating of the soul from the
    body must take place. It seems more probable that the kindling of
    his new sight is a further symbol of the Thomist doctrine that the
    state of blessedness is reached by means of vision, whence comes the
    love of the soul for God, and, from such love, joy that transcends
    all delight.

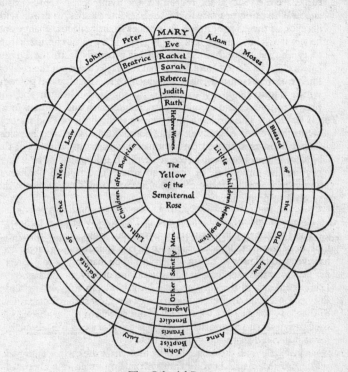

The Celestial Rose.

The River of Light: By a succession of images, Dante seeks to convey the gradualness of his approach to the ultimate vision. His first sight of the Empyrean is symbolical, a foreshadowing of the truth which he will behold. The river, flowing from an infinite height, symbolizes divine grace poured forth upon creation. The flowers on the banks are the souls of the redeemed, the living sparks represent the angels who minister grace to the souls. Dante has first to drink, with his eyes, of the river of grace. As he does so, its contours change and he sees it as a circular sea of light. This is said by most commentators to symbolize the light of glory which proceeds from the Divine Essence. In the *story*, Dante learns that it is reflected from the convex surface of the Primum Mobile, to which it gives that life and potency which is distributed by the angels to the stellar heaven and the planetary spheres and so, ultimately, to the earth and to mankind.

The White Rose: The circle of light, which is the light of God's glory, forms the yellow of the vast white rose which Dante next beholds. Its petals rising in more than a thousand tiers are the thrones of the blessed, whom Dante can perceive despite the distance, for he is now beyond the limitations of time and space. The rose in mediaeval literature was the symbol of earthly love; Dante's white rose is the symbol of divine love.

NOTES. l. 1–3: *Perchance six thousand miles away* etc.: When the earth's conical shadow falls level with the horizon, the sun is rising; at such an hour, noon is at its height a quarter of the globe away to the East.

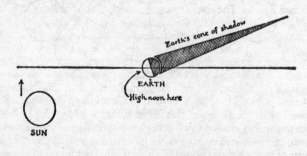

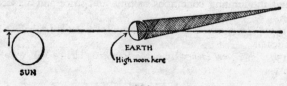

Note that as the sun approaches the horizon, earth's shadow is lowered. The figure "six thousand miles" eastward is intended to suggest a distance in time of about six hours. The circumference of the earth was estimated as 20,400 miles, of which the sun traversed 850 every hour. A quarter of 20,400 miles is 5,100. If noon is about 6,000 miles eastward from the observer, then where he stands it is about an hour before sunrise (i.e. the sun is 900 miles away from the horizon and it will take it just over an hour to reach it).

l. 7: . . . *the brightest handmaid of the sun*: i.e. Aurora.

l. 10: *the triumph-dance*: i.e. the joyous whirling of the angelic orders.

l. 12: *Seeming contained by that which it contains*: The Point of light is manifested as ringed by the angelic orders, whereas it is God who contains them.

ll. 38–9: "*We have won beyond the worlds, and move within that heaven which is pure light alone*": Beatrice tells Dante that they have ascended to the Empyrean.

l. 43: ". . . *and two-fold is the host of heavenly might*": i.e. the angels and the souls of the blessed.

ll. 44–5: ". . . *in that same guise*" etc.: i.e. manifested as though in the body.

ll. 52–4: "*Love, which in stillness holds this heaven rapt*" etc.: Every soul first entering the Empyrean is, like Dante, swathed in the light of glory. In this way the soul is rendered fit to see God. (Cf. *Prov.* xx. 27: "The spirit of man is the candle of the Lord".)

ll. 76–8: "*The stream . . . the topazes . . . the smiling shore are of their truth but shadow-prefaces* : These things are but symbols of what Dante will later behold. The river represents divine grace, the living sparks the angels, and the flowers the souls to whom they minister.

l. 85: "*As mirrors of mine eyes I then did make*": Dante eagerly receives yet more grace whereby he may see beyond these symbols. His eagerness is the measure of his merit. (Cf. Canto xxix. 64–6.)

ll. 100–108: *In yonder heaven the* "*lumen gloriae*" etc.: The light of God's glory ("lumen gloriae") gives to the minds of His creatures the power to behold Him. Manifested as a vast shining circle, it is reflected upward from the Primum Mobile, on which it strikes and to which it gives power and vitality. It is this perpetual reflection of the light of God which, cast back into the eyes of the blessed, ministers to their perpetual power of looking directly into His light itself. The same circle forms the yellow of the celestial rose.

ll. 121–2: *For* "*near*" *and* "*far*" *no reckoning is due* etc.: Dante has risen beyond the limiting conditions of time and space and all secondary causes.

l. 135: "*Ere at these nuptials thou be called to eat*": i.e. before Dante's own death.

l. 137: "*that great Henry*": i.e. the Emperor Henry VII, who died in 1313.

ll. 139–41: *"Bewitched by greed and blinded 'neath its sway"* etc.: These lines refer to the resistance offered by the Papacy and the Guelf party to the Imperial authority.

ll. 142–3: *"Then o'er the sacred forum will preside"* etc.: At the time of Henry's death, the Pope was Clement V, who first encouraged him to come to Italy to be crowned and then withdrew his support.

ll. 145–8: *"Him in the Holy Office no long term will God endure"*: Clement V died in 1314. Dante has already prophesied for him (through the words of Pope Nicholas III) a place in Hell among the other simoniacal popes (cf. *Inf*. xix. 79–83).

"where Simon Magus pays his score": i.e. in the third "bolgia" of Hell.

". . . to squirm behind the Anagni man, who'll deeper go": Pope Boniface VIII was born in Anagni. Pope Nicholas has already foretold that, when Clement comes, Boniface will slide further down the opening in the rock, pushing Nicholas before him (cf. *Inf*. xix. 73–5). Beatrice now confirms the prophesy, in similar terms.

CANTO XXXI

THE STORY. *Dante contemplates the snow-white rose, filled, rank upon rank, with the souls of the redeemed, to whom the angels, descending like a swarm of bees, minister peace and fervent love. Dante is so moved by the contrast between our world and this region of bliss that he falls into a stupor of silence and amazement. Turning then to hear Beatrice speak of this celestial scene, he finds her gone, and in her place a soul of extreme benevolence of aspect. This is St Bernard, who has come to lead Dante to the vision of God, as Beatrice has prepared his understanding in readiness for this final experience. Looking up, Dante has his first glimpse of Beatrice enthroned and utters his words of farewell. St Bernard bids him look even higher and Dante beholds, at the extreme edge of the rose, the glory of the Virgin, attended by countless angels.*

So now, displayed before me as a rose
    Of snow-white purity, the sacred might
    I saw, whom with His blood Christ made His spouse.

But the other, winging ever in His sight,   4
    Chants praises to the glory it adores,
    Its Maker's good extolling in delight.

As bees ply back and forth, now in the flowers   7
    Busying themselves, and now intent to wend
    Where all their toil is turned to sweetest stores,

So did the host of Angels now descend   10
    Amid the Flower of the countless leaves,
    Now rise to where their love dwells without end.

Their glowing faces were as fire that gives   13
    Forth flame, golden their wings; the purest snow
    The whiteness of their raiment ne'er achieves.

Down floating to the Flower, from row to row,   16
    Each ministered the peace and burning love
    They gathered in their waftings to and fro.

Between the Flower and that which blazed above   19
    The volant concourse interposed no screen
    To dim the splendour and the sight thereof;

22   For God's rays penetrate with shafts so keen
        Through all the universe, in due degree,
        There's naught can parry them or intervene.

25   Drawn from the new age and antiquity,
        This realm of saints, whose joy no dangers mar,
        Gazed on one sign in love and unity.

28   O trinal light, which shining as one star
        It fills them with delight to gaze on there,
        Look down on us, storm-driven as we are!

31   If the barbarians from regions where
        The sky by Helicè is daily crowned,
        Rotating with her son she holds so dear,

34   By Rome and all the wonders therein found
        Were moved to stupor when the Lateran
        Above all works of mortals was renowned,

37   I, coming to holiness from the profane,
        To the eternal from the temporal,
        From Florence to a people just and sane,

40   Into what stupor, then, must I needs fall!
        Truly, 'twixt it and joy I then preferred
        No sound to hear, no word to speak at all.

43   As when a pilgrim, to new life restored,
        Beholds a shrine, and hopes within him rise
        That of its wonders he may take home word,

46   So I amid the living light mine eyes
        Directed, gazing upon every row
        Now upwards and now down, now circle-wise.

49   To charity their faces sweetly woo,
        Made beauteous in our Maker's light and smile,
        And gracious dignity their gestures show.

52   Already now the general form and style
        Of Paradise my glance had taken in,
        But on no part had lingered yet a while.

55   And, with new-kindled eagerness to win
        My Lady's guidance, unto her once more I
        Turned me, to hear her speak of what I'd seen.

One thing I meant, another is my story:　　　　58
　　Not Beatrice, an elder there I saw,
　　Clad in the raiment of the saints in glory.

A joyfulness benign his features wore;　　　　61
　　Such gentle kindliness his air implied
　　As ever tender-hearted father bore.

"And she, where is she?" instantly I cried.　　64
　　"'Tis Beatrice who sends me unto thee
　　For thy desire's fulfilment," he replied.

"Lift up thine eyes, yonder thy Lady see　　　67
　　In the third circle from the highest place,
　　Enthroned where merit destined her to be."

Without a word I lifted up my gaze,　　　　　70
　　And there I saw her in her glory crowned,
　　Reflecting from herself the eternal rays.

The greatest height whence thunderings resound　73
　　Less distant is from mortal vision, though
　　Plunged in the deepest ocean it were found,

Than was my sight from Beatrice, and lo!　　76
　　By no material means made visible,
　　Distinct her image came to me below.

"O thou in whom my hopes securely dwell,　　79
　　And who, to bring my soul to Paradise,
　　Didst leave the imprint of thy steps in Hell,

Of all that I have looked on with these eyes　82
　　Thy goodness and thy power have fitted me
　　The holiness and grace to recognize.

Thou hast led me, a slave, to liberty,　　　85
　　By every path; and using every means
　　Which to fulfil this task were granted thee.

Keep turned towards me thy munificence　　88
　　So that my soul which thou hast remedied
　　May please thee when it quits the bonds of sense."

Such was my prayer and she, so distant fled,　91
　　It seemed, did smile and look on me once more,
　　Then to the eternal fountain turned her head.

94   The holy elder spoke: "That thou mayst draw
        Thy journey to a perfect close (and I
        By prayer and holy love am sent therefor),

97   Over this garden with thy vision fly,
        For looking on it will prepare thy gaze
        To rise towards God's luminance on high.

100   The Queen of Heaven, with love of whom I blaze,
        Since I her faithful servant Bernard am,
        Will grant us on our mission every grace."

103   Like one who, haply, from Croatia came
        To see the veil of St Veronica
        And held, unsated, by its ancient fame

106   Looks all he may, musing the while with awe:
        "Lord Jesus, Christ, true God, this likeness of
        Your face is, then, the form your features bore?"

109   So I there marvelled at the living love
        Of him who tasted, while a mortal man,
        By contemplation, of that peace above.

112   "O son of grace," thus he once more began,
        "Thou wilt not yonder joyous being know
        By fixing here beneath thy vision's scan.

115   Look on the circles, towards the utmost row,
        Until thou seëst our enthroned Queen
        To whom all in this realm devotion owe."

118   I looked above and, as the orient scene
        At dawn exceeds the beauty of the west,
        Where the declining sun has lately been,

121   So, mounting as from vale to mountain-crest,
        These eyes beheld, at the remotest rim,
        A radiance surpassing all the rest.

124   As here, where we await the pole, to him
        Entrusted once who drove so ill, the sky
        Flames brighter and the adjacent light grows dim,

127   So there, that oriflame of peace on high
        Was quickened at the heart, diminishing
        Its flame in equal measure outwardly.

About the heart I saw on outstretched wing   130
  More than a thousand angels jubilant,
  Distinct in radiance and functioning.

Their gladsome sporting and their festive chant   133
  Diffused, it seemed, a loveliness so gay
  That joy was in the eyes of every saint.

Were I endowed with wealth of words to say   136
  All I imagine, yet I dared not try
  The least part of their gladness to convey.

Bernard, who saw me gazing upon high   139
  Towards the glowing focus of his love,
  His own eyes turned to her so tenderly

Still greater ardour fixed mine own above.   142

THE IMAGES. *The White Rose*: See Canto xxx, under *Images*.

The Departure of Beatrice: Under the guidance of Beatrice, the figure of revealed theology or the true doctrines of the Church, Dante has seen anticipatory visions of the glory of God. Now, having been blinded and kindled to new sight by the light of that glory, he is ready to partake of the vision to which the soul attains after death. In her allegorical sense, Beatrice is no longer needed. Dante has passed beyond the intellectual comprehension of doctrine and has reached, by contemplation, the state of ecstasy in which the souls of the blessed (or of mystics) gaze directly upon God. In the literal sense, Beatrice on her departure is more than ever herself, the person whom Dante loves and to whom, in his farewell, he pours out his deepest gratitude, entreating her still to extend towards him her beneficence.

St Bernard: Although Beatrice can take him no further, for his final vision Dante still needs the guidance of one who can lead him onwards in contemplation and can implore grace for the ultimate boon. St Bernard, the type of the mystical contemplative, is chosen for this role. He is not only the image of contemplation; in his literal sense, he is one who has himself seen God in the first life, and, since he will implore the Virgin to intercede so that Dante too may share this vision, his devotion to the Mother of God has both a literal and an allegorical appropriateness.

The Virgin: For the second time (cf. Canto xxiii), Dante beholds the Virgin. On this occasion, though she appears in her bodily form, the imagery with which she is described reveals her as if all but divine. She is the Queen of Heaven, to whom the saints of her realm are devoutly subject; yet with them all, the Virgin, too, is adorned with the light of God; though Queen of them all, she, too, is one of redeemed humanity.

NOTES. ll. 2–4: ". . . *the sacred might . . . the other*": Dante now beholds the two-fold host of Heaven. "The sacred might . . . whom with His blood Christ made His spouse" are the souls of the redeemed, the saints of the Church Triumphant, whom Dante has already beheld, manifested as lights, in the eighth heaven. Now, as St Benedict has promised (Canto xxii. 61–3), he sees them in the guise of the bodies they will put on after the resurrection. "The other, winging ever in His sight" is the host of Angels, who minister peace and ardour to the saints; for ardour is here peaceful and peace ardent (cf. l. 17).

l. 19: . . . *that which blazed above*: i.e. the light of God.

l. 20: *The volant concourse interposed no screen*: The thronging Angels flying between the light of God and the saints in the rose cast no shadow, for in the purity of their nature they are transparent.

ll. 22–3: ". . . *God's rays penetrate . . . through all the universe, in due degree*": This recalls the first three lines of *Paradise* and adds the concept that nothing can dim the piercing light of God or the piercing vision of the blessed.

l. 26: . . . *whose joy no dangers mar*: The saints are secure in their joy for they have no fear that it will be diminished or withdrawn.

l. 27: *Gazed on one sign*: i.e. on the light of God.

ll. 31–2: . . . *regions where the sky by Helicè is daily crowned*: Helicè, or Callisto, one of Diana's nymphs, was dismissed when it was discovered she had been seduced by Jupiter, to whom she bore a son, Arcas. Jupiter transformed them both into constellations, Helicè becoming the Great Bear, and her son Arcas, the Little Bear. By the regions which have these constellations overhead throughout the year, Dante intends the far north, but no exact latitude is indicated.

l. 35: *the Lateran*: The Lateran palace in Rome was in Dante's time the usual residence of the Pope. Here it probably stands for the Eternal City itself, since the Lateran was believed to have been an imperial palace from the time of Nero until Constantine donated it to Pope Sylvester. If so, the time referred to here is the period when the seat of Empire surpassed in magnificence all the works of man.

l. 59: . . . *an elder there I saw*: The "elder" is St Bernard, the celebrated Abbot of Clairvaux (1091–1153). He launched the Second Crusade, in which Cacciaguida died. His devotion to the Virgin is apparent in many of his writings, especially in his *Homilies*, or sermons, on the Annunciation and in praise of her. In one of these, St Bernard calls her the sinners' ladder, "whose top, like the ladder which the patriarch Jacob saw, touched the heavens, and even passed through them until it reached the well of living waters which are above the heavens" (cf. Canto xxi).

For the allegorical significance of St Bernard's replacing Beatrice, see above, under *Images*.

l. 69: "*Enthroned where merit destined her to be*": The soul's enjoyment of heavenly bliss is due to grace and merit, the grace of God and the merit of the soul, which is free to choose between good and evil.

ll. 73–5: *The greatest height whence thunderings resound* etc.: The space which now separates him from Beatrice is greater than the distance between the highest region of thunder and the lowest depths of ocean.

l. 81: "*Didst leave the imprint of thy steps in Hell*": At the beginning of the *Divine Comedy*, Virgil relates that Beatrice descended to the Limbo to implore him to go to the rescue of Dante in the dark wood. (Cf. *Hell* ii. 52–117, esp. 82–4.)

l. 90: "*the bonds of sense*": i.e. the trammels of the body.

ll. 95–6: "*. . . and I by prayer and holy love am sent therefor*": The love of God and the prayers of Beatrice have brought St Bernard (as well as Virgil) to Dante's aid.

ll. 103–8: *Imagine one who . . . from Croatia came* etc.: To convey his awe at the presence of St Bernard, Dante asks the reader to imagine the feelings of a pilgrim from a remote region of Christendom gazing at the veil of St Veronica in Rome. It was believed that when Veronica wiped the blood and sweat from the face of Our Lord as He passed on His way to Calvary, His features were imprinted on the cloth. The relic, an object of deepest veneration, was displayed at St Peter's during January and in Holy Week. In the *Vita Nuova* (XI. i), Dante mentions the pilgrims passing through Florence on their way to see it.

ll. 110–11: *. . . who tasted, while a mortal man, by contemplation, of that peace above*: The question was raised by theologians as to whether St Bernard, in his contemplative life, had seen God in His essence. Dante evidently believes that he had, in fact, experienced immediate vision of the divine Being, and this belief largely accounts for Dante's awe on beholding him; as St Veronica's veil was imprinted with Christ's features, so St Bernard's countenance had envisaged God.

l. 113: *yonder joyous being*: i.e. the Virgin.

l. 123: *A radiance surpassing all the rest*: This is the glory of the Virgin Mary, who, though her radiance is unequalled and unexcelled, is yet among the ranks of redeemed humanity.

ll. 124–5: *. . . the pole, to him entrusted once who drove so ill*: The pole is the shaft of the chariot of the sun, which Phaëthon was once trusted to drive; too weak to hold the horses, he let them rush from their usual course and come so close to the earth that it was almost set on fire.

l. 132: *Distinct in radiance and functioning*: Each angel, being a separate species (cf. Canto xxix. 136–8), has his own specific beauty of light and activity.

CANTO XXXII

THE STORY. *St Bernard guides Dante's gaze amid the petals of the Rose, pointing out its main divisions and the principal souls enthroned therein. The different degrees of bliss enjoyed by children, who owe salvation solely to Christ, raises in Dante's mind the still unsolved problem of elective grace. St Bernard relates it to the mystery of predestination, which has already been shown to be inscrutable to mortal mind.*

St Bernard bids Dante fix his gaze first upon the Virgin, and then names other saints, ending with Lucia. Finally, as they both turn their gaze above, St Bernard begins his prayer.

Merged in his joy, that còntemplative soul
    These sacred words began, for me engaged
    In the fulfilment of a master's role:

4   "The wound which Mary tended and assuaged
    Was by the beauteous person at her feet
    Inflicted in surrender so ill-gauged.

7   Among the thrones of the third order sit,
    Below her, Rachel, and, as thou canst see,
    Thy Beatrice in the adjacent seat.

10   Sarah, Rebekah, Judith and then she,
    The ancestress of him who cried in grief
    At his wrong doing, *Miserere mei*,

13   Throne after throne, will greet thy vision if
    It keep with me as, naming them, I go
    Down through the rose, proceeding leaf by leaf.

16   As downwards to the seventh, so below,
    Are seated women of the Hebrew race,
    Parting the petals in unbroken row.

19   Since faith from two directions turned her gaze
    To Christ, these holy women form the wall
    Which indicates the parting of the ways.

22   Within this section of the Rose, where all
    The petals are mature, these saints mark well:
    Of faith in Christ-to-come they heard the call.

On yonder side, in semi-circles, dwell,   25
  Parted by empty spaces here and there,
  Those who believed in Christ Emmanuel.

And as we see the throne of glory where   28
  Our Lady is doth form a bastion
  With other thrones descending down her stair,

So, facing her, the throne of the great John   31
  Who endured the desert and a martyr's death
  And Hell, at last, until two years were gone,

The rose in its two sections severeth   34
  With Francis, Benedict, Augustine, and
  The rest who sit successively beneath.

Now marvel at God's plan, for on each hand   37
  Both aspects of the faith will, when complete,
  In equal measure in the garden stand.

Know that to here from where the petals meet,   40
  Up to midway, the lines of these partitions,
  No souls by their own merit have their seat,

But by Another's, under fixed conditions;   43
  For all these spirits were absolved from sin
  Ere they had reached control of their volitions.

Lend ear and thou wilt realize how thin   46
  Their voices are; look well and thou'lt make out
  Their infant faces and their childish mien.

Since now thou art perplexed by silent doubt,   49
  I will untie the knot and set thee free
  From subtle thoughts which twine thee round about.

In this wide kingdom no contingency   52
  Can find a place in the minutest fact,
  No more than sadness, hunger, thirst can be.

For here eternal law doth so enact   55
  All thou beholdest, that the measurements
  Between the ring and finger are exact.

Swift-sped to the true life, this child-folk, hence,   58
  Not *sine causa* in this Rose reside
  In varying degrees of excellence.

61   The King, within whose kingdom we abide
           Content in love and blissfulness so great
           No will has dared to long for more beside,

64   All minds in His glad semblance doth create;
           His grace thereon is variously conferred.
           Thou seest the effect: let that be adequate.

67   Plainly in Holy Scripture ye have heard
           This lesson in the story of the twins
           Who in the womb to enmity were stirred.

70   Since grace so early has her origins,
           So, as men's hair of divers shades doth grow,
           God's crown of light for every brow she wins.

73   Not, then, by merit, do these spirits go
           To dwell in varying degrees of bliss;
           Grace-given is the sight which grades them so.

76   In mankind's earliest ages true it is
           That innocent children came to Paradise,
           The faith of parents being enough for this.

79   Later it was required to circumcise
           Male infants, that their innocent wings might gain
           The power to bear them upward to these skies.

82   But since the Christian age such things were vain;
           For then, without true baptism in Christ
           Such innocence in Limbo must remain.

85   Now to that face which most resembles Christ
           Lift up thy gaze; its radiance alone
           Can grant to thee the power to look on Christ."

88   I looked, and on that countenance there shone
           Such bliss, bestowed by sacred minds who soar
           (For this created) through that lofty zone,

91   That nothing I had looked on heretofore
           Had held me breathless in such wonderment,
           Or unto God so close a likeness bore.

94   The angel who first thither made descent,
           Before her, sang "Hail, Mary, full of grace",
           His wings spread wide unto their full extent.

Response to the divine canticle of praise 97
   Was sung by all that court so blissfully,
   Still more serenely joyful was each face.

"O holy father, who dost bear for me 100
   To stay below, quitting thine own dear site
   To which thou'rt destined in eternity,

Which angel is it who in such delight 103
   Looks in Our Lady's eyes with love so burning
   That like a fire he seems, so radiant bright?"

Thus I deferred once more to the discerning 106
   Of one whom Mary's loveliness arrayed
   Even as the rising sun the star of morning.

"All joy and excellence that dwell", he said, 109
   "In soul or angel (and 'tis rightly so)
   In him is at its most sublime displayed;

For this is he who brought the palm below 112
   To Mary when the Son of God on high
   Bearing our fleshly burden willed to go.

But follow with thine eyes once more as I 115
   Continue, and the great patricians note
   Of this most just and pious sovereignty.

Those two on high, who, as thou canst make out, 118
   Being nearest to Augusta, are most blest,
   Of this our Rose are as a double root.

Upon her left is he, of all the rest 121
   The father, whose bold taste cost him so dear,
   Bequeathing to mankind such bitter taste.

Upon her right behold that reverend peer, 124
   Father of Holy Church, who holds the keys
   Of all the roseate joy assembled here.

And he who saw before his own decease 127
   All the sad seasons of the lovely bride
   Whom Christ with lance and nails had claimed as His,

Sits next to him; by Adam is the guide 130
   Whose people, nurtured by the Lord on manna,
   Were ingrate, fickle, mutinous beside.

133   Diagonal to Peter there see Anna,
            Gazing upon her daughter in such content
            Her look ne'er falters while she sings Hosanna.

136   And facing Adam sitteth she who sent
            Thy Beatrice to save thee from the path
            Where headlong to thy ruin thou wert bent.

139   But since the time of thy entrancement doth
            Grow short, like the good tailor spoken of,
            We'll cut our coat according to our cloth,

142   And here will stop, to turn our eyes above
            That thou, as far as may be, with thy gaze,
            Mayst penetrate into the Primal Love.

145   But (lest perchance thy wings should seem to raise
            Thee when they downward ply) 'tis well for thee
            That prayer should first be offered for thy grace,

148   Grace from Our Lady who can ever be
            Thy help in need; now follow as anon
            I pray, so that thy heart stray not from me."

151   And he began this holy orison.

THE IMAGES. *The Saints in the Empyrean*: Before beholding the Divine Essence, Dante must first prepare himself by contemplating the saints in glory. Those whom St Bernard indicates, beginning with the Virgin Mary, are all, in one way or another, connected with the story of the Redemption. In the almost rigid precision and symmetry of the ranks of the blessed, the perfection of the divine order is conveyed. God's plan for mankind, His heavenly kingdom, are as satisfying to the intellect as a geometrical design.

NOTES. ll. 4–6: "*The wound which Mary tended and assuaged*" etc.: The wound healed by Mary is the sin of man, redeemed by the Incarnation; the "*surrender so ill-gauged*" is the yielding by Eve to the serpent which led to the Fall; the "*beauteous person*" at Mary's feet is Eve.

l. 7: "*. . . the thrones of the third order*": i.e. the thrones in the third horizontal rank, counting from the top (cf. Diagram, p. 323).

l. 9: "*Thy Beatrice in the adjacent seat*": In the Limbo, Beatrice told Virgil that she was sitting by Rachel when the Virgin Mary sent Lucia to her, drawing her attention to the plight of Dante (cf. *Inf.* ii. 100–102). Rachel was the second wife of the Patriarch Jacob and the mother of Joseph and Benjamin (cf. *Gen.* xxix). She is mentioned in *Inf.* iv. (l. 60) as being among those released from Limbo on the descent of Christ into Hell, and appears to Dante in a dream in *Purg.* xxvi where she symbolizes the contemplative life. The Virgin Mary, Rachel, Lucia, Beatrice, and Virgil represent for Dante the stages of intervening grace which saves him from himself. Dante had, as it were, sunk beneath the Christian level and it was Virgil himself, to whose voice he was still responsive, who was able to show Dante the limitations of the Virgilian view of life.

ll. 10–12: *"Sarah, Rebekah, Judith, and then she, the ancestress of him"* etc.: Sarah was the wife of Abraham and mother of Isaac. Rebekah was the wife of Isaac and the mother of Esau and Jacob. Judith, the daughter of Meraris, murdered Holofernes while he slept, thereby saving Bethulia, which the Assyrians were besieging. In the apocryphal book which bears her name, Judith is represented as the ideal type of piety. "The ancestress of him who cried in grief at his wrong doing *Miserere mei*" is Ruth, the great-grandmother of David, the author of the penitential psalm beginning "Have mercy upon me, O Lord, for thy great goodness" (*Psalm* 1). The "wrong doing" of which he thus repents is his adultery with Bathsheba, the wife of Uriah, the Hittite. Bathsheba conceived a child by David and in order that he might marry her, David contrived that Uriah should be killed in battle. Bathsheba then became his wife and bore a son, who was Solomon (cf. *II Sam.* xi).

ll. 16–18: *"As downwards to the seventh, so below"*: St Bernard says that the line of thrones extending downwards from Mary is occupied by Hebrew women. The seven whom he has named are: Mary, Eve, Rachel, Sarah, Rebekah, Judith, and Ruth. The inclusion of Eve among "women of the Hebrew race" would seem to be justified inasmuch as she is the mother of all mankind and, in consequence, the ancestral mother also of Christ in His kinship with humanity. All the women named, with the exception of Judith, are wives of members of the House of David (of which Adam may be regarded as the ancestor). Rachel, the second wife of Jacob, is not in the direct line, for David was descended from Judas the son of Leah, Jacob's first wife. Rachel's importance, however, as the symbol of the contemplative life (cf. *Purg.* xxvii and *Images*) would seem to account for her being placed above Sarah, Rebekah, and Ruth. Between Sarah and David are the first fourteen generations mentioned by St Matthew (i. 1–17); and, according to the chronology indicated by Adam in Canto xxvi (ll. 118–23), the span of years from Eve until the birth of Christ is 5198.

ll. 19–21: *"Since faith from two directions turned her gaze"* etc.: St Bernard refers here to the distinctions between the saints of the Old and the saints of the New Covenant, those who believed in Christ to come and those who believed in Him as already come. The line of Old Testament women is at once the demarcation and the link between the two. The Virgin Mary is included among them since she had faith in Christ before His conception. (Cf. Canto xix. 103–5 and Canto xx. 103–5.)

ll. 22–3: "*. . . this section of the Rose, where all the petals are mature*": The thrones of the Old Covenant are all occupied, for the number of the elect of the Old Testament is complete.

ll. 25–7: "*On yonder side . . . dwell, parted by empty spaces here and there*" etc.: Among the thrones of the New Testament are a few vacant places (one of them awaits the soul of the Emperor Henry VII; cf. Canto xxx. 133–8). "*Those who believed in Christ Emmanuel*": i.e. those who believed in Christ already come ("Emmanuel", God-with-us).

l. 31: "*So, facing her*": The line of thrones headed by St John the Baptist is opposite that which is occupied by the women of the Old Testament. (Cf. Diagram, p. 323.)

ll. 32–3: "*Who endured the desert and a martyr's death and Hell, until two years were gone*": St John the Baptist was beheaded two years before the Crucifixion and thus was in Limbo for that length of time until Christ came to release him (cf. *Inf.* iv. 52–63 and *note*).

l. 35: "*. . . Francis, Benedict, Augustine*": i.e. St Francis of Assisi, St Benedict, and St Augustine of Hippo. Next to the Precursor of Christ comes His most perfect imitator. The exalted longing which Dante had expressed to see St Benedict (cf. Canto xxii. 58–63) is now fulfilled, according to the saint's promise. Note that St Benedict is placed opposite Rachel, the symbol of contemplation. St Augustine, the greatest of the Latin fathers of the Church, is the author of the *City of God*, a treatise in vindication of Christianity and the Christian Church.

ll. 38–9: "*Both aspects of the faith will, when complete, in equal measure in the garden stand*": It is not known whence Dante derived this notion that the elect of the New Covenant would be equal in number to those of the Old. Some commentators attribute it to Dante's love of symmetry; others see in it an indication that Dante believed the end of the world to be near at hand.

ll. 40–42: "*Know that to here from where the petals meet*" etc.: A line cuts horizontally across the two descending lines ("partitions"). Below this are the souls of children. (Cf. Diagram, p. 323.)

l. 43: "*. . . by Another's, under fixed conditions*": The souls of infants and children are saved, not through grace and the individual's choice between good and evil (as is the case with adults), but through the merits of Christ alone.

l. 45: "*Ere they had reached control of their volitions*": The children had died before reaching the age of reason, at which stage alone true choice is possible.

l. 48: "*Their infant faces and their childish mien*": Dante here departs from the teaching of St Thomas Aquinas, according to whom all the blessed will be as they were or would have been in youth. Dante, on the contrary, implies that the souls in Heaven show themselves to be of the same age and aspect which they possessed when they died; thus, children appear as children and adults as adults of varying ages.

l. 49: "*Since now thou art perplexed by silent doubt*": The doubt which

340

here perplexes Dante is the old one concerning election and predestination. St Bernard has indicated that the children are placed some higher, some lower ("under fixed conditions", l. 43), among the ranks of the blessed. Why, if they were all saved by equal merit (i.e. that of Christ), do they enjoy different degrees of bliss? This is the question which St Bernard proceeds to answer (ll. 52–84).

ll. 52–4: *"In this wide kingdom no contingency"* etc.: Nothing in Heaven is to be assigned to chance; everything is in accordance with the will of God, and whatever God wills is justice (cf. Canto xix. 85–90 and *note*).

ll. 56–7: *". . . the measurements between the ring and finger are exact"*: God's grace is more or less, in proportion to the greater or lesser merit of the soul that receives it. This does not mean that the soul *earns* grace by its merit, but that the relationship between grace and merit is such as to accord perfectly with divine justice, which is the will of God. This is so difficult a concept for mortal minds that it is not surprising that, even at the very culmination of his sublime vision, Dante is still in need of illumination concerning it.

ll. 59–60: *"Not 'sine causa' in this Rose reside in varying degrees of excellence"*: The Latin expression *sine causa* is a legalistic phrase, signifying "without cause", and is appropriate to the judicial nature of the mediaeval theology of the redemption.

l. 66: *"Thou seest the effect: let that be adequate"*: The gift of grace, "variously conferred" (l. 65), is so inscrutable as to elude all created mind. Compare the similar pronouncements on predestination by the Eagle (Canto xx. 130–38) and by St Peter Damian (Canto xxi. 83–99).

ll. 68–9: *". . . the twins who in the womb to enmity were stirred"*: St Bernard, to illustrate the inscrutable, unpredictable nature of grace, cites the case of Jacob and Esau, the twin sons of Rebekah and Isaac (cf. *Gen.* xxv. 21–6 *et sqq.*). St Paul also comments on the pre-natal predispositions of Jacob and Esau in the *Epistle to the Romans* (ix. 10–15): ". . . when Rebekah also had conceived . . . (For the children being not yet born, neither having done any good or evil, that the purpose of God according to election might stand, not of works, but of him that calleth;) it was said unto her, The elder shall serve the younger. As it is written, Jacob have I loved, but Esau have I hated. What shall we say then? Is there unrighteousness with God? God forbid. For he saith unto Moses, I will have mercy on whom I will have mercy, and I will have compassion on whom I will have compassion."

l. 71: *". . . as men's hair of divers shades doth grow"*: The comparison of the diversity of grace with the diversity of the colour of hair was probably suggested to Dante by Esau's having red hair (cf. *Gen.* xxv. 25: "And the first came out red, all over like an hairy garment; and they called his name Esau.").

ll. 76–81: *"In mankind's earliest ages true it is"* etc.: The faith of parents in the coming Messiah was sufficient in the early ages of the world until the time of Abraham. After that, until the birth of Christ, circumcision was required for salvation.

l. 84: "*Such innocence in Limbo must remain*": Here Dante causes St Bernard to contradict words which he had himself written on this question: "It is in God's hands; not mine be it to set the limit."

l. 85: ". . . *that face which most resembles Christ*": i.e. the face of the Virgin.

l. 89: ". . . *sacred minds*": i.e. angels who minister to the Virgin as others minister to the other souls (cf. Canto xxxi. 16–18).

l. 94: "*The angel who first thither made descent*": i.e. the Angel Gabriel, who descended to Mary to make the Annunciation.

ll. 109–11: "*All joy and excellence that dwell*" etc.: Just as God wills greater grace to some men than to others, so He vouchsafes more grace to one angel than to another. In Heaven this is a source of joy, for the will of the saints accords with the will of God. (Compare the words of Piccarda in Canto iii. 70–87.)

l. 112: . . . "*who brought the palm below*": In many representations of the Annunciation, the Angel Gabriel is shown holding a palm as a sign of the triumph that is to come.

l. 119: "*Augusta*": i.e. the Virgin.

ll. 121–2: ". . . *he, of all the rest the father*": i.e. Adam.

ll. 124–6: ". . . *that reverend peer*" etc.: i.e. St Peter.

ll. 127–9: "*And he who saw before his own decease*" etc.: i.e. St John the Evangelist, who, as author of the Apocalypse (as it was believed), foresaw the coming tribulations of the Church.

ll. 130–32: "*the guide*" etc.: i.e. Moses.

ll. 133–5: "*Diagonal to Peter there see Anna*" etc.: i.e. the mother of the Virgin (cf. Diagram, p. 323).

ll. 136–8: ". . . *she who sent thy Beatrice*" etc.; i.e. Lucia (cf. *Inf.* ii. 97–101 and *note*).

ll. 145–6: ' . . . *lest perchance thy wings should seem to raise thee*" etc.: There can be no true progress without the grace of God, which the soul must ever pray to have accorded to it through the intercession of the Virgin.

CANTO XXXIII

THE STORY. *St Bernard addresses to the Virgin a prayer for intercession for Dante that grace may be granted him to behold God. Conveying her acceptance of the prayer, the Virgin turns her eyes above and Dante, doing likewise, is enabled to penetrate with his vision to the True Light of which all other is the radiance or reflection. Therein he beholds the unity of all creation and all time, the Three Persons (manifested as three spheres), and, finally, Christ, one with the eternal being of Godhead. Here his powers of representation failed him and all that remains is the remembrance of his will and love wholly surrendered to the love of God.*

"O Virgin Mother, Daughter of thy Son,
Lowliest and loftiest of created stature,
Fixed goal to which the eternal counsels run,

Thou art that She by whom our human nature   4
Was so ennobled that it might become
The Creator to create Himself His creature.

Thy sides were made a shelter to relume   7
The Love whose warmth within the timeless peace
Quickened the seed of this immortal bloom;

High noon of charity to those in bliss,   10
And upon earth, to men in mortal plight,
A living spring of hope, thy presence is.

Lady, so great thou art and such thy might,   13
The seeker after grace who shuns thy knee
May aim his prayer, but fails to wing the flight.

Not only does thy succour flow out free   16
To him who asks, but many a time the aid
Fore-runs the prayer, such largesse is in thee.

All ruth, all mercy are in thee displayed,   19
And all munificence; in thee is knit
Together all that's good in all that's made.

This man, who witnessed from the deepest pit   22
Of all the universe, up to this height,
The souls' lives one by one, doth now entreat

25   That thou, by grace, may grant to him such might
         That higher yet in vision he may rise
         Towards the final source of bliss and light.

28   And I who never burned for my own eyes
         More than I burn for his, with all my prayers
         Now pray to thee, and pray they may suffice,

31   That of all mortal clouding which impairs,
         Thine own prayers may possess the power to clean
         His sight, till in the highest bliss it shares.

34   And further do I pray thee, heavenly Queen,
         Who canst all that thou wilt, keep his heart pure
         And meet, when such great vision he has seen.

37   With thy protection render him secure
         From human impulse; for this boon the saints,
         With Beatrice, thronging fold hands and implore."

40   The eyes which God doth love and reverence,
         Gazing on him who prayed, to us made plain
         How prayers, devoutly prayed, her joy enhance.

43   Unto the eternal light she raised them then:
         No eye of living creature could aspire
         To penetrate so fixedly therein.

46   And I, who now was drawing ever nigher
         Towards the end of yearning, as was due,
         Quenched in my soul the burning of desire.

49   Bernard conveyed to me what I should do
         By sign and smile; already on my own
         I had looked upwards, as he wished me to.

52   For now my sight, clear and yet clearer grown,
         Pierced through the ray of that exalted light,
         Wherein, as in itself, the truth is known.

55   Henceforth my vision mounted to a height
         Where speech is vanquished and must lag behind,
         And memory surrenders in such plight.

58   As from a dream one may awake to find
         Its passion yet imprinted on the heart,
         Although all else is cancelled from the mind,

So of my vision now but little part   61
   Remains, yet in my inmost soul I know
   The sweet instilling which it did impart.

So the sun melts the imprint on the snow,   64
   Even so the Sybil's wisdom that was penned
   On light leaves vanished on the winds that blow.

O Light supreme, by mortal thought unscanned,   67
   Grant that Thy former aspect may return,
   Once more a little of Thyself relend.

Make strong my tongue that in its words may burn   70
   One single spark of all Thy glory's light
   For future generations to discern.

For if my memory but glimpse the sight   73
   Whereof these lines would now a little say,
   Men may the better estimate Thy might.

The piercing brightness of the living ray   76
   Which I endured, my vision had undone,
   I think, if I had turned my eyes away.

And I recall this further led me on,   79
   Wherefore my gaze more boldness yet assumed
   Till to the Infinite Good it last had won.

O grace abounding, whereby I presumed   82
   So deep the eternal light to search and sound
   That my whole vision was therein consumed!

In that abyss I saw how love held bound   85
   Into one volume all the leaves whose flight
   Is scattered through the universe around;

How substance, accident, and mode unite   88
   Fused, so to speak, together, in such wise
   That this I tell of is one simple light.

Yea, of this complex I believe mine eyes   91
   Beheld the universal form – in me,
   Even as I speak, I feel such joy arise.

One moment brings me deeper lethargy   94
   Than twenty-five centuries brought the quest that dazed
   Neptune when Argo's shadow crossed the sea.

97　　And so my mind, bedazzled and amazed,
　　　　Stood fixed in wonder, motionless, intent,
　　　　And still my wonder kindled as I gazed.

100　　That light doth so transform a man's whole bent
　　　　That never to another sight or thought
　　　　Would he surrender, with his own consent;

103　　For everything the will has ever sought
　　　　Is gathered there, and there is every quest
　　　　Made perfect, which apart from it falls short.

106　　Now, even what I recall will be exprest
　　　　More feebly than if I could wield no more
　　　　Than a babe's tongue, yet milky from the breast;

109　　Not that the living light I looked on wore
　　　　More semblances than one, which cannot be,
　　　　For it is always what it was before;

112　　But as my sight by seeing learned to see,
　　　　The transformation which in me took place
　　　　Transformed the single changeless form for me.

115　　That light supreme, within its fathomless
　　　　Clear substance, showed to me three spheres, which bare
　　　　Three hues distinct, and occupied one space;

118　　The first mirrored the next, as though it were
　　　　Rainbow from rainbow, and the third seemed flame
　　　　Breathed equally from each of the first pair.

121　　How weak are words, and how unfit to frame
　　　　My concept – which lags after what was shown
　　　　So far, 'twould flatter it to call it lame!

124　　Eternal light, that in Thyself alone
　　　　Dwelling, alone dost know Thyself, and smile
　　　　On Thy self-love, so knowing and so known!

127　　The sphering thus begot, perceptible
　　　　In Thee like mirrored light, now to my view –
　　　　When I had looked on it a little while –

130　　Seemed in itself, and in its own self-hue,
　　　　Limned with our image; for which cause mine eyes
　　　　Were altogether drawn and held thereto.

As the geometer his mind applies   133
   To square the circle, nor for all his wit
   Finds the right formula, howe'er he tries,

So strove I with that wonder – how to fit   136
   The image to the sphere; so sought to see
   How it maintained the point of rest in it.

Thither my own wings could not carry me,   139
   But that a flash my understanding clove,
   Whence its desire came to it suddenly.

High phantasy lost power and here broke off;   142
   Yet, as a wheel moves smoothly, free from jars,
   My will and my desire were turned by love,

The love that moves the sun and the other stars.   145

THE IMAGES. *The Prayer to the Virgin*: In his prayer to the Virgin, St Bernard implores her to intercede for Dante that he may attain, now, to the vision of God and that, in his life henceforth, he may, under her protection, persevere in truth and righteousness, his affections and human impulses guarded from unworthiness. The prayer is also a hymn of praise to the Virgin. St Bernard, in life the most ardent worshipper in the Virgin-cult, now extols her as excelling all creatures, angelic or human, in lowliness, goodness, and vision. On earth, the historical and universal God-bearer, the vessel of Divine Grace, now, in Heaven, she is the one mediator to whom man must turn in prayer. In the *story*, the Virgin, from the very beginning, is the gentle Lady who is so moved to pity on Dante's account that for her sake "high doom is cancelled" (*Inf.* ii. 94–6). She it is who summons Lucy to her side, exhorting her: "Thy faithful votary needs thee, and I commend him to thy care"; and Lucy, in her turn, appeals to Beatrice, who swiftly seeks the aid of Virgil, who, alone, at this stage, can speak to, and be heard by, Dante. Now the story has come full circle. Grace, in its various manifestations, has brought Dante from the depths of Hell up to this height. As St Bernard prays for the Virgin's supreme intercession, all the saints, and Beatrice among them, fold their hands in the vast fellowship of prayer – prayer for one man's need.

The Vision of God: The final vision, the crown and climax of the whole work, consists of two revelations. First, Dante perceives in the Divine Light the form, or exemplar, of all creation. All things that exist in themselves ("substance"), all aspects or properties of being ("accident"), all mutual relations ("mode") are seen bound together in one single concept. The Universe is *in* God. Next, having glimpsed the whole of creation, Dante beholds the Creator. He sees three circles, of three colours, yet of one dimension. One seems to be reflected from the other, and the third, like flame, proceeds equally from both (the Father, Son, and Holy Ghost). Then, as he gazes, the reflected circle shows within itself the human form, coloured with the circle's own hue. As Dante strives to comprehend how human nature is united with the Word, a ray of divine light so floods his mind that his desire is at rest. At this point the vision ceases, and the *story* ends with the poet's will and desire moving in perfect co-ordination with the love of God.

NOTES. l. 8: "... *within the timeless peace*": in the eternal peace of the Empyrean.

l. 9: "*this immortal bloom*": i.e. the celestial Rose.

ll. 14–15: "*The seeker after grace who shuns thy knee*" etc.: Compare the words of St Bernard in his sermon on Christmas Eve: "Nihil nos Deus habere voluit, quod per Mariae manus non transiret." (God has willed that we should have nothing that did not come through the intercession of Mary.) The Roman Church still teaches that the Virgin Mary has always been the predestined channel of God's favours to man.

l. 39: "*With Beatrice, thronging fold hands and implore*": This is our last glimpse of Beatrice.

l. 40: *The eyes which God doth love and reverence*: The Virgin's eyes are loved by the Father and reverenced by the Son.

l. 54: *Wherein, as in itself, the truth is known*: The light of God alone is the true light, of which every other light is either the radiation or the reflection.

ll. 65–6: "*even so the Sybil's wisdom*" etc.: The Cumaean Sybil wrote her oracles on leaves which were scattered in the wind (cf. *Aeneid* III. 441 *et sqq.*; VI. 74 *et sqq.*).

ll. 85–7: *In that abyss I saw how love held bound* etc.: In the Divine Essence, Dante sees that all creation and all time are bound up, like the pages in a volume, in God.

l. 88: ... *substance, accident, and mode*: Substances, i.e. things existing in themselves, accidents, i.e. qualities residing in substances. and the relations between both are seen by Dante to be so fused together in God as to be indistinguishable.

ll. 91–3: *Yea, of this complex I believe mine eyes beheld the universal form* etc.: A "substantial form" is the distinguishing feature of a substance, that which makes it the thing it is and not another. The "form of the universe", therefore, would be the feature, property, or nature of the universe, that which makes it what it is. To glimpse that would be to read in the mind of God Himself the divine idea of all things, an experience which would defy description in mortal words. All Dante can do is to convey the exultation of spirit which is renewed in him when he speaks of recalling it.

l. 94: *lethargy*: forgetfulness, oblivion.

ll. 95–6: *Than twenty-five centuries brought the quest* etc.: The Argo, the first ship that ever sailed, caused the stupor of Neptune as its shadow passed over the water, on its way to Colchis for the Golden Fleece (25 centuries previous to Dante's vision would be 1200 B.C.). A moment after Dante's experience was over, it was plunged in deeper oblivion than an event thought to occur 2,500 years ago. (Dante also mentions the Argonauts in Canto ii. 16–18.)

ll. 118–20: *The first mirrored the next, as though it were rainbow from rainbow* etc.: The Son is begotten of the Father (as a second rainbow was thought to be "begotten" of the first; cf. Canto xii. 10–15); the Holy Ghost proceeds from the Father and the Son.

l. 127: *The sphering thus begot*: i.e. The Son.

ll. 130–31: *Seemed . . limned with our image*: The human features of Christ are perceptible to Dante within the "sphering" (l. 127).

ll. 133–5: *As the geometer his mind applies to square the circle* etc.: The problem of squaring the circle was formulated by the Greeks and was proved insoluble at the end of the last century. The problem is to construct a square with area equal to that of a given circle by using a straight line and compass only. The radius of the circle can be taken as a unit of length, so that the problem is to construct a square having a side $\sqrt{\pi}$ long. The point of the simile is that just as a circle is immeasurable in terms of a square, so is the deity inexpressible in terms of humanity.

ll. 136–8: *So strove I with that wonder – how to fit the image to the sphere* etc.: Dante's mind fails to grapple with the difficulty of reconciling the circle of Deity (the Son) and the human countenance of Christ.

ll. 140–41: *. . . a flash my understanding clove, whence its desire came to it suddenly*: By a flash of insight, or by an instantaneous participation of the bliss of souls in Heaven, Dante understands how the human and the divine are joined in God. To the souls who see Him in His essence, this union is as self-evident as axiomatic truth (cf. Canto ii. 40–45).

ll. 142–5: *High phantasy lost power and here broke off* etc.: At this point, the power of Dante's intellect to represent what it sees failed, and he can describe nothing more of his experience except to state his awareness that his will and desire were in accord with God's love. Compare St Paul, "I was not disobedient unto the heavenly vision".

APPENDIX

NOTE A: ASTRONOMY IN PARADISE

FOR the basic conceptions of the Ptolemaic system and their significance
for the *Divine Comedy* as a whole, the reader is referred to the section
entitled "Dante's Universe" which is contained in the first volume.[1]
The following additional explanation relates to the astronomical refer-
ences which occur in *Paradise*.

On the Wednesday of the week of his journey (which began on Good
Friday), after passing six hours in the Earthly Paradise, Dante ascends
at noon into the heavens. Since he is in the southern hemisphere, the sun
is due north; since it is the spring of the year (for the northern hemi-
sphere), the sun is at the equinox, or near it, and therefore on the
equator, and moving through the constellation of Aries. The moon,
which was opposite the sun on the first morning, has been proceeding
south and is now approaching the last degrees of Scorpio.

In the story, the first impression conveyed is one of vertical ascent,
from the Earth to the Moon, from the Moon to Mercury and from
Mercury to Venus. When he reaches Venus, Dante mentions particu-
larly the circling movement of the spheres. The souls who come to
greet him there are described as:

> . . . *quitting their reel that was on high*
> *Begun amid the exalted seraphim.*[2]

and Charles Martel says:

> "*Here, in one thirst, one wheeling, and one wheel*
> *We whirl with the celestial princes . . .*"[3]

Thus, four movements have so far been indicated: (1) Dante's vertical
ascent, (2) the vertical descent of the souls, (3) the vast circling of all the
spheres from east to west, tilting the former two movements out of the
perpendicular, and (4) the movement indicated (at the beginning of
the same canto) by the reference to the epicycle of Venus:

> '*Twas once believed that the fair Cyprian, whirled*
> *Radiant in the third epicycle . . .*[4]

This is the small circular movement which Venus performs independ-
ently, revolving upon a point on the great cycle performed by the
sphere. Since Dante and Beatrice are *in* the planet Venus, which is

---

1. *Hell*, pp. 292–5. See also M. A. Orr, *Dante and the Early Astronomers*
(2nd edition, revised by Barbara Reynolds, Allan Wingate, 1956).
2. Canto viii. 26–7.　　　3. *ibid.* 34–5.　　　4. *ibid.* 1–2.

carried round by its sphere at the same time as it revolves in its own epicycle, they and the souls with them experience both circlings.

When he has ascended from Venus to Mars, and thence onwards to the Sun, and Jupiter and Saturn, he passes beyond them all to the sphere of the constellations, which he enters among Gemini. From here Dante looks down and, with supernaturally strengthened vision, sees the little disk of the Earth; he sees the Moon (from the other side, which we now at last know from photographs, and on which he finds there are no markings); being able now to gaze fixedly on the Sun, he sees how Mercury and Venus circle in relation to it and understands how their positions alternate; and he sees Jupiter moving between Saturn and Mars.

After he has beheld the procession of the Church Triumphant, Dante looks down once more, this time that he may see how far he has circled with the spheres. He sees the Earth again and notes what parts are at that moment lighted by the Sun and what parts are in darkness. As the Sun is in Aries and he himself is in Gemini, he cannot see all the sunlit portion, but he can see that the shadow of night, sweeping westward over the globe, has covered it from the mouth of the Ganges almost to the coast of Phoenicia. The Atlantic Ocean beyond Cadiz is all in daylight and the sun is setting over Jerusalem. Since his previous glance, he has circled over an arc equal to 90 degrees, which means that he has been six hours in the eighth heaven. Another morning is now dawning over Purgatory and eighteen hours have passed since Dante left the Earthly Paradise.

The most impressive aspect, imaginatively, of the astronomy in *Paradise* is the turning of the heavens on their gigantic spindle. This motion is Dante's vision of the cosmic order and all words relating to it have for him a numinous quality. Something magical gets into his verse every time he mentions the poles or "the great wheels", as though they acted as an "Open Sesame" to unlock his poetry. It is difficult, in modern urban conditions, to recapture his impressions, but a planetarium (such as the one in Marylebone Road, London) enables one to visualize a great deal; in an aeroplane, too, on a clear night one may glimpse what Dante was seeking to convey, or sometimes even from earth, in a single moment, if one goes out at some late and unaccustomed hour and sees the Great Bear swinging high, and the Little Bear standing bolt upright on its tail.

NOTE B: PILGRIM OR FALCON?

In the first Canto, Dante says that he saw Beatrice, who had been facing east, turn to the left to gaze into the noonday sun:

> Quando Beatrice in sul sinistro fianco
> vidi rivolta e riguardar nel sole;
> aquila sì non lì s'affisse unquanco.

> E sì come secondo raggio suole
> uscir del primo e risalire in suso,
> pur come pellegrin che tornar vuole,

> Così dell'atto suo, per li occhi infuso
> nell'imagine mia, il mio si fece,
> e fissi li occhi al sole oltre nostr'uso.

> (ll. 46–54)

Sinclair's prose rendering of these lines is as follows:

... when I saw Beatrice turned round to the left and looking at the sun – never eagle so fastened upon it; and as a second ray will issue from the first and mount up again, like a pilgrim that would return home, so from her action, infused by the eyes into my imagination, mine was made, and beyond our wont I fixed my eyes on the sun.

The interpretation of Dante's "pellegrin" as a peregrine falcon rather than a pilgrim had been adopted by Dorothy Sayers already in 1947, when I heard her enter into a discussion of this passage with her friend, Ruggero Orlando. To her great delight, Orlando was able to bring visual corroborative evidence in support of her interpretation; being out one day with a party of friends who hunted with trained falcons, he had seen a peregrine swoop for its prey and then soar up again immediately; whereupon he cried out (to the surprise of his friends) "Olà! olà! il pellegrin di Dante!" [1] In 1956, S. A. Chimenz published a note on this passage in the *Giornale Storico della Letteratura Italiana* [2] in which he adduced textual evidence in support of the same interpretation. In the celebrated book on hawking by Frederick II of Sicily, *De arte venandi cum avibus* (a work which Dante knew well), there is a passage

1. The following description provides some vivid details: "The falcon is hunted by several people, mounted. You take up your position on the known line of flight of, say, a heron; then you unhood the falcon and cast her off. She mounts straight up out of sight. When the heron comes along, down comes the falcon like a stone. If she misses she has to gain height again, and at the same time keep up with the heron. A run like this may be ten miles across country. If the falcon misses, it can be quite a job with the lure to capture her." (From a letter signed "Colonel Gauntlett" to the *Sunday Times*, 4 October 1959.)
2. Vol. cxxxiii., pp. 180–85.

describing the method of training the peregrine to seize ducks on the water. Frederick recommends that if the bird misses its prey, the trainer should not send it up again if it is weary, but only *si ascendere vult*, 'if it wishes to ascend', a phrase which tallies closely with Dante's "che tornar vuole" (l. 51).

The image of the falcon swooping towards the shining surface of the water and immediately soaring up again is one which corresponds vividly with the image of the incidence and reflection of light. Dante had already referred to this V-shaped movement of the falcon in *Inferno* xxii. ll. 130-2:

> *Just as the wild-duck, with a falcon close*
> *Upon her, all of a sudden dives down quick,*
> *And up he skirrs again, foiled and morose . . .*

In this context, the image is, appropriately, savage rather than sublime, but it shows that Dante had observed or at least visualized this particular movement of the falcon.

The two chief objections to the interpretation of "pellegrin" as "falcon" are: (1) that Dante nowhere else in any of his works uses the word in the sense of falcon, but always the word "falcone"; and (2) that the double movement, of swooping and soaring, is associated with the occasions on which the falcon misses its quarry, an association which renders this interpretation inappropriate to the context; for the sight of Beatrice gazing up at the sun has the eventual effect, at least indirectly, of causing Dante to ascend into the heavens. Moreover, if the correspondence between Beatrice and a falcon is pressed, it is in danger of issuing in the grotesque, for the intention of the falcon which catches its prey is to take it somewhere and eat it.

However, it is not Beatrice's gaze which is compared either to a falcon or a pilgrim, but the ray of light, to which her gaze has been compared. To recapitulate:

(1) the image of Beatrice gazing up at the sun strikes into Dante's vision and turns his gaze likewise up towards the sun;

(2) a ray of light striking down upon a shining horizontal surface is reflected upwards;

(3) a peregrine falcon striking down upon its prey rises again into the air;

or: a pilgrim, or traveller, wishes to return home, or turns toward home.

If the falcon interpretation is accepted, the first movement is compared to the second and the second to the third; allegorical appropriateness links the first two, visual similarity the second and third. If the pilgrim interpretation is accepted, allegorical appropriateness links all three, but the visual similarity between the second and third is not so striking.

NOTE C: ANIMAL OR SILKWORM?

In Canto xxvi, when the soul of Adam responds in delight to Dante's words, it stirs beneath its covering of light:

> Tal volta un animal coverto broglia,
> sì che l'affetto convien che si paia
> per lo seguir che face a lui la 'nvoglia;
>
> e similmente l'anima primaia
> mi facea trasparer per la coverta
> quant'ella a compiacermi venia gaia.
>
> (ll. 97–102)

These lines are rendered by Sinclair as follows:

> Sometimes an animal that is covered up stirs so that its impulse is made to appear by the wrappings that follow its movement; and in like manner the primal soul showed me through its covering how gladly it came to do me pleasure.

The simile, thus interpreted, is often cited as an extreme instance of Dante's choice of simple, homely comparisons. But what animal is intended here? A cat in a sack? A falcon in its hood? A horse beneath its glittering caparison? A pig in a poke? All these, and others, have been put forward as suggestions. Dorothy Sayers, for instance, says: "Cutting clean into and through these immaterial heavens of pure intellectual light comes this concrete, commonplace, almost comic snapshot of something seen in any country town in the world on market-day. Nothing could be more vivid: nothing more characteristically Dantesque." [1]

There is little evidential support for departing from the orthodox interpretation, yet I am inclined to suspect that a suggestion put forward by A. Valgimigli [2] may be the right one. It had at any rate the distinction of being considered "ingenious and reasonable" by Moore. Valgimigli thought that the "animal coverto" was a silkworm in its cocoon. The verb "broglia" (which is now antiquated in Italian) was translated by Benvenuto da Imola to mean "vibrat, vel tremit" ("shakes or trembles"). This meaning would accord well with the vibrations of the cocoon as the caterpillar spins, or to the movement of the caterpillar itself to and fro inside the cocoon, which in the early stages would be a thin semi-transparent sack. If "broglia" means, as some commentators think, "breaks out", it may refer to the emerging of the chrysalis and

1. *Introductory Papers on Dante*, pp. 30–31.
2. See W. W. Vernon, *Readings on the Paradiso*, II, p. 325, footnote. This interpretation was perhaps in the minds of those early commentators who understood "coverto" to mean "in its covering or shell".

the accompanying movement of the cocoon at that stage. If the verb, as seems likely, has some connotation of intricacy (cf. *imbroglio*), then what Dante may mean is: "sometimes a silkworm moves so much as it spins that ("broglia *sì* che") the cocoon moves in response, so that the eagerness of the creature is apparent". The "talvolta" would then convey that this does not always happen, only sometimes, and this would accord with the behaviour of silkworms.[1]

The use of the word "animal" for an insect offers no difficulty. Dante has already used it in that sense in Canto viii, ll. 52-4, where Charles Martel says:

> "La mia letizia mi ti tien celato
> che mi raggia dintorno, e mi nasconde
> quasi animal di sua seta fasciato." [2]

Here the soul is completely concealed. In Canto xxvi, the soul of Adam is concealed, but the quivering of the light which conceals it makes apparent the soul's eagerness to reply, just as an animal's movements inside a sack show its desire to get out? . . . or just as the trembling of a cocoon reveals the movement of the silkworm inside?[3]

1. I am indebted to Dr Charles Goodhart for details concerning the movements and visibility of silkworms, but he is no way responsible for the construction I have put upon them.

2. For translation, see p. 116. It is, in any case, an error, if a common one, to suppose that the word "animal" means only a mammal, as contrasted with fishes and insects. Anything alive that isn't a plant is an animal.

3. See also Canto v. 124-6, where the soul of Justinian is described as "nestling in its own light's core", an image not dissimilar from that conjured up by the more explicit simile used in Canto viii.

GLOSSARY OF PROPER NAMES

THIS list contains all the names of persons and places mentioned in the *Paradiso*, together with references to the *Inferno* and *Purgatorio* if they have already been mentioned there, with an indication of all the passages in which they occur. If sufficient information about them has already been given in the "Images" or "Notes", the relevant reference only is inserted; if not, a brief description or explanation is here included. All references are given by Canto and Line (not by page); if the actual name is not mentioned in Dante's text, the reference relates to the line which identifies the person or place in question. Names of actual inhabitants, or places forming part of the geography, of Dante's Three Kingdoms are shown in capital letters, thus: CACCIAGUIDA; PRIMUM MOBILE; names of persons and places which are merely referred to in the text or notes are shown in italic type, thus: *Leda*; *Catria*.

Where the English form of the name differs from the classical or Italian form, the form used in the English text is given first, followed by the original or more correct form in brackets, thus: GRATIAN (Franciscus Gratianus); *Caieta* (Gaeta).

For the Italian personages the main entry will be found sometimes under the Christian name and sometimes under the family name, according to which is the more familiar, or figures the more prominently in the poem; but a cross-reference is given in every case. Thus, information about CHARLES MARTEL will be found under CHARLES, with a cross-reference under MARTEL; but information about *Can Grande della Scala* will be found under *Scala, della*, with a cross-reference under *Can Grande*.

> N.B. Both here and in the notes, the myths and stories of antiquity are given as they were known in Dante's day, i.e. in versions that are frequently post-classical and, by modern standards of scholarship, garbled and debased. One god or hero is often confused with another who happened to have a similar name or attributes; the Greek legends in particular have, since the time of Homer, suffered many alterations and additions in passing through the hands of generation after generation of Greek and Latin story-tellers. Here and there a few of the more flagrant corruptions have been pointed out, but for the most part the tale is told as it was known to Dante.

Acone: village in Tuscany, the exact situation of which is now uncertain. (*Para.* XVI. 65 and *note*.)

ADAM: father of mankind. (*Inf.* III. 116; IV. 55; *Purg.* IX. 10; XI. 44; XXIX. 85; XXXII. 37 and see Images; XXXIII. 62 and *note* 61–3; *Para.* VII. 147; XIII. 37–9; XXVI. 79–142 and see Images; XXXII. 121–3, 130, 136.)

Adige: river of Italy. (*Inf.* XII. 5 and *note*; *Purg.* XVI. 115 and *note*; *Para.* IX. 44.)

Adimari, name of a powerful Florentine family. (*Para.* XVI. 115–20 and *note*.)

AENEAS: a Trojan prince, son of Anchises by the goddess Venus; the hero of Virgil's *Aeneid*. Troy having fallen, he escapes with his father, his young son Ascanius, and a number of his followers, his wife Creusa having been lost in the confusion. He is told by the Penates (household gods), whose images he has piously brought away with him, that his destiny is to settle in Italy. After many wanderings by sea, in the course of which Anchises dies, his fleet is wrecked by the spite of Juno, but Aeneas with seven of his ships is saved by Neptune and brought to the coast of Africa. Here the Trojans are hospitably received by Dido, queen of Carthage, who, breaking her oath of fidelity to her dead husband, Sychaeus, falls in love with Aeneas, and, when he again sails for Italy at the bidding of Mercury, kills herself. Aeneas lands in Sicily, celebrates the funeral games of Anchises, and leaves some of his followers to found a colony there. The rest sail on and visit Cumae; here, guided by the Sybil, Aeneas makes the descent into Hades, where he sees the punishment of the wicked and the placid after-life of the virtuous. Among the latter he meets Anchises and learns from him that he is destined to be the ancestor of the Roman people, who are to possess the empire of the world. (This is the famous Book VI of the *Aeneid*, from which Dante derived so much of the geography and machinery of his *Inferno*.) Aeneas then sails up the mouth of the Tiber and lands in Latium; here the fulfilment of an oracle shows that the Trojans have reached their destined goal. Latinus, the king of the country, welcomes Aeneas and offers him the hand of his daughter Lavinia, previously betrothed to Turnus, prince of the Rutuli. Juno, with the aid of the fury Alecto, stirs up war between the Trojans and the Latins, and after a number of engagements, in which allies are called in on both sides, the Rutulians are routed. Turnus challenges Aeneas to single combat; and Juno at length comes to an agreement with Jupiter that Aeneas shall be the victor, on condition that Latium shall keep its own name. Thus in Aeneas and Lavinia the Trojan and Latian lines are united and the way is open for the foundation of the city and Empire of Rome. (*Inf.* II. 32; IV. 122; XXVI. 93; *Purg.* XVIII. 137 and *note* 132–8; XXI. 97 (*Aeneid*); *Para.* VI. 3; XV. 27.)

Agapetus I (Agàbito, Agàpito): Pope, 535–6. He is mentioned by Justinian (*q.v.*), as having convinced him of the error of his heretical belief that there was but one nature in Christ. (*Para.* VI. 16 and *notes*, 14–16.)

AGOSTINO, Fra: see Austen.

Aguglione, Baldo d': see D'Aguglio, Baldo.

Ahasuerus: king of Persia, the story of whose marriage to the Jewess

Esther is told in the Bible (*Bk of Esther*); identical with *Xerxes* (*q.v.*).

Alagna: see Anagni.

Alba (Alba Longa): the most ancient town in Latium, built according to tradition by Ascanius, the son of Aeneas (*q.v.*). (*Para.* VI. 37–9 and *note.*)

Alberic (Alberichi): name of an ancient noble family of Florence mentioned by Cacciaguida (*q.v.*) as being already in decline in his day. (*Para.* XVI. 89.)

Albert I of Austria: emperor. (*Purg.* VI. 97 and *note*; *Para* XIX. 115–17 and *note.*)

ALBERT OF COLOGNE (Albertus Magnus): surnamed the "Universal Doctor" on account of his vast learning. His soul is pointed out to Dante as being among the great theologians and others who loved wisdom and truth. (*Para.* X. 98 and *note.*)

Alcides: see Hercules.

Alcmaeon: son of Amphiaräus. (*Purg.* XII. 50 and *note*, 49–51; *Para.* IV. 103 and *note.*)

Alderotti, Thaddeus: celebrated physician of the latter half of the thirteenth century, reputed to have founded the scientific school of medicine at the University of Bologna. Dante seems to have taken rather a severe view of him for he cites him as an instance of the self-seeker. (*Para.* XII. 84 and *note*, 82–5.)

ALIGHIERI, DANTE: see DANTE ALIGHIERI.

Alighiero: the son of Cacciaguida (*q.v.*) and great-grandfather of Dante. (*Para.* XV. 91–6 and *note*; see also Genealogical Table, Alighieri.)

Alvernia, Mt: mountain in the Casentino, east of Florence. (*Para.* XI. 106–7 and *note.*)

Amidei: noble Florentine family; their murder of Buondelmonte de' Buondelmonti (*q.v.*), who had jilted a lady of their house, caused the Guelf-Ghibelline split in Florence. (*Para.* XVI. 136–9 and *note.*)

Amyclas: a poor fisherman to whom Julius Caesar went secretly one night asking to be ferried across the Adriatic. (*Para.* XI. 69 and *note.*)

Ananias: "the disciple at Damascus", who healed St Paul's blindness by laying his hands upon him (*Acts* IX. 10–18). (*Para.* XXVI. 12 and *note.*)

Anchises: father of Aeneas (*q.v.*). (*Inf.* I. 74; *Purg.* XVIII. 137; *Para.* XV. 25–7 and *note*; XIX. 130–31 and *note.*)

ANGELS: the lowest Order in the Celestial Hierarchies, ranking last in the third Hierarchy; they preside over the Heaven of the Moon. (*Para.* XXVIII. 126 and *notes* to 72–139.)

ANNE (ANNA) ST: mother of the Virgin. (*Para.* XXXII. 133–5.)

ANSELM, Archbishop of Canterbury: author of the famous treatise on the Atonement, "Cur Deus Homo", he is placed among the doctors of the Church in the Heaven of the Sun, where he is pointed out to Dante by St Bonaventure (*q.v.*). (*Para.* XII. 137 and *note.*)

Antandros: city of Great Mysia, on the Adramyttian Gulf, at the foot of

Glossary

Mt Ida. The Emperor Justinian (*q.v.*) mentions it, together with the Simois (*q.v.*) and the tomb of Hector, to indicate the Troad, the region whence the Eagle first arose (i.e. whence Aeneas sailed for Italy after the fall of Troy) and to which it returned (in the person of Julius Caesar after the Battle of Pharsalia). (*Para.* VI. 67 and *note*, 67–72.)

Anthony, St: the Egyptian hermit (251–356 A.D.) (*Para.* XXIX. 124 and *note*.)

Apollo: son of Jupiter and Latona, who gave birth to him and his twin sister Diana on the island of Delos. Apollo was the god of song and the leader of the Muses (*q.v.*); hence Dante invokes his aid at the beginning of his most daring and arduous enterprise (*Para.* I. 13 *sqq.* cf. II. 8). As Apollo was the god of the Sun and Diana the goddess of the Moon, Dante speaks of them together as "the twin eyes of heaven" (*Purg.* XX. 132), and of the Sun and Moon as "the two children of Latona" (*Para.* XXIX. 1). Apollo was also known as the Delphic god, from his temple and oracle at Delphi (*Para.* I. 32; XIII. 25 and *note*; cf. *Purg.* XII. 31 and *note*.)

Aquasparta (Acquasparta): see Matteo d'Acquasparta.

AQUINAS, ST THOMAS (Tommaso d'Aquino, 1225 or 7–1274): the greatest of the scholastic theologians, the "Common Doctor" of the Church, whose great work in systematizing Christian Doctrine according to Aristotelian philosophic method dominated the thought of the Middle Ages, and is still officially accepted as fundamental to the exposition of Catholic theology.

Born at Rocca Secca in Campania, the son of the count of Aquino; entered the Dominican Order at the age of 17; studied under St Albertus Magnus of Cologne (*q.v.*); debated in Paris, 1245; taught in Cologne, 1248; Doctor of Theology (Sorbonne), 1257; lectured in Paris, Rome, Bologna, etc.; wrote exhaustive commentaries on the works of Aristotle, and many theological works, including the *Summa contra Gentiles* (dealing with the principles of natural religion) and the monumental *Summa Theologica* – usually referred to briefly as the *Summa* – a complete systematization of Christian theology; died at Fossa Nuova, near Terracina, on the way to attend the Council of Lyons in 1274; canonized, 1323 (two years after Dante's death).

The work of St Thomas in "baptizing" secular philosophy into the Christian faith, and so reconciling reason with revelation, was of incalculable value, especially at that period, when the rediscovery of classical learning and literature was threatening to disturb people's minds by the apparent dilemma of having to choose between the two. St Thomas maintained and demonstrated that the knowledge that God exists could be arrived at by the use of reason, and that revelation, although transcending reason, at no time contradicted it.

Dante studied the works of St Thomas closely, and the theological structure of the *Comedy* owes more to him than to any other single theologian, although the poet supplemented his teaching by that of many other authorities, and did not hesitate to differ from him, now and again, in points of detail. References to relevant passages from St Thomas will be found from time to time in the *notes*.

Dante places St Thomas in Paradise, in the Heaven of the Sun, among the Doctors of the Church. (*Para.* x–xiii; *notes, passim*; cf. *Purg.* xx. 69 and *note*.)

Arca Dell': name of an ancient noble family of Florence. (*Para.* xvi. 92.)

ARCHANGELS: the lowest Order but one in the Celestial Hierarchies, ranking next above the Angels (*q.v.*); they preside over the Heaven of Mercury. Beatrice mentions them as forming, together with Principalities (*q.v.*) and Angels, the third Celestial Hierarchy. (*Para.* xxviii. 124–6 and *notes* 72–139.)

Ardinghi: ancient noble Florentine family, mentioned by Cacciaguida (*q.v.*) as among the great families existing in his day. (*Para.* xvi. 93.)

Argo: the ship Argo, built by Argus, son of Phrixus, in which the Argonauts sailed to Colchis in search of the Golden Fleece (see also Jason). (*Para.* xxxiii. 96 and *note*; cf. *Inf.* xxviii. 84 and *note*.)

Ariadne: daughter of Minos and Pasiphaë. When deserted by Theseus, whom she had helped to slay the Minotaur, she was found on the island of Naxos by Bacchus, who made her his wife. On her death, she was placed among the stars as the constellation known as Ariadne's Crown (Corona Borealis), the symbol of the garland she had worn at her marriage. (*Inf.* xii. 19–20; *Para.* xiii. 14–15 and *note*.)

ARISTOTLE: the great Athenian philosopher, founder of the Peripatetic School (384–322 B.C.). He was Plato's most brilliant pupil, but later diverged considerably from his master's teaching. His works were rediscovered and translated in the Middle Ages (largely through the work of Arabian scholars), and became enormously influential. The work of St Thomas Aquinas (see AQUINAS) incorporated the Aristotelian system of philosophy into Catholic theology. All Western philosophy derives ultimately from the twin Platonic and Aristotelian traditions.

The works of Aristotle were voluminous, and covered every branch of learning known in his day: Dialectics and Logic (the *Organon*); Philosophy (the *Physics* and other works on natural science; the *Metaphysics*; two treatises on *Mathematics*): Politics (the *Ethics*, the *Politics*, the *Economics*); Art (the *Poetics*, the *Rhetoric*). Only the major works are mentioned in this list, but there are many others.

For Aristotle, human thought proceeds by abstraction from the data provided by the senses; i.e. investigation into the nature of being starts from the observation of individual things sensibly existing. It is in this feature that his philosophy contrasts most forcibly with the Platonic idealism, for which (especially in its later developments) the world of existence is only the shadow of the world of essences. Aristotle analyses the individual existent into Matter (undifferentiated "stuff") and Form (structural organization), and the process by which a thing comes to attain its proper end (to be what it was intended to be) into the passage from Potentiality to Actuality. Neither Form nor Matter has any real existence by itself – every individual existent being a Form-Matter complex. The soul of the individual man is the "form" of the human body, both soul and body being thus considered as essential parts of the actualized personality. It is obvious that this concept lends itself readily to incorporation into orthodox Christian doctrine (e.g. of the sanctity of the material universe, sacramentalism, and the resurrection of the body) as opposed to the Gnostic doctrines of the inherent evil of matter derived from the Neo-Platonists. God is "the unmoved Mover", source of all change, motion and process – a definition which has left its mark on Thomist theology. Dante was well acquainted with all the works of Aristotle that were available in Latin in his time, and refers to them many times. (*Inf.* IV. 131; VI. 106; (*Ethics*) XI. 80; (*Physics*) XI. 101; *Purg.* III. 43; God as the unmoved Mover, *Para.* XXIV. 130–34 and *note*; XXVI. 37–8 and *note*.)

Arius: presbyter of Alexandria (d. A.D. 336), the originator of the Arian heresy that the Father and the Son were not "one substance", a doctrine which was condemned by the Council of Nicaea in 325. (*Para.* XIII. 127 and *note*.)

Arno: river of Italy. (*Inf.* XIII. 146; XV. 113; XXIII. 95; XXX. 65; XXXIII. 83; *Purg.* V. 126; XIV. 16; XIV. 24 and *note*; *Para.* XI. 107.)

Arrio: see Arius.

Arrigucci: name of an ancient noble family of Florence. (*Para* XVI. 107–8 and *note*.)

Assisi (Ascesi): town in Umbria, birthplace of St Francis (*q.v.*). (*Para.* XI. 43–54 and *note*.)

Athens: city of Greece. (*Purg.* XVIII. 92 and *note*; *Para.* XVII. 47 and *note*.)

Augustine, St: Father of the Latin Church (A.D. 354–430) (*Para.* X. 120 and *note*; XXXII. 35.)

Augustus, Caesar: see Caesar Augustus.

Ausonian Horn (Ausonia): the Southern part of Italy, of which the curve was thought to resemble a horn. (*Para.* VIII. 61 and *note*.)

AUSTEN (Fra Agostino): one of the earliest followers of St Francis (*q.v.*), whom he joined in 1210. In 1216 he became head of the Franciscan Order in Terra di Lavoro. (*Para.* XII. 130 and *note*.)

Avellana, Fonte: Benedictine hermitage on north-eastern slope of Mt Catria (*Para.* XXI, *note to* ll. 109–110).

Babylon: city in Egypt, symbol of terrestrial life or exile from the celestial. (*Para.* XXIII. 134; cf. *Inf.* Glossary under Babel.)

Bacchus: in Greek mythology, god of wine. (*Inf.* XX. 59; *Para.* XIII. 25; cf. Ariadne.)

Bagnoreggio: (now Bagnorea), village in Tuscany, birthplace of St Bonaventura (*q.v.*).

Bari: town of S. Italy in Apulia on the Adriatic coast; mentioned by

Charles Martel (*q.v.*) as one of the extreme points of the Kingdom of Naples. (*Para.* VIII. 62.)

Bartolomei, Enrico: see Henry of Susa.

Bartomeo della Scala: see Scala, Bartolommeo della.

Barucci: name of an ancient Ghibelline family of Florence. (*Para.* XVI. 104 and *note*.)

Bears: the constellations of the Great Bear (also called Ursa Major, the Plough or the Wain) and of the Little Bear (Ursa Minor, Arcas or Boötes), which contains the Pole star. (*Inf.* XI. 114; *Purg.* I. 26; IV. 65; XXX. 1 and *note*; *Para.* II. 9; XIII. 7–9 and *note*; XXXI. 32–3 and *note*.)

BEATRICE: daughter of Folco Portinari, born in Florence 1266. In the *Vita Nuova* (*New Life*) Dante says that he first saw and fell in love with her when she was 8 years and 4 months old and he was nearly 9. She was married to Simone dei Bardi, and died in 1290. See *Inf.* Introd. pp. 26 *sqq.* and The Greater Images, p. 67; *Purg.* Introd. pp. 25 *sqq.*; *Para.* Introd. pp. 49 *sqq.* and *notes passim*.

BEDE: the Venerable Bede, Anglo-Saxon monk and celebrated historian. (*Para.* X. 131 and *note*.)

Belisarius: famous general of the Emperor Justinian (*q.v.*) who overthrew the Vandal kingdom in Africa and reconquered Italy from the Goths (A.D. 505–65). (*Para.* VI. 25 and *note*.)

Bella, Della: one of the Florentine families which received knighthood from the Marquis Hugh of Brandenburg (*Para.* XVI. 127–32 and *note*).

Bellincion Berti: a Florentine of the ancient Ravignani family, father of the "good Gualdrada" (*Inf.* XVI. 37). (*Para.* XV. 112–3 and *note*.)

Belus: King of Tyre, father of Dido (*q.v.*).

BENEDICT, ST: founder of the Benedictine Order and of the monastery of Monte Cassino. (*Para.* XXII. 28–99 and *note*; beheld by Dante in glory, in bodily form, in accordance with his promise, XXXII. 35.)

Berengar, Raymond: Count of Provence. (*Para.* VI. 134 and *note*, 128; see also *Images*, under Romèo.)

BERNARD, ST, of Clairvaux: This famous Abbot of the Benedictine Order was born of noble parents in the village of Fontaines, near Dijon, in Burgundy, in 1091. At the age of 24 he was selected to be the head of a branch of the monastery of Cîteaux, and, setting out with a small band of devoted followers, he chose a site in the diocese of Langres in Champagne, where he made a clearing and founded his famous abbey of Clairvaux. His influence grew; in 1130, after the death of Pope Honorius II, he secured the triumph of Innocent II over his rival Anacletus; and in 1140, at the Council of Sens, he was influential in the condemnation of Peter Abelard for heresy. In 1144, after the capture of Edessa by the infidels, he preached a new Crusade (the disastrous Second Crusade, 1147–49), the failure of which was a blow from which St Bernard never recovered. A few years after his death (1153), he was canonized by Pope Alexander III. Among those who fell in the Second Crusade was Dante's great-great-grandfather, Cacciaguida (*q.v.*).

St Bernard's writings consist of epistles, sermons, and theological treatises, most of which are characterized by an ardent devotion to the Virgin Mary, especially his Homilies on the Annunciation and on the Praises of the Virgin. In *Paradise* he is the symbol of contemplation whereby man attains the vision of the Deity. It is he who replaces Beatrice when she returns to her place among the blessed in the Celestial Rose and who points out to Dante the principal saints, explains the arrangement of the thrones of the Elect and solves his doubts as to the salvation of infants. In the final canto, St Bernard offers up to the Virgin on Dante's behalf the famous prayer (adapted by Chaucer in the *Seconde Nonnes Tale*, vv. 29–56), imploring her intercession that Dante may attain the vision of God and that she will henceforth have him in her keeping. At the end of his prayer, St Bernard signs to Dante to look upwards (as he was already doing), and Dante beholds God. (*Para.* XXXI. 51 *sqq.*; XXXII, XXXIII *passim*; see also *notes* and *Images.*)

Bernard of Quintavalle: the first follower of St Francis (*q.v.*). (*Para.* XI. 79–81 and *note.*)

Bernardone, Peter: father of St Francis (*q.v.*). (*Para.* XI. 62, 89.)

BOETHIUS: Roman statesman and philosopher, born at Rome about A.D. 475, died at Pavia 525. From a position of honour and influence, he fell into disfavour with Theodoric, King of the Ostrogoths, who suspected him of plotting against him. He was imprisoned at Pavia and finally put to death by torture. During his imprisonment, he wrote his most celebrated work, *De Consolatione Philosophiae* (*On the Consolation of Philosophy*), a work which was well known to Dante. (*Para.* X. 124–9 and *note.*)

BONAVENTURA, ST: General of the Franciscan Order and Bishop of Albano. He was born (in 1221, at Bagnoreggio, now Bagnorea) as Giovanni Fidanza, but on being miraculously cured as a child from a dangerous illness his name was changed to "Bonaventura" ("happy chance", or "good fortune"). (*Para.* XII. 28–145 and *note.*)

Boniface VIII: Pope (Benedict Caietan) (*c.* 1217–1303); Pope, 1294–1303 (see *Inf.* Introd. pp. 34 *sqq.*) (*Inf.* XV. 112; XIX. 53 and *note*; XXVII. 70, 85; *Purg.* XX. 87 and *note* 85–7; *Para.* IX. 126; XII. 88–9; XXVII. 19–27; XXX. 148 and *note.*)

Boreas: the North Wind. (*Para.* XXVIII. 80–81 and *note.*)

Bostichi: name of an ancient noble Florentine family, mentioned by Cacciaguida (*q.v.*) as having been prominent in his day. They are said to have been Guelfs and to have fled with the rest of the party from Florence after the Battle of Montaperti in 1260. (*Para.* XVI. 93.)

Bougia (Bougie): city on the coast of Africa. (*Para.* IX. 92 and *note.*)

Brennus: leader of the Senonian Gauls who in 390 B.C. besieged the Capitol. (*Para.* VI. 44 and *note.*)

Glossary

Brenta: river of Italy. (*Inf.* XV. 7; *Para.* IX. 127.)

BRUTUS: Marcus Junius (85–42 B.C.), son of M. Brutus the Tribune and Servilia, half-sister of Cato of Utica. Trained by his uncle Cato in the principles of the aristocratic party, when the Civil War broke out in 49 B.C., he joined Pompey, although the latter had put his father to death. After the Battle of Pharsalia in 48 B.C., Julius Caesar not only pardoned him but raised him to high favour, making him governor of Cisalpine Gaul (46 B.C.) and praetor (44 B.C.) and promising him the governorship of Macedonia. Under the persuasion, however, of Cassius (*q.v.*), he took part in the conspiracy to murder Caesar in the hope of re-establishing the Republic (Ides of March, 44 B.C.). After Caesar's death, he took possession of Macedonia, and was joined by Cassius, who commanded Syria. In 42 B.C. their united forces were defeated by Octavian (afterwards Augustus) Caesar and Mark Antony at the Battle of Philippi, and Brutus committed suicide. (*Inf.* XXXIV. 65; *Para.* VI. 74.)

Bryson: Greek philosopher. (*Para.* XIII. 124 and *note*.)

Buondelmonti: the leaders of the Guelf party in Florence. Originally residing in the castle of Montebuono in the Valdigreve near Florence, they transferred to Florence in 1135 when their castle was destroyed. (*Para.* XVI. 66 and *note*; 135 and *note*.)

Buondelmonti, Buondelmonte de': a member of the aforesaid family who was murdered by the Amidei (*q.v.*) in revenge for an insult to their family. The murder gave rise to a feud between the partisans of both families, whence arose the Guelf and Ghibelline factions in Florence. (*Para.* XVI. 139–47 and *note*.)

CACCIAGUIDA: great-great-grandfather of Dante. Nothing is known of his life apart from what Dante hears in the Heaven of Mars, although his existence is attested by a document which refers to his two sons. He was born in Florence in the Sesto di Porta San Piero about the year 1090. He was baptized in the Baptistery of San Giovanni in Florence, where Dante himself was baptized (cf. *Inf.* XIX. 17 and *note*) and hoped to receive the poet's crown of laurel (cf. *Para.* XXV. 1–9). He had two brothers, Moronto and Eliseo; his wife came from the valley of the Po and from her the name of Alighieri descended (cf. Genealogical Table, Alighieri). He followed the Emperor Conrad III on the Second Crusade (which had been preached by St Bernard of Clairvaux, *q.v.*) and was knighted by him. He died in battle against the Infidel about the year 1147. (*Para.* XV, XVI, XVII. *passim*; see also *Images*, XV.)

Cadiz: sea-port on the south-west coast of Spain, regarded in Dante's time as the western limit of the habitable globe, the mouth of the Ganges being the eastern limit. (*Para.* XXVII. 82 and *note*.)

CAESAR: (1) Caius Julius, Dictator of Rome (100–44 B.C.). The son of C. Julius Caesar the praetor, he liked to claim descent from the Trojan hero Aeneas (*q.v.*), founder of Rome. A brilliant general and strong adherent to the democratic party, he was made Consul, 59 B.C.; his conquest of Gaul (59–51 B.C.) made him the idol of the people and the army. His rival, Pompey (*q.v.*), jealous of his rising power, joined the aristocratic party and headed an armed opposition against him; but Julius, crossing the river Rubicon which separated his own province from Italy, marched upon Rome, and being everywhere received with acclamation, made himself master of all Italy (49 B.C.). After defeating Pompey's adherents in Spain, he crossed over into Greece and decisively overthrew Pompey at the Battle of Pharsalia (48 B.C.). He was made Dictator and, after a period of further military triumphs, was offered the kingship; this, however, he reluctantly refused, for fear of offending the people. On the Ides of March, 44 B.C., he was assassinated in the Capitol by a band of conspirators, led by Brutus and Cassius (*q.v.*). His successor, Augustus (*q.v.*, below), was the first Roman Emperor, and the name Caesar became part of the Imperial title. (*Inf.* I. 70; IV. 123; XXVIII. 97; see also *Images* to XXXI; *Purg.* XVIII. 101 and *note*, 100–103; *Para.* VI. 57–72 and *notes. passim*; XI. 67–9 and *note*.)

(2) Caesar Augustus (Caius Julius Caesar Octavianus): First Roman Emperor (63 B.C.–A.D. 14). He was the great-nephew of Julius Caesar and adopted by him as his heir. After the assassination of Julius, he assumed the name of Caesar, and became, with Lepidus and Mark Antony, one of the triumvirs who took over the government of the Republic. He gradually gathered all the great offices of state into his own hands; in 32 B.C. he accepted the title of Imperator. The defeat of Antony at Actium (31 B.C.) and the death of Lepidus (12 B.C.) left him in fact and in name sole master of the Roman Empire. The epithet "Augustus", conferred on him by the Senate in 27 B.C., was borne by his successors as part of the Imperial title. The "Augustan Age" was marked by a brilliant flowering of Latin literary genius. (*Purg.* VII. 6; XXIX. 116 and *note* 115–16; *Para.* VI. 73–81 and *notes*.)

(3) Caesar, the Third (Tiberius Claudius Nero): adopted son and successor of Augustus, Roman Emperor (A.D. 14–37). Dante, regarding Julius Caesar as the first Emperor, speaks of Tiberius as the third Caesar. (*Para.* VI. 82–90 and *note*, 87.)

Cagnano: river of Italy. (*Para.* IX. 49.)

Caieta (Gaeta): town in southern Italy in the north of Campania, situated on a promontory at the head of the Gulf of Gaeta. (*Inf.* XXVI. 92 and *note*; *Para.* VIII. 62.)

Cain (with Thornbush, the Man in the Moon): (*Inf.* XX. 124 and *note*; *Para.* II. 49–51 and *note*.)

Calahorra: city of Castile. (*Para.* XII. 52 and *note*.)

Calfucci: name of an ancient noble family of Florence. (*Para.* XVI. 106 and *note*.)

Calixtus I: Bishop of Rome (217–22). (*Para.* XXVII. 43–5.)

Glossary

Campi: village near Florence. (*Para.* XVI. 51 and *note*.)

Can Grande della Scala: see Scala, della, Can Grande.

Caponsacco: member of an ancient noble family of Florence. (*Para.* XVI. 121–2 and *note*.)

Casale (Casal): town in Piedmont. (*Para.* XII. 125 and *note*.)

Cassino: the monastery of Monte Cassino, founded by St Benedict (*q.v.*) in the year 529, situated in the north of Campania, a few miles from Aquino. When St Benedict first visited the spot it was the centre of pagan worship, with a temple of Apollo and a grove sacred to Venus, both of which he destroyed. (*Para.* XXII. 37–42 and *note*.)

CASSIUS: (Caius Cassius Longinus): Roman statesman and general. After distinguishing himself as a soldier in the campaign against the Parthians (53–51 B.C.) he returned to Rome. In 49 B.C. he was tribune of the plebs, but when the civil war broke out, he joined the aristocratic party and fled from Rome with Pompey, whose fleet he commanded in 48 B.C. After the Battle of Pharsalia he went to the Hellespont and, accidentally falling in with Julius Caesar, surrendered to him. Caesar not only pardoned him but made him praetor and promised him the governorship of Syria. Cassius, however, repaid his generosity by heading a conspiracy to murder Caesar, and persuading M. Brutus (*q.v.*) to join it. After Caesar's death (Ides of March, 44 B.C.) he claimed the governorship of Syria according to Caesar's promise, although the Senate had given it to Dolabella. He defeated Dolabella and, after plundering Syria and Asia, joined Brutus in Macedonia in opposition to Octavian (Augustus) Caesar and Mark Antony. At the Battle of Philippi (42 B.C.) Cassius was defeated by Antony and took his own life. (*Inf.* XXXIV. 67; *Para.* VI. 74.)

Catellini: name of an ancient noble family of Florence mentioned by Cacciaguida (*q.v.*) as being already in decline in his day. (*Para.* XVI. 88.)

Catona: town in Calabria, a few miles north of Reggio, mentioned by Charles Martel (*q.v.*) to indicate the southern limit of the Kingdom of Naples. (*Para.* VIII. 62.)

Catria: one of the highest peaks of the Apennines, on the borders of Umbria and the Marches. (*Para.* XXI. 109–10 and *note*.)

Cerchi: name of a wealthy Florentine family of low origin who came from Acone (*q.v.*). When Florence was split into Guelf and Ghibelline factions (1215), the Cerchi sided with the former; when the Guelf party itself was split into Bianchi (Whites) and Neri (Blacks), the Cerchi, who by this time had become very wealthy and powerful through commerce, became the leaders of the Whites. (*Para.* XVI. 65.)

Certaldo: village in Tuscany, on the road between Florence and Siena. (*Para.* XVI. 51 and *note*.)

CHARLEMAGNE: emperor of the West (742–814), son of Pepin le Bref, King of the Franks; received the Imperial Crown from Pope Leo III, Christmas Day, 800. As a defender of the Christian faith in wars against heretics and Saracens, he was canonized in 1165. Dante places

him in Mars, the Heaven of the Warriors. His wars and his Twelve
Peers, of whom his nephew Roland (*q.v.*) and Roland's friend, Oliver,
are the best known, became legendary and were celebrated in the
early *chansons de geste* and many later epics. (*Inf.* XXI. 16; *Para.* VI. 95;
XVIII. 43 and *note*.)

CHARLES I OF ANJOU (1220–85): King of Naples and Sicily, count of
Anjou and Provence, son of Louis VIII of France and Blanche of
Castile. Invited by Pope Urban IV to assume the crown of Naples,
and urged by Pope Clement IV to take possession of the kingdom, he
entered Italy in 1265, was crowned King of Sicily and Apulia and
defeated Manfred at Benevento. The Sicilians, revolting against
French rule, invited Conradin (son of the Emperor Conrad IV) to
expel him. He defeated Conradin at Tagliacozzo in 1268, but in 1282
the Sicilian "underground movement" (surreptitiously aided, as was
believed, by Pope Nicholas III and others) broke out into open in-
surrection, ending in a fearful massacre of the French (the "Sicilian
Vespers") and the end of their rule in Sicily. Charles died in 1284
while trying to regain the kingdom. (*Inf.* XIX. 99 and *note*; see also
Inf. Introd. p. 25; *Purg.* VII. 109: XI. 137; XX. 67 and *note*; *Para.* VIII.
72 and *note*.)

Charles (Carlo) II: king of Naples, count of Anjou and Provence (1243–
1309); son of Charles I of Anjou and Beatrix of Provence. (*Purg.* V.
69; XX. 79 and *note*; *Para.* VI. 106 and *note*; XIX. 127–9 and *note*.)

CHARLES MARTEL: titular King of Hungary, grandson of Charles I of
Anjou and son of Charles II and of Mary, daughter of Stephen IV of
Hungary. (*Para.* VIII. 31–148 and *notes passim*; IX. 1–9 and *note*;
see also *Images* to VIII.)

CHERUBIM: the highest Order but one in the Celestial Hierarchies, rank-
ing next after the Seraphim (*q.v.*); they preside over the Eighth
Heaven (Heaven of the Fixed Stars). In the *Inferno* (XXVII. 114), Guido
da Montefeltro relates that he was carried off to Hell by one of the
black Cherubim and thrust into the 8th bolgia of the 8th Circle. From
this it would appear that Dante conceived of the fallen members of
the angelic Orders as presiding over circles of Hell corresponding
numerically to those ruled by their heavenly counterparts. (*Para.*
XXVIII. 98–9 and *note*, 133–5; see also under *Images* to this canto.)

Chiana: river in Tuscany. (*Inf.* XXIX. 47; *Para.* XIII. 24 and *note*.)

Chiarmontesi: name of an ancient noble family of Florence, referred to
by Cacciaguida (*q.v.*), of whom a member was guilty of fraud while
holding office as overseer of the salt-customs. (*Purg.* XII. 105 and
note; *Para.* XVI. 105 and *note*.)

Chiusi (Clusium): one of the twelve ancient Etruscan cities. (*Para.* XVI.
74 and *note*.)

CHRIST: The name of Christ is mentioned thirty-nine times in the
Comedy, five times in *Purgatory* and thirty-four times in *Paradise*. (It is
not once mentioned in *Inferno*, though He is referred to there by vari-

ous periphrases; cf. *Inf.* Glossary, under Christ.) When the name of Christ occurs at the end of a line, Dante does not rhyme with it, but repeats the name itself. There are four instances of this in *Paradise*: XII. 71, 73, 75; XIV. 104, 106, 108; XIX. 104, 106, 108; XXXII. 83, 85, 87. The other twenty-two mentions of His name in *Paradise* occur in the following: VI. 14; IX. 120; XI. 72, 102, 107; XII. 37; XVII. 51; XIX. 72; XX. 47; XXIII. 20, 72; XXV. 15; XXVI. 53; XXVII. 40; XXIX. 98, 109; XXXI. 3, 107; XXXII. 20, 24, 27, 125.

Other references: (1) as the Son of God: X. 1; VII. 119. (2) as the Son of God and Mary: XXIII. 136-7. (3) as the Son of Mary: XXIII. 108, 120. (4) as the Lamb of God: XVII. 33. (5) as the Blessed Lamb: XXIV. 2. (6) as our Lord: XXIV. 35; XXXI. 107. (7) as our Emperor: XXV. 41. (8) as the Redeemer: xiii. 40-42. (9) as the Bridegroom of Poverty: XI. 31-3, 64, 70-72. (10) as the Bridegroom of the Church: XII. 43. (11) as the Bridegroom: iii. 101; xxv. 24. (12) as the Word: VII. 30; XXII. 40-42; XXIII. 73. (13) as Wisdom: XXII. 37. (14) as Power: XXIII. 37; XXVII. 36. (15) as Light: XIII. 55; XXIII. 28-33; XXXIII. 119, 125. (16) as the true God: XXXI. 107. (17) as our Bliss: XIII. 111. (18) as He who lightens every wrong: XVIII. 6. (19) as He that hath the saving power: XX. 114. (20) as the Sun: XXIII. 28, 72. (21) as our Hope: XXIII. 105. (22) as our Pelican: XXV. 113.

Christ's twofold nature as God and Man is referred to in *Para.* II. 41-2; VI. 13-21; VII. 35-6; XIII. 26-7; XXIII. 136; XXXIII. 4-6. As the Second Person of the Trinity, He is referred to in *Para.* VII. 30; X. 1, 51; XXIII. 136-7; XXVII. 24; XXXII. 113 *sqq.*

CHRYSOSTOM, St John: Greek father of the Church (*c.* 344-407). (*Para.* XII. 137 and *note*.)

Cianghella: a Florentine woman of ill repute. (*Para.* XV. 127 and *note*.)

Cincinnatus (Lucius Quintius Cincinnatus): Dictator of Rome (458 B.C.). He was the Roman model of frugality and integrity. Living modestly on his farm, which he cultivated himself, he was called from the plough to assume the dictatorship in order to deliver the Roman army from the Aequians. When he accomplished this task, having held the dictatorship for only sixteen days, he returned to his plough. He was appointed dictator a second time in 439, when he was over eighty. (*Para.* XV. 129.)

Cirrha: town in Phocis, about 15 miles south-west of Delphi, where Apollo (*q.v.*) had his temple and oracle. The name was also applied to one of the peaks of Mt Parnassus (*q.v.*). (*Para.* I. 35-6 and *note*.)

Clemence, daughter of the Emperor Rudolph and widow of Charles Martel (*q.v.*). Some commentators understand the reference to be to her daughter, also named Clemence. (*Para.* IX. 1 and *note*.)

Clement V (Bertrand de Goth): Pope, 1305-14. It was he who, under pressure from Philip the Fair, transferred the Holy See to Avignon, where it remained from 1309 to 1377 (*Inf.* XIX. 83 and *note*; *Para.* XVII. 82-3; XXVII. 58-9 and *note*; XXX. 142-8 and *notes*.)

Glossary

Cleopatra: queen of Egypt (68–30 B.C.): mistress of (a) Julius Caesar (*q.v.*), (b) Mark Antony. When Antony's defeat by Octavius (Augustus) Caesar (*q.v.*) was followed by his suicide, she killed herself by the bite of an asp. (*Inf.* V. 63; *Para.* VI. 76.)

Cletus (Anacletus): Bishop of Rome of the first century (76 or 78 to 88 or 90). (*Para.* XXVII. 40 and *note.*)

Clymenë: mother of Phaëthon by Apollo. (*Para.* XVII. 2 and *note.*)

Colchis: country of Asia Minor, famous as the land to which Jason (*q.v.*) and the Argonauts sailed in search of the Golden Fleece. (*Para.* II. 16.)

Conrad III (1138–1152): Emperor, the first of the Hohenstaufen. In 1147, in company with Louis VII of France, he led the Second Crusade. Among his followers was Dante's great-great-grandfather, Cacciaguida (*q.v.*) who was knighted by him. (*Para.* XV. 139–44; see also under *Images* to this canto.)

CONSTANCE: Empress, mother of Frederick II. (*Purg.* III. 112 and *note*; *Para.* III. 109–120 and *notes*; IV. 97–8.)

CONSTANTINE THE GREAT: Emperor of Rome (A.D. 272–337; Emperor, 306), son of the Emperor Constantius Chlorus. During his campaign against Maxentius, in 1312, he is said to have seen a shining cross in the heavens, with the words "In hoc signo vinces" – "in this sign thou shalt conquer." He defeated Maxentius near Rome, embraced Christianity, and so became the first Christian Emperor. Later, he transferred the seat of Empire from Rome to Byzantium. It was Constantine who convened the great Council of Nicaea, which gave its name to the Nicene Creed. For the legend of the "Donation of Constantine" see *note* to *Inferno* XIX. 115. Dante places Constantine in the Heaven of Jupiter, among the spirits of the Just. (*Para.* XX. 55–7 and *note*; reference to his transfer of the seat of Empire from west to east is made by Justinian, *q.v.*, VI. 1–3 and *note*; cf. *Inf.* XXVII. 94 and note.)

CORNELIA: daughter of Scipio Africanus the Elder; wife of Tiberius Sempronius Gracchus (*fl.* 169 B.C.) and mother of the two famous Tribunes, Tiberius and Caius. She is celebrated as a model Roman matron of the old school, who brought up her sons in the utmost rectitude; after her death, the people of Rome erected a statue to her, inscribed: "The Mother of the Gracchi". (*Inf.* IV. 128; *Para.* XV. 129.)

Corso Donati: brother of Forese Donati, Florentine leader of the "Black" party. (*Purg.* XXIV. 82 and *note*; *Para.* XVII. 50–51 and *note.*)

Costanza: see Constance.

Creusa: daughter of Priam and Hecuba, wife of Aeneas, *q.v.* (*Para.* IX. 98 and *note.*)

Croatia: country south-west of Hungary, between the river Save and the Adriatic. Mentioned by Dante as a remote region of the Empire. (*Para.* XXXI. 103.)

CUNIZZA: sister of Ezzelino (Azzolino) da Romano (cf. *Inf.* XII. 109; XIII. 115 and *note*). (*Para.* IX. 13–66 and *notes*; see also under *Images* to this canto.)

Cupid: god of love, son of Venus. (*Purg.* XXVIII. 65 and *note*; *Para.* VIII. 7–9.)

Cyprian: epithet of Venus, goddess of love, the planet Venus (*q.v.*). (*Para.* VIII. 1–3.)

Daedalus: the cunning artificer who, in classical legend, lived in Crete and made the image of a heifer for Pasiphaë, the labyrinth in which Minos kept the Minotaur, and wings for himself and his son Icarus. (*Inf.* XII. 13 and *note*; XVII. 109 and *note*; XXIX. 116; *Para.* VIII. 125.)

D'Aguglio, Baldo: a lawyer who in 1320 deserted from the White to the Black Guelfs. (*Para.* XVI. 55–6 and *note*.)

DAMIAN, PETER: see Peter Damian.

Daniel: prophet of the Jews. (*Purg.* XXII. 146 and *note* to 140–54. *Book of Daniel*: *Para.* IV. 13 and *note*; XXIX. 133–5 and *note*.)

DANTE ALIGHIERI: poet. Born in Florence in Tuscany, May–June 1265, son of Alighiero Alighieri, and his first wife Bella (family name uncertain). Baptized at Church of San Giovanni Battista (St John Baptist).

First meeting with Beatrice Portinari (*q.v.*), May 1274. Fought on the Guelf side at Campaldino, 11 June 1289. Enrolled in Apothecaries' Guild, 1295 or 1296. Spoke in Consiglio dei Cento, 1296. Ambassador to San Gimignano, 1299.

Married, not later than 1298, Gemma Donati, by whom he had issue: Pietro, Jacopo, Giovanni (?), Antonia (?), Beatrice.

Elected to priorate to serve 15 June to 15 August 1300. Said to have been sent with embassy to Pope Boniface VIII, October 1301. Exiled from Florence with White Guelfs: 1st Decree, 27 January 1302; 2nd Decree, 10 March 1302. Joined Ghibelline party, but appears to have left them *c.* 1304 and taken refuge with Bartolommeo della Scala at Verona.

Lived a wandering life of which little record remains. With the Malaspini family, 1306–7; said to have visited Paris about this time; in Italy (probably as guest of Guido Novello), 1310–11, when he wrote letters in the Imperial cause to the Florentines and to the Emperor Henry VII. Excluded from decree of pardon the same year; 3rd Decree of exile (including his sons Pietro and Jacopo) published 6 November 1315. Refused to return to Florence under amnesty of 1316.

After visiting Verona again as guest of Can Grande della Scala, went to live at Ravenna, under the protection of Guido Novello, with his banished sons and his daughter Beatrice. Sent on embassy to Venice, July 1321. Died of fever on his return to Ravenna, 14 September 1321.

Works (dates conjectural, but order pretty certainly established): *La Vita Nuova* (*The New Life*), probably between 1292 and 1295; *Il Canzoniere* (*Song-book*), collection of lyrics of various dates; *Il Convivio* (*The Banquet*), *c.* 1307–9 (unfinished); *De Vulgari Eloquentia* (*Of Writing in the Vulgar Tongue*), probably about the same time as *Il Convivio* (unfinished); *De Monarchia* (*Of Monarchy*), probably about

1311; various *Letters* (chiefly political) in Latin; two Latin *Eclogues*, addressed to Giovanni del Virgilio, 1319; a scientific treatise, *Quaestio de Aqua et Terra*, of which the authenticity has been much disputed. A number of other minor works have been attributed to him from time to time.

The *Commedia* (the word "Divina" is not part of Dante's own title for the work) is thought by some to have been begun before Dante's exile, and Boccaccio states that the first draft of it was in Latin. As we have it, however, the *Inferno* cannot have been completed before 1314. The *Purgatorio* seems to have been partly or wholly written by 1319; some place its completion before 1312. Of the *Paradiso*, the twenty-seventh canto cannot have been written before 1315, and the poem was apparently finished only a short time before the author's death in 1321. (See *Para.* Introd. pp. 34 *sqq.*)

Danube: river. (*Inf.* XXXII. 25; *Para.* VIII. 65.)

DAVID: king of Israel. (*Inf.* IV. 58; XXVIII. 136 and *note* to 134; *Purg.* X. 64–5 and *note*; *Para.* XX. 37–42 and *note*.)

Decii: famous Roman family, three members of which, father, son, and grandson, sacrificed their lives for Rome. (*Para.* VI. 47.)

Demophoön: son of Theseus and Phaedra. He accompanied the Greeks against Troy and on his way home gained the love of Phyllis, daughter of the King of Thrace, whom he promised to marry when he had been home to Athens. As he was longer in returning than Phyllis expected, she believed he had forsaken her and put an end to her life. (*Para.* IX. 101 and *note*.)

DEVIL: see Satan.

DIDO: queen of Carthage (see AENEAS). (*Inf.* VI. 61, 85; *Para.* IX. 97–8.)

Dion (Dione): daughter of Oceanus and Thetis and mother of Venus by Jupiter. (*Para.* VIII. 7–9; reference to "Dion's daughter", Venus, occurs XXII. 144.)

DIONYSIUS, the Areopagite: the Athenian whose conversion to Christianity by St Paul is mentioned in the *Acts*, XVIII. 34. He was believed in the Middle Ages to be the author of a number of works which are now known to be writings of Neo-Platonists of the fifth and sixth centuries. In particular, the work on the Celestial Hierarchy, attributed to Dionysius and translated into Latin by John Erigena, was the accepted text-book on angelology. (*Para.* X. 115–17 and *note*; XXVIII. 130–32 and *note*; 136–7.)

Dionysius, King of Portugal (Dionysius Agricola) (1279–1325): son of Alphonso III and Beatrice, daughter of Alphonso X of Castile; he married Isabella, daughter of Pedro III of Aragon. (*Para.* XIX. 139–40 and *note*.)

Dominic, St: (1170–1221), founder of the Dominican Order. (*Para.* X. 95 and *note*; XI. 36, 38–9; XII. 32–105 and *notes*, *passim*; see also under *Images* to this canto.)

DOMINIONS: the fourth Order in the Celestial Hierarchies, ranking first in the second Hierarchy; they preside over the Heaven of Jupiter. (*Para.* XXVIII. 122–3 and *notes* to 72–139.)

Donati, Corso: see Corso Donati.

Donati, Piccarda: see Piccarda.

Donato, Hubert (Donati, Ubertino): one of the Donati family of Florence who married a daughter of Bellincion Berti (*q.v.*). (*Para.* XVI. 119 and *note*.)

DONATUS (Aelius Donatus): celebrated grammarian of the fourth century. (*Para.* XII. 137 and *note*.)

Dyrrachium (Durazzo): the ancient Epidamnus, town in Greek Illyria (the modern Albania) on a peninsula in the Adriatic. Caesar was here repulsed by Pompey's troops in 48 B.C., and forced to retreat, with considerable losses, towards Thessaly, where on 9 August he defeated Pompey decisively at the Battle of Pharsalia. (*Para.* vi. 64.)

Earthly Paradise: see Eden.

Ebro: river of Spain. (*Purg.* XXVII. 3 and *note*; *Para.* IX. 89.)

Eden: the Garden of, equivalent in Dante's cosmography to the Earthly Paradise. (*Para.* VII. 87; XXVI. 110; 139–42 and *note*.)

Egidio, St: see Giles.

Egypt, symbol of life on earth: (*Para.* XXV. 55.)

Eliseo: brother of Cacciaguida, *q.v.* (*Para.* XV. 136–7; cf. Genealogical Table, p. 397.)

Elysium: the abode of the Blessed in classical mythology. (*Para* XV. 27.)

Ema: small stream in Tuscany. (*Para.* XVI. 143 and *note*.)

Empyrean: the highest Heaven, the abode of the Deity (cf. chart at end of book). (*Para.* XXII. 61–72; XXVII. 99–120.)

England: *Para.* XIX. 121–3 and *note*.

Esau: eldest son of Isaac and Rebecca, twin-brother of Jacob. (*Para.* VIII. 131; XXXII. 68–70 and *note*.)

Europa: daughter of Agenor, King of Phoenicia, sister of Cadmus. Jupiter, enamoured of her, assumed the form of a bull and mingled with a herd close to where Europa and her maidens were sporting on the shore. Encouraged by its tameness, she mounted on the bull's back, which immediately swam out to sea with her and carried her off to Crete. There she became the mother of Minos, Rhadamanthus and Sarpedon. (*Para.* XXVIII. 83–4.)

Eurus: name given by the ancients to the east or south-east wind. (*Para.* VIII. 67.)

EVE: mother of mankind. (*Purg.* VIII. 99; XI. 63; XII. 71; XXIX. 24; XXX. 52; *Para.* VII. 147; XIII. 37–9; XXXII. 5–6 and *note*.)

Fabii: name of an ancient patrician family of Rome, which claimed descent from Hercules and from the Arcadian, Evander. It produced a long line of distinguished men, among whom the most famous were:

Q. Fabius Vibulanus, three times Consul (484–479 B.C.); Q. Fabius Maximus Rullicanus, six times Consul (322–296); he was also eminent as a general in the second Samnite war; Q. Fabius Maximus Gurges, three times Consul (292–265); W. Fabius Maximus Cunctator, five times Consul (233–209). This last member was appointed to the command of a fresh army after the defeat of the Romans at Lake Trasimene in the Second Punic war. His defensive and delaying policy on this occasion earned him the surname "Cunctator", which means "delayer". (*Para.* VI. 47.)

Famagosta: town in Cyprus. As a seaport it was of considerable importance in the Middle Ages. (*Para.* XIX. 145–8 and *note*.)

Fazio da Signa: a Florentine lawyer. He was Gonfaloniere della Giustizia in Florence in 1316 and several times Prior. He was sent as ambassador to Clement V in 1310 for the purpose of organizing the opposition to Emperor Henry VII when he entered Italy; consequently his name is on the list of those condemned by the Emperor in 1313. (*Para.* XVI. 56–7 and *note*.)

Felix: Don Felix Guzman, father of St Dominic (*q.v.*). (*Para.* XII. 79 and *note* to 81.)

Feltro (Feltre): a town in Venetia, on the road between Bassano and Belluno. In Dante's day it was under the lordship of its own bishops. (*Para.* IX. 52 and *note*.)

Ferdinand IV: king of Castile and Leon (1295–1312). Some commentators think the reference is to Ferdinand's grandfather, Alphonso X. (*Para.* XIX. 124–6 and *note*.)

Ferrara: city of Italy, in the north-east of Emilia, a few miles from the south bank of the Po. Some commentators think this may be the place to which Cacciaguida (*q.v.*) alludes as the region of the Po valley whence his wife came. (*Para.* IX. 58; XV. 137.)

Fiesole: town of Italy, near Florence. (*Inf.* XV. 62 *sqq.* and *note*; *Para.* XV. 126; XVI. 121.)

Fifanti: name of a Ghibelline family expelled from Florence in 1258. (*Para.* XVI. 104 and *note*.)

Fighine (Figline): village near Florence. (*Para.* XVI. 51 and *note*.)

Filippi: name of an ancient noble family of Florence mentioned by Cacciaguida (*q.v.*) as having been in decline already in his day. (*Para.* XVI. 89.)

Florence: in Italy, on the river Arno, chief city of Tuscany, and birthplace of Dante. (For history see *Inf.*, Introd., pp. 29 *sqq.*) (*Inf.* VI. 49 *sqq.*; VI. 61; X. 92; XIII. 143 *sqq.* and *note*; XVI. 75; XXIV. 144; XXVI. 1; *Purg.* VI. 127 *sqq.*; XIV. 51 and *note*; XX. 75; XXIII. 102 and *note* to XXIII. 101; *Para.* IX. 127; XV. 97–129; XVI. 25–154; XXXI. 39.)

Foulquet (*Folco*) *of Marseilles*: troubadour poet (*fl.* 1180–1195). (*Para.* IX. 67–142 and *notes*, *passim*; see also under *Images* to this canto.)

FRANCIS, ST, OF ASSISI (Francesco Bernardone) (1182–1226): son of a rich wool merchant, he lived the usual pleasant life of a young man of means until, after a severe illness at the age of 25, he experienced a change of heart and vowed to devote himself to a life of religion. Publicly renouncing all his worldly goods, and stripping off even his clothes, he made himself "the Bridegroom of Poverty". Later, he founded the Order of the Cordeliers, who, in accordance with Christ's injunction (*Matt.* x. 9, 10; *Mark* vi. 8, 9; *Luke* ix. 3, 4), possessed no money, went barefoot, and wore only a single garment, girt with a cord. The Order, called Friars Minor (Frati Minori) in token of humility, was sanctioned by Pope Innocent III, and in 1212 made its home in and about the little church of the Portiuncula, near Assisi, presented to it by the Benedictines. In 1219 Francis went to Egypt in a vain attempt to convert the Sultan; and returning in 1221 founded the Tertiary Order of Franciscans, for penitents of both sexes, who, while still living in the world, wished to live a dedicated life and keep the Rule of the Order in a form adapted to their condition. (Some think that Dante may have been a tertiary of the Order – see *note* on the "rope girdle", *Inf.* xvi. *Images*). In 1223 the Order was confirmed by a bull of Pope Honorius III. In 1224 Francis had an ecstatic vision and received the "Stigmata" (marks of Christ's wounds) in his hands, feet, and side. He died, at Assisi, at the age of 45 (4 Oct., 1226), and in 1228 was canonized by Pope Gregory IX.

In *Paradise* Dante tells the story of St Francis and of his Order in the words of St Thomas Aquinas (*q.v.*); and later sees Francis himself among the ranks of the Blessed in the Empyrean. (*Inf.* xxvii. 112; *Para.* xi. 36–129 and *note*; xiii. 32; xxii. 90; xxxii. 35.)

FREDERICK II, EMPEROR (1194–1250): *Inf.* x. 119; xiii. 58; xxiii. 66 and *note*; *Para.* iii. 120 and *note*.

FREDERICK II, KING OF SICILY: born 1272, reigned 1296–1337; third son of Peter III of Aragon. On the death of Alfonso II in 1291, James, the second brother, succeeded to the throne of Aragon, leaving Sicily to Frederick, the youngest; but a few years later, ignoring this arrangement, he tried (at the instigation of Pope Boniface VIII) to hand Sicily over to Charles II (of Anjou), King of Naples. The Sicilians rose in protest, renounced their allegiance to James, and offered the crown to Frederick, who succeeded in holding it against all comers. Frederick seems to have been an excellent and well-loved ruler. He assisted the Emperor Henry VII (*q.v.*) against Robert of Naples; but, after Henry's death, ceased to interest himself in Italian affairs, devoting himself exclusively to the defence of Sicily. It is probably this preoccupation with his own kingdom, to the neglect of national and imperial interests, that accounts for Dante's poor opinion of him, and for the place assigned to him in Purgatory. (*Purg.* vii. 119; *Para.* xix. 130–38 and *note*.)

GABRIEL: Archangel; the angel of the Annunciation. (*Purg.* x. 34; *Para.* iv. 47; ix. 138; xiv. 36; xxxii. 103–114.) Some commentators think that the archangel Gabriel is intended in *Para.* XXIII. 94–108, but this is not the view taken in this translation.

Gaeta: see Caieta.

Galaxy, the: (Milky Way). (*Para.* XIV. 99.)

Galicia: province in Spain. (*Para.* XXV. 18 and *note*.)

Galigaio: name of an ancient noble family of Florence. (*Para.* XVI. 102 and *note*; cf. *Inf.* XXV. 148.)

Galli: name of an ancient noble Ghibelline family in Florence. (*Para.* XVI. 103 and *note*.)

Galuzzo: borough of Florence. (*Para.* XVI. 52 and *note*.)

Gangalandi: one of the Florentine families which received knighthood from Hugh of Brandenburg (*q.v.*). (*Para.* XVI. 127–32 and *note*.)

Ganges: river of India; regarded as eastern limit of horizon, reckoned from meridian of Jerusalem. (*Purg.* II. 5 and *note*; XXVII. 4 and *note*; *Para.* XI. 51.)

GEMINI: Constellation of the Twins (Sun in Gemini mid-May to mid-June). (*Purg.* IV. 61, 62 and *note*; *Para.* XXII. 111–123 and *notes*; see also *Images* to this canto.)

Genoa: town in Italy. (*Para.* IX. 90.)

Giandonati: one of the Florentine families who received knighthood from Hugh of Brandenburg (*q.v.*). (*Para.* XVI. 127–32 and *note*.)

Giano della Bella: a famous Florentine tribune who, though of noble birth, brought into effect the "Ordinamenti di Giustizia" (Ordinances of Justice) which restricted the power of the nobles in Florence. (*Para.* XVI. 131–2 and *note*.)

Giles, St (Egidio) of Assisi: one of the three earliest followers of St Francis (*q.v.*). (*Para.* XI. 83–4 and *note*.)

Giuda: name of an ancient Florentine, mentioned as representing the Giudi family. Cacciaguida (*q.v.*) refers to him as having been a virtuous citizen. (*Para.* XVI. 122–3 and *note*.)

Giuochi: name of a Ghibelline family who held office in Florence in the twelfth century. (*Para.* XVI. 104 and *note*.)

Glaucus: a fisherman of Anthedon in Boeotia, who became a god of the sea by eating a herb or weed sown by Saturn. Dante compares the change which he undergoes on gazing at Beatrice to the transformation which took place in Glaucus. (*Para.* I. 67–9.)

Goat: Constellation of Capricorn. (*Purg.* II. 56 and *note*; *Para.* XXVII. 68–9 and *note*.)

GODFREY, DUKE (Gottifredi): Godfrey of Bouillon, leader of the First Crusade and among the first to enter Jerusalem when the city was liberated, after a siege of five weeks, in 1099. (*Para.* XVIII. 47 and *note*.)

GRATIAN (Franciscus Gratianus): founder of the science of canon law. (*Para.* X. 103–5 and *note*.)

Greci: name of an ancient noble family of Florence mentioned by Cacciaguida (*q.v.*) as having been already in decline in his day. (*Para.* XVI. 89.)

Gregory, St (Pope Gregory I, the Great): born *c.* 540. Educated for the law, at the age of about 30 was elected Prefect of Rome, and held office for three years. On his father's death he retired from public life and devoted his fortune to founding monasteries and charitable institutions, eventually becoming a monk of the Order of St Bene-dict in a monastery which he had built in Rome. About 579 he was made abbot, and in 590 was elected Pope in succession to Pelgius II. He was an active and vigorous pontiff, checking the Lombard aggres-sions, tightening up ecclesiastical discipline in France and Italy, and constantly combating paganism and heresy. Bede relates how, on see-ing some Anglo-Saxon slaves in the market at Rome, he was fired with enthusiasm for the conversion of this fair-haired race – "not Angles, but Angels". His writings include the *Moralia* (a commen-tary on *Job*), *Homilies* (on *Ezekiel* and the Gospels), the *Dialogues* and *Letters*. He died at Rome in 604. (*Purg.* X. 74–5 and *note*; *Para.* XXVIII. 133–5 and *note*.)

Gualdo: a town near Perugia. (*Para.* XI. 47–8 and *note*.)

Gualterotti: name of a Florentine Guelf family of noble descent. (*Para.* XVI. 133–5 and *note*.)

Guglielmo: see William.

Guidi: a great Lombard family, with possessions in Tuscany and Ro-magna; their castle was in Romena. Dante mentions several of them in the *Inferno*. (*Para.* XVI. 64–5 and *note*.)

Guinivere (Ginevra): wife of King Arthur. (*Para.* XVI. 14–15 and *note*.)

Haakon: King of Norway (1299–1319). (*Para.* XIX. 139–40 and *note*.)

Hannibal: Carthaginian general (247–183 B.C.), son of Hamilcar Barca; the great adversary of Rome. Having overrun Spain, he entered Italy and, in the Second Punic War, defeated the Romans at the Battles of Lake Trasimene (217 B.C.) and Cannae (216 B.C.). He was eventually defeated by Scipio (*q.v.*) and killed himself to avoid capture. (*Inf.* XXVIII. 11 and *note*; XXXI. 117; *Para.* VI. 49.)

Hebrews(Jews): (*Purg.* IV. 83; *Para.* V. 49; VII. 47 and *note* to 40–51; XXIX. 102.)

HECTOR: son of Priam, king of Troy, chief of the Trojan heroes in the *Iliad*. He was killed by Achilles. (*Inf.* IV. 122; *Para.* VI. 68.)

Helicè (Callisto): mother of Arcas, the Little Bear. (*Para.* XXXI. 31–3 and *note*.)

Henry II of Lusignan: King of Cyprus. (*Para.* XIX. 146–8 and *note*.)

HENRY VII, Emperor: (born 1268, son of Ermesinde, grand-daughter of Conrad, Count of Luxemburg, he was Henry IV of Luxemburg); elected emperor as Henry VII in 1308 at the instance of Pope Clement V in opposition to the French candidate, Charles of Valois; crowned at Aix, 6 January 1309. The following year he sent ambassadors to Flor-ence, announcing that he intended to come to Italy to receive the im-perial crown. (This ceremony had been neglected for the last sixty years, so that Dante had some grounds for maintaining that Frederick II was "the last Emperor of the Romans", his successors having been neither crowned nor anointed (cf. *Para.* III. 120). Henry crossed the Alps in 1310, and was at first well received, but presently encountered bitter opposition. On reaching Rome he found St Peter's in the hands of King Robert of Naples, and his coronation had to take place, without ceremonial, at St John Lateran. The violent opposition of the Guelfic League, headed by the Florentines, obliged him to ally himself with the Ghibellines and to hasten back to Tuscany, with the intention of besieging Florence; an enterprise to which Dante, who hoped great things from Henry's reign, passionately urged him, though refusing himself to bear arms against his native city. Under pressure from France, Clement V withdrew his support from Henry, and the siege had to be abandoned. Next year Henry set out with the intention of reducing Naples, but suddenly fell ill and died at Buonconvento near Siena (24 August 1313).

Henry was a prince of great parts and piety, eager to heal the internecine feuds which devastated Italy, and to unite the Empire under a just rule; and in him Dante saw the promise of that ideal emperor by whom the civil government of the world might be established on a secure and peaceful basis (see *Inf.* Introd , pp. 43–8). In *Paradise* he is shown the seat that awaits Henry in the Empyrean. (*Purg.* VII. 96; *Para.* XVII. 82–3 and *note*; XXX. 133–8 and *note*.) (See A. H. Cooper-Prichard, *History of the Grand-Duchy of Luxemburg*.)

Henry of Susa (Enrico Bartolomei): Archbishop of Embrun and Cardinal of Ostia (1261; d. 1271), author of a famous commentary upon the Decretals. (*Para.* XII. 83 and *note*.)

Hercules (Gk Heracles): in classical mythology, a demi-god, renowned for his enormous strength; the son of Zeus by Alcmene the wife of Amphitryon. Of the famous twelve Labours which he had to perform in the service of King Eurystheus, two are alluded to in the *Inferno*: the capture of the Oxen of Geryon, which the monster Cacus stole from him as he was driving them back (XXV. 25 *sqq.* and *note*), and the carrying off of Cerberus from Hades (VI. 18 and *Images*; IX. 98 and *note*). After his death at the hand of his wife Deianira (XII. 67 and *note*) he was taken up to Olympus and became one of the Immortals. He was also honoured with a constellation, which lies beneath the head of the Dragon, between the Lyre and the Crown. In *Paradise*, reference is made to the love of Hercules for Iole (*q.v.*). (*Inf.* XXV. 33; XXVI. 107; XXXI. 132; and *note* to XXXI. 101–21; *Para.* IX. 100–101 and *note*.)

Hezekiah: king of Judah (*II Kings*, 1–6; *II Chron.* XXXII, 26). (*Para.* XX. 49–54 and *note*.)

Hippolitus (Ippolito): son of Theseus and Hippolytë, Queen of the Amazons. Theseus afterwards married Phaedra, who fell in love with her step-son and wrongfully accused him to his father of having attempted to dishonour her. Theseus thereupon cursed his son, who was obliged to flee from Athens. (*Para.* XVII. 47 and *note.*)

Hugh of Brandenburg (Ugo di Brandimborgo): marquis, Imperial Vicar of Otho III. He is said to have conferred knighthood on five Florentine families (the Giandonati, the Pulci, the Nerli, the Gangalandi, and the Della Bella). (*Para.* XVI. 127–32 and *note.*)

HUGH OF ST VICTOR (Ugo di San Vittore): mystic and theologian of the twelfth century. (*Para.* XII. 133 and *note*)

Hungary: In Dante's day and for two centuries after his death, Hungary was an independent kingdom. The first king was St Stephen (1000–1038) and the last king of his line, Andrew III (1290–1301), was on the throne at the assumed date of the action of the *Comedy*. Charles Martel (*q.v.*), the friend of Dante, on the death of his mother's brother, Ladislas, became titular king of Hungary and was crowned at Naples, but never reigned, the kingdom being seized by Andrew III, first cousin of his mother's father. The crown however eventually came to the son of Charles Martel (Charles Robert), who reigned from 1308–1342. (*Para.* XIX. 142–3 and *note.*)

Hyperion: the father of Apollo. (*Para.* XXII. 142–3 and *note.*)

Icarus: son of Daedalus (*q.v.*). (*Para.* VIII. 126.)

ILLUMINATO DA RIETI: one of the earliest followers of St Francis (*q.v.*), whom he accompanied into Egypt. (*Para.* XII. 130 and *note.*)

Importuni: name of an ancient noble family of Florence. (*Para.* XVI. 133–5 and *note.*)

Infangato: name of a Florentine, mentioned by Cacciaguida (*q.v.*) as representing the ancient Florentine family of the Infangati and as an example of a virtuous citizen in his day. (*Para.* XVI. 122–3 and *note.*)

Innocent III: Pope, elected 1198. (*Para.* XI. 92–3 and *note.*)

Iphigenia: daughter of Agamemnon and Clytemnestra. (*Para.* V. 68–71 and *note.*)

Ippolito: see Hippolitus.

Iris: daughter of Thaumas and Electra. Originally the personification of the rainbow, she was regarded as the messenger of the gods and (among later writers) of Juno in particular. (*Para.* XII. 12; XXVIII. 32–3.)

Isaiah: prophet. (Quoted, *Para.* XXV. 91–3 and *note.*)

Isère (Isara): river of France. (*Para.* VI. 59.)

ISIDORE, ST, OF SEVILLE (Isidorus Hispalensis): born *c.* 560, died at Seville, 636, author of many learned works, including an encyclopaedia of the scientific knowledge of his age, *Etymologiarum Libri XX*, or *Origins*. (*Para.* X. 130 and *note.*)

Jacob: the patriarch, twin brother of Esau (*q.v.*). (*Inf.* IV. 59; *Para.* VIII. 130; XXII. 70–72 and *note*; XXXII. 67–9 and *note.*)

JAMES II, king of (1) Sicily, (2) Aragon: second son of Peter III of Aragon (*q.v.*). On Peter's death in 1285 his eldest son Alfonso succeeded to the crown of Aragon, and James to that of Sicily. When Alfonso died in 1291, James succeeded to Aragon, leaving the government of Sicily in the hands of the youngest brother, who became King Frederick II (*q.v.*). James died at Barcelona in 1327. (*Purg.* VII. 119; *Para.* XIX. 136-8 and *note*.)

James, King of the Balearic Islands: youngest son of James I of Aragon, and brother of Peter III. He is referred to as the uncle of Frederick of Aragon (*q.v.*), both of whom are reproached for the unworthiness of their reign. (*Para.* XIX. 136-8 and *note*.)

JAMES, ST: the Apostle. (*Purg.* XXXII. 76 and *note* to 73-81; *Para.* XXV. 13-96; present 97-end, XXVI *passim*, XXVII. 1-75.)

Janus: ancient Roman deity who presided over the beginning of everything. He was the guardian of gates and consequently is represented as having two faces, since every gate or door looks two ways. He was the deity of the beginning of the year; hence the first month was named Januarius after him. At Rome, Numa is said to have dedicated to him a covered passage (often referred to as a temple), which was opened in time of war (indicating that the god had gone forth to help the army) and closed in time of peace (indicating that the god had returned to protect the city). (*Para.* VI. 81 and *note*.)

JASON: the Greek hero who led the Argonauts to fetch the Golden Fleece from the hands of Aietes, king of Colchis. (*Inf.* XVIII. 86; *Para.* II. 16-18.)

Jephthah: the Gileadite, a judge of Israel. (*Para.* V. 66 and *note*.)

Jerome, St: Father of the Latin Church. (*Para.* XXIX. 37-9 and *note*.)

Jerusalem, symbol of eternal life. (*Para.* XXV. 56.)

JESUS CHRIST: see Christ.

Jews, the: see Hebrews.

JOACHIM OF FLORA: abbot of Calabria (*c.* 1130-1202). (*Para.* XII. 139-141 and *note*.)

Joanna: mother of St Dominic (*q.v.*). (*Para.* XII. 80 and *note* to 81.)

John Baptist, St: church of, in Florence. (*Inf.* XIX. 17 and *note*; XV. 134-5; XVI. 47 and *note*; XXV. 8-9.)

JOHN THE BAPTIST, ST: forerunner of Christ. (*Purg.* XXII. 152 and *note* to 140-54; *Para.* IV. 29; XXXII. 31-3; Florence referred to as his sheepfold, XVI. 25.)

JOHN, ST: the Apostle and Evangelist, son of Zebedee and Salomë, younger brother of St James the Apostle; he has been regarded as the author of the Gospel according to St John and of the Book of Revelations and there is little doubt that Dante so regarded him. (*Inf.* XIX. 106; *Purg.* XXIX. 104 and *note* to 93 *sqq.*; XXXII. 76 and *note* to 73-81; *Para.* IV. 29; XXIV. 126 and *note*; XXV. 100-29; XXVI. 1-69; XXXII. 127-9; Book of Revelations quoted, XXV. 94-6.)

John XXII (Jacques Duese): Pope, born *c.* 1244 at Cahors in Guienne; succeeded Clement V (after a vacancy of more than two years) in August, 1316; died at Avignon, 1334. (*Para.* XXVII. 58-9 and *note*.)

Jordan: river of Palestine. (*Purg.* XVIII. 134 and *note*; *Para.* XXII. 94.)

Joshua: son of Nun. (*Purg.* XX. 111 and *note* to 103–17; *Para.* IX. 125; XVIII. 38 and *note*.)

Jove (Jupiter): Roman deity, identified with the Greek Zeus, the son of Chronos and Rhea, "father of gods and men" and chief of the Olympian deities. His spouse was Juno (Gk Hera), and his weapon the thunderbolt. (*Inf.* XIV. 52; XXXI. 43, 92; *Purg.* XXIX. 120; XXXII. 112; *Para.* IV. 63; for the planet and heaven bearing his name, see Jupiter.)

Juba: son of Hiempsal, King of Numidia; he supported Pompey against Caesar. After the death of Pompey he joined Marcus Porcius Cato and Metellus Scipio. When the latter was defeated by Caesar at Thapsus he committed suicide (46 B.C.) (*Para.* VI. 70,)

Judith: daughter of Meraris, heroine of the *Book of Judith* in the Apocrypha. (*Para.* XXXII. 10 and *note*.)

JULIUS CAESAR: see Caesar (1).

Juno (Gk Hera): the goddess wife of Jove, (*q.v.*). She was the enemy of the Thebans, on account of Semelë (*q.v.*), and of the Trojans, on account of the judgement of Paris. (*Inf.* XXX. 1 and *note*; *Para.* XII. 12.)

Jupiter: Roman deity; see Jove.

JUPITER: planet, the sixth in order from the earth, its position being between Mars and Saturn. (*Para.* XVIII. 68–70; 95; 115; XX. 17; XXII. 145–6; XXVII. 14; see also Astronomical Note, p. 350, and Diagram of Paradise at end of book.)

JUPITER, HEAVEN OF: the sixth Heaven in Dante's conception of Paradise. It is presided over by the Dominions (*q.v.*). (*Para.* XVIII–XX. *passim*.)

JUSTINIAN: surnamed "the Great", Emperor of Constantinople, A.D. 527–65. He made a valiant effort to hold together the decaying fabric of the Empire, and by the help of his famous generals, Belisarius (*q.v.*) and Narses, overthrew the Vandals in Africa and the Ostrogoths in Italy. He is chiefly renowned for his great codification of the Roman Law. His four compilations, the *Digesta* or *Pandectae*, the *Codex Justinianus*, the *Institutiones* and the *Novellae Constitutiones*, known jointly as the *Corpus Juris Civilis*, contain a summary of the work of earlier jurists together with the Imperial Constitutions of his own time, and make up the "Roman Law" as received in Europe. Dante (to whom Justinian's figure must have been familiar from the great mosaics in the Church of San Vitale at Ravenna) places this great Christian Emperor in the Heaven of Mercury. (*Purg.* VI. 88; *Para.* V. 121 *sqq.* and *note*; VI. 1 *sqq.* see also under *Images* to this canto.)

La Malta: see Malta.

Lamberti: a Florentine family of which the notorious MOSCA (cf. *Inf.* XXVIII. 106) was a member, and to which reference is made by their arms (golden balls on a field azure). (*Para.* XVI. 110–11 and *note*.)

Lapo Salterello: a Florentine lawyer and judge. (*Para.* XV. 128 and *note*.)

Lateran, the: the palace at Rome which in Dante's day was the usual residence of the Pope. (*Para.* XXXI. 35–6 and *note*.)

Latona (Gk Leto): mother of Apollo and Artemis (Diana) by Zeus (Jupiter). (*Purg.* XX. 131 and *note*; ref. to her daughter, Diana, the Moon, *Para.* X. 68; XXII. 139–41; ref. to both her offspring, XXIX. 1–6 and *note*.)

LAVINIA: daughter of Latinus and wife of Aeneas (*q.v.*). (*Inf.* IV. 126; *Purg.* XVII. 34; 37 and *note*; *Para.* VI. 3.)

Lawrence, St: martyr. (*Para.* IV. 83, and *note*.)

Leda: daughter of Thestius, wife of Tyndareus, King of Sparta, and mother by Jove of Castor and Pollux and Helen. Jove, assuming the form of a swan, made love to Leda, who brought forth two eggs, from one of which issued Helen, and from the other the twin-brothers, Castor and Pollux. At their death, Jove placed the twins among the stars as the constellation of Gemini. Hence Dante speaks of it as "Leda's lovely nest". (*Para.* XXVII. 98.)

Linus: Bishop of Rome of the first century. (*Para.* XXVII. 40 and *note*.)

LOMBARD, PETER: see Peter Lombard.

LUCRECE (Lucretia): wife of Lucius Tarquinius Collatinus. Having been outraged by Tarquin, the son of Tarquinius Superbus (*q.v.*), she stabbed herself, calling upon Collatinus to avenge her. (*Inf.* IV. 127; *Para.* VI. 41.)

LUCY, ST (LUCIA): She is traditionally associated with the especial gifts of the Holy Ghost, and it is possible that in the "Three Blessed Ladies" (Mary, Lucy, and Beatrice) who interest themselves in Dante's salvation we are to see an analogue of the Holy Trinity of Father, Son and Spirit – or, in St Hilary's phrase, Basis, Image, and Gift – Mary, the absolute Theotokos, corresponding to the Basis; Beatrice, the derived God-bearer, to the Image; Lucia, the bond and messenger between them, to the Gift. (*Inf.* II. 97 and *note* to Images; *Purg.* IX. 55, 88 and *Images*; *Para.* XXXII. 136–8.)

Luna (Luni): city of Italy, near Carrara. (*Inf.* XX. 47 and *note*; *Para.* XVI. 73.)

MACARIUS, ST: probably St Macarius the Younger, of Alexandria. (*Para.* XXII. 49 and *note*.)

MACCABAEUS, JUDAS: the great Jewish warrior, whose valour is glorified in the *Book of Maccabees* (I. III. 3–4.). (*Para.* XVIII. 40 and *note*.)

Macra: small river in Tuscany. (*Para.* IX. 89.)

Maia: daughter of Atlas and Pleionë, mother of Mercury by Jove (Jupiter). (*Para.* XXI. 143.)

Malehaut, the Lady of: one of Queen Guinevere's companions. (*Para.* XVI. 14–15 and *note*.)

Malta: name of an ecclesiastical prison on Lake Bolsena, or possibly in Viterbo. (*Para.* IX. 53 and *note* to 52–60.)

Mars: God of War – ancient patron of Florence. (*Inf.* XIII. 144 and *note* to 143; XXIV. 145; XXXI. 51; *Purg.* XII. 32 and *note* to 31–3; *Para.* IV. 63; VIII. 132; statue of, *Para.* XVI. 47 and *note*; 145 and *note*.)

MARS: the fifth planet, according to the Ptolemaic system (see Astronomical Note and Diagram of Paradise). (*Purg.* II. 14; *Para.* IV. 63; XIV. 100 *sqq.*; XXII. 145–7; XXVII. 13–15.)

MARS, HEAVEN OF: the fifth Heaven in Dante's conception of Paradise. It is presided over by the Virtues (*q.v.*). (*Para.* XIV–XVIII. *passim.*)

Marsyas: a satyr of Phrygia who was rash enough to challenge Apollo (*q.v.*) to a musical contest. The Muses (*q.v.*) gave their decision in favour of Apollo who, to punish Marsyas for his presumption, bound him to a tree and flayed him alive. (*Para.* I. 19–21 and *note*.)

MARY, B.V.: the Mother of Christ. (*Inf.* II. and *note*; *Purg.* III. 39; V. 101; VIII. 37; XIII. 50; XX. 97; *examples from life of*: *Humility* (Annunciation), X. 34–45 and *notes*; *Generosity* (Marriage at Cana), XIII. 28 and *notes* to 25, 29; *Meekness* (Finding of Christ in the Temple), XV. 88 and *note* to 87–9; *Zeal* (Visitation), XVIII. 100 and *note*; *Liberality* (Nativity), XX. 20 and *note*; *Temperance* (Marriage at Cana), XXII. 142 and *note* to 140–54; *Chastity* (Annunciation), XXV. 128 and *note*; *Para.* IV. 30; XIV. 36; XV. 133–4; XXI. 91–3 and *note*; XXIII. 73–4; 88–111; 118–126; as Queen of Heaven, XXXI. 100–102; 115–42; XXXII. 4; Prayer St Bernard (*q.v.*), XXXIII. 1–39; the Virgin raises her eyes to God, XXXIII. 40–45.)

Matteo d'Acquasparta: monk of the Franciscan Order. (*Para.* XII. 125 and *note*.)

Mediterranean, the: regarded as the largest expanse of water with the exception of the great Ocean. (*Para.* VIII. 63; IX. 82–5 and *note*.)

Melchisedech: priest and king of Salem. (*Gen.* XIV. 18.) (*Para.* VIII. 125.)

Melissus: philosopher of Samos. (*Para.* XIII. 125 and *note*.)

Mercury: Roman god of commerce, son of Jupiter (*q.v.*) and Maia (*q.v.*). (*Para.* IV. 63.)

MERCURY, planet: the second planet from the earth, according to the Ptolemaic system (see Astronomical Note, p. 350, and Diagram of Paradise at end of book). (*Para.* IV. 63; V. 93; VI. 112; XXIII. 144.)

MERCURY, THE HEAVEN OF: the second Heaven in Dante's conception of Paradise. It is presided over by the Archangels (*q.v.*). (*Para.* V. 91 *sqq.* VII. *passim.*)

Michael, St: the Archangel, chief of the angelic host. (*Inf.* VII. 11 and *note*; *Purg.* XIII. 51; *Para.* IV. 47.)

Minerva: the Roman goddess of wisdom, identified with the Greek Pallas Athenë. Dante speaks of her as lending the breeze to the vessel of his poetic enterprise (*Para.* II. 8; cf. *Purg.* XII. 32 and *note* to 31–3; XII. 43 and *note*; XXX. 68.)

MINOS: in classical mythology, the legendary king of Crete who after death became a judge in the Underworld. (*Inf.* V. 5 *sqq.* and *note*; XX. 36; XXVII. 124; XXIX. 119; *Purg.* VII. 98; reference to the daughter of Minos, Ariadnë, *q.v.*, *Para.* XIII. 14–15.)

Modena: town in Italy. (*Para.* VI. 75.)

Montemario (Montemalo): the ancient Clivus Cinnae, a hill outside Rome. (*Para.* XV. 110 and *note.*)

Montemurlo: a castle on a hill between Prato and Pistoia. (*Para.* XVI. 64–5 and *note.*)

MOON: the first planet from the earth, according to the Ptolemaic system (see p. 350 and Diagram of Paradise at end of book). (*Inf.* VI. 64; X. 79–80; XV. 19; XX. 125–7; XXVI. 131; XXIX. 10; XXXIII. 26; *Purg.* IX. 1–3; X. 14–15; XVIII. 28; 76–8; XIX. 2; XX. 132; XXIII. 119–20; XXVIII. 33; XXIX. 53; 78; *Para.* I. 115; explanation of the spots on the moon: II. 29–148, *passim*; see also *notes* and *Images* to this canto; X. 14–15, 67–9; XVI. 82; XXII. 139–40; XXIII. 25–6; XXVII. 132; XXVIII. 20; 23; XXIX. 1–6; 97–9.)

MOON, THE HEAVEN OF: the first Heaven in Dante's conception of Paradise. It is presided over by the Angels (*q.v.*). (*Para.* I–IV. 84, *passim.*)

Moronto: brother of Cacciaguida (*q.v.*). (*Para.* XV. 136–7; cf. Genealogical Table, p. 397.)

MOSES: the Law-Giver of Israel. (*Inf.* IV. 57; *Purg.* XXXII. 80; *Para.* IV. 29; XXIV. 136; XXVI. 41; XXXII. 130–32.)

Mucius: Caius Mucius Scaevola, Roman citizen, celebrated for his fortitude. (*Para.* IV. 84 and *note.*)

Muses: the nine Muses, inspirers and patronesses of the Arts, dwelt upon Mt Parnassus, of which, according to Dante, one peak (Nyssa) was dedicated to them, and the other (Cyrrha) to Apollo. They were said to be daughters of Zeus (Jupiter) and Mnemosynë (Memory). (*Inf.* II. 7; XXXII. 10; *Purg.* I. 8; XXII. 102; XXIX. 37; *Para.* I. 13–18; II. 9; XVIII. 82–7; XXIII. 55–60.)

NATHAN: the Prophet, sent by God to reprove David for causing the death of Uriah the Hittite. (*II Sam.* XII. 1–2). (*Para.* XII. 136 and *note.*)

Navarre: kingdom in the Pyrenees. (*Inf.* XXII. 121; *Para.* XIX. 143–4 and *note.*)

Nazareth: village of Galilee. (*Para.* IX. 137.)

Nebuchadnezzar: king of Babylon (604–561 B.C.). (*Para.* IV. 14–15 and *note.*)

Neptune: in Roman mythology, god of the sea. (*Inf.* XXVIII. 82; *Para.* XXXIII. 96.)

Nerli: name of an ancient noble family of Florence. (*Para.* XV. 115–17 and *note*; XVI. 127–32 and *note.*)

Nicosia: town in Cyprus. (*Para.* XIX. 145–8 and *note.*)

Nile: river of Egypt. (*Inf.* XXXIV. 45; *Para.* VI. 66.)

NIMROD: Biblical king. (*Inf.* XXXI. 77 and *note*; *Para.* XXVI. 126.)

Noah: the patriarch. (*Inf.* IV. 56; *Para.* XII. 18 and *note.*)

Nòcera: town near Perugia. (*Para.* XI. 47–8 and *note.*)

Glossary

Ormanni: name of an ancient noble family of Florence mentioned by Cacciaguida (*q.v.*) as being already in decline in his day. (*Para.* XVI. 89.)

OROSIUS, PAULUS (Paolo Orosio): Spanish priest and historian of the fifth century A.D. His chief work, the *Historiarum adversus Paganos vii. Libri*, usually known as the *Ormista*, a history of the world from the Creation to A.D. 417, was written as a companion to St Augustine's *City of God*, and is based on Livy, Justin, Tacitus, Suetonius, and other Roman historians. It was a favourite historical text-book in the Middle Ages, and Dante was indebted to it for many points, e.g. in the *Inferno*, the story of Semiramis (v. 54–60), the character of Alexander the Great (XII. 107), and, in all probability, the account, quoted from Livy, of the Battle of Cannae (XXVIII. 10–11). In the *Paradiso*, Dante places Orosius in the Heaven of the Sun, among the Doctors of the Church. (*Para.* X. 118–20 and *note*.)

stia, "*him of Ostia*": see Henry of Susa.

Pachynus: promontory at the south-east extremity of Sicily, now called Cape Passaro. (*Para.* VIII. 68)

Padua: town of Italy, in Venetia. (*Inf.* (Paduans)· XV. 7; XVII. 71; *Para.* IX. 46.)

Paean: see Apollo.

Palermo: capital of Sicily. (*Para.* VIII. 75 and *note*.)

Pallas: son of the Trojan, Evander, slain by Turnus while fighting for Aeneas (*q.v.*). (*Para.* VI. 36.)

Parmenides: a Greek philosopher of the sixth century B.C. (*Para.* XII. 124 and *note*.)

Parnassus: mountain range a few miles north of Delphi, consisting of two peaks, one of which (Nyssa), according to Dante, was dedicated to the Muses (*q.v.*) and the other (Cyrrha) to Apollo (*q.v.*). (*Purg.* XXII. 65 and *note*; XXXI. 140; *Para.* I. 16–18 and *note*.)

PAUL, ST: the Apostle. (*Inf.* II. 28 and *note*; II. 32; *Para.* XVIII. 131, 136; XXI. 127–9; XXIV. 61–69; healing of his blindness by Ananias, *q.v.*, XXVI. 12 and *note*; XXVIII. 138–9 and *note*.)

Pelorus: the promontory at the north-east extremity of Sicily, now called Cape Faro. (*Para.* VIII. 68; cf. *Purg.* XIV. 33 and *note*.)

Peneian frond: the laurel, into which Daphne was metamorphosed when pursued by Apollo (*q.v.*). Daphne was the daughter of Peneus, a river-god. (*Para.* I. 32–3.)

Pera, Della: name of an ancient noble family of Florence. (*Para.* XVI. 124–6 and *note*.)

Perugia: city of Italy, in Umbria. (*Para.* VI. 75; XI. 46–8 and *note*.)

Peter Bernardone: see Bernardone, Peter.

PETER, ST: the Disciple and, according to tradition, the first Bishop of Rome. (*Inf.* II. 24; XIX. 91, 94; *Purg.* IX. 127; XIII. 51; XIX. 99 and *note*; XXI. 54 (Peter's Vicar); XXII. 63; XXXII. 76 and *note* to 73–81;

Para. IX. 141; XVIII. 131, 136; XXI. 127–9; XXII. 88; XXIV. 19–154; XXVII. 19–66; XXXII. 124–6, 133.)

PETER DAMIAN: a Father of the Church; he entered the Benedictine monastery of Fonte Avellana on the slopes of Mt Catria (*q.v.*), of which in 1041 he was appointed Abbot. (*Para.* XXI. 43–135 and *notes*.)

PETER LOMBARD: theologian of the twelfth century. (*Para.* X. 106–8 and *note*.)

PETER MANGIADOR (Petrus Comestor): historian and ecclesiastic of the twelfth century. (*Para.* XII. 134 and *note*.)

PETER OF SPAIN (Petrus Hispanus): Archbishop of Braga, Cardinal Bishop of Tusculum and, from 1276 to 1277, Pope, under the title of John XXI. (*Para.* XII. 134 and *note*.)

PETRUS COMESTOR: see Peter Mangiador.

PETRUS HISPANUS: see Peter of Spain.

Phaedra: wife of Theseus and step-mother of Hippolitus (*q.v.*). (*Para.* XVIII. 46 and *note*.)

Phaëthon: son of Clymenë by Apollo. (*Inf.* XVII. 107 and *note*; *Purg.* IV. 72; XXIX. 118; *Para.* XVII. 1–3 and *note*.)

Pharsalia: territory in Thessaly, scene of the decisive battle between Pompey (*q.v.*) and Julius Caesar (*q.v.*). (*Para.* VI. 65.)

Philip IV ("the Fair") of France (Philippe le Bel): born 1268, reigned 1285–1314; second son of Philip III and brother to Charles of Valois. By his marriage in 1284 to Juana, daughter of Henry I of Navarre, he became father of three kings of France and Navarre: Louis X, Philip V, and Charles IV. His reign was marked by a bitter quarrel with Pope Boniface VIII (*q.v.*), which arose over the taxation of the clergy. By the Bull *Clericis Laicos* the Pope declared church property to be exempt from all secular obligations. Philip retorted that if the clergy were not to be tributary to France, then neither should France be tributary to the Pope; and promptly cut off papal supplies by prohibiting the export of money and valuables from France. Eventually, Boniface excommunicated Philip, who replied by seizing the Pope's person at Anagni (see *Purg.* XX. 86–90 and *notes*.). After the death of Boniface, and the short pontificate of Benedict XI, Clement V succeeded, by Philip's influence, to the Papacy, and became a mere tool in Philip's hands; during his pontificate the Papal See was transferred to Avignon (see *Purg.* XXXII. 151–60 and *note*). Dante also refers (*Purg.* XX. 93–5) to Philip's persecution and suppression of the Order of the Knights Templars (1313). Philip was killed in 1314 by an accident during a boar-hunt. (*Inf.* XIX. 85 and *note*; *Purg.* VII. 109 and *note*; XX. 86 *sqq.*; XXXII. 152; *Para.* XIX. 118–20 and *note*.)

PICCARDA DONATI: sister of Corso and Forese Donati. (*Purg.* XXIV. 11 and *note*; *Para.* III. 34–120; see also *notes* and *Images* to this canto.)

Pius I: Bishop of Rome of the second century (A.D. 140). (*Para.* XXVII. 43–5.)

PLATO: the great Athenian philosopher (pupil of Socrates and founder of the Academic School (*c.* 428–347 B.C.). Although his *Dialogues* had not, for the most part, been translated into Latin by the beginning of the fourteenth century, so that Dante was directly acquainted only with the *Timaeus*, yet through the writings of the Neo-Platonists, Platonic thought had had a profound influence from very early days upon the development of Christian philosophy.

Of especial importance is the Platonic doctrine of "Ideas" – the eternal archetypes or universal patterns in the Divine Mind, conceived as the "most real 'existences'," of which particular and material things are only, as it were, the types and shadows. Thus in contrast with Aristotelianism (cf. under ARISTOTLE), Platonism is concerned with the world of essence rather than with that of experience.

The *Timaeus* is a mystical and figurative account of the creation of the world by God the Artificer ("the Demiurge"); the Cosmos is "made in his image", the imperfection of all actually existing things being attributed to the inherent limitations of matter. This line of thought, while in itself not irreconcilable with Christian orthodoxy, was developed by later writers, under Oriental influence, so as to lead to the conception that matter was in itself not only finite but actually evil, and so to the Gnostic and Dualist theory that the material creation was the work of the Devil. (This heresy Dante specifically repudiates.) The Neo-Platonic doctrine of the (active) "Divine Mind", proceeding from the "One" who is the ultimate Being beyond Mind, was on the one hand taken up into the Christian doctrine of the First and Second Persons of the Trinity, while on the other it was expanded into various Gnostic heresies of a Godhead declining by successive and subordinate "emanations" into materiality. In its orthodox form, it appears in the Fourth Gospel, the Nicene Creed, and the theology of St Augustine and his followers; so that Platonism has thus been – perhaps less explicitly but quite as firmly as Aristotelianism – incorporated into the body of Christian philosophy. (*Inf.* IV. 134; *Purg.* III. 43; his doctrine of the multiple soul, *Purg.* IV. 5 *sqq.* and *note*; *Para.* IV. 22 *sqq.* and *notes, passim*.)

Po: river of northern Italy. (*Inf.* V. 98; XX. 78; *Purg.* XIV. 91; XVI. 115 and *note*; *Para.* VI. 51; valley of, XV. 136–7.)

Polyhymnia: muse of sacred poetry. (*Para.* XXIII. 55–7.)

Pompey (Cneius Pompeius Magnus, "the Great"): born 106 B.C., died 48 B.C. As a young man he distinguished himself as one of Sulla's most successful generals in the war against Marius and his party, especially in the African campaign. He was made Consul with Crassus in 70 B.C. and in 59 B.C. joined Julius Caesar (*q.v.*) and Crassus in the triumvirate. In 55 B.C. he was Consul for a second time with Crassus. His rivalry with Caesar came to a head in 49 B.C., when civil war broke out, and in the following year Pompey was decisively defeated by Caesar at the Battle of Pharsalia. Pompey fled to Egypt where he was murdered by order of Ptolemy's ministers. (*Para.* VI. 53, 72.)

POWERS: the sixth Order in the Celestial Hierarchies, ranking last in the second Hierarchy; they preside over the Heaven of the Sun. (*Para.* XXVIII. 122–3 and *note* to 133–5.)

Prague: capital of Bohemia. (*Para.* XIX. 117 and *note*.)

Pressa, Della: member of an ancient Ghibelline family who were exiled from Florence in 1258. (*Para.* XVI. 100–101.)

PRIMUM MOBILE (Crystalline Heaven): the ninth Heaven in Dante's conception of Paradise. Its existence was first conceived by Ptolemy to account for the movement of the Heaven of the Fixed Stars. It is the highest of the revolving heavens and imparts motion to all the rest. (*Inf.* IX. 29; *Purg.* XXVIII. 104; XXXIII. 90; *Para.* I. 123; II. 113 *sqq.*; XIII. 24; XXIII. 112–117; XXVII. 99; XXIX. 145; XXX. 39; 106–8 and *note*.)

PRINCIPALITIES: the seventh Order in the Celestial Hierarchies, ranking first in the third Hierarchy; they preside over the Heaven of Venus. (*Para.* VIII. 35, 37 and *note*; XXVIII. 124–6 and *note* to 133–5.)

Provençals: inhabitants of Provence, former province of France, at one time independent. Their sufferings under the rule of Charles of Anjou (*q.v.*) are seen as a just retribution for their ingratitude to Romèo (*q.v.*). (*Para.* VI. 130.)

Ptolemy: king of Egypt. (*Para.* VI. 69.)

Pulci: one of the Florentine families which received knighthood from Hugh of Brandenburg (*q.v.*). (*Para.* XVI. 127–32 and *note*.)

PURGATORY, MT: Reference is made to the First Cornice. (*Para.* XV. 93.)

PYRRHUS: king of Epirus. (*Inf.* XII. 134, but cf. Glossary; *Para.* VI. 44.)

Quintius: see Cincinnatus.

Quirinus: name given to Romulus after his death, when he had been raised to the rank of a divinity. (*Para.* VIII. 131.)

RABANUS MAURUS: Archbishop of Mayence. (*Para.* XII. 139 and *note*.)

RACHEL: wife of the Patriarch Jacob and mother of Joseph and Benjamin. (*Inf.* II. 102 and *note*; IV. 60; *Purg.* XXVII. 104 and *Images* to this canto; *Para.* XXXII. 8 and *note*.)

RAHAB: the harlot of Jericho. (*Para.* IX. 115–126 and *note*.)

Raphael (Raffaelle): the Archangel. (*Para.* IV. 48.)

Ravenna: town on the sea-coast of Italy, near the mouth of the Po; the birthplace of Francesca da Rimini. (*Inf.* V. 97 and *note* to 88; XXVII. 40; *Para.* VI. 61.)

Ravignani: name of an ancient noble family of Florence. (*Para.* XVI. 97 and *note*.)

Raymond Berengar: see Berengar, Raymond.

REBECCA: wife of Isaac and mother of Esau and Jacob. (*Para.* XXXII. 10 and *note*.)

Red Sea: (*Inf.* XXIV. 90; *Purg.* XVIII. 134; *Para.* VI. 79.)

Glossary

RENOUARD: a legendary Saracen convert. (*Para.* XVIII. 46 and *note.*)

Rhine: river of Germany. (*Para.* VI. 58.)

RHIPEUS (Ripheus, Rifeo): Trojan hero, slain during the sack of Troy. (*Para.* XX. 67 *sqq.* and *note*; 100–105, 118–129 and *notes*; 147–8; see also *Images* to this canto.)

Rhodope: Phyllis, daughter of Sithon, King of Thrace. Believing Demophoön to have forsaken her, she put an end to her life. (*Para.* IX. 100 and *note.*)

Rhone: river of France. (*Inf.* IX. 112 and *note*; *Para.* VI. 60; VIII. 58.)

Rialto: one of the islands on which Venice was built, mentioned as the eastern limit of the March of Treviso. (*Para.* IX. 26.)

RICHARD OF ST VICTOR: celebrated scholastic philosopher and theologian. (*Para.* X. 131–2 and *note.*)

ROBERT GUISCARD: Duke of Apulia and Calabria. (*Para.* XVIII. 48 and *note.*)

ROLAND: nephew of Charlemagne (*q.v.*). He was an historical personage, but little is known of him beyond the many legends and poetical traditions that have clustered about his name. Dante places him in Mars, the Heaven of the Warriors. (*Inf.* XXXI. 18 and *note* to 16; *Para.* XVIII. 40 and *note.*)

Rome, Romans: (*Inf.* I. 71; II. 20; XIV. 105; XV. 77; XVIII. 28; XXVI. 60; XXXI. 59; *Purg.* VI. 113; XVI. 106 and *note*; XIX. 108; XXI. 89; XXII. 145; XXXII. 101; *Para.* IX. 140; XV. 126; XIX. 102; XXXI. 34–6 and *note.*)

ROMÈO: seneschal of Raymond Berengar (*q.v.*). (*Para.* VI. 127–142; see also under *Images* to this canto.)

ROMUALDUS, ST: founder of the Order of Reformed Benedictines. (*Para.* XXII. 49 and *note.*)

Rubicon: small river of northern Italy which falls into the Adriatic a few miles north of Rimini. During the period of the Roman Republic it formed the boundary between the province of Cisalpine Gaul and Italy proper. When Julius Caesar (*q.v.*) crossed it in 49 B.C. at the head of his army, he declared war by this action against the Republic. (*Para.* VI. 62.)

RUDOLPH I OF HAPSBURG: born 1218, emperor 1272–92; eldest son of Albert IV, count of Hapsburg; founder of the Imperial House of Austria. While serving in Germany under Ottocar, king of Bohemia, he heard that he had been elected emperor in preference to Ottocar and Alphonso of Castile. Ottocar refused to acknowledge Rudolph, but was defeated in battle and obliged to cede Austria and other provinces. A second rebellion led to Ottocar's defeat and death in 1278. Rudolph allowed Ottocar's son Wenceslas to succeed to the throne of Bohemia, but retained Austria and the other ceded provinces for his own sons, Albert and Rudolph. (*Purg.* VI. 103; VII. 94 and *note*; *Para.* VIII. 72.)

RUTH: wife of Boaz, great-grandmother of David. (*Para.* XXXII. 10–12 and *note.*)

Sabellius: theologian of the third century. (*Para.* XIII. 127 and *note*.)

Sacchetti: name of a Guelf family who left Florence after the Battle of Montaperti (1260). (*Para.* XVI. 104 and *note*.)

Salterello, Lapo: see Lapo.

Samuel: the Prophet. (*Para.* IV. 29.)

Sannella, Della: name of an ancient noble family of Florence mentioned by Cacciaguida (*q.v.*) as having been of importance in his day. (*Para.* XVI. 92.)

Saone: river of France. (*Para.* VI. 59.)

SARA: wife of Abraham. (*Para.* XXXII. 10 and *note*.)

Sardanapalus: king of the Assyrian empire of Ninus. (*Para.* XV. 107 and *note*.)

Satan: (*Para.* XXVII. 26–7; XXIX. 55–7.)

SATURN: the seventh planet from the earth, according to the Ptolemaic system (see Astronomical Note, p. 350, and Diagram of Paradise at end of book). *Purg.* XIX. 3 and *note* to 1–3; *Para.* XXII. 145–7.)

SATURN, THE HEAVEN OF: the seventh Heaven in Dante's conception of Paradise. It is presided over by the Thrones (*q.v.*). (*Para.* XXI–XXII. 99.)

Scala, della (or in its Latin form *Scaliger*): noble family of Verona. Their name means "of the Ladder", and they bore the canting arms: a ladder surmounted by an Imperial eagle. They first rose to prominence in the middle of the thirteenth century, when Mastino della Scala was appointed first podestà of Verona and then (1262) Captain of the People. Their sovereignty over Verona lasted for 100 years, during which time Verona enjoyed unexampled peace and prosperity. The three sons of Alberto all succeeded him in the government of the city, and Dante, during the period of his exile, owed, and expressed, a great debt of friendship to the family. See below under Bartolommeo and Can Grande.

Scala, Bartolommeo della: eldest son of Alberto della Scala; lord of Verona, September 1301–March 1304. He was Dante's host at Verona during the early years of his exile (see *Inf.* Introd. p. 38) and is alluded to in *Para.* XVII. 71–5, to which see also *note*.

Scala, Can Francesco della, commonly called *Can Grande*: third son of Alberto della Scala; born 1291; died 1329. Joint lord of Verona with his brother Alboino, 1308. On Alboino's death on 1311 he became sole lord of Verona, Imperial Vicar-General in Verona (1311), Vicenza (1312), Vicenza and Verona (1317). A great Ghibelline prince; a patron of the arts and a generous friend to the exiled members of his party, including Dante and Guido da Castello (see *Inf.* Introd. p. 50). He is thought by many commentators to be the "greyhound" of *Inf.* I. 101–11 and (possibly) the DXV of *Purg.* XXXIII. 43–5. In *Para.* XVII. 78 *sqq.* Dante speaks of him in the highest terms of praise. It was to Can Grande that Dante sent the first "fair copy" of the *Paradiso*, about half a dozen cantos at a time, as it was completed; and to him that he addressed the letter (cf. Introd. to this volume, pp. 36 *sqq.*) which explains the purpose of the *Comedy* as a whole and the manner in which the allegory is to be interpreted. The letter opens with a fervent eulogy of Can Grande's bounty and munificence. Can Grande is said to have been tall, handsome, gracious in act and bearing and also in speech, and a bold warrior. A statue of him on horseback is to be seen at Verona.

Scipio (Publius Cornelius Scipio Africanus Major): Roman general (born *c.* 235, died *c.* 183 B.C.); fought against Hannibal at Cannae (cf. *Inf.* XXVIII. 11 and *note*); was appointed to the command of the army in Spain, captured New Carthage (Cartagena) (210 B.C.), and drove the Carthaginians out of Spain; crossed into Africa and there gained a decisive victory over Hannibal at the Battle of Zama (202 B.C.). For these services he earned the title Africanus. After being twice Consul, and serving in the war against Antiochus the Great, he was accused of accepting bribes, and eventually left Rome and died in exile. (*Inf.* XXXI. 116; *Purg.* XXIX. 115 and *note*; *Para.* VI. 52; XXVIII. 61–3 and *note*.)

Scotland: (*Para.* XIX. 121–3 and *note*.)

Seine: river of France. (*Para.* VI. 59.)

Semelë: daughter of Cadmus, king of Thebes, who became, by Jupiter, the mother of Bacchus. In revenge, Juno, disguised as Semelë's old nurse, persuaded her to ask Jupiter to show himself to her in his divine splendour as the god of thunder; he did so, and Semelë was struck by lightning and burnt to ashes. Juno also revenged herself on Semelë's three sisters, Ino, Agavë, and Autonoë. (*Inf.* XXX. 1 and *note*; *Para.* XXI. 6 and *note*.)

SERAPHIM: the highest Order in the Celestial Hierarchies, ranking first in the first Hierarchy. They preside over the Primum Mobile or Crystalline Heaven. (*Para.* IX. 77–8; XXVIII. 98–9; see also *note* to 133–5.)

Sicily: island in the Mediterranean, divided from Italy by the Straits of Messina. (*Para.* VIII. 70; XIX. 130 and *note*.)

SIGIER OF BRABANT: doctor of philosophy and professor at the University of Paris. (*Para.* X. 133–8 and *note*.)

Signa: see Fazio de' Mori Ubaldini.

Sile: small river of northern Italy in Venetia. (*Para.* IX. 49.)

Simifonti: fortress in the Valdelsa, south-west of Florence. (*Para.* XVI. 62.)

Simois: river in the Troad. (*Para.* VI. 67.)

Simon Magus: the magician. (*Inf.* XIX. 1 and *note*; *Para.* XXX. 147.)

Sinigaglia (Senigallia, Sena Gallica): town in Italy, on the Adriatic, to the north-west of Ancona. (*Para.* XVI. 75 and *note*.)

Sixtus I: Bishop of Rome of the second century (119–127.) (*Para.* XXVII. 43–5.)

Sizii: name of an ancient noble family of Florence. (*Para.* XVI. 107–8 and *note*.)

Soldan (*Sultan*) *the*: of Egypt, was also called in Dante's time the "Sultan of Babylon" – hence, by a confusion between the two Babylons, Dante refers to the kingdom of Semiramis as "the land the Soldan rules over". (*Inf.* V. 60 and *note*; XXVII. 90; *Para.* XI. 101 and *note*.)

Soldanieri: name of an ancient noble family of Florence mentioned by Cacciaguida (*q.v.*) as having been of importance in his day. (*Para.* XVI. 92.)

SOLOMON: King of Israel. (*Para.* X. 109–114; XIII. 89–107 and *note*; XIV. 35–60.)

Solon: celebrated Athenian legislator, one of the Seven Sages of Greece. (*Para.* VIII. 124.)

Sorgue: river of France. (*Para.* VIII. 59.)

Spain: (*Inf.* XXVI. 103; *Purg.* XXVI. 40 and *note*; *Para.* VI. 64; see also under Cadiz.)

Stephen Ouros: King of Rascia (Dalmatia). (*Para.* XIX. 140–41 and *note*.)

Subasio, Mt: mountain in the north of Umbria. (*Para.* XI. 45 and *note*.)

SUN: the fourth planet from the earth, according to the Ptolemaic system (see p. 350 and Diagram of Paradise at end of book). At the beginning of Dante's journey (*Inf.* I. 38–40), the sun has risen among the stars which were with him at the Creation, that is, according to tradition, the constellation of Aries. It is a week past the equinox, therefore the sun was in about 7 degrees of Aries; by the end of the journey it has reached the middle of Aries. (*Inf.* I. 38, 60; II. 128; VI. 68; VII. 122; XI. 91; XXIV. 2; XXVI. 117; XXVIII. 56; XXIX. 105; XXXIII. 54; XXXIV. 96, 105; *Purg.* I. 39, 107; II. 1, 56; III. 16, 96; IV. 16, 56, 81, 119, 138; V. 39; VII. 26, 54, 85; VIII. 133; IX. 44; XII. 74; XIII. 13, 67; XV. 5; XVI. 107; XVII. 6, 9, 52; XVIII. 80, 110; XIX. 10, 39; XXI. 101; XXII. 61; XXIII. 114, 121; XXV. 2, 77; XXVI. 4, 23, 45; XXVII. 5, 61, 66, 68, 79, 133; XXVIII. 33; XXIX. 6, 78, 117, 118; XXX. 25; XXXI. 121; XXXII. 11, 18, 56; XXXIII. 104; *Para.* I. 47, 54, 63, 80; II. 33, 80; III. 1; V. 133; VII. 12; IX. 8, 69, 85, 114; X. 41, 48, 53, 76; XI. 50; XII. 15, 51; XV. 76; XVII. 123; XVIII. 105; XIX. 5; XX. 31; XXII. 56; XXIII. 8, 12, 29, 79; XXV. 54, IX. 8, 69, 85, 114; X. 41, 48, 53, 76; XI. 50; XII. 15, 51; XV. 76; XVII 123; XVIII. 105; XIX. 5; XX. 31; XXII. 56; XXIII. 8, 12, 29, 79; XXV. 54, 119; XXVI. 120, 142; XXVII. 28, 69, 86; XXIX. 99; XXX. 8, 25, 75, 105, 126; XXXI. 120; XXXII. 108; XXXIII. 64, 145; as the son of Latona: XXIX. 1–6; as the son of Hyperion: XXII. 142; as the lantern of the world: I. 38; as the universal lamp: XX. 1; as the chief minister of Nature: X. 28; as father of all life below: XXII. 116; as he who brings the morn and leaves the night: XXVII. 137; as a measure of time: XXVI. 119–20. See also under *Images* to relevant cantos and *notes, passim*.)

SUN, THE HEAVEN OF: the fourth Heaven in Dante's conception of Paradise. It is presided over by the Powers. (*Para.* X. 28–XIV. 81.)

Swabia (Suevia, Soave): ancient duchy in the south-west of Germany. (*Para.* III. 119 and *note*.)

Sychaeus (Sicheo): uncle and husband of Dido (*q.v.*). He was a wealthy Phoenician merchant who was murdered for the sake of his wealth by Dido's brother, Pygmalion. (*Inf.* V. 62; *Para* IX. 98 and *note*.)

Sylvester, St: one of the earliest followers of St Francis (*q.v.*). (*Para.* XI 83–4 and *note*.)

Tagliamento: river of northern Italy, mentioned by Cunizza (*q.v.*) as one of the boundaries of the March of Treviso. (*Para.* IX. 44.)

Thaddeus: see Alderotti, Thaddeus.

THOMAS AQUINAS, ST: see Aquinas.

THRONES: the third Order in the Celestial Hierarchies, ranking third in the first Hierarchy; they preside over the Heaven of Saturn. (*Para.* IX. 61–3 and *note*; XXVIII. 104–5; see also *note* to 133–5.)

Tiber: river on which Rome stands. (*Inf.* XXVII. 30; *Purg.* II. 101 and *note*; *Para.* XI. 107.)

Timaeus: name of a work by Plato (*q.v.*). (*Para.* IV. 48.)

Titus (Flavius Sabinus Vespasianus): Roman Emperor. (*Purg.* XXI. 82 and *note*; *Para.* VI. 92 and *note*.)

Tobit: name given in the English version of the Vulgate to the Jew who was healed of blindness by the Archangel Raphael. (In the Latin version he is called Tobias, which in the English version is the name of his son.) (*Para.* IV. 48 and *note*.)

Torquatus (Titus Manlius): Roman hero, twice Dictator (353, 349 B.C.) and three times Consul (347, 344, 340 B.C.). (*Para.* VI. 46.)

Tosinghi: name of an ancient noble family of Florence. (*Para.* XVI. 112–14 and *note*.)

TRAJAN (M. Ulpius Trajanus): Roman Emperor A.D. 98–117; born at Italica near Seville A.D. 52. After serving with distinction in the East and in Germany he was made Consul in 91, and in 97 was adopted by the Emperor Nerva and given the title of Caesar. He succeeded Nerva as Augustus in 98, being the first emperor who was born out of Italy. A good commander, he was loved and respected by his troops, whose fatigues and privations he shared, and was victorious in his wars against the Dacians (102–3, 104–6) and the Parthians (115–16). As a ruler he won the affection of his people by his simple and laborious life, his love of justice and his sincere concern for their welfare. He constructed a number of great roads in the Empire, built libraries and a theatre in Rome, and laid out the Forum Trajanum, in the centre of which stood the famous Column of Trajan, commemorating his victories. He was succeeded by Hadrian. (*Purg.* X. 76 and *note* to 74; *Para.* XX. 44–8 and *note*; 100–17 and *notes*; 147–8.)

Trespanio: borough of Florence. (*Para.* XVI. 52–3 and *note*.)

Trinacria: name used by Virgil and other Latin poets for Sicily (*q.v.*).

Trivia: "the goddess of the three ways", a name applied to Diana (or to the Moon) by Virgil and other Latin poets because Diana's temple was often placed where three roads met. (*Para.* XXIII. 25–7.)

Tronto: river of central Italy. (*Para.* VII. 63.)

Troy (Ilium; Gk Ilion): ancient coast-town in Asia Minor. It was taken and sacked by the Greeks under Agamemnon, after ten years' siege for the recovery of Helen. The siege is described in Homer's *Iliad*, and the sack in Virgil's *Aeneid*. (*Inf.* I. 74–5; XIII. 11; XXVIII. 10 and *note*; XXX. 14, 22, 97, 113; *Purg.* XII. 61, 62; *Para.* XV. 126.)

Glossary

Tupino (Topino): stream in Umbria. (*Para.* XI. 43.)

Tuscany: that district of Italy which lies, for the most part, between the Apennines and the Mediterranean, extending roughly from the Gulf of Genoa in the north to Orbitello in the south It is watered by the Arno, and Dante's birthplace, Florence, was its chief city. Many Tuscan towns are mentioned in the *Comedy*, and on two occasions the spirits of Hell recognize Dante by his Tuscan speech. (*Inf* X. 22; XXII. 99; XXIII. 76, 91; XXIV. 122; XXVIII. 108; XXXII. 66; *Purg.* XI. 59, 110; XIII. 149; XIV. 17, 103, 124; *Para.* XXII. 117.)

Typhoeus (Typhon, Tifeo): hundred-headed monster who defied Jove and on being quelled by a thunderbolt was buried under Mt Aetna, the eruptions of which were said to be caused by his struggles to regain his liberty. (*Para.* VIII. 69.)

Ubald, St (Ubaldo Baldassini): Bishop of Gubbio; born 1084; 1129–60. (*Para.* XI. 44 and *note*.)

Uberti: name of the famous Ghibelline family of which Farinata (*Inf.* X. 32 *sqq.*) was a member. (*Para.* XVI. 109–10 and *note*.)

Uccellatoio, Mt: name of a hill outside Florence. (*Para.* XV. 109 and *note*.)

Ughi: name of an ancient noble family of Florence mentioned by Cacciaguida (*q.v.*) as having been in decline already in his day. (*Para.* XVI. 88.)

Ugo di Brandimborgo: see Hugh of Brandenburg.

Ugo di San Vittore: see Hugh of St Victor.

Ulysses (Odysseus): prince of Ithaca; hero of Greek mythology, renowned for his cunning. His exploits at the siege of Troy are recounted in Homer's *Iliad*, and his wanderings in the *Odyssey*. (*Inf.* XXVI. 55 *sqq.* and *notes*; *Purg.* XIX. 22 and *note*; XXVII. 82–3 and *note*.)

Urban I: Bishop of Rome, of the 3rd century (222–230). (*Para.* XXVII. 43–5 and *note*.)

Urbisaglia (Urbs Salvia): once an important town but in Dante's day, as now, a collection of ruins in the province of the Marches. (*Para.* XVI. 73.)

Ursa Major, Ursa Minor: see Bears, constellations of.

Val di Greve (Valdigreve): valley of the Greve, small river of Tuscany. (*Para.* XVI. 66.)

Var (Varo): river of southern France. (*Para.* VI. 58 and *note*.)

Vatican: the Vatican hill at Rome on the right bank of the Tiber on which are situated the Church of St Peter and the Vatican Palace, which latter has been the usual residence of the Pope ever since the Papacy returned from Avignon in 1377. In Dante's time the papal residence was the Lateran palace (cf. Lateran). The Vatican hill, believed to be the scene of the martyrdom of St Peter and of many early Christians, was the most sacred territory of all Rome. (*Para.* IX. 139 and *note*.)

Vecchio, Del: name of an ancient noble family of Florence. (*Para.* XV. 115–17 and *note*.)

Glossary

Venus (goddess of love): (*Purg.* XXVIII. 65 and *note*; *Para.* VIII. 1–3 and *notes*.)

VENUS: the third planet from the earth, according to the Ptolemaic system (see Astronomical Note, p. 350, and Diagram of Paradise at end of book). (*Purg.* I. 19 and *note*; XXV. 132; XXVII. 94 and *note*; *Para.* VIII. 1–3 and *notes*; 11–12; 19; IX. 33, 110; XXII. 144.)

VENUS, THE HEAVEN OF: the third Heaven in Dante's conception of Paradise; it is presided over by the Principalities (*q.v.*). (*Para.* VIII, IX. see also *notes*, *passim* and *Images* to these cantos.)

Verde: river of Italy, now the Garigliano. (*Purg.* III. 131; *Para.* VIII. 63.)

Verona: city of Italy, in Venetia. (*Inf.* XV. 122 and *note* to 121; XX. 68; *Purg.* XVIII. 118; *Para.* XVIII. 70–71.)

Veronica, St: reference is made to her veil ("la Veronica") believed to bear the impression of the face of Our Lord. (*Para.* XXXI. 103–8 and *note*.)

Vicenza: city of Italy, in Venetia. (*Para.* IX. 47.)

VIRGIL (P. Vergilius Maro): Roman poet (70–19 B.C.). Born at Andes (now Pietole), near Mantua. His great epic, the *Aeneid*, tells the story of Aeneas, and celebrates the origins of the Roman people and empire (see Aeneas). Author also of the *Georgics* and of the *Eclogues*, one of which (*Ec.* IV.) looks forward to the birth of a Wonder-Child who should restore the Golden Age, and was held in the Middle Ages to be an unconscious prophecy of Christ (*Purg.* XXII. 70–72). In mediaeval legend, Virgil had the reputation of being a White Magician. In the *Divine Comedy* he guides Dante through Hell and accompanies him through Purgatory. (For references in *Inf.* and *Purg.*, see Glossaries to these volumes; *Para.* XV. 26; XVII. 19–21; XXVI. 118.)

VIRGIN MARY: see Mary.

VIRTUES: the fifth Order in the Celestial Hierarchies, ranking second in the second Hierarchy; they preside over the Heaven of Mars. (*Para.* XXVIII. 122–3 and see *note* to 133–5.)

Visdomini: name of an ancient noble family of Florence. (*Para.* XVI. 112–14 and *note*.)

Wain: see Bears, constellations of.

Wenceslas IV: king of Bohemia, 1278–1305. (*Purg.* VII. 101; *Para.* XIX. 124–6 and *note*.)

William, Count of Orange: defender of Christendom. (*Para.* XVIII. 46 and *note*.)

William II: king of Sicily and Naples (1166–89). (*Para.* XX. 61–6 and *note*.)

Xerxes: king of Persia, 485–465 B.C.; identical with Ahasuerus (*q.v.*). (*Purg.* XXVIII. 71 and *note*; *Para.* VIII. 124.)

Zephyrus (Zephyr, Zeffiro): the West Wind. (*Para.* XII. 46.)

BOOKS TO READ

GENERAL

UMBERTO COSMO, *A Handbook to Dante Studies*, tr. David Moore (Basil Blackwell, 1950).

DOROTHY L. SAYERS, *Introductory Papers on Dante* and *Further Papers on Dante* (Methuen, 1954 and 1957).

C. S. SINGLETON, *Dante Studies* (Harvard University Press, 1954).

MICHELE BARBI, *Life of Dante*, tr. P. G. Ruggiers (University of California Press, 1954).

PARADISE

EDMUND GARDNER. *Dante's Ten Heavens* (Constable, 1900).

P. H. WICKSTEED, *From Vita Nuova to Paradiso* (Longmans, 1922).

SHEILA RALPHS, *Etterno Spiro, a Study in the Nature of Dante's Paradise* (Manchester University Press, 1959).

MEDIAEVAL PHILOSOPHY, ETC.

ÉTIENNE GILSON, *Dante the Philosopher*, tr. David Moore (Sheed and Ward, 1948).

F. J. POWICKE, *Christian Life in the Middle Ages* (Clarendon, 1935).

EDMUND GARDNER, *Dante and the Mystics* (Dent, 1913).

P. H. WICKSTEED, *Dante and Aquinas* (Dent, 1913).

KENELM FOSTER, *The Life of St Thomas Aquinas* (Longmans, 1959).

D. J. B. HAWKINS, *A Sketch of Mediaeval Philosophy* (Sheed and Ward, 1946).

S. J. CURTIS, *A Short History of Western Philosophy in the Middle Ages* (Macdonald, 1950).

DANTE'S POLITICS

A. P. D'ENTRÈVES, *Dante as a Political Thinker* (Clarendon, 1952).

JOSEPH LECLER, *The Two Sovereignties* (Burns, Oats and Washburne, 1952).

CHARLES TILL DAVIS, *Dante and the Idea of Rome* (Clarendon, 1957).

MEDIAEVAL ASTRONOMY

M. A. ORR, *Dante and the Early Astronomers* (2nd ed., Allan Wingate, 1956).

ITALIAN EDITIONS

Readers who wish to know the original Italian text of *Paradise* will find the following editions and commentaries of great assistance:

Testo Critico della Società Dantesca Italiana, La Divina Commedia, ed. Giuseppe Vandelli (Hoepli, Milan).

Books to Read

La Divina Commedia, commentata da Manfredi Porena (Zanichelli, Bologna, 1954).

La Divina Commedia, a cura di Natalino Sapegno (Ricciardi, Milan, 1957).

The Divine Comedy (Italian text with prose translation) by J. D. Sinclair (John Lane, Bodley Head). This edition contains excellent commentaries, in English. (First published 1939, revised 1948.)

Among Italian critics, the names of Bruno Nardi (*Dante e la Cultura Medievale*, *Nel Mondo di Dante*), Michele Barbi, and Attilio Momigliano, as well as those mentioned above, are paramount. Reference to Umberto Cosmo's *Handbook to Dante Studies* will direct the reader in the field of Italian studies on Dante. (See also list of books recommended in *Hell* and *Purgatory* in this series.)

DESCENT OF DANTE FROM CACCIAGUIDA

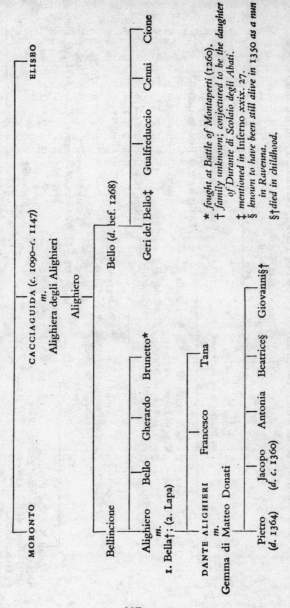

MORONTO   CACCIAGUIDA (c. 1090–c. 1147)   ELISBO
m.
Alighiera degli Alighieri

Alighiero

Bello (*d.* bef. 1268)

Geri del Bello‡   Gualfreduccio   Cenni   Cione

Bellincione

Alighiero   Bello   Gherardo   Brunetto*
m.
1. Bella†; (2. Lapa)

Francesco   Tana

DANTE ALIGHIERI
m.
Gemma di Matteo Donati

Pietro   Jacopo   Antonia   Beatrice§   Giovanni†
(*d.* 1364)   (*d. c.* 1360)

* *fought at Battle of Montaperti* (1260).
† *family unknown; conjectured to be the daughter
of Durante di Scolaio degli Abati.*
‡ *mentioned in Inferno* xxix. 27.
§ *known to have been still alive in 1350 as a nun
in Ravenna.*
§† *died in childhood.*

397

KINGS OF FRANCE, 1223–1350

(Table showing connexion between Royal Houses of France, Navarre, Hungary and Naples.)

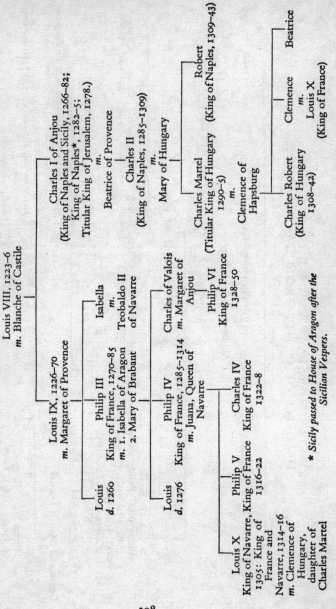

Louis VIII, 1223–6
m. Blanche of Castile

Louis IX, 1226–70
m. Margaret of Provence

Charles I of Anjou
(King of Naples and Sicily, 1266–82;
King of Naples*, 1282–5;
Titular King of Jerusalem, 1278.)
m.
Beatrice of Provence

Charles II
(King of Naples, 1285–1309)
m.
Mary of Hungary

Philip III
King of France, 1270–85
m. 1. Isabella of Aragon
2. Mary of Brabant

Isabella
m.
Teobaldo II
of Navarre

Charles Martel
(Titular King of Hungary
1290–5)
m.
Clemence of Hapsburg

Robert
(King of Naples, 1309–43)

Philip IV
King of France, 1285–1314
m. Juana, Queen of
Navarre

Charles of Valois
m. Margaret of
Anjou

Philip VI
King of France
1328–50

Charles Robert
(King of Hungary
1308–42)

Clemence
m.
Louis X
(King of France)

Beatrice

Louis
d. 1260

Louis
d. 1276

Charles IV
King of France
1322–8

Louis X
King of Navarre,
1305: King of
France and
Navarre, 1314–16
m. Clemence of
Hungary,
daughter of
Charles Martel

Philip V, King of France
1316–22

* Sicily passed to House of Aragon after the
Sicilian Vespers.

398

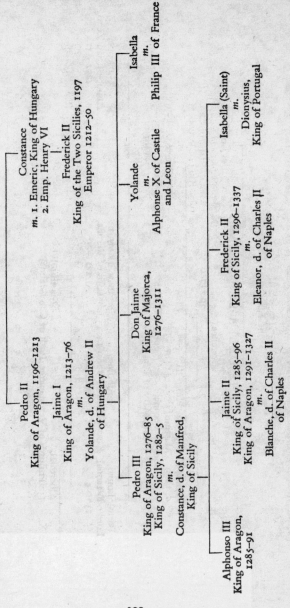

Pedro II
King of Aragon, 1196–1213

Constance
m. 1. Emeric, King of Hungary
2. Emp. Henry VI

Frederick II
King of the Two Sicilies, 1197
Emperor 1212–50

Jaime I
King of Aragon, 1213–76
m.
Yolande, d. of Andrew II
of Hungary

Don Jaime
King of Majorca,
1276–1311

Yolande
m.
Alphonse X of Castile
and Leon

Isabella
m.
Philip III of France

Pedro III
King of Aragon, 1276–85
King of Sicily, 1282–5
m.
Constance, d. of Manfred,
King of Sicily

Alphonso III
King of Aragon,
1285–91

Jaime II
King of Sicily, 1285–96
King of Aragon, 1291–1327
m.
Blanche, d. of Charles II
of Naples

Frederick II
King of Sicily, 1296–1337
m.
Eleanor, d. of Charles II
of Naples

Isabella (Saint)
m.
Dionysius,
King of Portugal

THE DELLA SCALA FAMILY

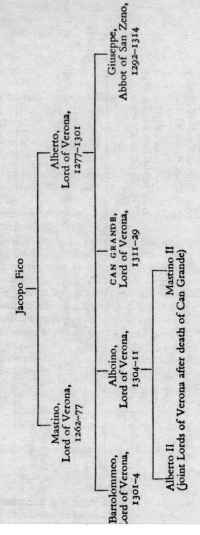

Jacopo Fico

Mastino,
Lord of Verona,
1262–77

Alberto,
Lord of Verona,
1277–1301

Bartolommeo,
Lord of Verona,
1301–4

Alboino,
Lord of Verona,
1304–11

CAN GRANDE,
Lord of Verona,
1311–29

Giuseppe,
Abbot of San Zeno,
1292–1314

Alberto II
(joint Lords of Verona after death of Can Grande)

Mastino II